Frontiers of Test Valid

This book examines test validity in the behavioral, social, and educational sciences by exploring three fundamental problems: measurement, causation, and meaning. Psychometric and philosophical perspectives receive attention along with unresolved issues. The authors explore how measurement is conceived from both classical and modern perspectives. The importance of understanding the underlying concepts as well as the practical challenges of test construction and use receive emphasis throughout. The book summarizes the current state of the test validity theory field. Necessary background on test theory and statistics is presented as a conceptual overview where needed.

Each chapter begins with an overview of key material reviewed in previous chapters, concludes with a list of suggested readings, and features boxes with examples that connect theory to practice. These examples reflect actual situations that occurred in psychology, education, and other disciplines in the US and around the globe, bringing theory to life. Critical thinking questions related to the boxed material engage and challenge readers. A few examples include:

What is the difference between intelligence and IQ?
Can people disagree on issues of value but agree on issues of test validity?
Is it possible to ask the same question in two different languages?

The first part of the book contrasts theories of measurement as applied to the validity of behavioral science measures. The next part considers causal theories of measurement in relation to alternatives such as behavior domain sampling, and then unpacks the causal approach in terms of alternative theories of causation. The final section explores the meaning and interpretation of test scores as they apply to test validity. Each set of chapters opens with a review of the key theories and literature and concludes with a review of related open questions in test validity theory.

Researchers, practitioners, and policymakers interested in test validity or developing tests will appreciate the book's cutting-edge review of test validity. The book also serves as a supplement in graduate or advanced undergraduate courses on test validity, psychometrics, testing, or measurement taught in psychology, education, sociology, social work, political science, business, criminal justice, and other fields. The book does not assume a background in measurement.

Keith A. Markus is a Professor in the Department of Psychology at John Jay College of Criminal Justice of The City University of New York (CUNY).

Denny Borsboom is a Professor in the Department of Psychology at the University of Amsterdam.

Multivariate Applications Series

Sponsored by the Society of Multivariate Experimental Psychology, the goal of this series is to apply statistical methods to significant social or behavioral issues, in such a way as to be accessible to a nontechnical-oriented readership (e.g., non-methodological researchers, teachers, students, government personnel, practitioners, and other professionals). Applications from a variety of disciplines such as psychology, public health, sociology, education, and business are welcome. Books can be single- or multiple-authored or edited volumes that (1) demonstrate the application of a variety of multivariate methods to a single, major area of research; (2) describe a multivariate procedure or framework that could be applied to a number of research areas; or (3) present a variety of perspectives on a topic of interest to applied multivariate researchers.

Anyone wishing to submit a book proposal should send the following: (1) author/title; (2) timeline including completion date; (3) brief overview of the book's focus, including table of contents and, ideally, a sample chapter (or chapters); (4) a brief description of competing publications; and (5) targeted audiences.

For more information, please contact the series editor, Lisa Harlow, at Department of Psychology, University of Rhode Island, 10 Chafee Road, Suite 8, Kingston, RI 02881-0808; phone (401) 874-4242; fax (401) 874-5562; or email LHarlow@uri.edu.

What if There Were no Significance Tests?, co-edited by Lisa L. Harlow, Stanley A. Mulaik, and James H. Steiger (1997)

Structural Equation Modeling with LISREL, PRELIS, and SIMPLIS: Basic Concepts, Applications, and Programming, written by Barbara M. Byrne (1998)

Multivariate Applications in Substance Use Research: New Methods for New Questions, co-edited by Jennifer S. Rose, Laurie Chassin, Clark C. Presson, and Steven J. Sherman (2000)

Item Response Theory for Psychologists, co-authored by Susan E. Embretson and Steven P. Reise (2000)

Structural Equation Modeling with AMOS: Basic Concepts, Applications, and Programming, written by Barbara M. Byrne (2001)

Conducting Meta-Analysis Using SAS, written by Winfred Arthur, Jr., Winston Bennett, Jr, and Allen I. Huffcutt (2001)

Modeling Intraindividual Variability with Repeated Measures Data: Methods and Applications, co-edited by D. S. Moskowitz and Scott L. Hershberger (2002)

Multilevel Modeling: Methodological Advances, Issues, and Applications, co-edited by Steven P. Reise and Naihua Duan (2003)

The Essence of Multivariate Thinking: Basic Themes and Methods, written by Lisa Harlow (2005)

Contemporary Psychometrics: A Festschrift for Roderick P. McDonald, co-edited by Albert Maydeu-Olivares and John J. McArdle (2005)

Structural Equation Modeling with EQS: Basic Concepts, Applications, and Programming, Second Edition, written by Barbara M. Byrne (2006)

A Paul Meehl Reader: Essays on the Practice of Scientific Psychology, co-edited by Niels G. Waller, Leslie J. Yonce, William M. Grove, David Faust, and Mark F. Lenzenweger (2006)

Introduction to Statistical Mediation Analysis, written by David P. MacKinnon (2008)

Applied Data Analytic Techniques for Turning Points Research, edited by Patricia Cohen (2008)

Cognitive Assessment: An Introduction to the Rule Space Method, written by Kikumi K. Tatsuoka (2009)

Structural Equation Modeling with AMOS: Basic Concepts, Applications, and Programming, Second Edition, written by Barbara M. Byrne (2010)

Handbook of Ethics in Quantitative Methodology, co-edited by Abigail T. Panter & Sonya K. Sterba (2011)

Longitudinal Data Analysis: A Practical Guide for Researchers in Aging, Health, and Social Sciences, co-edited by Jason T. Newsom, Richard N. Jones, and Scott M. Hofer (2011)

Structural Equation Modeling with MPlus: Basic Concepts, Applications, and Programming, written by Barbara M. Byrne (2012)

Understanding the New Statistics: Effect Sizes, Confidence Intervals, and Meta-Analysis, written by Geoff Cumming (2012)

Frontiers of Test Validity Theory: Measurement, Causation and Meaning, written by Keith A. Markus and Denny Borsboom (2013)

Frontiers of Test Validity Theory

Measurement, Causation, and Meaning

Keith A. Markus
and
Denny Borsboom

Routledge
Taylor & Francis Group

NEW YORK AND LONDON

First published 2013
by Routledge
711 Third Avenue, New York, NY 10017

Simultaneously published in the UK
by Routledge
27 Church Road, Hove, East Sussex BN3 2FA

Routledge is an imprint of the Taylor & Francis Group, an informa business

© 2013 Psychology Press

Library of Congress Cataloging in Publication Data
Markus, Keith A.
   Frontiers in test validity theory : measurement, causation and meaning /
   Keith A. Markus and Denny Borsboom.—1 Edition.
   pages cm
   Includes bibliographical references and index.
   1. Psychometrics. I. Borsboom, Denny. II. Title.
   BF39.M277 2013
   150.28'7—dc23
   2012047896

ISBN: 978–1–84169–219–7 (hbk)
ISBN: 978–1–84169–220–3 (pbk)
ISBN: 978–0–203–50120–7 (ebk)

Typeset in Sabon
by Swales & Willis Ltd, Exeter, Devon

Certified Sourcing
www.sfiprogram.org
SFI-00453

Printed and bound in the United States of America
by Edwards Brothers, Inc.

Contents

About the Authors

Keith A. Markus is a Professor in the Department of Psychology at John Jay College of Criminal Justice of The City University of New York (CUNY). He received his PhD in Psychology from the CUNY Graduate School. His research interests focus on causal models and causal inference, test validity, statistical inference, and applications of latent variable modeling. He has served as Associate Editor of *Psychological Methods* and of *Structural Equation Modeling: A Multidisciplinary Journal*. Dr. Markus teaches courses in psychometrics, structural equation modeling, program evaluation, and other topics in quantitative methods.

Denny Borsboom is a Professor in the Department of Psychology at the University of Amsterdam where he received his PhD in Psychology in 2003. His research has focused on the conceptual background of psychometric models, validity theory, and network modeling. He has published on these issues in journals like *Behavioral and Brain Sciences*, *Psychological Review*, *Psychometrika*, *Psychological Methods*, and *Annual Review of Clinical Psychology*. In addition, he authored the monograph *Measuring the Mind: Conceptual Issues in Contemporary Psychometrics*, which was published by Cambridge University Press. Dr. Borsboom teaches courses in Research Methods, Network Analysis, and Psychometrics. He is a member of the Psychometric Society Board of Trustees.

Preface

There is much to capture the imagination in test validity theory. Unfortunately, the challenges and unsolved puzzles of test validity often do not come across as readily as they do in other areas of testing. In this book we seek to throw Pandora's Box wide open and shine a light on the fantastic trove of complex and interconnected problems at the frontiers of test validity theory. In so doing, we hope to attract renewed attention and stimulate further advances in this critical domain of test theory. Arguably, there is no other domain as critical to effective test design, construction, interpretation and use. If scores derived from a test do not inform us about the desired construct, then it makes little difference how reliable, how precise, or how free from biases the scores may be. However, validity theory is not a topic of intense research focus, in either practical testing, scientific research, or research into psychometric methods. New breakthroughs in test validity theory do not flood related journals. Certainly, the rate of progress does not compare to progress in reliability estimation methods or new statistical models for test item scores. For a field that commonly holds validity to be the central psychometric issue in testing, this is a rather surprising situation.

The explanation for this situation may in part rest with the fact that test validity is a very unusual specialization within a very unusual sub-field. Most students attracted to behavioral science disciplines such as psychology, sociology, education, or political science are not attracted to these disciplines by their love of mathematics. Test theory, then, represents an unusual sub-field within behavioral science disciplines because it represents the most mathematical sub-field for most such disciplines. In contrast to test theory as a whole, test validity represents the least mathematical specialization within the most mathematical sub-field of less mathematical disciplines. So, the path to a specialization in test validity involves an unusual winding route with relatively little traffic to follow. In this book, the reader will find both a guided tour of existing work and also reports of some new expeditions into uncharted territory.

Students seeking entry into the problems and puzzles of test validity theory will find the book useful, particularly students who have completed a first course in testing or measurement. Test developers and test users seeking additional conceptual tools to put to use in validating their tests or testing programs will also find it useful. Additionally, members of the same audience seeking to sharpen their test validity reporting practices will find it useful. Finally, the book breaks sufficient new ground that we also hope that test validity specialists will find useful contributions to existing theory between its covers.

We have tried to present the material in a way that makes it accessible to a broad audience and does not assume a great deal of prior familiarity with the material. It is not possible, however, to embed within a book on test validity theory a comprehensive introduction to test theory or comprehensive discussion of the relevant statistical or philosophical background. As such, necessary background is often introduced in small doses without any attempt to provide encyclopedic coverage. We present mathematical and statistical material in conceptual overview, without presenting the details of areas like axiomatic measurement theory, item response theory, or structural equation models. We assume no background in relevant philosophical material. Nonetheless, such material receives tightly circumscribed introduction without any attempt to present broader contexts beyond the purposes at hand. If we have succeeded in our goals, readers who bring considerable background knowledge to the book will find that the material in the book engages with that background without oversimplification or distortion. Readers who come to the book with less background will find the treatment readable and understandable.

The book explores each of the above frontiers of test validity theory in turn: measurement, causation and then meaning. The treatment is progressive in the sense that one need not scratch too deeply below the surface of current testing practices to encounter problems related to measurement. If one digs a little deeper, questions related to causation begin to emerge. Questions of meaning emerge at even deeper levels beneath the surface of everyday practice. However, the treatment is also progressive in the sense that later chapters often assume material introduced in earlier chapters. Readers with less background will therefore find it advantageous to read the chapters in order. In contrast, readers with more background will find that chapters of specific interest to them stand alone. Throughout the book, however, we draw not only from the literature of test theory, but also from broader theoretical and philosophical sources that directly inform issues involved in test theory. To facilitate reading chapters in isolation, each of the remaining chapters begins with a box containing a brief summary of material assumed from prior chapters.

The book devotes a subsection containing three or four chapters to each of these three frontiers, yielding ten core chapters. Each core chapter includes boxed examples threading a single central example through the various issues explored in the chapter. We have attempted to choose a range of examples that reflect the breadth of testing across various disciplines including psychology, education, and others. Each core chapter also includes a list of further reading at the end, which includes key references for that chapter, and suggestions for readers who want to further explore issues taken up in that chapter. In one form or another, the last chapter in each section takes up open questions that remain fertile areas for further research and further contributions to test validity theory. Taken together, each of the three main sections presents the reader with a range of theoretical options and unpacks each of those options in some detail. However, each of these three frontiers could easily support a full-length book treatment in and of itself. As such, none receive a comprehensive treatment.

In chapter 1, we first tackle the formidable challenge of constructing a systematic terminology for use in the remainder of the book. We then review how test validity reached its current state of development and then introduce the three central problems of measurement, causation and meaning. In chapter 2 we canvass central ideas in measurement theory and relate them to testing. In chapter 3 we contrast various statistical models of observed scores in relation to their assumptions. In chapter 4 we explore persistent difficulties in sorting out the roles of axioms and of latent variables in understanding measurement in behavioral sciences. A picture emerges from the three chapters in Part One of measurement, construed more narrowly, and testing, construed more broadly, as theoretically diverse fields in which different testing applications call for different theoretical approaches.

In chapter 5 we explore the viability of a non-causal approach to such models based on domain sampling and also the prospects for reconciling domain sampling with a causal theory of measurement. In chapter 6 we contrast various causal models relating observed scores to latent variables, or to the construct measured by the test. In chapters 7 and 8 we canvass several broad approaches to understanding causation and what they add to a non-causal statistical interpretation of test score models. The picture that emerges from the chapters that comprise Part Two arrays various causal and non-causal interpretations of statistical models of test item scores as contrasting alternatives open to the test developer that involve a series of trade-offs between evidence required to support them and the conclusions that they in turn support.

In chapter 9 we consider the role of values, in the sense of what is considered to have worth or merit, in test validation. In chapter 10 we develop an approach to modeling test score interpretation. In chapter 11 we probe questions along the frontier of test validity theory and meaning. Part Three comprises a set of forays into the terra incognita of what stands as the least well-understood frontier of test validity theory, but also a frontier that at some level encompasses all else and allows for no external vantage point. Exploration of this frontier remains too preliminary for a clear overall picture to emerge. Nonetheless, current approaches to test validation in terms of validity arguments offer a useful guide to this largely unexplored region.

In chapter 12 we integrate the material from the three main sections and relate this material to the practical task of test validation. Written as a dialog between the authors, chapter 13 offers both a retrospective look at the material covered in the earlier chapters and also a prospective look at the broader context of that material. Together constituting Section Four, these chapters allow us to address the interrelationships between the issues explored in the previous sections and the broader relationships with test validity theory and test validation practice. In the end, however, a single book can merely begin a process of exploration that we expect to see continue for decades to come. If nothing else, we hope that the chapters that follow will put to rest any perception that test validity theory in its current form represents a nearly completed project with little room remaining for new contributions or advances. Nothing could fall further from the truth.

Acknowledgements

We would like to thank Lisa Harlow for inviting the book proposal and shepherding it through the revision process. In addition, we are grateful to Debra Riegert for patiently answering many questions and attending to many details while serving as the book's editor, originally at Erlbaum and then Taylor & Francis. We would also like to thank several reviewers for helpful comments on both the proposal and draft chapters including Terry Ackerman, the University of North Carolina at Greensboro, Brian Habing, the University of South Carolina, Derek Briggs, the University of Colorado, Boulder, Jean Powell Kirnan, the College of New Jersey, and Joseph J. Palladino, of the University of Southern Indiana.

This book was originally conceived as an update to Jackson and Messick's (1978) classic collection of measurement papers augmented with commentaries of the editors, in the style of Hofstadter and Dennett (1981). However, a simple cocktail napkin calculation demonstrated the infeasibility of this project. The result would have exceeded 700 pages. Nonetheless, we tip our hats to these four individuals for having partly inspired the present book. We hope that, like their books, the current work captures the imagination and inspires the reader to ask novel questions about the foundations of psychological testing.

The authors thank the following research assistants for contributing library research about various tests used as examples in the book: Elenore Altman (GRE, SVII), Nick Cromie (GRE, SVII), Clara Davis (various testing standards), Ruby Goldman (LSAT), Sam Hawes (PCL-R, WAIS II), Chia-ying Lin (PCL-R, MacCat), Michelle Loughlin (GRE), Ginger Menkal (16pf), Kerri Norton (ECST-R, SVII), Kellie Smith (WAIS II, U.S. State reading tests), Marina Sorochinski (16pf), Rula Thasites (TOEFL), Sharleen Yuan (GRE). We would like to thank Lisa Haney for producing the illustration and Laura Ruzzano for compiling the index. We would also like to thank Michael Kane for helpful comments on several draft chapters.

KM would like to thank the CUNY Research Foundation for two one-year grants (PSC-CUNY grant 67457-00-36 2004–2005 and 66729-00-35 2005–2006) and the John Jay College Forensic Psychology Research

Institute for a one-year grant (2007–2008) that helped support early work on this book. KM would also like to thank the participants who contributed thoughtful and thought-provoking comments and questions when he presented material from the book while it was being written.

DB was supported by NWO innovational research grants 451-03-068 and 452-07-005. DB would like to thank Conor Dolan, Angélique Cramer, and Rogier Kievit for their comments on parts of the manuscript. In addition, DB is grateful to the members of the talking-measurement mailing list for many stimulating discussions about measurement in physics and psychology. In addition, the current work integrates and systematizes the results of informal interactions with many different researchers, whom DB would like to thank for their willingness to engage in discussions on the measurement foundations of psychology.

Considering both planning and writing, the production of this work took a decade, and many people suffered from the side effects of what they have come to know as 'the book'. Thus, KM and DB would both like to thank the countless individuals and organizations who received answers, manuscripts, feedback, grades, research proposals, reviews, action letters, and all manner of other responses later than they otherwise would have during the writing of this book.

1 Introduction
Surveying the Field of Test Validity Theory

This book treats test validity theory from perspectives emphasizing measurement, causation, and meaning. This chapter provides a foundation for what follows with respect to key concepts used throughout the book. An introduction to key terminology appears in the next section. A brief overview of test validity theory and an overview of the key concepts of measurement, causation and meaning as they relate to test validity occupy the following two sections.

1.1. Terminology

There was a time, toward the middle of the last century, when the demand that one define one's terms could fluster even the most nimble theoretician. In the decades since, it has become clear that defining terms and developing their use do not separate so easily that one can fully complete the former before embarking on the latter. Nonetheless, merely using terms without introducing them—on the assumption that everyone else will understand them precisely as the author understands them—is the surest path to talking at cross purposes. Therefore, the present section will help the reader carve out some basic vocabulary used throughout the remainder of the book. Further refinement and elaboration of the concepts introduced here will await later chapters.

What follows may seem like surplus of terms at this early stage. The reader need not keep all of these distinctions in memory. However, much of the terminology introduced here foreshadows important distinctions developed in later chapters. The distinctions made below will each serve an important purpose in later chapters. Some terms and distinctions may seem novel, but the terminology presented conforms as much as possible to standard use of the terms within the testing literature. Our goal is to avoid misunderstandings while addressing a field in which authors often write about similar topics in very different terms.

1.1.1. *Testing, Assessing, and Measuring*

Authors often used the terms '*testing*', '*assessing*', and '*measuring*' interchangeably. However, just as often, authors use these terms to distinguish closely related ideas. In this book, the term 'measurement' has a narrow sense that involves strict quantities or magnitudes measured on at least an interval scale (chapter 2). That is to say, the term 'measuring' only applies when one has standardized units that remain consistent across the range of possible values, as with lengths or temperatures. On rare occasion, however, we will also make use of the broader sense of the term because of its pervasive use in certain contexts (e.g., measurement models). In such cases, we will clearly mark this context as an exceptional use of the term. The term 'testing' applies more broadly. It covers any technique that involves systematically observing and scoring elicited responses of a person or object under some level of standardization. In other contexts, the term 'assessment' might apply more broadly to include non-systematic or non-standardized methods. However, because the present book is restricted to test validity theory, 'testing' and 'assessment' will largely function interchangeably in the present context. The term 'testing' places more emphasis on systematic observation, whereas the term 'assessment' places more emphasis on scoring. We understand outcomes assessment as a special case distinguished primarily by the fact that the variable assessed by the test or assessment instrument serves as an outcome variable in some context. As illustrated in this paragraph, throughout the book single quotes are used to refer to terms.

1.1.2. *Attributes, Constructs, and Latent Variables*

Consider the sentences "The intelligence construct has spurred considerable controversy in the research community" and "The employer uses IQ-scores to assess applicants' standing on the intelligence construct." In the first of these sentences, the term 'construct' denotes a word or concept used by intelligence researchers, sometimes referred to as a *theoretical term*. As such, the term 'construct' indicates the *signifying term*. In the second sentence, the term 'construct' instead denotes an *attribute* that the tested persons have. Philosophers have used the term 'property' in a similar manner, sometimes referring to the term (a predicate in logic) and sometimes referring to the attribute that the term signifies (Putnam, 1975a, chapter 19). Following the same pattern, much behavioral science literature uses the term 'variable' sometimes to refer to the attribute and sometimes to refer to the signifier of the attribute (Markus, 2008a). It is worth noting that dichotomous variables correspond to simple properties, such that each individual either has or lacks the property in contrast to properties one can have to some degree or in some quantity. For example, having a height of two meters constitutes a simple property. Multi-valued variables, categorical or quantitative, correspond to complex properties involving mutually exclusive simple properties, such as height in general (Rozeboom, 1966). In some cases an attribute is associated with a particular test, such as a passing score on a particular certification test or a particular score on a college admissions test. In other cases, many different tests assess the same attribute and people have this attribute independent of any particular test. For example, several tests could all assess the level of mastery of the same curriculum in college-level calculus.

In this book, these terms always refer to the actual property tested or intended for testing. They never indicate the theoretical term, label, or symbol used to refer to this property. The term 'construct' always assumes a substantive interpretation of this property. The term 'latent variable' allows for content-free statistical models that capture probabilistic relationships with latent variables without specifying the specific property that the latent variable represents. Finally, the term *'construct label'* refers to the label given to the construct—the theoretical term used in scientific discourse, for instance. In keeping with these distinctions, we always understand a latent variable as a simple or complex property of test takers. What makes the variable latent is the fact that researchers do not directly observe it, possibly but not necessarily because it cannot be directly observed. The formalism of a latent variable makes it possible to represent statistical relationships with some latent variable, whatever it may be, without specifying the substance of that variable. For example, a common factor model makes it possible to estimate shared variance between items without specifying or making any assumptions about the content of that shared variance.

1.1.3. Items, Indicators, and Indices

Each individual stimulus that is incorporated in a test with the goal of eliciting a response from the test taker constitutes a test *item*. For instance, an item may be "*Spring* stands to *Season* as *Jupiter* stands to . . .?" The response to the item is the *item response*; for instance, a response to the example item could be "Planet" or "Solar system." The coding of the response, for instance as correct or incorrect, or as 0 or 1, is the *item score* and the process of coding responses into numbers is *item scoring*. Here, the response "Planet" would be coded as correct, and would typically be scored 1, while the response "Solar system" would be coded as incorrect, and be scored as 0.

In the context of models that relate item responses to latent variables, items are used as *indicators*. Item scores are then interpreted as indicator scores. These indicator scores may be used to assess or to measure a construct. Recall that the terms 'assess' and 'measure' apply to indicators only when the indicator scores are used to gauge a person's standing on a construct, not to merely summarize performance. This means that, in the measurement model, the indicator variables are dependent variables, and the latent variable is an independent variable (chapter 6). In the present example, the test user may interpret the item score as an indicator of the construct *verbal reasoning*. In educational testing, the term indicator can refer to a parcel of items combined for reporting purposes. We will not use the term in this sense.

In contrast, an item score can also function as an *index*. This applies to indicators when the model equation is reversed. This means that the indicators are used to form a composite score, which may be used as a *summary* of the item responses. For instance, in the current example, a number of similar items may be administered to the test taker. In this case, the total number of correctly answered items would be an index or summary of the person's performance. In some cases the term 'index' may also apply to situations where a construct is *predicted* from the item scores. For instance, the item scores may in this case be used to predict a property that was not assessed, for instance future performance on a job. In the measurement model, the indicators then function as independent variables, whereas the latent variable (future performance on a job) is a dependent variable that is predicted from the items. When test scores are used in this way, i.e., as predictors of an external variable, then that external variable may also be designated a *criterion variable* or *criterion*. A criterion may be a construct or an observable, depending on context, where the term 'observable' refers to something that can be directly observed. In most cases of interest, the criterion carries surplus meaning over the observed score and in such cases the criterion is best thought of as a construct. For example, the choice of one observable over another typically has a theoretical rationale. The data alone do not force such choices upon the researcher.

In many contexts, test theory assumes that indicators come from homogeneous *domains* of items, whereas indices more typically reflect a small number of heterogeneous-theory-determined attributes that comprise the composite variable. In still other contexts, indicators may serve as *samples* from heterogeneous domains. In this case, the response behavior is considered to be a sample from a larger domain of behaviors that characterizes a person. For instance, in the current example, a correct response to the item may be considered a sample from a person's responses to all possible items of the verbal analogy type. The response is then used to infer, from the administered items, the person's response behavior on items that were not actually administered. This inferential process is called *generalization*. Generalization is horizontal inference: one makes inferences from one set of properties (administered verbal analogies) to other properties of the same kind (other verbal analogies). This contrasts with assessment and measurement, which are vertical inference strategies: one makes an inference from one class of properties (administered verbal analogies) to properties of a different kind (constructs involved in analogical reasoning).

1.1.4. Test Validity and Validation

When it appears on its own in the present book, the term *validity* generally refers to test validity and not to broader applications such as the validity of inferences or research designs. *Validation* refers to the process of investigating and documenting test validity. Both validity and validation are evolving concepts that have taken on a variety of meanings in the past century. We briefly chart this historical development in the next section.

1.2. The Development of Test Validity Theory

Throughout the history of test validity theory, one can discern three interacting processes: *expansion, unification,* and *partition*. Expansion occurs when test developers encounter applied problems that existing validity theory does not cover. At such times, new concepts and validation procedures enter validity theory. Examples of expansion typically involve new types of validity evidence incorporated into the validation process. Unification occurs as a form of theoretical integration. It results when theoretical innovation treats aspects of validity formerly treated as disparate as special cases of a common overarching concept, emphasizing their commonalities as part of test validity. Examples of unification typically involve reinterpretation of existing validation strategies. Partition occurs when authors press distinctions between cases treated similarly under existing validity theory. This process occurs when authors emphasize the differences between elements of validation treated together under existing theory. Examples of partition typically involve the introduction of typologies of test development and test validation activities.

Superimposed over this dynamic interplay between these three processes, one also finds a successive development in the underlying philosophical assumptions. The chapters in successive editions of *Educational Measurement* on validity (Cureton, 1951; Messick, 1989) and validation (Cronbach, 1971, Kane, 2006) offer useful guideposts to this development. Cureton (1950) developed test validity theory in a manner consistent with a form of descriptive empiricism, reflecting both behaviorism in psychology and positivism in the philosophy of science. Here, one finds an emphasis on the idea that claims are not meaningful unless operationalized in terms of observables. Correlations provide the currency of the realm. Sometimes correlations inform claims about the identity of the correlates, such as what the test measures and what the test developer intends to measure. Other times, correlations inform claims about prediction, claims that what the test measures at one time predicts what the test user wants to predict at a later time. Cronbach (1971) developed test validity in a way that shifted toward an explanatory (logical) empiricism. The primary innovation here involves the idea that inferred theoretical variables (e.g., extroversion, reading ability, job knowledge) explain patterns of observed test behavior rather than simply summarizing such behavior. The relevant notion of explanation involves subsuming observed test behaviors under general scientific laws (Hempel, 1965). Messick (1989) reworked a broad range of test validity concepts under a form of constructivist realism. The constructivist part was already well entrenched in validity theory, as earlier authors had long emphasized the underdetermination of theory by data: the idea that observed test behaviors do not fully determine the abstractions from them introduced by theory (Loevinger, 1957). Different theories can summarize the same data differently, and abstracting from data to theory thus involves choices that cannot be driven only by the data. The realist component, however, marked a break with earlier validity theory (congruent with Donald Campbell's advocacy of critical realism during a similar period, both reflecting shifts in the philosophy of science). Messick emphasized psychological constructs as actually existing properties reflecting real dimensions of variability between people (or other objects of measurement) rather than just convenient summaries of observable test behaviors (c.f. Norris, 1983). In the most recent chapter in the series, Kane (2006) moved test validity theory in a direction consistent with philosophical pragmatism. Earlier approaches sought to articulate the universal nature of validity, validation, and truthful claims about tests and test use. Kane's approach is pragmatic in the sense that he instead presents an approach to test validity that treats all of these things as highly context specific. One constructs an interpretive argument and validates relative to that interpretive argument. The interpretive argument leads to standards for validity, validation evidence, appropriate to the intended interpretation. The distinctive character of pragmatism is the view that there are no foundations that transcend individual or collective perspectives on the world, but, instead, knowledge of the world develops from within such perspectives. As such, a validation effort might prove adequate for one context, but not for another. When the interpretive argument changes or expands, a need for new validation evidence can result.

Corresponding to this philosophical progression, one finds in the four *Educational Measurement* chapters an interesting narrowing of focus over the decades. Cureton (1951) devoted a substantial portion of the chapter to the problem of choosing the right attribute to measure. Cronbach (1971) more or less assumed that the test developer had decided what to measure and focused a good deal of attention on the myriad of other factors that could also impact test responses. Messick (1989) assumed both that the test developer knew what he or she wanted to measure and that he or she had developed a standardized procedure that controlled for extraneous factors. Messick primarily focused on what was involved in collecting evidence that the standardized procedure measured the desired attribute. Kane (2006) more or less assumed that the test developer has selected an attribute and developed a standardized procedure that measures it with at least partial success. Kane focused on providing a detailed account of producing a persuasive argument to justify test use to outside audiences.

1.2.1. Descriptive Empiricism

It seems fitting that the acronym of the subtitle of this book forms the Roman numeral MCM, because the year 1900 is a good starting point for the history of test validity theory. Pearson invented the correlation coefficient in 1896. The coefficient was immediately applied to test scores (e.g., Wissler, 1901). The concept of test validity was first introduced to indicate the extent to which a test measures what it purports to measure (e.g., Buckingham, 1921). The correlation with a criterion measure (of what the test purports to measure) provided an index of this and was widely referred to as a validity coefficient (e.g., Hunkins & Breed, 1923). Favoring a more theory-neutral approach, Nunally and Burnstein (1994) described the absolute value of the correlation coefficient as the validity coefficient.

Using the terminology outlined above, we would paraphrase this in terms of the test assessing what it purports to assess, to avoid assuming too much about the level of measurement or the quantitative attributes of the construct assessed. Correlations with other variables remain a basic tool in the test validator's toolkit, although few users today would interpret such correlations as providing a complete summary of a test's validity. Historically, however, the correlation between test score and criterion has been of great importance.

The validity coefficient applied most naturally in cases where a test was used to provide a prediction before the criterion measure became available. For instance, universities may use high school grade point average as a predictor of success in college; the army may use personality test scores as predictors of behavior in combat situations; and companies may use task performance ratings as predictors of performance on the job. Other uses involved situations in which a test provided a shorter, more economical alternative to a longer but definitive measure. For instance, in medicine, a symptom profile (e.g., coughing, fever, headache) is often the first choice to assess someone's condition (e.g., influenza) even though it is inferior to other tests (e.g., blood tests).

In still other contexts, test developers created tests based on detailed content specifications rather than to predict or approximate a specific criterion measure. For instance, educational tests, like exams, are traditionally put together according to content specification, rather than on the basis of test–criterion correlations. An example may be an arithmetic examination. Such a test requires adequate content coverage of several distinct arithmetic skills (addition, subtraction, multiplication and division). Content often takes precedence over test–criterion correlations in these cases. Suppose that the answer to the question 'Do you like beans?' happened to do better than arithmetic items in predicting arithmetic ability. Even if this were so, few would propose replacing arithmetic exams by inquiries into one's taste for beans.

Out of this context grew a distinction between criterion-related validity and content validity. These categories were initially connected to discrete types of tests that required discrete types of evidence (Goodenough, 1949). Content-based tests required evidence that showed the items to be representative samples of the domain. Such evidence would typically take the form of expert judgment. Tests for predictive use required evidence that showed the test scores to be adequate predictors of a criterion. Such evidence would typically take the form of a test–criterion correlation. The addition of content validity reflects the process of expansion, and the separation between the two reflects partition.

Cureton (1951) drew on behavior domain theory to unify content and criterion validity under one theoretical treatment. From this perspective, content validation involves showing that a test samples representatively from the domain that the test is intended to cover. Criterion validation involves showing that the test samples representatively from a domain that currently predicts a future criterion of interest. In some cases, the tested domain represents an intermediate outcome and the criterion an ultimate outcome (e.g., learning national history leads to more effective citizenship). In other cases, the testing domain represents an outcome that will then transfer to another outcome (e.g., teaching Latin transfers to improve English skills). The folding of the two types of validation into behavior domain theory provides an example of unification.

1.2.2. Explanatory Empiricism

By the 1950s it had become evident that these two categories did not exhaust the universe of testing situations. In some cases, test developers found it hard to operationalize what the test measured in terms of a domain of content, skills, or behavior. For example, intelligence research involves positive correlations across a sweeping range of cognitive ability tasks, possibly an open set with no finite domain (this phenomenon is known as the *positive manifold*). More narrowly, the specific domain of responses that reflect a particular personality trait might vary across cultures even though it makes sense to speak of the same personality trait across cultures. In other cases, no single criterion serves as a gold standard. For example, no one measure may fully exhaust the idea of aggression, no one observer may provide a definitive assessment of job performance. Drawing on the notion of a hypothetical construct (MacCorquodale & Meehl, 1948), Cronbach and Meehl (1955) sought to address this problem through a new type of validity: *construct validity*.

Instead of operationalizing what the test measured in terms of a content domain or criterion, construct validity articulated what the test measured in terms of how test scores relate to a network of other observables, as predicted by theory.

For instance, suppose that a theory of verbal reasoning says that verbal reasoning is positively related to the amount of educational instruction received, but not to extraversion. Further suppose that the test score on a verbal analogies test correlates positively with time spent in school, but not with an extraversion subscale. Then the test score behaves in accordance with what would be expected on the theory in question, at least in these respects. In turn, this delivers some evidence for the interpretation of test scores in terms of the theory. Thus, the validity of test score interpretations in terms of a theory is bolstered by tests of that theory through use of the relevant test scores. A wide variety of observations bear on the empirical evaluation of the same theory. This idea of a hypothetical construct allowed for multiple operationalizations, reinforcing a shift away from identifying what a test measured with a single operationalization in terms of either content or a criterion (Campbell & Fiske, 1959).

This model reflects changes in empiricist models of science. Whereas descriptive empiricism characterized validity as a matter of identity between the test domain and the intended domain, this logical empiricist approach posits hypothetical constructs as explanatory of test responses. Nothing explains itself, so this entails taking test scores as distinct from constructs in a way that the earlier approaches did not. Moreover, explanation was understood at the time as subsumption under laws (Hempel, 1965). This is reflected in Cronbach's (1971) and Cronbach and Meehl's (1955) accounts where the identity of hypothesized constructs is fixed by the system of laws into which the theory situates the construct. These laws were operationalized in the testing context as patterns of correlation between the construct and other variables.

The three basic types of content validity, criterion validity, and construct validity formed the foundation for the 1985 Standards for Educational and Psychological Testing (AERA, APA & NCME, 1985), influenced other professional standards and testing legislation, and organize many textbook treatments of test validity even today. This tripartite approach offers another example of partition because different types of validity were deemed appropriate for different types of tests. Beyond these three basic types, however, the process of expansion led to several more types of validity added to these three. For instance, Campbell and Fiske (1959) introduced the notions of *convergent validity* and *discriminant validity* in the context of multimethod–multitrait matrices of data. Such analyses take relatively higher correlations between scores intended to assess the same construct as support for convergent validity, and lower correlations between scores intended to assess different constructs as support for discriminant validity. A further distinction divides convergent validity into *trait validity* based on measures of the same construct and *nomological validity* based on measures of related constructs (Geisinger, 1992). In other contexts, the term *discriminant validity* refers to a form of *criterion-related validity*: the ability of test scores to discriminate between members of two groups (e.g., pathological and not). Discriminant validity in that sense further divides into sensitivity and specificity when combined with a cut score for the test (Fombonne, 1991). Sensitivity refers to the proportion of true positives out of the group one wishes to detect (e.g., pathological group) whereas specificity refers to the proportion of true negatives out of the group one wishes to distinguish from the detected group (e.g., not pathological). Though they don't use the word 'validity' in their names, the literature on validation of clinical scales often treats these as two further subtypes of validity. *Criterion validity* combined two previously distinct subtypes: *concurrent validity* and *predictive validity*, which differed with respect to the timing of criterion data collection (concurrent with versus following the test score collection). The term *incremental validity* came into use to refer to the extent to which a test added to a set of other predictors in a regression equation predicting a criterion variable (Sechrest, 1963). *Ecological validity* refers to generalizability of validity across settings and *population validity* to generalization across populations of test takers (Geisinger, 1992). *Synthetic validity* refers to the validity of a battery of tests built up from validity evidence for individual tests included in the battery (Lawshe, 1952). *Face validity* most often refers to the extent to which a test appears to test takers to assess what it is intended to assess (Mosier, 1947).

Whereas the tripartite approach to validity reflected partition, and various additional forms of validity reflected expansion, a process of unification also began taking shape during this period. Loevinger (1957) and Cronbach (1971) proposed subsuming other forms of validity under construct validity (see also Guion, 1980). However, this idea remained more or less an undercurrent in validity theory for many decades until it reached its culmination in Messick's (1989) validity chapter and the 1999 *Standards* (AERA, APA & NCME, 1999).

1.2.3. *Constructivist Realism*

Although Messick's work reflected a continuation of the unification begun much earlier in the test validity literature, the work also reflects an important shift from empiricist assumptions about how science works to a realist view. In the empiricist views that informed earlier work, observations serve as the basic elements from which theories develop. Useful constructs help to organize and simplify laws holding between observations of various types. In contrast, realism takes references to unobserved properties at their word: Constructs like anxiety, extraversion, math ability, competency to perform a certain task, and intelligence exist as attributes of individuals independent of our attempts to assess them. As such the idea of things with independent existence displaces the idea of observations as the central idea in realist thinking. Researchers use psychometric models to model the behavior of test scores in relation to these independently existing attributes of test takers (Borsboom, Mellenbergh, & Van Heerden, 2003). However, nature does not provide us with a universal lexicon of things that exist (Putnam, 1983, chapter 12). As such, researchers painstakingly develop terminology to describe entities and attributes, sometimes with false starts (phlogiston, feeble-mindedness) and corrections along the way. For this reason, Messick adopted a constructivist realism that understands constructs used in scientific research as approximations of existing entities constructed through scientific practice and through applied practice. There may be no such personal attribute as general vocabulary in a given language and such references to general vocabulary may fail to refer to anything. Nonetheless, one can understand the use of the term as a first attempt to formulate a means of referring to what turns out to be a cluster of closely related attributes that differ in terms of oral versus written language, recognition versus recall, and so on. This also allows for the possibility that separate groups of researchers can construct different vocabularies for discussing the same cluster of attributes, as may have been the case with intelligence researchers disagreeing about general intelligence versus multiple dimensions of intelligence.

Realism in measurement theory and test validity theory may seem to conflict with two central ideas: that one should not reify common factors and that classical test theory does not apply to platonic true scores. The first idea is that one should not always assume that a common factor corresponds to an existing attribute. This should be clear from the fact that one can rotate a factor solution to produce infinitely many alternative factor representations of the same data. It certainly seems unlikely that each of these sets of factors has an independent existence. However, this does not conflict with the use of factor analysis to make abductive inferences to the best explanation of the observed data (Haig, 2005). It simply means that positing a real attribute differs from attributing an independent existence to the common factor itself. At best, common factors exist as elements of mathematical models that researchers use to represent existing attributes of test takers.

The second idea comes from Lord and Novick (1968) who developed an example in which interpreting true scores as the correct answer failed to comport with classical test theory. They referred to such true scores as platonic true scores. The example involved a dichotomously scored test in which the correct answer had to be either zero or one, but the classical true score had to be a mean somewhere between zero and one. Similarly to the above case, there stands a critical distinction between the true score of classical test theory, on the one hand, and the attribute that is taken to have an independent existence, on the other. A true score remains test dependent. An attribute is a property of test takers independent of any particular test. As such, positing real attributes does not imply interpreting true scores as platonic true scores.

Messick formulated a validity theory that was unified, but not unitary. It was unified because, at a theoretical level, it subsumed many lines of evidence under a generalized notion of construct validity. However, the theory was not unitary because it allowed for considerable diversity in which particular lines of evidence or which types of theoretical rationales were drawn together for any given test. The general character of Messick's (1989) validity theory allowed previously discrete *types of validity* to be recast as distinct *types of validity evidence* for a single validity judgment. According to Messick's theory, all validity comes down to demonstrating that a test assesses as much as possible of what it should (minimize construct underrepresentation) and as little as possible of what it should not (minimize construct-irrelevant variance). All sources of invalidity, in this view, fall into one of these two exhaustive types (Messick here elaborated on an idea introduced by Cook and Campbell, 1979).

However, the generality and flexibility of the unified theory also placed a substantial new burden on individual test developers. They were required to conceptualize and chart their own validation agenda specific to the needs of their individual tests. This was a burden many were simply not prepared to bear, perhaps reasonably so. Not every cook needs to perform the tasks of a chef, and not every builder needs to perform the tasks of an architect. Such concerns have led to renewed efforts at partition. Perhaps the most controversial element of Messick's (1989) theory, however, involved the idea that the consequences of test interpretation and use should contribute to the basis for the integrated judgment on the appropriateness of test score interpretation and use (Borsboom & Mellenbergh, 2007; Messick, 1998; Popham, 1997; Reccase, 1998). Messick's position here was, however, consistent with earlier work. For instance, Cronbach (1988) viewed consequences as providing direct evidence for test validity, albeit acknowledging that some may prefer not to call it that, whereas Messick (1989) presented consequences as merely providing indirect evidence pointing to possible sources of construct underrepresentation or construct-irrelevant variance.

1.2.4. Pragmatism

A diverse range of views fall under the general label of pragmatism. Indeed, the three philosophers who founded pragmatism, Charles Sanders Peirce, John Dewey, and William James, disagreed on many key points, right down to the name. Later philosophers have further developed various aspects of classical pragmatism but rejected others. Kane's (1992, 2006, 2009) approach to validation reflects shift from realism toward pragmatism in the following sense. Although Kane did not originate the concept of a validity argument, he made argument a central organizing idea in ways that emphasized several issues associated with pragmatism. Moreover, Kane introduced the interpretive argument as the basis for the validity argument, taking the place of a more formal scientific construct theory in Messick's approach (Kane, 2006). This shift makes validation more dynamic over time and more closely tied to communication and dialog. Kane's approach shifts the emphasis away from abstract arguments constructed in accordance with timeless universal standards toward context-specific arguments constructed at a particular time and place for a particular purpose. The goal of validation is to provide a line of reasoning that will support the acceptability of the test interpretation in question. This interpretation depends upon choices that go beyond what the data can determine. The desired conclusions of the argument depend upon the specific interpretation at hand. Practical concerns can encourage a change in interpretive argument even if the underlying construct theory remains relatively stable. More importantly, the criteria that make for a good argument depend in part on the formulation of the interpretive argument and on what assumptions are deemed plausible. Broadly speaking, Kane's approach can be read as turning away from fixed universal foundations for validation practice and instead grounding validation in context-specific features of the effort to accomplish something using testing. Kane might not accept the classical pragmatist idea equating truth with what works, but his approach to validation focuses on building an argument for test use that an audience will accept at a particular time and in a particular context (c.f., Zumbo, 2009). Justifying a testing practice to two different audiences, for example, may require that the test developer integrate very different perspectives with different concerns and different assumptions. This approach thus reflects a dramatic contrast with the idea of a single validation effort guided by universal standards of scientific evidence that seems to guide earlier validity literature. This general pragmatic shift animates Kane's treatment of a variety of specific validity issues. For example, Kane (2006) attempted to reconcile Cronbach's (1971, 1988) and Messick's (1989) views of the role of consequences through the context-dependent aspect of validity arguments. In Kane's view, consequences bear on the validity argument if and when legitimate stakeholders have concerns about them. This view follows directly from the need to make validity arguments specific to the context that they address.

Interpretive arguments summarize evidence for conclusions about individual test takers (Kane 1992, 2006). For instance, suppose that John fails to solve relatively easy verbal analogies. The test user may interpret this as indicating a low level of verbal reasoning ability. Kane (2006) distinguishes four components of such interpretations: scoring of test responses, generalization to a domain of test responses, extrapolation beyond test responses, and decisions based on test scores. This interpretation, however, requires evidence. One piece of evidence is the test score itself. However, other evidence is usually required. For instance, one has to rule out plausible alternative explanations to the low score (e.g., there are no indications of test anxiety, John stands nothing to gain by scoring low on the test, he can read adequately, etc.). In addition, one requires positive evidence about the functioning of the test in general, in order to support the hypothesis that the test indeed assesses verbal reasoning ability. This argument, that focuses on the test in general rather than on John's specific case, is a validity argument. The validity argument draws from validity evidence, theory, and plausible supposition to support the premises required to back up the interpretive argument. In Kane's (2006) approach, test developers and test users should begin by spelling out the interpretive argument, then probe that argument for weakness, and finally build their validation efforts around the weak points in the argument. In this way, Kane's work seeks to provide more concrete guidance to test developers and users regarding how best to proceed with validating a test for a specific purpose.

The view of validity and validation presented in the most recent versions of the *Standards* and *Educational Measurement* reflect efforts at unification but also incorporate elements of partition by allowing broad differentiation between specific applications within the unifying concepts. For example, Kane (2006) organizes his chapter around a series of contrasting types of test validation applications. From the beginning, however, the idea of unifying test validity under one organizing principle has met with objections. The perspectives on validity advocated in the field have remained diverse despite the canonizing efforts of the *Standards* and *Educational Measurement* in their various editions. Cronbach devoted three and a half pages to addressing criticisms from Bechtoldt (1957) and Brodbeck (1957, 1963). Similarly, in an early caution against an overly broad understanding of validity, Ebel (1961) concluded that "The term 'valid' is not to be made synonymous with the term 'good'" (p. 646). More recently, Cervone and Caldwell (2008) argued for a view that makes the appropriate understanding of measurement and validity highly specific to individual substantive contexts. Since the publication of Messick's work, a number of authors have advocated various ways of restoring validity to a purely descriptive factual basis by partitioning concerns about value implications and consequences from validity itself (reviewed in chapter 9). Borsboom, Mellenbergh, and Van Heerden (2004) and Borsboom et al. (2009) argued in favor of understanding validity in terms of what holds true independent of the available evidence rather than as a summary of the extent to which evidence supports the belief. Whereas much recent literature takes validity as the result of validation, this view takes validity as a precondition for successful validation. Michell (2009) argues that the concept of validity itself results from a lack of clarity about measurement and could be profitably eliminated by more precise efforts to tie measurement to quantitative structure. The papers collected by Lissitz (2009) present a broad range of contemporary perspectives on test validity. In the present book, we consider alternative positions without attempting to adjudicate between them. Instead, we intend to make as clear as possible the differences and communalities between positions.

1.3. Measurement, Causation, Meaning, and Test Validity

The present book focuses on three fundamental concepts as they relate to test validity: measurement, causation and meaning. Many take measurement, in some sense of the term, as the fundamental goal of testing. The term 'measurement' permeates the literature on test theory. Moreover, of these three basic concepts, measurement is probably the best understood at a theoretical level. Nonetheless, many complexities remain in bridging the gap between the theory of measurement and testing practice. Unquestionably, we understand the concept of causation substantially less well than that of measurement. In recent years, progress has been noteworthy in this area both in the general theory of causation and in methodological literature on causal estimation and causal inference. Increasingly, discussion of causal relationships in measurement models has cropped up alongside measurement applications of structural equation models. Nonetheless, the surface has barely been scratched in terms of working out the complex connection between test validity and causation. Finally, the concept of meaning applies wherever one finds talk of test score interpretations. Talk of test score interpretations comes up wherever test scores play a role in informing decisions. Today test-driven decisions range from cradle to grave. Nonetheless, the theoretical understanding of meaning in the context of test validity remains underdeveloped and undertheorized. Greater attention to these three fundamental areas holds the potential to move forward our general understanding of test validity.

1.3.1. Measurement and Test Validity

In many contexts 'testing' and 'measurement' serve as interchangeable terms. As noted earlier, the present book restricts 'measurement' to a more narrow sense that assumes quantitative properties in what is measured. Such quantitative properties involve more than just continuity or moreness and lessness. As examples, consider some common types of tests: a language arts ability test for elementary school students, a test of physical fitness for military recruits, and a test of psychopathic traits used for clinical assessment. If the test scores have any variance beyond error variance, then clearly some test takers show more language arts ability, more physical fitness, or more psychopathic traits than others. Technically, however, no test scores, and indeed no numbers representable by computers, are truly continuous. There are always gaps without numbers in between. Nonetheless, suppose that one focuses on the underlying attribute rather than the score itself (over the objections of committed empiricists who only believe in observed scores). Let us grant the continuity of these. Is the difference between a score at the 10th percentile and a score 1 point above the same as the difference between a score at the 90th percentile and a score 1 point above? If not, then one can test the attribute but not measure it in the strict sense adopted here. Thus understood, measurement is an ideal to which many tests aspire but one that few tests attain.

Even if rarely realized, measurement remains an important and influential regulative ideal and a clear understanding of measurement remains important to testing. The concept of measurement shapes the ways that tests are constructed, and the ways that test scores are interpreted and validated. Moreover, different approaches to measurement do not necessarily agree on the details and can thus have different implications for testing practice. For example, axiomatic measurement theory often assumes that observable variables must show quantitative structure. In contrast, latent variable theory allows for latent variables with quantitative structure imperfectly measured by observed indicators that do not themselves show such structure. Whether or not one expects observed test scores to show quantitative structure will have an effect on how one designs the test. For example, sum scores of dichotomous items cannot show such structure for finite tests due to lack of continuity. Test score interpretation will also be affected, because the former approach requires equal intervals in test scores whereas the latter need not. Indeed, a latent variable model might explicitly assume that equal intervals on the latent variable do not lead to equal intervals in observed test scores along the range of latent variable values. Finally, this difference in assumptions will also affect test validation because one seeks to establish support for different sets of assumptions, and these will require different lines of support.

1.3.2. Causation and Test Validity

Do construct values cause test score values? Some authors have argued that they typically should (Borsboom et al., 2004), and others that they only sometimes should (Bollen & Lennox, 1991; Foster & Cone, 1995; Kane, 2009). From a descriptive empiricist perspective (Cureton, 1951), they never should because constructs are only patterns in the data. A convenient redescription of the data cannot cause the data. Many latent variable models naturally lead to such causal assumptions and the concept of causation helps to distinguish test validity that one can plausibly project into other times and contexts from spurious correlation that might not generalize as dependably. On the other hand, behavioral observation measures simply attempt to operationalize an observed behavior without relating it to any latent construct (Foster & Cone, 1995; Kane, 2009) and formative models take the indices as causes of the latent construct (Bollen & Lennox, 1991; Edwards & Bagozzi, 2000). However, even if one can agree on a causal path diagram, there remains room for alternative interpretations of the same diagram (Markus, 2002). Such alternatives differ in their understanding of causation itself (Markus, 2010). For example, one can interpret causal diagrams in a way that does not require distinctness between causes and their effects (Markus, 2008b).

1.3.3. Meaning and Test Validity

For test developers and applied test users, nothing comes more naturally than talk of meaning and interpretation of test scores. Do parents misinterpret their children's educational test scores, drawing incorrect conclusions about their children's performance? Do clinical measures retain their meaning when applied to new immigrant populations? Do employers or public administrators over-interpret job performance scores, basing decisions on them that the scores do not fully support? Do precinct-level performance measures retain their meaning when municipal or state governments make the scores objects of policy initiatives? Such talk appears in test theory and psychometric literature as well. References to interpreting common factors have a long history in the literature on factor analysis. The literature on scaling theory often makes reference to what one can or cannot infer from a given score, or score difference. By and large, however, test theory has remained somewhat less fluent with respect to talk of test score meaning and interpretation than have test developers and users.

One source of this disparity may be the colloquial division of occupational interests between numbers people and words people. As noted above, testing as a sub-discipline tends to attract numbers people. However, meaning and interpretation have traditionally fallen into the domain of words people. More specifically, there is a traditional view of mathematics as providing timeless and universal truths, outside the reach of interpretation. As geometry discovered with Euclid's axioms, however, the same formal mathematical system can have different interpretations (what is a line? what is a plane?) and these can have very different practical implications (such as the sum of the angles of a triangle varying with the degree of curvature of the surface on which the triangle resides). Closer to home, the basic concepts of both classical and modern test theory are also open to different interpretations: true scores, common factors, latent variables, and probabilities all have literatures exploring alternative interpretations. As such, the idea that mathematical descriptions somehow bypass the problems of interpretation and meaning seems less plausible today than it may once have seemed.

In this light, gaining more than just an informal understanding of talk about test score interpretations and meaning has value in illuminating this aspect of test theory in general and test validity theory in specific. What sort of thing is an interpretation? Of what does it consist? How can one compare two interpretations? How can test score interpretation inform mathematical descriptions of test scores? How might answers to these questions inform and guide test validation?

These three concepts, measurement, causation, and meaning, provide the central components to the exploration of test validity theory presented in the remaining chapters. Each raises important questions and practical problems that a theory of test validity should address. Each also plays a central role in informing and guiding the practice of test development and test validation.

1.4. Further Reading

Angoff, W. H. (1988). Validity: An evolving concept. In H. Wainer & H. I. Braun (Eds.), *Test validity* (pp. 19–32). Mahwah, NJ: Erlbaum.

Borsboom, D., Mellenbergh, G. J., & Van Heerden, J. (2004). The concept of validity. *Psychological Review, 111*, 1061–1071.

Geisinger, K. F. (1992). The metamorphosis of test validation. *Educational Psychologist, 27*, 197–222.

Hubley, A. M. & Zumbo, B. D. (1996). Dialectic on validity: Where we have been and where we are going. *The Journal of General Psychology, 123*, 207–215.

Kane, M. T. (2001). Current Concerns in Validity Theory. *Journal of Educational Measurement, 38*, 319–342.

Lissitz, R. (2009). *The concept of validity: Revisions, new directions, and applications*. Charlotte, NC: Information Age Publishing. (Chapter 1).

Newton, P. E. (2012). Clarifying the consensus definition of validity. *Measurement: Interdisciplinary Research and Perspectives, 10*, 1–29.

2 Philosophical Theories of Measurement

Connections With Other Chapters

Chapter 1 has outlined the major historical developments in validity theory. Throughout these developments, the idea of measurement has been prominent. This chapter outlines the most important theories of measurement that in the past have been developed by philosophers and measurement theorists. The chapter relates these theories to the case of measurement in the social sciences and outlines their relevance to the concept of validity.

Measurement plays an important role in our daily lives, and has probably done so since the dawn of humanity. Ancient ruins testify to the presence of measurement procedures long before anything remotely resembling modern science was around. To construct even the simplest building requires one to engage in measurement procedures, however primitive, to assess dimensions such as length and height. Moreover, the ease with which human beings acquire such concepts and learn to evaluate them suggests that measurement procedures are grounded in very basic perceptual and cognitive abilities, rooted in our evolutionary ancestry.

The assessment of attributes that we may label as psychological is equally basic to human functioning. For instance, human beings appear to routinely assess psychological differences in the dominance of other human beings. In fact, the ability to assess individual differences in traits like dominance is not limited to primates, but can be observed in many social animals at different positions of the phylogenetic scale including mammals, birds and fish. This suggests that the ability to do so is essential to an animal's chances of survival.

Many measurement procedures used in science can be viewed as refinements of basic perceptual abilities common to human beings. Such abilities involve both physical and psychological dimensions. Thus, it is not surprising that measurement procedures have been developed for the assessment of psychological attributes such as attitudes and personality traits as well as physical attributes such as lung capacity or body mass. However, the differences between measurement procedures in the natural sciences and the social sciences are revealing. Whereas the application, development, and refinement of measurement instruments in the natural sciences have led to an increased understanding of how these instruments work and what they measure, many psychological measurement procedures fail to provide a full understanding of what psychological tests measure or how they measure it.

For example, despite the general acceptance of intelligence tests, we lack an equally well-accepted theory of what constitutes intelligence. This has led at least one critic to maintain that no such thing as psychological measurement exists, and that the idea that psychological measurement is a case of applied science is flawed because there is no psychological science to apply in this case (Michell, 1997). While few psychologists would subscribe to this position, it is evident that there exist doubts on the scientific underpinnings of many of psychology's measurement procedures even among methodologists of a more moderate opinion (Messick, 1989; Borsboom, Mellenbergh, & Van Heerden, 2004). For instance, as will be discussed in more detail later in the chapter, many contributors to the literature have taken transitivity (e.g., if A > B, and B > C, then A > C) as basic to measurement. However, few real-world tests attain clear unidimensionality and yet without this feature scores need not conform to transitivity. To illustrate, if person *A* demonstrates more creativity than person *B*, and person *B* more than person *C*, one cannot necessarily conclude from this, given a multidimensional attribute, that person *A* demonstrates more creativity than person *C*. That is, whether or not such a conclusion is valid depends on the way the different dimensions are organized. In many such possible organizations, transitivity will be violated.

How do these issues relate to validity theory? Although the meaning of the term 'validity' is subject to debate, as is the preferred way of going about validation research (e.g., Cronbach & Meehl, 1955; Loevinger, 1957; Messick, 1989; Borsboom, Mellenbergh, & Van Heerden, 2004), this much seems beyond contention: In order to answer the question of what a psychological test measures, one needs to have an idea of what measurement is. From this point of view, it must be considered surprising that this issue has received little attention in the validity literature. Most treatises on the topic of validity appear to proceed under the assumption that one can give a reasonable verdict on the validity of measurement procedures without specifying an account of measurement itself. However, as the present chapter will make clear, measurement can be conceptualized in several different ways. Given the different consequences that follow from choosing a definition of measurement, the idea that one can answer the question of what it is that psychological tests measure without fleshing out the meaning of the term 'measurement' may be crucially mistaken (Michell, 2009).

It is therefore important to have a clear idea of how measurement can be conceptualized. The purpose of the present chapter is to elucidate the ways in which this can be done, and to assess the consequences of several available conceptualizations. We will outline the basic tenets of some of the main contenders, which are classical measurement theory, operationalism, axiomatic measurement theory, and latent variable theory. In addition, we discuss their possible application to psychological measurement procedures. The central questions that we aim to address are (a) which sorts of attributes allow for measurement in the first place, (b) whether it is likely that psychological attributes are of that sort, and (c) how we should evaluate proposed procedures for psychological measurement in the light of the available philosophical theories. This last question, of course, lies at the foundation of test validity theory.

2.1. The Classical Theory of Measurement

One of the most intuitive ways of thinking about measurement is according to what has been called the *classical* theory of measurement (Michell, 1986; not to be confused with classical test theory as put forward, for instance, by Lord & Novick, 1968). According to this theory, "[s]cientific measurement is properly defined as *the estimation or discovery of the ratio of some magnitude of a quantitative attribute to a unit of the same attribute*" (Michell, 1997, p. 358, italics in the original). This definition closely aligns with paradigm cases of measurement, e.g., length or weight measurement. For instance, one estimates the length of a rod (or rather, the ratio of the rod's length to a unit such as a centimeter) by assessing how many units make up a length that equals that of the rod. A familiar way of doing this is by simply holding a tape measure next to the rod and reading off the corresponding number of units from the tape measure.

This definition has two important consequences. First, as conventionally interpreted, it implies a *realist* philosophy of measurement. That is, we *estimate* or *discover* the relevant relations between magnitudes, which means that these relations existed prior to the act of measurement. Hence, those who subscribe to the classical theory of measurement are committed to the position that these relations (rod x is twice as long as rod y, object x is π times as heavy as object y, time interval t_2–t_1 is half as long as time interval t_3–t_4) exist independently of our determination of them. Therefore, the existence of such relations is not the consequence of our act of measurement, but a precondition for measurement to be possible at all.

Second, the class of attributes that allows for measurement is *restricted*. Since measurement involves the estimation of discovery of *ratios* of magnitudes, only attributes that possess such relations are candidates for measurement. These attributes are said to have *quantitative structure*.

The idea of quantitative structure has been made precise by Hölder (1901; see Michell & Ernst, 1996, for an English translation) by means of a set of axioms to which the structure of the attribute should conform in order for it to be quantitative.

An important condition to consider is expressed in Hölder's first axiom: Given some quantity Q with levels $(a, b, c, . . .)$, either (i) $a = b$, (ii) there exists c in Q such that $a = b + c$, or (iii) there exists c in Q such that $b = a + c$. This axiom can be used to illustrate two important characteristics of quantitative attributes. The first characteristic was described by Aristotle (*Metaphysics, Book V*) in terms of divisibility into divisibles. Any magnitude can be analyzed into component parts that are themselves instances of the same magnitude. As an illustration, any length can be split up in two parts that are themselves also lengths, which can again be split up in parts that are themselves also lengths, etc. Rozeboom (1966) viewed this as the defining property of a quantitative attribute. In this respect, a magnitude contrasts with a multitude, which is divisible into *in*divisibles; e.g., a multitude of people is divisible into individual persons, but these persons are not themselves further divisible into other persons. A more detailed consideration of the difference between magnitudes and multitudes is given by Cooper and Humphry (2010).

The second characteristic of a quantitative attribute is *additive structure*. This means that one can add two lengths to produce a third; moreover, as is demanded by Hölder's other axioms, the order in which this is done does not matter for the result (i.e., $a + b = b + a$), and the same holds for the manner in which one groups the magnitudes (i.e., $\{a + b\} + c = a + \{b + c\}$). Thus the combination of levels of the attribute is *commutative* and *associative*. The internal structure of a quantitative attribute is therefore such that the combinations of its levels are structurally similar to the mathematical operation of addition, hence the term *additive structure*. It should be noted that additive structure, in this sense, is *not* a property of the numbers that are assigned to the levels of the attribute. Additions of numerical assignments will behave in accordance with the laws of addition trivially; this holds not only for adding length measurements, but also for adding IQ-scores, football numbers, and postal codes. The point is not that one can add arbitrarily assigned numbers, but that the attribute *itself* satisfies additive structure. Hence additivity here refers to a condition on the structure of attributes, and not to the question of what one can practically do with a set of numerical assignments.

A final note about Hölder's conditions, and the classical theory of measurement that is based on them, is that they require the attribute to be continuous. That is, the attribute must be infinitely dense: between any two levels of the attribute, there must be a third, and there can be no gaps in the structure of the attribute.

It is important to draw attention to the property of continuity, because in this theory continuity does not imply quantitative structure (as is sometimes thought in methodological circles). Attributes can be continuous but not quantitative; this will happen as soon as an attribute satisfies the continuity condition but does not possess additive structure. For example, library call numbers are continuous because each book receives a unique number and it is always possible to add a new book between any two existing books. Nonetheless, the subject matter of two books with call numbers differing by an equal amount do not themselves differ by an equal quantity of some aspect of the subject matter. This issue is sometimes not clearly perceived in psychology. For instance, Borgatta and Borhnstedt (1980, p.29) state that "if the variables are continuous, they must also by definition, be interval." This appears to be a view that is quite widely espoused in psychology. However, assuming that the use of the term 'interval' here refers to a quantitative structure, this statement is false. Continuity is an ordinal condition that does not imply quantitative structure as defined by Hölder (1901); and, as far as we know, there exists no argument to support the thesis that continuity implies quantitative structure. The standard example is a stretchy measuring tape on which one can always identify a point between any two other points, but equal numerical distances between numbered points need not correspond to equal physical distances, due to the stretchiness of the tape.

If an attribute is not only continuous, but in addition possesses quantitative structure, then that means that any two levels of the attribute stand in a special relationship to each other; namely, they have a *ratio*. It is the estimation or discovery of such ratios that the classical theory views as definitional with respect to the term *measurement*. Normally, the estimation of ratios happens by choosing an arbitrary level of the quantitative attribute as a *unit* (for instance, the meter), and estimating the ratio in which other levels of the attribute stand to that unit. This definition is well suited to dealing with measurement as it occurs in physics; e.g., the measurement of length with a tape measure or weight with a balance scale. As described, measurement procedures can be used to achieve what psychologists know as a *ratio scale* (Stevens, 1946).

Alternatively, attributes with a quantitative structure may admit for measuring the *differences* between any two levels of an attribute. In this case one can construct an *interval scale*. Formally, interval scales are ratio scales that work on the differences between attribute levels, rather than on these levels themselves. Although interval scales and ratio scales differ in their levels of representation (i.e., they are representations of attribute levels or of differences between them), in the classical view, both require attributes to have a quantitative structure. Also, it is important to realize that, in the classical view, quantitative structure is something that an *attribute* does or does not have. In contrast, the terms *ratio level* and *interval level* refer to properties of *scales* (i.e., to representations of an attribute, rather than to the attribute itself). So, although there are interval and ratio *scales*, there are no ratio and interval *attributes*. Attributes, in the classical view, are either quantitative or qualitative; if they are quantitative, they may be measured on either a ratio or interval level. On which level the scale operates depends on the measurement instruments at one's disposal. However, if attributes are qualitative, they cannot be measured at all.

Now, it is not obvious that there exist psychological measurement procedures that fit this definition (see Box 2.1). Nevertheless many would like to hold on to the idea that the procedures that go under the name of psychological measurement *do* deserve the label *measurement*. One way of alleviating the cognitive dissonance that one experiences when one attempts to retain the idea that psychological measurement could exist, even if no psychological attributes are quantitative, is to change one's definition of measurement so that it may also apply to weaker structures, such as ordinal ones. Perhaps unsurprisingly, this is exactly the route that psychology took when it was first confronted with criticisms of the quantity assumption. The main player in this move was S. S. Stevens; and the resulting theory is what is now known as the *representational* theory of measurement. To this theory we will turn shortly. However, to understand the motivation for this theory, we first need to delve slightly deeper into the way that measurement was conceptualized in physics at the beginning of the 20th century.

Box 2.1. Is Intelligence Quantitative?

As with most psychological attributes, the hypothesis that intelligence has quantitative structure is, at present, unsupported, either by theoretical arguments or by empirical research. It is, in this context, important to separate intelligence (the attribute) from IQ (the score), and to note that the hypothesis of quantitative structure does *not* pertain to IQ-scores. In fact, IQ-*scores* are extremely unlikely to possess interval or ratio properties as measures of intelligence, even if intelligence were to be quantitative. The reason for this is that they are based on a more or less arbitrary collection of items; adding or removing items will yield a different score distribution, and hence will give rise to different IQ-scores. Hence it would be a very unlikely coincidence if, say, the current edition of the WAIS would have *precisely* the right set of items to map onto the attribute of intelligence in the way an interval scale does. It is not certain, however, that there exist no *functions* of item responses that yield interval measures of intelligence. For instance, according to latent variable models like the Item Response Theory (IRT) model to be discussed later, this possibility does exist via the construction of trait estimates (which, unlike IQ-scores, are theoretically independent of the particular items that they are based on). For this to be possible, according to the classical view of measurement, it must however be the case that intelligence *itself* has quantitative structure, and it is *this* hypothesis that is currently unsupported. Every single study that has been done on the concept of intelligence is consistent, for instance, with the hypothesis that intelligence is an ordinal attribute rather than a quantitative one; the reason for this is that the additivity of intelligence has never been put to the test. This omission partly springs from theoretical limitations. From a theoretical point of view, we do not know how to combine levels of intelligence and check whether they support additivity the same way that we know how to combine lengths or weights (Section 2.2). At the level of IQ-scores, it is certainly unlikely that two people with an IQ of 50 will match a person with an IQ of 100 when solving a problem. Perhaps IQ does combine lawfully, but does so in other ways—however, we currently do not know whether or how this is the case. In fact, we do not even know whether we are really *interested* in testing the hypothesis that intelligence is quantitative because we do not see the hypothesis that it is quantitative as *central* to the functioning of IQ-tests or the theories of intelligence research. Most researchers will be happy if intelligence has a bona fide ordinal structure that can reasonably be approximated by the ordering induced by IQ-scores—and this hypothesis by itself is hard enough to test.

2.2. Addition and Concatenation

The classical theory of measurement, as formulated by Michell (1986; 1997; 1999), makes a clear distinction between the ontological conditions that have to be satisfied for measurement to be possible (i.e., the attribute must be quantitative) and the epistemological process by which one estimates the values of the attribute (i.e., by making some comparison to a unit; the manner in which this is done is left unspecified). However, measurement theorists did not always accept such a separation between ontology and epistemology. In fact, when the philosophical theory of measurement crystallized in the beginning of the 20th century, several theorists maintained that measurement requires a very specific epistemological process that serves both to ascertain the quantitative structure of attributes and to furnish the scaling efforts that lead to a measurement scale.

The most influential of these theorists was Norman Campbell. Campbell (1920) set out to provide a general theory of *fundamental measurement*. For Campbell, fundamental measurement referred to measurement procedures that do not require the prior determination of other quantities than the one measured. This class contrasts with *derived* measurement, which refers to the determination of quantities on the basis of other quantities. An example is the determination of density, which requires the prior determination of mass and volume. Fundamental measurement is thus fundamental in the sense that it does not depend on the measurement of other attributes. How does such measurement work?

According to Campbell, the crucial point lies in the presence of an *empirical* counterpart to the numerical operation of addition. Such an empirical operation is often called a *concatenation operation*. A concatenation operation is an operation that literally adds two objects to each other. An example for the case of length is laying two rods end-to-end; this amounts to *empirically adding* the lengths of these objects. Another example is putting two objects in one pan of a pan balance. This empirically adds the weights of these objects.

If a concatenation operation exists, then the quantitative structure of an attribute can be tested experimentally. Suppose, for instance, that one has a pan balance and four weights *a*, *b*, *c*, and *d*. One puts *a* and *b* in one pan of the balance and *c* in the other. Suppose that the weights balance each other. One concludes that the concatenation of *a* and *b* is equally heavy as object *c*. One may then check whether first putting *a* in the pan, and *b* secondly, makes a difference in the behavior of the balance scale, when compared to first putting *b* and then *a*. This is not so; whether *a* or *b* is put in first, the concatenations *a* + *b* and *b* + *a* are balanced by *c* in either case. Hence *commutativity* is confirmed. Further, one may combine *a* and *b* and *c* in one arm of the balance; suppose it is balanced by *d*, which is on the other side. Checking whether {*a* + *b*} + *c* is equal to *a* + {*b* + *c*} is then easy; one tests whether the order of concatenation (*a* and *b* first; *c* added, versus *a* first; *b* and *c* added) makes a difference with respect to d; if both cases are balanced by *d*, then *associativity* is confirmed. The concatenation operation thus has *empirical* properties which are the exact mirror image of the *numerical* operation of addition. When this is so, the road to fundamental measurement is open.

With the presence of a concatenation operation, the construction of a measurement scale is simple. In Campbell's words:

> If these experimental propositions, corresponding to the laws of addition, are true (and in the case of weight they are) we can proceed at once to measurement. We know that Number 2 is that which results from the addition of the Number 1 to the Number 1; that the Number 3 results from the addition of the Number 2 to the Number 1; and so on for all other Numbers.
>
> (Campbell, 1920, p. 180)

Campbell further noted the arbitrary nature of the choice of the unit corresponding to the number 1. He also noted that, once started, one can readily extend the process of concatenation arbitrarily far along an infinite series of numbers.

Campbell's account of fundamental measurement, although impressive, places an extremely heavy burden on the existence of a specific way of assigning numbers to objects (i.e., through concatenation). Campbell was clear on his position with respect to this issue: "In order that a property should be measured as a fundamental magnitude, involving the measurement of no other property, it is necessary that a physical process of addition should be found for it" (Campbell, 1920, p. 267). Without a concatenation operation, therefore, fundamental measurement could not exist. By this requirement, Campbell defined measurement through a restriction on the epistemological processes that are involved in the assignment of numbers to objects.

When Campbell put forward his account of fundamental measurement, it was immediately obvious that the nascent methods of psychological measurement, as were emerging in the fields of psychophysics (Fechner, 1860; Stevens, and Davids, 1938), ability testing (Binet, 1916; Terman, 1916), and attitude measurement (Thurstone, 1927) did not conform to it. No psychological concatenation operations existed, and hence no psychological measurement was fundamental in Campbell's sense. At the same time, psychological attributes were not determined through derived measurement by means of lawful composition of other measurements, in the way that density is derived from mass and volume. The question thus arose whether such methods were methods of measurement at all.

With a famous gathering of measurement experts (including Campbell himself), known as the *Ferguson Committee*, the British Association for the Advancement of Science attempted to reach a conclusion on whether psychological assessment methods were worthy of the name measurement. The committee never reached unanimous agreement, but the influential opinion of the hardliners in the committee was, as Guild (cited in Reese, 1943, p. 6) put it, that "to insist on calling these other processes [i.e., psychological assessment] measurement adds nothing to their actual significance, but merely debases the coinage of verbal intercourse. Measurement is not a term with some mysterious inherent meaning, part of which may be overlooked by physicists and may be in the course of discovery by psychologists." Hence, according to this viewpoint, psychological measurement was unrealized in practices that went by that name. Of course, psychologists who had invested in the concept of psychological measurement could not let these charges go unanswered. Their response cumulated in the representational theory of measurement.

2.3. The Representational Theory of Measurement: Stevens' Version

There is a crucial difference between Campbell's formulation of fundamental measurement and the classical theory of measurement that we started out with. Whereas, in the classical theory, measurement procedures are attempts to *estimate ratios of magnitudes*, in Campbell's view measurement procedures are methods to *assign numerals to objects*. In this sense, Campbell stood with one foot in a realist framework and the other in a representationalist framework, which views as the essence of measurement the representation of empirical relations in a number system. This view was first explicitly articulated by Russell in 1903, and formed the basis of the response of psychologists, which started with the work by Stevens (1946) and would eventually culminate in the *Foundations of Measurement* (Krantz, Luce, Suppes, & Tversky, 1971).

The basis of representationalist thinking consists in drawing attention to the fact that the assignment of numerals to objects is an act of representation, much like the construction of a map of, say, Amsterdam is. The numeral that was assigned to object *a* thus *stands for something else*, just like the sign 'Amsterdam Central Station' on your map stands for the main train station in Amsterdam. What is that something else in the case of measurement? It is obvious that, in the classical theory, the assigned numeral is taken to be an estimate of a magnitude (or rather, the ratio of the magnitude to a unit), and in this sense stands for the magnitude in question. However, this is not the only interpretation that is open to the measurement theorist.

An alternative interpretation is that the numeral that is assigned to object *a* represents the empirical relation that object *a* bears to other objects *within a specified measurement procedure*. In such an interpretation, "object *a* weighs 12 kilograms (kg)" means something like "if you do such and such with *a* (for instance, follow Campbell's concatenation procedure) then you will find this and that (for instance, that *a* will be assigned the numeral '12')." Now this is obviously true in any scheme of thinking about measurement, including the classical theory, in the sense that if an object really weighs 12 kg, then a good measurement procedure will show this to be so. One can, however, go one step further to claim that the term 'weight' refers to *nothing but* the outcomes of such a procedure.

Taking such a perspective involves the definition of theoretical terms like weight *in terms of* the measurement procedure. This comes down to a semantic reduction of theoretical concepts to procedural schemes. The doctrine of *operationalism*, which was invented by Bridgman in 1927, maintains exactly this thesis: "We evidently know what we mean by length if we can tell what the length of any and every object is, and for the physicist nothing more is required." and "In general, we mean by any concept nothing more than a set of operations; *the concept is synonymous with a corresponding set of operations*." (Bridgman, 1927, p. 5, italics in the original).

Understood this way, Bridgman's point of view was quickly discredited in philosophy of science for two reasons. First, the idea that a term (e.g., 'length') can be synonymous with a succession of actions (e.g., laying a tape measure next to an object and reading off the value printed at its end) appears to be a category mistake. This is because synonymy is a relation between two linguistic entities (words or concepts or symbols), and actions are not linguistic. Hence it is unclear how actions can enter into the relation of synonymy. Second, the idea that a theoretical concept is synonymous with a set of operations entails that two different sets of operations could not possibly measure the same concept. Hence, the literal interpretation of Bridgman's definition implies that, say, mercury thermometers and electronic resistance thermometers cannot both measure temperature, because they involve different operations and work according to different principles (Suppe, 1977; Green, 2001). Needless to say, this flies in the face of scientific practice. Box 2.2 illustrates the shortcomings of operationalism in a psychological context. More recent scholarship has suggested more defensible interpretations of Bridgman: we need not pursue these here.

In psychology, however, operationalism had a profound influence on the thinking of psychologists. One reason for this is that it provided the following opening in thinking about measurement: If measurement is really nothing but the assignment of numerals according to some well-defined procedure, and there is nothing more to the meaning of a theoretical term than is captured in the procedures used to measure it, then there is no principled objection to the thesis that *any* well-defined procedure to assign numerals is a measurement procedure. So the class of measurement procedures is then restricted only by an appropriately specific description of the way that the numerical assignments are carried out. Obviously, upon this viewpoint, psychological measurement *does* exist; in fact, it is impossible *not* to be engaged in measurement provided that one follows a consistent scheme of numerical assignment.

S. S. Stevens (1946) took this theoretical opportunity and initiated a view that was based upon exactly this line of reasoning. Stevens broadened the conception of measurement to include not only the magnitudes of the classical theory, or the fundamental and derived measurement schemes of Campbell (1920), but in fact anything from the classification of people according to their hair color to the measurement of length by a tape measure. Rather than restricting the concept of measurement in some way, he divided measurement procedures into subtypes depending on the procedures for numerical assignment that were followed; weight and length measures then came out on one end of the spectrum (namely as *ratio scales*), and the classification of people according to their hair color on the other end (namely as *nominal* scales)[1]. In-between was a suitable open range for all sorts of psychological measurement procedures to grow.

Stevens' move may be criticized for many reasons (see, for instance, Michell, 1997; 1999), but not for theoretical incoherence. It is an immediate logical consequence of operationalist thinking that differences between measurement procedures (now conceived of as schemes for numerical assignment) must originate from differences in the way that the numbers are assigned. This is precisely what Stevens maintained: "[W]e may say that measurement, in the broadest sense, is defined as the assignment of numerals to objects or events according to rule" (Stevens, 1946, p. 677), in which a rule may refer to any standardized procedure.

One can hardly overestimate the impact of this view on psychology. The definition of measurement as the assignment of numerals according to rule became the standard definition of measurement in psychology (Michell, 1997). The idea that measurement scales can be characterized in terms of their mathematical group structure laid the basis for axiomatic measurement theory (Suppes & Zinnes, 1963; Krantz, Luce, Suppes, & Tversky, 1971, see also Section 2.4). And the scales of measurement, now taught to every student in the behavioral sciences and prominently figuring in many introductory books on statistics, were born when Stevens linked classes of empirical operations used in measurement procedures to distinct scale types. The *nominal* scale originates when the empirical operation is the determination of equality; the *ordinal* scale when the empirical operation is the determination of greater or less; the *interval* scale when the empirical operation is the determination of equality of intervals or differences; and the *ratio* scale when the empirical operation is the determination of equality of ratios.

Although Stevens' insights were undoubtedly rich and fruitful for subsequent theorizing, it must however be noted that, on a literal reading of his theory, the price to be paid for his liberal conception of measurement is rather high. In Stevens' conceptualization, the question is no longer *whether* one is measuring—one is always doing this, provided one is consistently assigning numerals according to rule—but *on which scale* one is measuring. The answer to that question depends on the empirical operations that were performed in the measurement procedure. And the answer to *that* question, when interpreted literally, is a will-o'-the-wisp. There is basically nothing in Stevens' conceptualization that prevents me from saying that I have measured the concept *nothingness* on a ratio scale, by gauging the equality of ratios of people's hair color to their political convictions. You may object that this measurement procedure is nonsensical, but in the absence of a rationale that says why it is nonsensical, you are merely expressing a value judgment and not providing a scientifically credible critique. If I can provide a consistent rule that specifies when two ratios of hair color and political convictions are to be considered equal, then I am thereby assigning numerals according to a rule for determining the equality of ratios; and since, according to Stevens, this is the defining operation for a ratio scale, that is the end of it.

Although it is improbable that Stevens had this particular interpretation in mind when he wrote his influential paper, it is clear that, if the representational theory is to avoid the absurd consequences that follow from a literal reading of his theory, additional specifications for what counts as a method for determining the relevant equalities are required. Clearly, it is not sufficient that, say, a method for determining the equality of intervals is followed; there must also be a justification that the method actually *does* determine the equality of intervals for some property. The classical view fences off this problem by insisting that we are not talking about the assignment of numerals but rather about the determination or estimation of (ratios of) attribute values. The price that is paid for this move, however, is that one commits to realism about attribute values. And one may not want to pay this price. In this case, the objection to Stevens' operationalism can be accommodated by adopting a more restrictive approach to what counts as a relevant representation in the context of measurement. In this approach, which has sometimes been called the *axiomatic* theory of measurement, the concept of a measurement scale is retained, but it is grounded in the empirical relations that must hold for the construction of a scale to be possible, rather than in the operations used to arrive at the scale.

Box 2.2. Intelligence and IQ-scores

Traditionally interpreted, an operationalist like P. W. Bridgman identified properties with the procedures used to measure them; i.e., he would have defined intelligence as the procedure used to measure intelligence. In psychology, however, the term operationalism is often used to refer to a related but somewhat different position, namely, that there is no distinction between *measurement outcomes* and *measured properties*. For instance, this position holds that IQ-scores *are* levels of intelligence. For many measurement specialists working today, however, the distinction between measurement outcomes (IQ-scores) and the property being measured (levels of intelligence) is an important one that should not be blurred, and collapsing the distinction is very hard to defend. The primary reason for this is that, by the equation IQ-score = level of intelligence, all the properties of IQ-scores are automatically transferred to levels of intelligence. This is inherent to the relation of identity: If two things are identical, then they must share *all* of their properties (otherwise they could be distinguished, and would thus by definition not be identical). So, if IQ-scores were the same as levels of intelligence, then that would mean that levels of intelligence can be added, squared, divided, and multiplied; that they are linearly ordered (i.e., form a line) and are therefore unidimensional, which means that a single number says all there is to know about a person's level of intelligence; and that there exists a maximum level of intelligence—namely, the maximum attainable score on an IQ-test. This is hard to believe. Moreover, equating IQ-scores with levels of intelligence implies that it is impossible that IQ-scores *measure* levels of intelligence—for they *are* levels of intelligence. Also, it implies that there are as many kinds of intelligence as there are IQ-tests, since each test will give a somewhat different ordering of people by IQ-scores, and that the number of potential intelligences is infinite, because the number of potential IQ-tests is. The implausible consequences of equating IQ and intelligence (more generally: measurement outcomes and the property measured) indicate that they cannot be identical.

2.4. The Representational Theory of Measurement: The Axiomatic Approach

The axiomatic approach to measurement exploits the idea that measurement requires an isomorphism between the numerals that are assigned to objects and the empirical relations that obtain between these objects. Although the notion of an isomorphism can be treated in a mathematically sophisticated way, for present purposes it is sufficient to understand the concept as we often encounter in daily life, which is as a navigation device. In a street map of a city, for instance, the streets in the city correspond to the lines on your map in a systematic way: if you have the map, you can use it to deduce how the streets are organized, and if you know how the streets run, you can use that knowledge to deduce what the map looks like. Thus, the directional relations among the streets are isomorphic to those among the lines on your map.

The idea of the representational theory is that a similar logic applies to measurement. Here, the numerals assigned in a measurement procedure provide a map, which tells us how the corresponding objects are related. For instance, suppose that object A has a mass of 1 kg, while object B has a mass of 2 kg. Then we may deduce, among other things, that if we place each object in the arm of a sufficiently precise balance scale, the scale will tilt towards object B. The numerical relations (e.g., 2 is larger than 1) provide a map of the empirical relations (B is heavier than A). This is the way that the notion of isomorphic mapping functions in the representational theory.

Extending this line of thinking, the whole set of empirical relations between objects (with respect to a given attribute like weight) may be considered to make up an *empirical relational system* (Krantz, Luce, Suppes, & Tversky, 1971). Consider again the ordering of objects with respect to their weights. If an appropriate method of assessment is followed (this may, but need not, be the placement of objects in the opposite pans of a balance scale), it turns out that for any two objects *a* and *b*, either *a* is heavier than *b*, *b* is heavier than *a*, or there is no observable difference between *a* and *b*. If one were to put these relations in a very large matrix with the objects listed in both rows and columns, and entered '»' in a cell when the object corresponding to that row outweighed the object corresponding to the column, '«' when the reverse was true, and '~' if no difference was observed, that matrix would be an example of an empirical relational system. Table 2.1 displays such a system for the weights of an eraser, a pencil and a pen, where we assume that the relations between them are assessed with a sufficiently precise balance scale.

The act of measurement involves the subsequent construction of a numerical relational system that is isomorphic to the empirical relational system. For instance, if *a* » *b*, we may choose to assign a higher number to *a*; if *a* « *b*, we assign a lower number to *a*; and if *a* ~ *b*, we assign an equal number to *a* and *b*. If this can be done in such a way that each and every relation occurring in the empirical relational system can be read off from the numerical one, then the numerical system is isomorphic to the empirical relational system[2]; in this case, the systems are isomorphic with respect to the relation of 'heavier than'. Note that, because no quantitative information is present in the relational systems, this would not be a metric scale, but an ordinal one.

In axiomatic measurement theory, the specification of an empirical relational system is prior to the scaling efforts. One first hypothesizes the expected scale of measurement and then empirically tests that hypothesis. It is also important to note that empirical relational systems such as the upper-left quadrant of Table 2.1 are purely qualitative: they do not contain numerical information. However, if a given empirical relational structure can be shown to hold, a quantitative representation of this structure can be constructed, such as the one in the lower-right quadrant of Table 2.1. The link between a set of empirical relations and a numerical representation is provided by a *representation theorem*, which mathematically proves, for a given empirical relational system, that there exists an isomorphic numerical representation. An isomorphic representation is an assignment of numerals to objects such that every relation between the numerals has

Table 2.1 An Empirical Relational System of Weights.

	Eraser	Pencil	Pen	1	2	3
Eraser	~	>>	>>			
Pencil	<<	~	>>	← Same		
Pen	<<	<<	~	↓		
1				~	>>	>>
2				<<	~	>>
3				<<	<<	~

Note: The column entry bears the tabled relation to the row entry.

a parallel relation between the objects. So, for instance, if object a has a higher number than b, then a is heavier than b. That the theory does not assume the prior existence of quantitative attributes, but constructs such attributes on the basis of qualitative relations, is one of the main philosophical differences with the classical measurement theory approach[3].

After a representation theorem has been proven, the level of uniqueness of the representation is to be established. This is done on the basis of a *uniqueness theorem*. A uniqueness theorem specifies the classes of transformations that can be applied to a representation without destroying the isomorphism that the representation bears to the empirical relational system. On the basis of these classes of transformations, Stevens' measurement scales are constructed.

For instance, if a representation is unique up to any one-to-one transformation, then the scale is nominal. This means that it only represents the relation of being equal to; i.e., if two people have the same hair color, then they get the same number, but that number only serves to indicate that they are equivalent. No ordinal or quantitative information can be deduced from the number itself. Reversing the numbers 1 and 2 on Table 2.1 would fail to capture the relative weights of the objects and disrupt the isomorphism. Weight is not measured on a nominal scale.

If a representation is unique up to a monotonic transformation, then the scale is ordinal. A monotonic transformation is any transformation that does not change the order of the numbers assigned to objects. If we denote the original value of the assigned number as x, and the transformed value as $x_{transformed}$, then examples of monotonic transformations are $x_{transformed} = \sqrt{x}$, $x_{transformed} = e^x$, and $x_{transformed} = \log(x)$. If scale values can be monotonically transformed without loss of information, then the scale represents the ordering of objects according to the attribute measured, but does not provide quantitative information. For example, if we square the numbers in Table 2.1 to get 1, 4, and 9, this retains the proper ordering of the weights of the eraser, pencil and pen.

The quantitative scales arise smoothly from this conceptualization when one demands that, apart from orderings, the representations also uniquely preserve *distances* between objects on the measured attribute. It is easy to see that such a representation must be unique up to (at least) linear transformations (i.e., transformations of the form $x' = ax + b$, where a and b are fixed constants), since a nonlinear transformation does not leave distances intact, and therefore cannot have the desired property. For example, if we transform the numbers in Table 2.1 according to $x' = ax + b$, using $a = 2$ and $b = 10$, we get 12, 14, and 16. Either scale correctly indicates that the pen outweighs the pencil by the same amount as the pencil outweighs the eraser. When the representation is in fact unique up to linear transformations, we have an interval scale. An interval scale is metric, but does not have a fixed zero point, as can be seen from the fact that translations ($x' = x + b$) are allowed. The temperature scales of Celsius and Fahrenheit are standard examples of interval scales. Their metric is defined in terms of a difference between two arbitrary levels of the attribute temperature; for instance, the Celsius scale is fixed by setting the difference between the temperature at which water freezes and boils at sea level to 100 degrees.

Finally, a ratio scale requires that the representation is unique up to transformations of the form $x' = ax$, where a is a fixed constant; this means that the origin of the metric is fixed, and only changes in the unit are allowed (this is the function of the parameter a). When one represents objects by numbers, and also represents the empirical concatenation operation of Campbell (1920) by the mathematical operation of addition, then one gets a ratio scale (Krantz, Luce, Suppes, & Tversky, 1971). For example, one can multiply the weights 1, 2, and 3 by 10 to get 10, 20, and 30. In this case, the values still correctly represent the pencil as weighing twice as much as the eraser.

Although the technical expositions needed to prove the theorems that establish the uniqueness of a representation are far too involved to address here, a feeling for their relevance can be conveyed by considering an example. Suppose that one assigns numerals to objects according to the pan balance method of Campbell, discussed above, and resulting in the weights given in Table 2.1. This implies that the concatenation of the eraser and pencil will balance the pen, because 1 + 2 = 3. Suppose that the numerical assignments have been made with care, so that this is indeed found to be the case. When one now applies a transformation to the scale values (say, $x' = 3x$), then the numerical representation continues to function adequately (in this case, we get 3 + 6 = 9, which correctly represents the fact that the concatenation of the pencil and the eraser balances the pen). But when one applies a non-multiplicative linear transformation (say, $x' = 3x + 10$), the representation fails (in this case, we get 13 + 16 > 19, which falsely implies that the concatenation of the eraser and pencil outweighs the pen). Thus, the scale values may be multiplicatively transformed, but not generally linearly transformed, if the numerical relational system is to stay isomorphic with the empirical relational system. Hence, Campbell's fundamental measurement gives a ratio scale.

Ratio scales have a fixed origin, which is usually taken to correspond to an absolute zero point. Considering temperature, for instance, it can be seen that the Kelvin scale is at the ratio level according to the axiomatic measurement theory. This contrasts with the view of Campbell, for whom degrees Kelvin was not a fundamental measurement scale for temperature, since the concatenation of materials, e.g., two fluids of different temperatures, does not behave in accordance with mathematical addition; that is, the combination of two quantities of water, of which one has a temperature of 275 degrees Kelvin and the other 300 degrees Kelvin, does not give one a composite that has a temperature of 575 degrees Kelvin. In this case, the temperature of the concatenation is an average of the original temperatures, weighted by the volumes of the added quantities.

Even a representation in terms of weighted averages, however, only holds for particular materials—for example, the concatenation of nitric acid, sulphuric acid, and glycerol, also known as nitroglycerin, behaves rather differently (as the reader is advised not to verify at home).

The axiomatic theory of measurement is based on some very good ideas, and is the favorite theory of measurement among many philosophers. However, in science, the theory has been less than thriving. Axiomatic measurement theory is not regularly applied in the analysis of real data, neither in the natural nor in the social sciences. It has found some practical applications in psychophysics (Levelt, Riemersma, & Bunt, 1972), and theoretical ones in economics (e.g., Wakker, 1989), but one has to know where to look in order to find them. In regular scientific work, the theory appears not to play a role, and at least in psychology the theory has not brought the progress that some expected (Cliff, 1992).

One of the reasons for this is that the theory makes very strong assumptions with regard to the structure that empirical data should satisfy. Even the ordinal scale level, for instance, requires transitivity (if $c \gg b$ and $b \gg a$ then $c \gg a$) across the full set of objects to which the measurement structure is to apply. In psychology, violations of transitivity are common, although it is generally hard to see where they come from. For instance, if the structure of test scores differs both over people and across time, and the scores also contain some noise, violations of transitivity may be expected and need not necessarily be assigned too much weight. On the other hand, such violations may also indicate that something is wrong at the theoretical level (for instance, the attribute in question has been conceptualized wrongly) or at a more practical level (for instance, the testing procedure used was not sufficiently standardized). It is not easy to disentangle these factors in the absence of strong theory, which unfortunately is the rule rather than the exception in psychological research. Box 2.3 provides an example.

If a basic requirement like transitivity is already hard to substantiate, the requirements that need to be met in order to create stronger scales, like interval or ratio scales, are even harder to satisfy. As may be expected, at that level things do not become easier, since the axiomatic structures become more precise and fine-grained (e.g., Luce & Tukey, 1964). With the possible exception of some basic scales in psychophysics, there currently exist few psychological testing procedures that meet such requirements (see chapter 4 for some putative examples) and hence an adherent to the axiomatic theory of measurement should be extremely skeptical about the existence of measurement in psychology.

2.5. The Latent Variable Perspective

In considering the most important contending theories of measurement, we have encountered only one theory that would allow one to say that

Box 2.3. What is the Scale Level of IQ?

Many psychologists think that IQ-scores are ordinal, but that the assumption that they form an interval scale is a harmless idealizing assumption which is useful because it facilitates statistical analyses. Several reasons can be adduced for this viewpoint. One is that, if intelligence is unidimensional (i.e., intelligence differences between people can be adequately represented on one line), and IQ-scores depend exclusively on intelligence, then the assumption that IQ-scores have interval properties comes down to the assumption that the relation between IQ-scores and intelligence levels is *linear*. Now, it is well known from statistics that linear functions can do a good job in approximating many nonlinear ones, so that even if the relation between IQ and intelligence is not linear (i.e., IQ-scores are not of the interval level), assuming that it is linear may still be reasonable. In fact, as long as the relation between IQ-scores and intelligence is nondecreasing (meaning that there is no point on the scale where the correlation between IQ and intelligence becomes negative), this approximation is likely to be quite good. On the other hand, the assumptions underlying this conclusion (intelligence is unidimensional and the only cause of systematic differences in IQ-scores) are far from trivial. In statistical analyses of IQ-tests, more than one (first-order) factor is always needed to achieve a reasonable fit to the data. This suggests that a person's level of intelligence is not a unitary trait in the sense that more than one number is needed to represent a person's position relative to others (for instance, not one but three numbers: one for spatial ability, one for numerical ability, and one for verbal ability). If that is true, IQ-scores are not ordinal or interval measures of intelligence levels, because IQ and intelligence do not have the same dimensionality. In that case, the answer to the question of whether IQ-scores are ordinal or interval is simply: neither. However, the analysis can be carried further; for if differences in verbal, numerical, and spatial ability are themselves caused by differences in some general ability (a second order factor often indicated as 'g'), then differences in IQ may indirectly reflect differences in *that* factor; in which case the question of whether the relation to the second-order factor is sufficiently close to linear to justify an interval scale assumption is again open.

psychological measurement exists (i.e., Stevens' definition of measurement as merely the assignment of numerals according to rule, which implies that every consistent numerical assignment procedure is a measurement procedure). The classical view is highly restrictive with respect to the sorts of variables that could be measured. These have to be quantitative magnitudes, and it is highly questionable—if not downright far-fetched—to presume that common psychological attributes like intelligence, attitudes, or personality traits, are of this kind. The axiomatic theory of measurement is considerably more liberal, but even in this theory the axiomatic structures laid down appear to be too strict for the noisy data that psychologists typically have at their disposal. In contrast, Stevens' theory seems to make measurement trivially easy, and thus cannot provide an adequate basis for the critical evaluation of psychological measures as required for test validation (although it does not make levels of measurement above the nominal level trivially easy).

However, an intermediate set of empirical requirements to be met for the term 'measurement' to apply is available; in the past century, a collection of models has been proposed that allow for perturbations in the data (and hence a less than perfect satisfaction of the axioms of representationalism) because they view the measurement problem statistically. These models are known as latent variable models. We now examine a general theoretical perspective that could be based on this class of models.

Latent variable models work as follows. First, we assume that a psychological attribute has a certain structure; this assumption has to be motivated on the basis of substantive theory. It may be an unordered categorical, ordered categorical, or a continuous structure. A set of observed variables, each of which may also be (un)ordered categorical or continuous, are assumed to depend statistically on this unobserved structure. The relation of statistical dependence relation means that one assumes that not the data themselves but their expected values depend on the latent structure in a lawful manner. For instance, a typical latent variable model would say that an observed random variable x depends on latent variable θ through a function like $E(x|\theta) = \alpha\theta + \varepsilon$, where α is a regression parameter and ε represents measurement error. Many commonly used latent variable models can be derived from this basic equation by using appropriate probability distributions and link functions (link functions are simply transformations of the expected value of the item score; e.g., the natural logarithm of the expected value—$\ln[E(X)]$—could be link function; see also Mellenbergh, 1994).

Of course, a single equation of this type contains more unknowns than knowns and hence neither has a unique solution nor testable consequences. However, when a number of observed variables depend on one and the same latent variable, and a functional relation with the latent structure is assumed for each of them, then the parameters of the model can be uniquely estimated; in that case, the model also has testable consequences, which render it falsifiable. One straightforward and insightful consequence is *local independence*. Local independence follows from the hypothesis that the different observables depend on one and the same latent structure. Because apart from random error the observables depend *only* on the latent variable, conditioning on that latent variable renders the observables statistically independent.

It is a matter of some contention how the dependence of item scores on the latent variable should be interpreted here. In the statistical formulation of a latent variable model, for a single item, the word 'dependence' merely means that some general regression equation with nonzero regression parameter relates the item score to the latent variable; i.e., the item score and latent variable are *correlated*. However, a latent variable model for a number of items is not identical to the hypothesis that each of the items is merely correlated to the latent variable. Many items may be correlated to the latent variable, but only a subset of them will actually fit a latent variable model, e.g., be consistent with the assumption of local independence. Why, then, should one at all *expect* local independence to hold? Not many answers to this question are available. One holds that variation in the latent variable is the *common cause* of the variation in item scores. In fact, local independence is indistinguishable from the screening-off effect in common cause models (i.e., the latent variable screens off or removes the correlation between its indicators), which has been much discussed in the philosophical literature (e.g., Reichenbach, 1956; Glymour, 2001).

To see how a causal interpretation of a latent variable model works, it is useful to consider a simple analogy. Suppose one counts the number of firefighters, police cars, and ambulances present at a number of fires. These will be correlated: the more firefighters, the more police cars, the more ambulances. The reason for this is that all of these variables depend on the size of the fire. Hence variation in the size of the fire is the common cause of the variation in these variables, just like differences in psychological attributes like intelligence may be considered the common cause of differences in responses to a set of IQ-items. If we now consider a single level of the common cause (say, fires of a given size, or a given level of intelligence) we will find that the observables (say, the number of firefighters and the number of ambulances, or the scores on two IQ-items) are no longer correlated. The reason for this is that their common cause is now no longer a variable, but has become a constant, so that the variation left is random variation (error). Hence, although the variables are correlated in the general population (of fires), these correlations are screened off by the common cause (the size of the fires). In psychometric theory, one would say that the item scores are locally independent (i.e., uncorrelated in a subpopulation with the same level of the psychological attribute).

It is clear that the common cause model provides a reasonable motivation for demanding local independence. However, other motivations for using this requirement may also be formulated. For instance, the item scores may covary systematically and thus exhibit local independence for other reasons, such as some fundamental law of co-occurrence. Van der

Maas et al. (2006), for instance, have shown that if items assess distinct attributes that, however, mutually influence each other, the resulting covariance matrix can show an exact correspondence to local independence. In addition, one can conceive of chance experiments that generate patterns of data that are in agreement with local independence but where a causal interpretation is not straightforward (Holland, 1992; see also chapter 6). Thus, there may be other reasons for systematic covariation than causal dependence on a common latent variable.

Nevertheless, in a measurement context, the causal interpretation of latent variable models is *prima facie* attractive (see Borsboom, Mellenbergh, and Van Heerden, 2003, who also discuss various problems with this view). And in the case of the emergency vehicles example, it certainly seems more plausible than a fundamental law of co-occurrence. However, the possibility of specifying a non-causal interpretation serves as a reminder that the causal interpretation is not inherent in the statistical model, but added to it in a given substantive application (discussed further in Part II).

With sufficient observed variables, local independence imposes restrictions on the data. The feasibility of these restrictions, as well as the goodness of fit of the model, can then be handled as a model selection problem (e.g., see the 2006 Special Issue on model selection of the *Journal of Mathematical Psychology*). In this way, the evaluation of measurement models is scientifically accessible by statistical means. This is not to say that evaluating the empirical adequacy of latent variable models is an easy task; however, it is not radically different from ordinary statistical model selection.

Latent variable models can be seen as a crossbreed of the classical measurement theory and representationalism. They share with the classical theory a tendency toward a realist perspective; the attributes measured, in a latent variable model, are susceptible to a realist interpretation[4]. On the other hand, as in representationalism, these attributes are not required to be quantitative; there exist several models that conceptualize attributes categorically, either as unordered or as ordered latent classes. Unlike the scales of representationalism, however, these latent variables are not constructed from an observable empirical relational system. Rather, they are hypothesized to be common causes of a set of measures. Because observed data are assumed to reflect the underlying latent structure imperfectly (i.e., they are subject to error), latent variable models can naturally cope with the fact that, in real applications, data that conform strictly to the axioms of representationalism are scarcely observed.

Latent variable models are sufficiently liberal to accommodate the data encountered in real measurement situations, and they are sufficiently restrictive to be scientifically testable. For these reasons, the models have become increasingly popular to tackle measurement problems in psychology. This does not mean that these models do not present theoretical problems of their own: they do, and several of the most important ones will be discussed in chapters 3, 4, and 6.

2.6. Chapter Conclusion

In the present chapter, we have attempted to give an overview of the most important developments in measurement theory that have occurred in the past century, and have highlighted their strengths and weaknesses. The *classical theory of measurement* couples a commitment to the existence of quantitative attributes with a restriction on the meaning of measurement. That is, measurement exclusively applies to the estimation or discovery of quantitative relationships between levels of measurements of an attribute; i.e., their ratios. Truly quantitative measurements of attributes are rare in psychology, if they exist at all. Hence, one who adopts this theory might conclude that, in view of the current state of affairs, psychological measurement does not exist.

In Stevens' *operationalist* variant of representationalism, one reaches exactly the opposite conclusion: every situation where people are assigning numerals to objects according to rule is a measurement situation, and hence measurement is ubiquitous in psychology. The problem is not to find out whether one is measuring something, but to find out at which level of measurement the numerical assignment procedure is situated. Although Stevens' definition of measurement appears to be widely accepted in psychology (at least in the sense that it is the default definition of measurement in textbooks), it is questionable whether a definition of measurement that views every conceivable numerical assignment procedure as a measurement procedure provides an adequate definition of measurement on which to ground test validation. Something more appears to be needed. Conversely, however, it seems useful to have a general term to cover all procedures that assign variable values to cases; from this point of view, the question becomes whether that term should be measurement.

The *axiomatic* variant of representationalism gives a sensible extension of Steven's theory by requiring that one needs an established *empirical relational system* in order to speak of measurement. Measurement then involves the construction of a numerical representation of this relational structure that is, up to a certain level, *isomorphic* with it. Different measurement scales are specified by considering up to what kind of transformation of the assigned scale values the isomorphism is retained. Axiomatic theory has not become widely used in psychological research, and one plausible reason for this is that establishing an empirical relational structure that lives up to the strict axioms of the theory has turned out to be quite difficult. One of the primary reasons for this is that measurement procedures in psychology appear to be influenced by many situational and person-specific factors that are not linked to the attributes that are the objects of measurement; that is, they are noisy and it is difficult to make them depend on a manageable number of (experimental) conditions (Trendler, 2009). Axiomatic measurement theory has, so far, not been able to produce a way of handling such situations because it applies its constraints on measurement directly to the observed measures, and thus noise in the system must also conform to the constraints of measurement. A strict adherent to the theory would therefore have to say that psychological measurement is extremely rare, if it exists at all, for the simple reason that for the overwhelming majority of measurement scales in use, representation and uniqueness theorems have not been proven—and perhaps cannot be proven given the noise in the observed measures.

The *latent variable perspective* handles the problem of measurement error by explicitly assuming that data contain noise, and by modeling the expected values of observed variables. In this way, latent variable models circumvent the problem that empirical relational systems are hard to establish. One could say that these models shove the relational systems under the carpet of unobservability, which means that the fact that they cannot be established on the basis of observation is no longer a principled problem. However, the price that is paid for this move is that the structure of the latent attribute cannot be established on the basis of an observed empirical relational system (as, for instance, the level of measurement can be established on this basis in axiomatic measurement theory). The empirical data, after all, are noisy and may be related to a multitude of latent structures in a multitude of ways.

Thus, the incorporation of a latent structure leads to an underdetermination problem: how do we decide which of the many available latent structures is the correct one? Other problems that surface upon this interpretation of the measurement problem are (a) that it is hard to see what a reasonable interpretation of the expected values figuring in latent variable models may look like, and (b) that, although the general structure of latent variable models mimics a common cause structure, it is not obvious how a causal relation between the measured attribute and the observed data is to be conceptualized, as will become clear in chapters 3, 4, and 6.

The theories of measurement relate to validity as follows. In the classical theory of measurement, one would have a hard time establishing the thesis that psychological tests measure anything at all, so that the question of *what* they measure is beyond the purview of contemporary psychology as long as this foundational issue is not resolved. In any case, psychological research should first and foremost focus on establishing the quantitative structure of attributes, before using the rhetoric of measurement. In contrast, Stevens' operationalism renders the question of whether measurement really occurs in psychology moot; measurement is always taking place, as long as numerals are assigned in a consistent fashion according to his rules for assignment. In this view, however, is it rather hard to envision what validation research may look like. Since the operationalist view is that a theoretical attribute is *defined* in terms of a set of measurement operations, the question of whether that attribute is really being measured through these operations is self-contradictory.

For the axiomatic theorist, restrictions on the term measurement are in place, but they are different from the quantity requirement of the classical theory: measurement only occurs when an empirical relational system satisfies the axiomatic requirements of the theory and is isomorphically mapped into a numerical relational system. Hence, validation research is inextricably connected to establishing such an empirical relational system and describing it axiomatically. Finally, in a latent variable perspective, a primary question of validity would be whether the data-generating mechanism is as the latent variable model portrays it to be, i.e., whether the causal mechanisms involved in the production of datasets are adequately specified (Borsboom, Mellenbergh, & Van Heerden, 2004).

It is, at the very least, questionable whether validity theory can gloss over such differences, since the very meaning of the validity concept appears to be intertwined with the conceptualization of measurement one adheres to. Thus, a major issue to be resolved for any theory of validity is what kind of relation between theoretical attributes and observed data we have in mind when speaking of measurement. The next chapters will consider this question in greater detail, and flesh out the philosophical and practical consequences that are attached to this question.

2.7. Further Reading

Bridgman, P. W. (1927). *The logic of modern physics*. New York: Macmillan.

Campbell, N. R. (1920). *Physics, the elements*. Cambridge: Cambridge University Press.

Michell, J. (1997). Quantitative science and the definition of measurement in psychology. *British Journal of Psychology, 88*, 355–383.

Stevens, S. S. (1946). On the theory of scales of measurement. *Science, 103*, 667–680.

Suppes, P. & Zinnes, J. L. (1963). Basic measurement theory. In: R. D Luce, R. Bush, & E. Galanter (Eds.). *Handboook of mathematical psychology* (pp. 3–76). New York: Wiley.

3 Psychometric Models

Connections With Other Chapters

In chapter 2, the most influential philosophical theories of measurement were discussed. Although these theories are important to psychometrics, they do not directly guide psychometric practice. Instead, this role is played by statistical modeling approaches. This chapter discusses the most important of these models: classical test theory, modern test theory, and generalizability theory. The relation between the construct of interest and the observed test score is conceptualized differently in each of these models. We link these differences to validity theory. In addition, the relation of validity to important psychometric concepts, such as reliability and measurement invariance, is analyzed.

The previous chapter discussed the properties that observations should have in order to be considered measurements, according to different conceptions of what measurement is. Although such theories are important, in psychometric practice they play a background role. In the foreground, psychometric practice is guided by a more statistical approach to test scores. That is, psychometrics generally starts off from the interpretation of the observations as *data*, for which an adequate *statistical model* should be found. This approach gave birth to the major psychometric models currently used: the classical test theory model, the modern test theory model, and the generalizability model. Each of these approaches could be described as data-oriented, in the sense that their main use lies in the analysis of empirical data (rather than, say, in characterizing tests theoretically or in proving properties of measurement structures). As such, they are heavily informed by practical concerns.

One important practical concern in setting up useful statistical models is that they should not be tied too closely to content. That is, if one has a statistical model that can only be used for one specific content area (e.g., to model mathematical reasoning) this limits the practical usefulness of the model (e.g., one could not use the same model for verbal reasoning). Thus, like most models that are developed from a primarily statistical point of view, psychometric models are generic. That is, they are content-neutral statistical structures, which can in principle be applied to any substantive domain. As a result, one can use psychometric models to discover the reliability of one's test scores, but these models will not say what one is measuring. That information, in current practice, is brought to the scene by the researcher and by the substantive context. Thus, the person using the model has to interpret the results by attaching them to the substantive domain studied.

The general idea of psychometric modeling is that, if the data fit the statistical model sufficiently well, then this content-neutral way of working offers a generic method to ascribe psychometric properties to items. The modeler can do this without having to make up a substantive theory of how the items are answered or what they measure. For instance, a researcher might want to know which of the items was most difficult, or which of the items measure the same attribute, or whether the composite score constructed from a set of items is reliable. Psychometric models are built to answer these questions just by looking at the data, i.e., without a need for the modeler to even know what the data are about. This decoupling of substantive theory and statistical model is, in a sense, the success story of psychometrics. This is because it has allowed people to use psychometric models in fields where no formalized substantive theory exists (i.e., where theories are purely verbal, as is the case in many areas of psychology and education). However, the weak ties of psychometric models to content may also be the germ of many validity problems. Thus, it is important to address the way the most important psychometric models relate to validity issues.

In this chapter, we aim to give a conceptually oriented description of the most important psychometric models and to relate these to important concerns in validity theory. First, we will address the basic assumptions of classical test theory. Second, we will give an overview of two extensions of the classical test model, namely generalizability theory and Item Response Theory (IRT). For each of these models, we concentrate on the issue of how they picture the relation between observable item or test scores, and theoretical constructs. We close off with a discussion of the relation between validity and important psychometric concepts such as reliability, measurement invariance, and predictive utility.

3.1. Psychometric Models

This section describes the basic ingredients of the models most often used in the psychometric analysis of test scores: the classical test theory model, the generalizability theory model, and the modern test theory model. The aim of this section is to familiarize the reader with the conceptual and statistical apparatus of these models, without going into too much mathematical detail.

3.1.1. Classical Test Theory

The system of classical test theory is by far the most often used model for analyzing test data. Its assumptions are simple, but its payoff is surprisingly rich. As Novick (1966) showed, and Lord and Novick (1968) later worked out in detail, the most basic form of classical test theory requires just one assumption, namely that the test score obtained from an individual *i* is a realization of a random variable which has a probability distribution or density with finite variance. This assumption allows the decomposition of *i*'s test score into a constant *true score*, τ_i, and a variable *error score*, E_i, according to the definitions (not to be mistaken for assumptions):

$$\tau_i = E(X_i), \text{ and}$$
$$E_i = X_i - \tau_i$$

Here $E(X_i)$ denotes the expectation of subject *i*'s test score. From this it follows, among other things, that the expectation of the error score equals zero. Extending this model from the individual to a population renders the true score defined on X a random variable as well, usually denoted T_X. Through straightforward applications of probability calculus, classical test theory then yields the fundamental result that the variance of the observed variable equals the sum of the true score variance and error variance: $Var(X)=Var(T)+Var(E)$. This result is used to deliver the main concept of classical test theory: *reliability*.

Reliability is defined as the ratio of true score variance to test score variance: $r^2(X,T_X)=Var(T_X)/Var(X)$. This definition is intuitive: reliability will equal one if there is no error variance, because in that case $Var(X)$ will equal $Var(T_X)$, and it will approach zero as $Var(E)$ becomes larger relative to $Var(T_X)$. Thus, reliability ranges between zero (complete unreliability) and one (perfect reliability). The quantity $r^2(X,T_X)$ can be interpreted as the proportion of variance in the true scores that can be linearly predicted from the observed scores. The square root of reliability is the correlation between the test scores and true scores. Note that, like any other correlation, reliability is a population-dependent statistic. Thus, in different populations test scores will ordinarily have different reliabilities (see Box 3.1).

Although classical test theory offers an important psychometric framework for thinking about test scores, it has two major drawbacks. First, classical test theory is not equipped to address the generalizability of results to other assessments (e.g., involving other items, other people, other occasions, other testing situations, etc.). Second, the definition of true scores as expected test scores makes them test-specific, so that the theory does not allow for the calibration of different items on a common scale. There are two extensions of the theory that admit a better treatment of these problems, namely generalizability theory and modern test theory. Generalizability theory addresses the extension of classical test theory to other modes of assessment; modern test theory formalizes and utilizes the idea that different items are calibrated to measure the same attribute. These theories also offer more sophisticated ideas on the place of validity in psychometric models.

Box 3.1. Who's Reliable?

Reliability is often presented as a property of a test or subtest; e.g., when such claims are made as "the test was shown to have adequate reliability." However, reliability is not a property of a test in itself. This is because reliability is population dependent.

For instance, consider tests for arithmetic as implemented in the online testing program Maths Garden (http://www.mathsgarden.com), which will be the leading example in this chapter. The Maths Garden uses a large set of arithmetic items from various domains (e.g., counting, addition, multiplication, etc.) that allows schools to adaptively test and track progress of their pupils. The reliability of the tests administered depends on which population is chosen. Take, for instance, the entire set of addition items that result in a sum of at most 100 (i.e., $1 + 1, 1 + 2, \ldots, 49 + 50, 50 + 50$). For pupils aged, say, 5–6 years old, many of these items (roughly, all number combinations with at least one element above 10) are uninformative with respect to their competence at adding numbers. Since such items will add pure noise into the system, the total score reliability will be very low in this group. If we added the scores of pupils aged 8–9, for whom more of the items are informative, total test score reliability would be much higher. So, there is no such thing as *the* reliability of the Maths Garden addition test. If reliability is not a property of the test per se, then it becomes an interesting question to ask what it *is* a property of. One solution is to say that it is a property of a given set of *test scores* rather than of tests, i.e., of the set "all responses to Maths Garden items given by 5–6 year olds." This is consistent with the fact that the reliability coefficient is, statistically speaking, the result of a test-by-population interaction. So, this interpretation naturally accommodates the fact that the value of the reliability coefficient is different in different groups. However, by itself, this interpretation appears to be too weak for reliability to function as a sensible guiding statistic in, say, choosing between two tests to administer in a *new* population. For this to work, one would have to assume, minimally, that the new population is sufficiently similar to the population previously tested, so that the reliability in this population will resemble that in the old population. For instance, if a school decides to participate in the Maths Garden rather than in another system based on superior reliability, this makes sense only if there is a sufficient resemblance of their 5-6 year olds to the pupils already in the system. Thus, if one chooses one test over another on the basis of reliability, one expresses the expectation that the scores that arise from administering the test will behave similarly to the ones that yielded the reliability coefficient on which one based the decision. This implies robust regularities in the world which are not licensed by a passing reference to the characteristics of an existing dataset of test scores. Thus, even the apparently simple attribution of reliability involves implicit assumptions regarding robust characteristics of the test score distribution that generalize across situations.

3.1.2. Generalizability Theory

Generalizability theory arose, historically, out of an attempt to give a consistent and widely applicable definition of reliability. The originators of the theory, Cronbach, Gleser, Nanda, and Rajaratnam (1972) started out by considering the question of what reliability is. Their answer was that reliability is a special instance of *generalizability*, a concept that quantifies to what extent the results of a test administration can be generalized to different items, situations, or raters.

The theory arises logically from classical test theory. As we have seen, within classical test theory reliability indicates the squared correlation between test scores and true scores. This quantity can be mathematically shown to equal the correlation between the test scores and scores on a so-called parallel test. This is a test for which the observed score distributions are exactly equal to the original test for each individual. Therefore, the test scores on the original and parallel tests are realizations of the same random process (i.e., are draws from the same distribution). In this interpretation, reliability quantifies the degree to which conclusions based on one test are generalizable to a parallel test.

Naturally, one may state that one's interest is not merely in generalization to parallel test items, but, say, to different testing situations or, if performance was rated, to another set of raters. Classical test theory does not handle such cases as it lacks the definitional framework to address them. It can only assess random error. Generalizability theory broadens the apparatus of classical test theory to handle other sources of variation besides random error.

The main concepts that allow generalizability theory to take care of the problem at hand are that of a *universe of admissible observations* and a measure, defined on that universe, which is called the *universe score*. The universe of admissible observations is the set of observations that the researcher deems of interest. This set is defined by the researcher in advance. For instance, if we consider the performance of a group of students on a number of essay assignments that are judged by different raters, we could define the universe of admissible observations to be all possible essay assignments judged by all possible raters. Next, we define a given person's universe score to be the score that the person would get if he or she took all possible assignments and had them judged by all possible raters.

Upon this setup, the variance in observed scores can be dissected into three sources: variance that is due to variance in universe scores, variance due to sampling of items (the essay assignments), and variance due to variance among raters. For a single individual, the expected value of the observed score for subject i on a given assignment j, as judged by rater r, is considered to be

$$E(X_{ijr}) = \mu + \alpha_i + \beta_j + \gamma_r + E_{ijr},$$

This is analogous to the way that effects of different experimental conditions are represented in analysis of variance: μ is an intercept, α_i is the person effect, β_j is the item effect, γ_r is the rater effect, and E_{ijr} is an error term (i.e., the part of the score X_{ijr} that cannot be predicted from the modeled factors). If we have a number of tested individuals, who take a number of different items that are rated by a number of different raters, under assumptions similar to those of classical test theory the variance of the observed scores decomposes additively:

$$Var(X) = Var(\alpha_i) + Var(\beta_j) + Var(\gamma_r) + Var(E).$$

Upon this decomposition, generalizability theory defines the *coefficient of generalizability* or *G-coefficient*, ρ^2, analogous to classical test theory; namely, as the ratio of person variance to observed score variance:

$$\rho^2 = Var(\alpha_i)/Var(X_{ijr}).$$

This coefficient says how much of the observed score variance is due to variance in persons. As this coefficient gets higher, more variance is attributable to differences between people, so that the ordering of people on the score on a particular item judged by a particular rater generalizes well to the scores they get when they take other items and/or are judged by other raters. Clearly, if no variance is attributable to items or raters, for instance because there is only one item and only one rater in the universe of admissible operations, then the generalizability coefficient ρ^2 reduces to reliability, $r^2(X, T_X)$, as defined in classical test theory.

3.1.3. Modern Test Theory and the Latent Variable Model

The last great addition to the arsenal of psychometric models that we discuss is modern test theory. Modern test theory, like generalizability theory, takes care of some limitations of classical test theory, but it does so in a different fashion. Instead of conceptualizing the observed test scores as samples taken from a universe of admissible observations, the models of modern test theory consider the observed test scores to be a function of a latent variable.

For a single observable variable (an item response), the Item Response Function (IRF) describes how the item response behaves as a function of the latent variable. For instance, an often-used function is a logistic function, which says that the probability of a correct response increases with the position of a person on a continuous trait according to the model:

$$P(X_{ij} = 1) = \exp(\beta_j - \theta_i)/(1 + \exp(\beta_j - \theta_i)),$$

Where exp(.) denotes the exponential function, β_j is a threshold parameter, and θ_i is a person parameter assigning to each individual a value on the latent trait. This function defines the Rasch (1960) model and has been particularly attractive to researchers in educational testing, because it guarantees favorable measurement properties, and has some characteristics that match the substantive structure of educational tests. For instance, the function is increasing in θ. Hence, if we take θ to represent ability, the function says that more able people have a higher chance of correctly answering the item which is substantively plausible. The item parameter β controls the location of the IRF, so if we consider a person with a given value of θ, then this person has a lower chance of correctly answering items with a higher β parameter. Hence, the parameter β is often interpreted as item difficulty; items with higher β are more difficult.

For a single item, the model does not imply testable hypotheses because it uses two parameters (θ and β) to represent one probability $P(X_{ij} = 1)$; so, like the equation of classical test theory, it is vacuously true. This changes when we consider multiple items that depend on one and the same latent variable (i.e., that measure the same attribute in latent variable theory, as discussed in chapter 2). If each of these items depends only on that latent variable (an assumption known as unidimensionality) then the model implies conditional independence of the item responses given that latent variable. This is called *local independence*. Local independence imposes testable predictions on the data structure. Hence, it renders the model as a whole falsifiable. As a result, and in contrast to the classical test theory true score, the introduction of a latent variable in an IRT model should be taken to have empirical content, i.e., to say something empirically informative about the world.

The IRF may be any function, and which function should be considered sensible depends on the substantive situation at hand. The proliferation of different IRT models in the psychometric literature arises from taking different functions for the IRF. For instance, the demand that the function is monotonically increasing leads to nonparametric IRT (Mokken, 1971), a logistic function with a slope parameter leads to Birnbaum's (1968) model, additionally including a guessing parameter leads to the 3-parameter logistic model (Hambleton & Swaminathan, 1985), assuming a peaked IRF leads to an ideal point model (Chernyshenko, Stark, Drasgow, & Roberts, 2007), a linear function leads to the single factor model (Mellenbergh, 1994), and so on. If one drops the assumption that θ should be continuous (i.e., one considers the possibility that θ is typological), one opens up an additional models class commonly indicated as finite mixture models (McLachlan & Peel, 2000). Currently, there also exist mixed forms of these models, both at the observed end (e.g., when some observed variables are dichotomous and others continuous) and at the latent end (e.g., with continuous latent trait models nested in latent classes). We do not provide an extensive discussion of the different models here, but would like to note their existence. In this book, we will limit ourselves to a discussion of some aspects of models that are particularly interesting from the point of view of validity theory.

One such property of latent variable models is that they offer a window on measurement precision that is quite different from the classical test theory and generalizability theory approaches. In classical test theory, measurement precision is viewed as reliability, which is the squared correlation between true scores and test scores. In generalizability theory, it is the generalizability coefficient. Both refer to a percentage of variance (in the universe scores or true scores) that could be linearly predicted from the test scores. These quantities are unconditional, and hence they are influenced by the amount of variance in the population considered. Because that variance is typically not constant over populations, reliability and generalizability are best defined and interpreted with respect to a given population (Box 3.1). They are not properties of the test, but of a test-by-population interaction. A particularly illustrative case occurs when we consider a single person. Since the expected value of the test score is a constant for an individual, it has no variance, so that both the classical test theory reliability and the generalizability coefficient take the value zero for an individual person.

This situation is different for latent variable models, as they offer the possibility of evaluating measurement precision conditionally on the latent variable. For instance, considering the logistic IRT model, the information given by a dichotomous item is largest at $\theta = \beta$ (which is where IRF is steepest) and levels off when θ gets larger or smaller than β (where the slope of the IRF gets flatter). This can be quantified using the information function, which measures the amount of information a given item offers for any position on the latent variable. The approach readily generalizes to the level of the test score. Thus, in modern test theory, it is possible to define measurement precision conditional on the latent variable (Mellenbergh, 1996). This, in turn, means that measurement precision has a meaningful value for a subpopulation (or individual) with a given value of θ. It does not take the value zero when the latent variable is held constant. This opens up the possibility of considering the most optimal test to administer given a level of θ, and also means that the optimal test is not the same for each level of θ. This property of IRT models is exploited in adaptive testing (Van der Linden & Glas, 2007). It is useful to note that, in the common factor model, the information is constant over θ under standard assumptions (most importantly, homoscedastic error variance), so the common factor model does not allow for adaptive testing. In the factor model, a given test or item is equally informative for all levels of θ.

3.2. Test Scores, Constructs, and Validity

Each of the psychometric models discussed above suggests a different relation between test scores and constructs. For instance, in the generalizability model, the items are considered to be samples, and thus it makes sense to think about validity in terms of sampling relations. A relevant question would be: how representative is the sample of items for the domain from which they were sampled? In the latent variable model, item scores are modeled as effects of a latent variable, and this suggests thinking about validity in causal terms. For instance, one might ask whether there is an effect of the construct on the item scores, and wonder what the nature of that effect is. Thus, different models suggest different conceptualizations of validity. Although this does not imply that using a model ties the modeler to one of these conceptualizations, it is useful to consider how each of the models relates to validity.

3.2.1. Validity as a Relation Between Test Scores and True Scores

The focal concept of classical test theory is the *true score*. This terminology makes it seductive to equate true scores to psychological constructs, but this can be misleading. For instance, every person has a true score associated with the response to the question *do green ideas sleep furiously?*, scored 1 (yes), $\sqrt{2}$ (no), or 2^{10} (don't know). Nonetheless, it would be far-fetched to conclude that the question therefore measures a psychological construct. However, if we equate true scores to psychological constructs, then logically every test corresponds to a construct, and we cannot avoid this conclusion.

In addition, the true score is typically different for any two different tests. If one equates true scores to constructs, then tests that yield different true scores logically could not measure the same construct. This is unreasonable. For instance, Celsius and Fahrenheit thermometers will have different expected readings and hence different true scores, but they arguably both measure the same attribute. Thus, if one wants to claim that two tests can in fact measure the same attribute, as one typically would, then that attribute cannot logically be equated with the true score, because true scores are scale-specific and attributes are not.

Finally, if one thinks of true scores as psychological constructs, then it is natural to think of the correlation between test scores and true scores as a measure of validity. However, this correlation is already in use for a different purpose: it defines the *reliability* of the test scores, as discussed above. So, if one thinks that validity of the test scores equals the correlation between the test scores and the true scores, one is thereby equating validity and reliability. Most scholars view that as an undesirable move. As a result of these implications, the identification of constructs with true scores is difficult to maintain.

3.2.2. *Validity as a Relation Between Test Scores and External Variables*

Classical test theorists have typically refrained from conceptualizing validity as a relation between test scores and true scores for the reasons discussed above. Instead, they have considered validity to be a relation between test scores and other variables. These other variables typically take the form of external criteria (e.g., success on the job, study grades, behavioral measures). This conception of validity is the cradle of the so-called *validity coefficient*: the correlation between the observed scores and a criterion to be predicted from them. Typically, however, this correlation is confounded by the unreliability of the test scores and of the criterion measure itself. In this case, one may think of validity as the correlation between the true scores on the test and the true scores on the criterion measure. In either case, validity is the correlation between test scores and some criterion variable. Generically speaking, this idea defines the notion of *criterion validity*.

The research program of criterion validity is straightforward: Gather test scores, gather criterion scores, and compute the correlation between the two. The higher the correlation, the higher the validity of the test scores. The result of such an endeavor, the validity coefficient, also has a clear interpretation: it is the square root of the proportion of variance in the criterion scores that can be linearly predicted from the test scores. Indeed, this research program has been of great use in the development of psychological tests. Early psychometric work featured a wholesale reduction of validity to test-criterion correlations. However, there are some consequences that follow immediately from the idea that validity is nothing but a correlation between test scores and criterion variables that many theorists have found unattractive.

First, it follows from a reduction of validity to a test-criterion correlation that a test is valid for anything with which it correlates (Guilford, 1946). Given that zero correlations are rare in the social sciences, this literally means that every test is, to some degree, valid for everything. So, in this view the question 'are you sad?' has some validity for the variable *life expectancy* and the question 'are you male?' has some validity for the variable *annual income*, because these variables are correlated nonzero in the population. This is a straightforward consequence of the way criterion validity is set up, which many find undesirable.

Second, it follows from criterion validity that validity is population-specific. This means that *the* validity of a test does not exist. Because the correlation is attenuated by restriction of range, for instance, validity coefficients are so too. In a population with little variance on the observed scores, the validity coefficient will be lower when compared with a population with larger variance (assuming reliability is the same in both cases). There have been attempts to correct for all effects that might possibly attenuate validity coefficients—a program known as validity generalization (Schmidt & Hunter, 1977). This program aims to establish *the* validity coefficient by defining it with respect to the general population. However, it is unclear whether this program is internally consistent (Thomas, 1989).

Third, because correlations are symmetric, criterion validity is too, so that one can also reverse any validity relation. Thus, one may say that SAT scores predict grade point average in college, but the reverse holds just as well. Statistically, of course, this is perfectly sensible, but it becomes problematic when validity is interpreted with respect to measurement rather than prediction. There is an asymmetry between, for instance, differences in temperature and differences in test scores (e.g., thermometer readings), in the sense that thermometers measure temperature but temperature is hard to understand as a measure of thermometer readings. Criterion validity cannot represent this difference.

The underlying issue here is that criterion validity captures a predictive relation, rather than a measurement relation. However, many issues in validity theory relate to measurement, rather than to prediction. Thus, although offering a clearly specified and useful research program, criterion validity is not a good candidate to define validity generally. In accordance, validity theorists (Messick, 1989; Kane, 2001) have come to think of criterion validity as offering a specific type of validity evidence, rather than as a definition of validity. This interpretation has the advantage of being able to support the important place of criterion-related evidence in considering validity, while avoiding the reduction of validity to a correlation coefficient.

3.2.3. Validity as a Relation Between Test Scores and Universe Scores

Generalizability theory offers an interesting view of the relation between test scores and constructs. Namely, one may frame this relation in terms of the relation between samples (test scores) and populations (universe scores). That is, if the attribute that the researcher aims to assess is identified with a (hypothetical) score on a universe of admissible observations, then the generalizability coefficient tells us how well the researcher can infer these scores from test scores. This coefficient, in turn, may be viewed as a measure of validity. Thus, within a generalizability context, validity may be considered to be the degree to which observed score differences generalize to the universe as a whole (McDonald, 2003).

Since the basic idea of generalizability theory is that item response behaviors are samples, the safeguards of and threats to validity are similar to those in the statistical theory of sampling. These turn on the representativeness of the sample with regard to the population. In this respect, a perfectly random sample of facets from the universe of admissible observations would optimally guarantee generalizability, just like a perfectly random sample from a population is statistically optimal for generalizing to that population. However, items can rarely be regarded as a random sample from a well-defined universe. Two questions then arise. First, to what extent do the chosen items represent or cover the domain as specified in the definition of the universe of admissible observations; for instance, is no intended part of the universe left out of the sample? Second, is the stable variance associated with the items restricted to the universe as defined; that is, is some of the variance in the test scores produced by unintended factors? In construct validity theory, similar concerns are usually denoted with the terms *construct underrepresentation*, which arises when the items fail to include certain parts of the intended domain, and *construct-irrelevant variance*, which arises to the extent that unintended factors produce stable variance in the test scores (e.g., see Messick, 1989, p. 34).

It is a matter of contention whether, if we allow a universe of admissible observations to be delineated purely by the content of items, such concerns necessarily should invoke psychological constructs. Suppose that one equates the construct with a universe score, and that one can define this score without reference to psychological constructs. For instance, one could define a universe score as *the expected score on all addition items involving numbers below one hundred*. Such a definition would seem quite neutral with respect to the question of which psychological processes and constructs underlie people's performance on these items. In that case, it would seem that validity indeed reduces to generalizability. Therefore, the degree of validity could be precisely quantified as the generalizability coefficient. The adequacy of that coefficient hinges only on standard statistical theory, and would for instance be guaranteed by the random sampling of items. Thus, one could quite readily *make* the required assumptions for validity true by setting up the test administration by taking random draws of items.

In contrast, if one needs psychological theory to delineate the universe score (e.g., *the expected score on all tasks that involve response inhibition*), then the very existence of such a universe depends on whether the theory adequately describes reality (for instance, does response inhibition delineate a well-defined universe of tasks?). In this case, issues of psychological theory and of construct validity would appear implicated by necessity. Arguably, this would be the case for the majority of tests.

3.2.4. Validity as a Causal Relation Between Test Scores and Latent Variables

In modern test theory models, item scores are regressed on a common latent variable. Conditional on that latent variable, item scores are random (i.e., they no longer correlate). This is similar to a common cause model, where the latent variable acts as a common cause of the item scores (see chapters 2 and 6). This opens up the possibility of defining validity within the terms of the model itself, e.g., without making reference to the correlation of the test scores with an external criterion.

This can be done by taking the latent variable to represent the attribute of interest. Suppose that the model accurately describes reality (i.e., the items do in fact measure the same attribute). Then the question of whether we measure what we want to measure turns on the question of whether the latent variable in the model (i.e., the attribute measured by the items) is in fact the attribute that we intended to measure in the first place (e.g., *general intelligence*, *extraversion*, etc.). This means that the phrases "the latent variable measured by these items" and, say, "general intelligence" co-refer to the same attribute (Borsboom, Kievit, Cramer, Zand Scholten, & Franic, 2009). The causal interpretation of the relation between test scores and constructs is the focus of chapters 6, 7, and 8 of this book.

3.3. The Relation Between Validity and Other Psychometric Concepts

Psychometric models by themselves constitute a set of axiomatic definitions and empirical assumptions that may be more or less plausible in a given testing situation. An important question within the context of this book is how psychometric properties, which are defined within test

Box 3.2. Universes and Abilities: The Case of Multiplication

In the Maths Garden, items are grouped based on their mathematical characteristics: there is an addition section, where children can play addition games, and there are sections where they can practice counting, multiplication, and so forth. The items in each of these sections are thus grouped together by reference to the fact that they require the same mathematical operation. For this reason, the items can be generated algorithmically. When a limit is set on the upper bound of the addition, counting, or multiplication items (e.g., the end result is under a fixed number), the sets of items that may be so generated are finite.

If we propose that, say, the multiplication items measure multiplication ability, then we have two choices of filling in the semantics of this proposition. In a generalizability theory scheme, the administered items are interpreted as *samples* from a universe. For instance, a test consisting of the multiplication items "$7 \times 9 = \ldots$," "$6 \times 3 = \ldots$," and "$5 \times 5 = \ldots$" may be considered a sample from the universe of items characterized as "$m \times n = \ldots$" with $m,n \in (1,10)$. A pupil's universe score is his or her total score (at the time of testing) on the 100 items that belong to this universe. The generalizability of the three-item test is the proportion of variance that it explains in the universe scores. The question "what is multiplication ability?" may, in this case, be considered fixed through the definition of the universe, and the question "how valid is the test?" may be considered reduced to the question of how well it explains the variance in the universe score. As McDonald (2003, p. 219) states, "at this point we conclude that reliability is generalizability is validity, which makes a considerable simplification in thought." One could in fact estimate the validity of a subtest directly in the Maths Garden case by administering all items in the universe, and regressing the subtest score on the universe score. We will go into the caveats of such a position in chapter 6.

In a modern test theory scheme of thinking, we would be inclined to say that the administered items are *signs* of an underlying attribute, which we interpret as multiplication ability. In the Maths Garden, items are selected by an adaptive testing scheme, so that children who are better are administered more difficult items. This involves the additional assumption that the ability measured is continuous, and that it is the only ability measured by the test. This entails that the scores should exhibit local independence: conditional on the latent variable measured, a pupil's answer to the item "$1 \times 1 = \ldots$" conveys no information about that pupil's answer to the item "$2 \times 2 = \ldots$" In this case, the latent variable must be something that functions as a common cause with respect to the differences in item scores observed between pupils.

This creates an interesting divergence in thought. Does one choose the position that multiplication ability is just the total score on the universe of items, reducing validity to a generalization relation, or does one choose the position that multiplication ability is something that gives rise to observed differences in item scores, suggesting that validity involves a causal relation between the ability and the test scores? Each of these interpretations has advantages and disadvantages, and we invite the reader to consider these; we will return to this fundamental issue in the coming chapters.

---

theoretic models, relate to the validity of tests and test score interpretations. This section seeks to sketch out some of the questions that present themselves in this respect. First, we discuss the relation between validity, on the one hand, and reliability, on the other. Second, we discuss the relation between validity, measurement invariance, and predictive invariance. Third, we discuss the place of validity in psychometrics.

3.3.1. Reliability and Validity

The relation between reliability and validity is a traditionally important issue in psychometrics. The relation is simplest in the classical test theory model. Here, the variance of the observed score for a given person is considered to be pure error (since the true score is a constant). In a population of people, the true score is no longer a constant but a variable, and hence we can consider the relation between true and observed scores. As noted earlier, the squared correlation between these variables equals reliability. If (and only if) we consider validity to be a correlation between the true score on the test and another variable (i.e., subscribe to a variant of *criterion validity*), it follows that the value of this correlation is bounded by the reliability of the test. This is expressed in the famous attenuation formula, which relates the correlation between the true scores of test and criterion as a function of their reliabilities:

$$r(T_X, T_Y) = r(X,Y)/\sqrt{(r^2(X,T_X) + r^2(Y,T_Y))}.$$

Assuming, for the sake of argument, that the reliability of the criterion $r^2(Y,T_Y)$ equals one, and that the correlation between the true scores on the test and on the criterion is one as well, it follows that the maximum correlation between the observed test scores and the true criterion scores is $\sqrt{(r^2(X,T_X))}$. So, for instance, if the test scores have a reliability of $r^2(X,T_X) = .81$, then the maximum correlation between the test scores and the true criterion scores equals $\sqrt{.81} = .9$. If the correlation between the true test scores and the true criterion scores is lower than 1, say, .6, then the maximum correlation between observed test scores and true criterion scores is further attenuated to become $.6*\sqrt{.81} = .54$. Thus, the square root of reliability is the upper limit for the correlation between the observed test scores and the true criterion scores. This relation is the basis for the commonly heard thesis that "reliability is the upper limit on validity." Strictly speaking, the thesis should state that the *square root* of reliability is the upper limit of validity. Of course, even within the framework of classical test theory, the stark dichotomous proposition that "unreliable tests cannot be valid" is not supported. For example, for reasons developed above, this proposition would imply that all tests are invalid when interpreted at the level of individual test takers, thus obliterating the entire field of psychological assessment. This proposition is best seen as a general maxim rather than a statement of a test theoretic fact.

However, suppose we consider the idea that validity is a property of a test score interpretation, rather than of a test or test score itself (Messick, 1989; Kane, 2006). Then it is less clear what the attenuation formula has to do with validity. The attenuation formula gives a maximum value for a correlation, but not for the degree to which empirical evidence and theoretical rationales support a test score interpretation (e.g., Messick, 1989). It is questionable whether such a degree of evidential support could be represented in a single number in the first place, but even if that could be done, there is no reason to believe that this number should be a function of the classical test theory concept of reliability. Rather, within the construct validity perspective, reliability is an epistemic condition that facilitates the determination of validity (Hood, 2009). That is, if reliability is so low that the relations between the test score and other variables become essentially random, it becomes virtually impossible to determine what the test measures. Otherwise put, unreliable variance is construct-irrelevant variance and one aspect of validity involves minimizing construct-irrelevant variance.

Thus, the relation between reliability and validity is straightforward in classical test theory, but the reason for this is that classical test theory gives a very restrictive meaning to the word validity since it equates this term with a test-criterion correlation. Because validity theory, at least since Cronbach and Meehl (1955), no longer defines validity in this way, the supposition that reliability puts an upper limit on validity should be considered to be dependent on a theory of validity to which few theorists now subscribe.

3.3.2. Measurement Invariance, Predictive Invariance, and Validity

The modern test theory model introduces a distinction between θ and $E(X)$. It thereby offers the possibility of examining whether $E(X)$ is the same for members of different groups who have the same position on θ. For instance, if we take X to be the score on an IQ-item, we may wonder whether the expected value of X given a value of θ is the same for males and females. Denoting the variable *sex* by S, this comes down to evaluating whether $E(X|\theta) = E(X|\theta,S)$. If this is not the case, then there exist values of θ for which the expected test score is not the same for males and females; when θ is taken to be *intelligence*, this means that males and females who are equally intelligent do not have the same expected score on the item. In this situation the item in question displays differential item functioning (DIF), which means that it is not *measurement invariant* (Mellenbergh, 1989; Meredith, 1993). In the older literature, the situation was often interpreted as one in which the item is *biased*, but this invites a further interpretation of the difference in expected scores that is not statistical in nature, so without further evaluation of this difference the neutral term DIF is preferable.

An interesting case of DIF without bias occurs in developmental psychology. There, one may observe significant shifts in the ordering of item difficulties in Piagetian tasks; items that are easier for earlier developmental stages can become harder for later stages and vice versa (Jansen & Van der Maas, 2002). It would be preliminary to label such cases of DIF as signs of invalidity, since they are inherent to the phenomenon of stagewise development, and can in fact be predicted from that theory. Similarly, Borsboom, Mellenbergh, and Van Heerden (2002) discuss the example of the question "Are you tall?" as asked in males and females; this question elicits implicit within-group comparisons, so that the height at which males consider themselves tall is different from the height at which women do. If such processes are explicitly modeled, however, the statistical phenomenon of DIF need not cause invalidity in the assessment. Finally, translated tests may lead to DIF while there is no invalidity. The Mini Mental Status Examination, designed to quickly assess deficits in cognitive functioning, has an item that asks the respondent to repeat the phrase "no ifs, ands, or buts." This item was translated into Spanish, in which it reads "no hay peros que valgan" (which roughly back-translates as "no buts"). Unsurprisingly, the item shows significant DIF, because even for one who does not know Spanish the item is easier in Spanish than in English (Borsboom, 2006b). Generally, if one understands where DIF is coming from, items that show DIF can be retained in a test; they just need to be treated differently in different groups. Invalidity arises only if items are treated indiscriminately, leading to adverse effects. Even then, however, the consequences can be minor or even absent, such as when different items have DIF in different directions so that the net effect at the level of the total score is zero.

In addition, DIF without invalidity can occur because the wrong statistical model is used. For instance, if one uses a linear factor model to model total scores on dichotomous items, and uses standard statistical procedures to assess measurement invariance (e.g., checking whether the slopes and intercepts in the factor model are invariant across groups), one may get spurious cases of DIF. The reason is that, if one adds dichotomous items, the relations between total scores and latent variable is nonlinear (since the total score is bounded). If groups then differ in the location of their respective population distributions on the latent variable, the slopes of the regression of the total scores on the latent variable will usually be different in these populations (Bauer, 2005). In such a situation, if there exist group differences on the latent variable, the most likely reason for *not* finding DIF is actually a lack of statistical power. There are many other such cases. In general, forcing the data into parametric relations that they do not sustain may cause differences in model parameters across groups, even though there is no DIF under the generating model and there would be no invalidity in the use of, say, total scores to compare groups.

At a more philosophical level, it is interesting to note that the possibility of defining DIF as the violation of $E(X|\theta) = E(X|\theta, S)$ depends crucially on the possibility of separating the expectation of the test score, $E(X)$, from the latent variable, θ. For this reason, the classical test theory model never had an adequate representation of measurement invariance. The reason that classical test theory cannot separate the true score from the expected observed score is that these are identical by definition: In classical test theory, $E(X|\tau) = E(X|\tau, S)$ cannot be false, since $E(X)$ and τ are axiomatically identical.

Instead, in classical test theory, bias was taken to involve a situation of *prediction invariance*, where the regression of the test score X on the criterion Y is different for two groups, so that $E(Y|X) = E(Y|X,S)$. Predictive invariance is sometimes espoused as indicative of test fairness in test standards (AERA, APA, & NCME, 1999; SIOP, 2003). Also, scholars have required that items should be both measurement invariant, in the sense that $E(X|\theta) = E(X|\theta, S)$, *and* feature invariant regressions, according to $E(Y|X) = E(Y|X,S)$ (e.g., Camilli, 2006). Unfortunately, this situation cannot exist when the groups differ with respect to θ (Millsap, 1997, 2007). Normally, prediction invariance implies violations of measurement invariance and vice versa (Borsboom, Romeijn, & Wicherts, 2008; Millsap, 2007; Wicherts & Millsap, 2009). Thus, by demanding predictive invariance, one may unintentionally be demanding violations of measurement invariance.

This is important because it indicates that validity cannot be unambiguously mapped to psychometric concepts like measurement invariance. For instance, if we interpret "lack of bias" to mean "measurement invariance", then validity requires measurement invariant items. Often, however, this will imply a violation of prediction invariance. If we take the other route, interpreting "lack of bias" as "prediction invariance," then validity requires predictively invariant items. This will ordinarily imply that there exist violations of measurement invariance. So we cannot have everything at the same time. In many cases, psychometric decisions thus are governed by a trade-off, because not all desirable properties of test scores can be maximized at the same time.

Box 3.3. Measurement Invariance, DIF, and Bias

In the Maths Garden, item parameters are continuously updated on the basis of incoming online item responses. New items are injected into the system with their parameters at starting values considered plausible by the test constructors and, based on the item responses, the parameters are dynamically updated. Part of the quality control procedures involves tracking the course that parameter estimates take in this process. Here, interesting things happen with respect to measurement invariance.

For instance, consider the item "4000 + 4000 = ..." When this item was first injected into the system, it received a high initial difficulty based on the fact that it involves high numbers; the intended audience for this item were children in the older age groups (say, 9–12). However, as will be obvious, the item is of an entirely different character as compared to its "neighbor" "3999 + 4001 = ..." So what happened, when the item was first injected, was that the older children uniformly answered the item correctly. This caused its difficulty parameter to drop so spectacularly that it was subsequently administered to the younger children (say, 5–6). Naturally, these children uniformly failed the item, so that its parameter estimate bounced back up, etc.

This behavior is probably caused by the fact that the item is not measurement invariant: for the older children, it as difficult as "4 + 4 = . . .," whereas for the younger children, it is radically more difficult. Technically, the item therefore violates measurement invariance, i.e., it shows Differential Item Functioning. It is questionable whether this should be interpreted as bias, however, because the item may in fact function well an addition item in both age groups individually. It may rather be considered a different item when administered to different age groups: Once a child has grasped the rule that underlies the addition items involving round tens, hundreds, thousands, etc., they suddenly all become equally difficult. This is perfectly sensible from a substantive viewpoint, and the shift in difficulties may not be a sign of anything being wrong—except, perhaps, in the psychometric model.

3.3.3. Psychometrics and Validity

In the above paragraphs, a number of psychometric properties received mention that are generally deemed desirable: predictive power (correlation or multiple correlation), reliability, generalizability, measurement invariance, and prediction invariance. Each of these psychometric concepts has received ample formal treatment in the psychometric literature. In addition, each of them has a mathematical expression within a formal model. It is noteworthy that, among the concepts that have been formalized in psychometrics, validity itself is conspicuously lacking.

Hence, the question arises of how validity should be related to psychometric properties. One possible response is in terms of what may be called an "umbrella model," in which validity is viewed as an overarching concept: a general verdict on the psychometric properties of the test taken together. Such a view was adopted by Messick (1989) who viewed validity as an integrative judgment of a wide set of relevant properties of the test and test scores, in the light of a specific interpretation of the test scores in terms of constructs. A pressing issue, under this viewpoint, is how the integration of information, which is necessary to form a judgment, should be conceptualized.

It is in general unlikely that all psychometrically desirable properties could be optimized simultaneously. For some properties (e.g., measurement invariance and predictive invariance) this may in fact be impossible. So, suppose that we have two intelligence tests: Test *A* and Test *B*. Suppose that scores on Test *A* are more reliable, behave in keeping with theoretically posited relations, and have predictive invariance. At the same time, these test scores violate measurement invariance and have limited predictive utility. Scores on Test *B* have high predictive utility and measurement invariance, and behave in keeping with theoretical relations, but violate predictive invariance and have low reliability. How do we integrate these pieces of information in a general verdict of the validity of interpretations of scores on Tests *A* and *B* in terms of intelligence? The information could be integrated in different ways. We could, for instance, use one of various decision theoretic models. Because such a model would serve to rank order (or scale) the tests with respect to their degree of validity (as defined in the model), the information integration procedure would in essence constitute a measurement process in itself. If one should ask about the justification for using such a procedure, one would essentially question the validity of a procedure designed to assess validity. An infinite regress looms, albeit not necessarily an inescapable one. For instance, a psychometrician committed to such an approach might argue that the impact of alternative validity criteria at higher levels on validity judgments at the lowest level (the test in question) diminishes to zero as the number of levels approaches infinity.

An alternative choice would be to restrict validity to one particular aspect of test functioning: for instance, to the question of whether the test actually measures the intended attribute (Borsboom, Mellenbergh, & Van Heerden, 2004). Such a move renders all other psychometric properties conditional on validity; one would not speak of the reliability of test scores per se, but rather of their reliability with respect to the measured attribute. Similar considerations apply to measurement invariance, generalizability, and so on. In such a view, psychometric functioning could only be truthfully assessed given validity. The drawback of this viewpoint is that psychometric models clearly do not assume a particular identity of, say, the latent variable that they present in the model formulation. For instance, methods for estimating reliability are loaded with assumptions, but not with the assumption that, say, the test in question actually measures any particular attribute. That is, perhaps the methods presume that *some* attribute is being measured, but certainly not that any particular attribute is being measured. Insofar as validity concerns the actual identity of latent variable and construct, this identity is fixed outside the realm of psychometric modeling. Moreover, even if the judgment of validity is restricted to just one attribute, practical decisions about test use generally will not be (chapter 9). As such, a restricted notion of validity does not eliminate the above concerns about integrating information about various properties into one judgment; it simply eliminates them from validity judgments.

Thus, it appears that one can view validity either as an integrative function of psychometric properties, or as a separate property that is orthogonal to psychometric functioning. This is an important issue, because one's viewpoint here determines what one takes as validity evidence. On the integrative viewpoint, for instance, high measurement precision would count as one piece of evidence for validity by itself (as validity is an overarching property which has reliability as one its constituents). In the orthogonal viewpoint, it would not, as high reliability is neither necessary nor sufficient for validity. Reliability is not necessary, because one may have an instrument that does in fact measure the intended attribute, but does so with low measurement precision. It is not sufficient, because one can have highly reliable test scores that measure nothing in particular or something other than what one intended to measure. The same holds for the relation between validity and other psychometric concepts. Chapter 9 addresses the dilemma of choosing between encompassing and restricted definitions of validity in greater detail.

3.4. Chapter Conclusion

The present chapter has outlined the basic ingredients of psychometric models currently in use, as well as studying the question of how the central terms in these models (true scores, universes, and latent variables) may be taken to relate to constructs. Clearly, how one tends to think of a construct determines one's psychometric taste. For those who think of constructs as causal variables that determine test scores, the latent variable model may seem more sensible. For those who tend to think of test items as samples taken from a universe of possible items, the generalizability model will appear more attractive. However, it should be noted that which model is most appropriate in a given context likely depends on the nature of the properties one intends to assess, as well as on how one defines such a construct and on what one's purposes in testing are. After all, some indicators may in fact be the effects of a common cause, whereas others may in fact be samples taken from a universe. Which model is more plausible would seem to depend on what is the case here. In addition, because both the content and the grouping of test items into scales are under our control, it is conceivable that a construct that functions as a common cause variable in one context may function as a universe score in another. As a result, it may be unwise to prefer any one model across the board.

The classical test theory model has very little to say about validity. Its semantics almost force it to consider validity from a predictive perspective. In contrast, the latent variable model and generalizability model hold the possibility of representing the construct inside the model formulation (e.g., as a latent variable of universe score). Thus it is sensible to devote more attention to these models in the present book. The conceptual cousin of the generalizability model, behavior domain theory, is the primary topic of chapter 5. Possible causal interpretations of latent variable models will be addressed in chapters 6, 7, and 8. The issue of how the identity of the construct is fixed, which involves questions of meaning and reference, will be taken up in the third part of the book.

3.5. Further Reading

Baker, F. *Fundamentals of item response theory*. Freely downloadable from: http://echo.edres.org:8080/irt/

Brennan R. L. (2001). *Generalizability theory*. New York: Springer.

Lord, F. M., & Novick, M. R. (1968). *Statistical theories of mental test scores*. Reading, MA: Addison-Wesley.

Mellenbergh, G. J. (2011). *A conceptual introduction to psychometrics*. The Hague: Eleven International Publishing.

4 Open Issues in Measurement Theory and Psychometrics

Connection With Other Chapters

Chapter 2 reviewed the most influential theories of measurement, and chapter 3 discussed psychometric models that are often used in analyzing test scores. Theories of measurement are of central importance to test score interpretations in terms of measurement. Psychometric models are of central importance to the statistical analysis of test scores. Both measurement interpretations and statistical analyses of test scores figure prominently in validation research. Hence it is important to analyze how measurement theory and psychometric models are connected. This chapter analyzes the relation between psychometric models and theories of measurement. In particular, it discusses the question of whether psychometric test scores can be justifiably interpreted as measurements.

The relation between measurement theories and psychometric models is highly relevant to validity. One commonly sees papers in which researchers claim that they have *measured* something, whereas the defense of this claim only involves psychometric *modeling*. For instance, one might claim that one has measured reading ability, and justify this claim through the supporting claim that a unidimensional Item Response Theory model fits the item scores. For such arguments to work, there must be a connection between the fit of the model and the status of test scores as putative measurements. Somehow the fit of the model must count as evidence for the measurement claim. That requires a link between psychometric models and theories of measurement.

That connection, however, is not a secure and settled part of test theory. Instead, it is an important open issue in psychometrics. On the one hand, there are those who think that psychometric models—especially those in Item Response Theory—are a special case of representational measurement theory as discussed in chapter 2 (e.g., Fisher, 1995; Roskam

& Jansen, 1984; Bond & Fox, 2001). Thus, these researchers think that using standard psychometric models provides a safe haven for test score interpretations in terms of measurement. Other scholars, however, have argued that there is no such equivalence. They hold that psychometric models simply assume measurable quantitative traits without ever testing the hypothesis that these traits are quantitative (Michell, 1997, 1999, 2008; Kyngdon, 2008). Finally, it has been argued that psychometric models do formulate bona fide measurement relations, but incorporate them as hypotheses that are intertwined with other assumptions in the model structure (Borsboom & Mellenbergh, 2004; Borsboom & Zand Scholten, 2008).

Perhaps the most essential turning points in the disagreements are the questions of (a) what measurement is, (b) whether or not it is required in psychological testing, and (c) whether or not psychometric tests instantiate it. These discussions are complicated because they involve disagreements on various levels. Some of these issues have to do with *meaning*, because whether one takes a psychometric model to establish measurement depends partly on how one defines measurement. In addition, the disagreements have to do with *norms*, because they depend on what level of justification is required for claiming, say, that an IQ-test measures intelligence. Finally, some of the disagreements have to do with *norms* that apply to *meaning*. For instance, authors typically disagree on what we should take measurement to mean.

The complicated, layered structure of this problem may explain why, even after a century of psychometrics, it is still subject to debate. In the present chapter we analyze the measurement debate, and evaluate what its consequences are for validation research. First, we discuss differences between theories of measurement and their relevance to psychometric modeling. The most important differences involve (a) whether a certain *structure* of attributes is required for measurement, and (b) whether or not *probabilities* may legitimately enter in measurement theory. Second, we will analyze possibilities to reconcile psychometric models and measurement theory.

4.1. Measurement and the Structure of Psychological Attributes

In chapter 2, several positions on measurement have been laid out. The following three positions are currently considered viable. First, the *classical theory*, which holds that measurement involves the estimation or determination of independently existing quantitative relations. These relations are expressed as the ratio of a magnitude to a unit magnitude of the same kind. Second, *representionalism*, which holds that measurement is the assignment of numerals according to rule. The rule must be such that the numerical assignments are isomorphic with a set of empirical relations. Third, *latent variable theory*, which holds that measurement involves determining the position of people in a latent space on the basis of sets of fallible indicators. This theory rests on the specification of a functional relation between the latent variable and its indicators.

There are some structural differences between these theories, but at other points they appear reconcilable. A particularly important issue concerns the question of whether a certain *structure* of attributes is required for measuring them. For instance, the classical theory holds that only certain *kinds* of attributes are measurable. This is because quantitative structure is a *sine qua non* for measurement. Representationalism and latent variable theory do not make this requirement. For instance, representationalism allows for nominal and ordinal measurement. Latent variable theory commonly involves categorical latent structures as well, for instance in the formulation of the latent class model. The classical theory thus holds on to a stricter definition of measurement than representationalism or latent variable theory. What is the basis for this restriction?

The most obvious route to defend the restriction is by claiming that the semantics of measurement are not negotiable. In this vein, one could argue that measurement always involves the estimation or determination of quantitative relations, because this is *what measurement truly is*. In philosophy, such a position is called *essentialist*, because it assumes that the definition of measurement has an *essence* that cannot be changed. In the classical view, the essence of psychological measurement involves three necessary conditions. First, the levels of psychological attributes must be quantitative so that they stand in quantitative relations to each other. Second, there must be a system of units of measurement that can be used to determine these relations. Third, there must be an empirical procedure to measure the attribute in the relevant units.

The latter two conditions—devising a system of units and forging a procedure to compare people—are engineering problems. They require one to solve what Michell (1997) called the *instrumental task* of measurement. However, the condition that psychological attributes must be quantitative is of a different nature. If psychological attributes are not quantitative, then psychological attributes are simply not measurable, period. In this case, psychological measurement is frustrated, however advanced our technologies may become. In contrast, if at least some psychological attributes are quantitative, then psychological measurement is possible for these attributes. However, as long as there is no way to compare the levels of attributes in terms of units, that possibility is not actualized. Psychological measurement then has the status of science fiction: It may someday become a reality, but not today.

Michell (1997) has argued that investigations into the structure of attributes cover a distinct part of the development of measurement. Contrasting this to the instrumental task, he called this the *scientific task* of measurement. The scientific task consists in testing whether attributes are quantitative or not. Testing the quantity hypothesis requires one to deduce empirical predictions from it. Examples of such predictions are the double cancellation conditions worked out in the theory of conjoint measurement (Luce & Tukey, 1964). For a researcher who intends to interpret test scores as measures in the strong sense of the classical theory, conjoint measurement therefore offers ways to test the hypothesis that the attribute in question is quantitative. It is beyond the scope of this book to discuss this method in detail. The reader is referred to Luce and Tukey (1964) and Krantz, Suppes, Luce, and Tversky (1971) for detailed discussions on conjoint measurement; Michell (1990) provides a good nontechnical treatment.

Reserving the term *measurement* for quantitative attribute has an important benefit. Such language use is continuous with the paradigm cases of measurement, i.e., those of length, mass, etc. On the other hand, there is also a disadvantage. The meaning of measurement in the past century has shifted so considerably that a restriction of the term's application may not be optimal in terms of communication. It is a fact of life that, in many quarters of science, the word 'measurement' has come to be used in a much wider sense than just the quantitative meaning. Researchers and test users often take measurement to refer to simple classifications (e.g., when taking symptoms as measures of a latent disease condition) or to orderings (e.g., when taking educational test scores to identify top students in the context of university admissions). This has been partly under the influence of Stevens' (1946) notions of ordinal and nominal measurement and the representationalist work that followed it, which were discussed in chapter 2.

Likewise, even in physics one reads about the measurement of categorical attributes—an impossibility in the classical theory. For instance, such language use is frequent in an important source like Bell (1964), who talks about measuring the *spin* of particles. Here, spin refers to a categorical variable with two levels, such that the measurement of spin should be considered nominal. Hence, the restrictive use of the term measurement is not strictly adhered to even in the exact sciences. In fact, the famous *measurement paradox* in quantum mechanics is ordinarily constructed as concerning problems in the detection of categorical states. Therefore it is a problem of nominal measurement. According to the classical theory, this is inappropriate. Should the measurement paradox then be relabeled the *naming paradox* or the *assessment paradox*? The message is clear: To insist on the restrictive definition of measurement runs the risk of taking a position so restrictive that one disconnects oneself even from the sciences that cover the paradigm cases of measurement. This is an unfavorable situation, in our view.

One could alternatively take the viewpoint that nominal and ordinal scales are in fact cases of measurement, be it at a lower level. In this viewpoint, Stevens' (1946) move represents a much-needed liberalization of measurement theory from the restricted meaning it had both in the classical theory (Michell, 1986) and in the fundamental measurement ideas of the 1920s (Campbell, 1920). In the context of representationalism, Stevens' move is a natural step to take. The reason is that representationalism takes numerical representation to be the key element of measurement. From this perspective there is no compelling reason to reserve the term for quantitative representations. In addition, bona fide quantitative attributes, such as length or temperature, can be measured at various scale levels—including nominal and ordinal ones. It therefore makes sense to admit this possibility within measurement theory. For instance, a thermostat may divide the set of temperatures into three categories—*too hot, too cold* and *just right*. This means the thermostat measures temperature on an ordinal scale at best. Few would object to the notion that the thermostat measures temperature in the process. However, according to the classical theory, this ordinal measurement cannot be measurement.

Similarly, if attributes like energy and mass are discontinuous (as one may in fact take 20th-century physics to have shown), the strict interpretation of measurement should imply that mass has in fact never been measured. The reason is that such attributes are not continuous and hence were never actually amenable to Hölder's (1901) axioms (Michell & Ernst, 1996, 1997). They just seemed to be, at a macrolevel. In our view, however, any theory of measurement should accommodate the fact that attributes like mass are measured in practice. Whether they are ultimately continuous or not is irrelevant. We would therefore suggest adapting Hölder's axioms rather than prescribing that the use of the word 'measurement' was inappropriate. In view of these considerations, we think that too strict a position on the semantics of measurement ultimately backfires. The more liberal notions of measurement, incorporated by representationalism and latent variable theory, accommodate such cases without problems.

Is a compromise possible? We suggest the following solution. We admit nominal and ordinal cases as cases of measurement, in accordance with the more colloquial usage of the term in scientific research. This is consistent with representationalism and with latent variable theory. However, at the same time we recognize that the term 'measurement' most naturally applies to metric scales, that are designed to measure quantitative attributes. The use of the word 'measurement' to indicate systematic determination of orders and similarities is legitimate, but it is clearly an extension of this original meaning. Moreover, we view the metric notion of measurement as an important one that should not simply be absorbed into the broader notion and treated as an alternative on par with the others. Therefore, we prefer to use the term 'assessment' to cover the more general case. Assessment may include measurement, but it also applies naturally to cases where scores are used to order or classify. In the context of validity, it is important to be mindful of the fact that reproducible individual differences need not imply that an underlying quantitative attribute exists or in fact is measured. Thus, if one intends the strict measurement interpretation of test scores, then specific tests of quantitative structure are appropriate.

Box 4.1. Measurement Units in Psychology

Is it possible in psychology to construct measurement scales that work analogously to those of physics? To do so, one first requires a unit of measurement. Second, one needs a procedure to concatenate units of measurement. If these are in place, then a person's level of ability may be obtained by counting how many units must be concatenated to match that level of ability.

A rare attempt to achieve such a unit-based representation has been undertaken in the Lexile framework for measuring reading ability (Stenner, Burdick, Sanford, & Burdick, 2006). To determine their reading ability, respondents are given a passage of text with a word missing from a sentence. The respondents have to choose which word should be used to complete the sentence. They choose this word from a number of options. Their choice constitutes an item response.

In the Lexile framework, the difficulty of a passage is modeled as a function of two factors. First, sentence length, which is a proxy for syntactic complexity. Second, the average frequency with which the words in the item are used in natural language. This is a measure of semantic rarity. The unit—called a *lexile* and indicated by the letter L—is defined as 1/1000th of the difference in difficulty between a very simple primer text, set at 200L, and a passage from an encyclopedia, set at 1200L. A person's level of ability is conventionally defined as the number of lexiles of a passage for which the person has a probability of 0,75 to give a correct response.

The lexile is argued to have the same meaning at each level of the reading ability scale. Therefore it is put forward as a unit that achieves a genuine interval scale. It is at present unclear whether the scientific community accepts this claim. However, the website of the company Barnes and Noble has not waited for scientific acceptance, and allows parents to search books in a range of complexity that matches the Lexile reading ability measure of their children.

4.2. Measurement and Probabilistic Models

The previous section discussed the question of what kind of attribute structure is required to speak of measurement. This is a major dividing line between the classical theory on the one hand, and representationalism and latent variable theory on the other. The question of whether, and if so how, probabilities may enter into measurement theory is another important dividing line. This line, however, divides latent variable theory and representationalism. Latent variable theory routinely invokes probabilities, while representationalism hardly ever does. The classical theory of measurement mainly concerns the character of quantitative attributes and the way that measurement scales relate to it, and could be viewed as neutral on this issue.

The introduction of probabilities in psychometric models is generally defended on the grounds that psychological data are noisy. This implies that, in psychology, deterministic models hardly ever fit the data. As a consequence, latent variable models have become popular in psychological research. From this, the appearance may arise that latent variable models are specific to psychology, whereas deterministic models are specific to physics. This, however, is not necessarily the case. Consider the analysis of how a standard sequence of weights is built, as described by Campbell (1920; discussed in chapter 2). In order to follow the required concatenation schemes, one needs relations like *object A balances object B*, *object B outweighs object C*, etc., to be deterministic (see chapter 2). This means that these relations should not present a single violation of the relevant axioms. For instance, in the case of mass, there should not be a single violation of transitivity. Thus, for all triples of objects tested, the results must be such that if object A outweighs object B, and object B outweighs object C, then object A outweighs object C.

Informally thinking through the thought experiment that would give rise to a ratio scale, we tend to admit deterministic relations. However, it is doubtful whether such relations would ever be encountered in practice, even in physics. To elucidate this matter, it is instructive to think through how the practice suggested by Campbell (1920) for constructing a standard sequence for mass would work out in practice.

Assume for simplicity that we are submitting to our measurement procedure a population of objects to measure the attribute mass M with levels m. We aim to construct a standard sequence in exactly the way Campbell (1920) reconstructs the procedure. Thus, we use a balance scale with two arms and represent concatenations of objects by the mathematical operation of addition symbolized as '+'. Finally, we take the relation A *balances* B as a model for the equality sign '=' (see chapter 2 for details).

The forces exerted at either end of the balance scale, say Left and Right, are F_L and F_R. Assume gravity constant at level $G = g$. F_L and F_R are a function of the mass of the object to the left and right, m_L and m_R, plus any unintentional forces exerted on either arm by the person operating the balance scale. Call the latter forces $F_{E,L}$ and $F_{E,R}$ for the extraneous forces exerted on the left and right arms. These may be thought of as producing measurement error. Assume a deterministic Newtonian universe, so that no probabilities need enter at this point. Then the forces exerted on the left and right arms are $F_L = m_L g + F_{E,L}$ and $F_R = m_R g + F_{E,R}$. The balance scale tips to the left when $F_L > F_R$. It tips to the right when $F_L < F_R$. It stays in balance when $|F_L - F_R| < F_B$, where F_B is the frictional force, i.e., the resistance produced by the balance scale itself.

F_B determines the precision of the balance scale. It is impossible to measure differences in weights that result in a force difference smaller than F_B, even if the balance scale is operated with perfection (such that $F_{E,L} = F_{E,R} = 0$). In turn, if the balance scale is operated perfectly, and the difference in weights produces a force larger than F_B, then the probability of the balance tilting to the "correct" side (i.e., the side with the larger mass) equals one.

In the special case that $F_{E,L} = F_{E,R} = 0$, the balance scale behaves according to a deterministic model, because its response only depends on the weight differences. In this case the Campbell scheme can always be used to create a standard sequence. The *Balance Response Function*, analogous to the Item Response Function in psychometrics, would look like the one in Figure 4.1. This function plots the probability of the balance scale outcomes as a function of the differences between weights.

The figure gives a graphical representation of the idea that the pan balance will tilt in the direction of the side with greater mass. This will happen deterministically whenever the difference between the forces exerted on the left and right sides exceeds the frictional force of the balance scale.

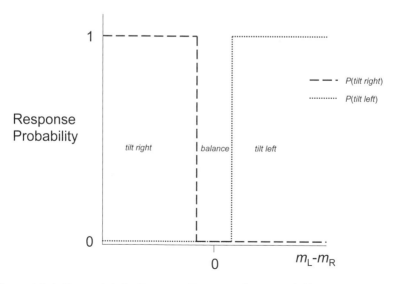

Figure 4.1 A Deterministic Response Function for Campbell's Balance Scale. m_L-m_R is the mass difference between the objects on the left and right arms of the pan balance.

Psychometrically speaking, this is the polytomous equivalent of a Guttman model.

Now, we can imagine increasing the precision of the balance scale by making F_B arbitrarily small so that the balance will tip for arbitrarily small differences between the weights. This could be done by, e.g., putting some oil on the fulcrum of the balance scale, using better materials, etc. As we increase the precision of the scale in this way, while keeping other things constant, the region in Figure 4.1, in which the scale is in balance, shrinks. Even if the region of balance determined by F_B becomes arbitrarily small, the model can still hold true provided there are no error forces that would upset the deterministic behavior of the scale in or around the region of balance. Such a situation, in which the error forces are absent and the balance scale is perfectly precise, would in fact seem to constitute the perfect Campbellian scheme.

However, neither perfect precision nor the absolute absence of error forces is an empirically realizible condition. This means the Campbellian scheme is, essentially, an idealization. In reality, where error forces can be minimized but not entirely eliminated, the adequacy of Figure 4.1 (which is needed for the construction of the balance scale in Campbell's construction recipe) implies that the precision of the balance scale must be limited. In other words, the deterministic relations required for Campbell's construction can only be realized if the balance scale used has some degree of *imprecision*.

One can also see this by approaching the balance scale from the opposite situation, i.e., by modeling error forces as random variables and letting their variance shrink. For instance, assume that the error forces have some bell-shaped distribution around zero, like a normal distribution. Then we get a response function like that in Figure 4.2. Clearly, this is analogous to the Item Response Function for a polytomous item in models like those of Samejima (1959). We can think of approaching the idealized Campbellian balance scale by creating improved observational conditions, so that our errors become progressively smaller. This means that the variance of the distribution of the error forces decreases. For a given level of imprecision of the balance scale, the response functions in Figure 4.2 will become steeper and tend towards those in Figure 4.1. When they are sufficiently small for the balance scale to produce deterministic data, Campbell's construction recipe is again possible. However, this only works when the balance scale has some imprecision. If precision is perfect, the construction will fail whenever there is random noise, however small.

In the presence of noise, Campbell's construction can only work if $F_B > 0$, that is, if there is a certain degree of *imprecision* in the instrument used. This is interesting because deterministic measurement models are usually associated with perfect measurements. In this case, however, the ability to construct a deterministic model of individual measurements depends

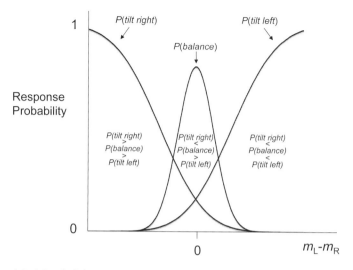

Figure 4.2 A Probabilistic Response Function for Campbell's Balance Scale.

on the measurement instrument being imperfect. This appears to be a rather general point that is easily extended to other kinds of measurement. The general rule would seem to be that the more precise the instrument, the smaller the chance that the item responses form patterns that can be described with a deterministic model.

Now, if one in fact did have a perfectly precise balance scale, an alternative way of constructing a standard sequence would be available. This is because one could use the probabilistic relations. For instance, one could balance two objects *repeatedly* against each other. Then one could take the equivalence relation, A~B, to be satisfied if and only if P(balance tilts to A) = .5. A standard sequence could then be constructed based on essentially the same procedure as Campbell (1920) described, only with the equivalence relation redefined in this way.

The difference between deterministic axiom systems, as typically presented in representational measurement theory, and probabilistic models, as typically presented in psychometrics, may be less principled than it seems at first sight. In particular, while representationalism does take axiomatic structures to be error-free, this does not imply that the axioms cannot apply to probabilities. As long as these probabilities are themselves in accordance with the relevant axiomatic system, they can be used to construct a scale in essentially the same way as is done in representationalism. Thus, the distinction between deterministic axiom systems and probabilistic models is less strict than may be supposed at first blush. In addition, psychometric models could be used to furnish physical measures if need be. Of course, this does not imply that fitting a psychometric model to a dataset delivers measures on a par with those of physics; it rather implies that there are no principled barriers between psychometric models and representationalism.

Box 4.2. Continuous Quantity and Qualitative Shifts

The Lexile framework has an outspoken goal and that goal is measurement. The central claim in the framework is that the Lexile system measures reading ability on an interval scale. Researchers associated with the framework conceptualize measurement according to classical theory of measurement (e.g., Kyngdon, 2008).

This means that they are bound to assume that reading ability, as measured by the Lexile system, is a continuous attribute with quantitative structure. Given this hypothesis and the further supposition that the item responses are described by a Rasch model, specific predictions can be deduced that can be used to test the hypothesis of quantitative structure. Specifically, the axioms of conjoint measurement should hold. This means that the empirically estimated probabilities should display a chacteristic trade-off between reading ability and item difficulty.

Kyngdon (2008) succinctly described the results of some preliminary tests and finds that they corroborate the hypothesis in question. This would imply that reading ability behaves as a continuous quantitative attribute. If such results are independently replicated and augmented with other tests, the conclusion that reading ability is quantitative may become well supported.

Such a conclusion would allow for powerful scientific applications, but it would also raise some difficult questions. For instance, at the level of the individual, learning language appears to have discontinuous features, as does any instance of rule-based learning. Learning a rule typically changes not only *how much* one can do, but also *what* one can do. It is an open question whether such changes could be described within a theory that treats reading ability as a continuous property.

4.3. A Possible Reconciliation Between Theories of Measurement

One may view the theories under consideration as yielding a definition of what measurement is. So interpreted, the classical theory, representationalism, and latent variable theory appear to be quite different theories. However, if one takes a step back and considers them to be concerned with different *aspects* of measurement and assessment processes, then the differences fade and significant communalities begin to stand out. The classical theory then appears mainly a restriction on the scope of representationalism. Latent variable theory is mainly a way to handle the interface between data and attributes, when empirical relational systems are indirectly assessed through the examination of noisy data. Viewing the matter in this way, the following picture emerges. The empirical relational systems of representationalism are idealized data structures. The representations of these idealized data structures characterize attribute structures. In turn, the models of psychometrics represent ways to connect these attribute structures to item responses in case the latter are contaminated by noise. A causal interpretation may be given to these models by taking the functional relation, which holds between the attribute and the item responses, to support counterfactuals (see chapter 7). If the attribute structure is quantitative, this allows for the construction of a system of units, and quantitative relations between (properties of) objects can be estimated on the basis of the data. This is a special and extremely powerful case, which lies at the basis of the success of quantitative theories in the natural sciences. The classical theory of measurement focuses on this particular situation.

Box 4.3. Causality and Measurement

The latent variable idea of measurement holds that individual differences in response probabilities are caused by individual differences in the latent variable as well as differences between items regarding difficulty. Direct tests of this hypothesis require manipulation of the latent variable, which is generally hard, and of the item difficulties, which is often easier. In the Lexile framework, the item difficulties are presumed a simple function of word frequency and sentence length, both of which are manipulable. As such, this allows for relatively straightforward tests of the measurement system. By tracking the natural growth of individuals, the validity of the system can be further checked at the level of the individual. Interventions, e.g., educational ones, may in addition be used to check whether increases and decreases in reading ability behave as hypothesized. Finally, a substantive theory of reading and the psychological or neurocognitive processes that lead up to individuals' item responses may elucidate why the measurements behave as they do. This is generally the weakest link in psychological measurement, and, in the case of the lexile, ideas on such issues remain sketchy as elsewhere.

4.4. Is Measurement Necessary in Psychological Testing?

The above reconciliation of theoretical perspectives leads to a view on measurement that is liberal when compared to a strict reading of representationalism, and even more liberal when compared to the classical theory of measurement. However, it is not trivial. Even in nominal systems, for instance, the above account still requires a latent class model to hold for a given set of item responses; for ordered attributes this becomes an ordered latent class model; for continuous attributes, a continuous unidimensional latent variable model; and for quantitatively continuous attributes, a continuous unidimensional latent variable model with metric properties.

If no such model holds, it is hard to defend the thesis that one is measuring something even under a liberal conception of measurement. And there are many cases of psychological tests for which a clean fit to any such psychometric model is a far cry. Does this invalidate the use of test scores? The answer to this must be: no, as long as no measurement interpretation is made. If no measurement model can be found to hold for the data, then there is little evidence for the thesis that the test scores can be interpreted as measurements, and hence this interpretation is unsupported.

However, test scores may be justifiably used for purposes other than measurement, like prediction, generalization, and selection. That is, the successful application of a measurement model to item or test scores supports the measurement interpretation, but the decision to use the test scores is not necessarily based on such an interpretation (and, we may add, probably never on such an interpretation alone). For instance, suppose one had recorded shoe size, running speed, and hand-eye coordination, and formed a composite by adding the resulting numbers. Then, surely, the interpretation of these composite scores as unidimensional measures of some linearly ordered continuous attribute would be difficult to support. But the composite scores may still predict success on a basketball team quite well. Therefore, in certain circumstances (e.g., in the absence of a better alternative) a coach could use these scores as a selection instrument for team membership. Similarly, if one's goal is merely generalization to behaviors outside the testing situation, as in generalizability theory, what one should support is the predictive utility of item scores, not necessarily their measurement properties.

Thus, the interpretation of test scores can take various forms and not all of them require a measurement model. The same holds for justifying the decision to use a test in a given situation. One can, for instance, be convinced that the democratic vote is a worthless system for measuring the quality of candidates' presidential qualities. Then one may nevertheless be an avid supporter of the use of the democratic vote as a selection instrument to decide who gets to occupy presidential office; for instance, because one judges the consequences of every alternative method of selection as worse. Thus, the justification of test score use may, but need not, involve evidential backup for a measurement interpretation of test scores. Chapters 9 and 12 take up this issue in detail.

> **Box 4.4. So What is Being Measured?**
>
> The Lexile framework is a well-developed psychometric system for which the hypothesis that something is indeed being measured enjoys some evidential support. The item difficulties are in addition reasonably modeled as a function of sentence length and word frequency. Thus, the model is not purely mathematical but has substantively meaningful components that serve to restrict the possible interpretations of the ability measured; at least, it should be something that allows a reader to better cope with increasing sentence lengths and rarer words, which rules out, say, extraversion or attitudes towards the death penalty. However it leaves open the precise character of the reading ability measured; this may be a composite of working memory, recognition abilities, lexicon size, and general knowledge. Interestingly, should any one of the functions that compose reading ability have discrete characteristics, the continuity, and hence the quantitative structure, of the ability would become questionable.

4.5. Chapter Conclusion

This chapter has explored the question of to what extent the measurement theories and models discussed in the previous chapters are reconcilable. Clear philosophical and practical differences between the theoretical systems exist. However, it appears that, when interpreted as dealing with distinct aspects of the measurement process, they are not completely at odds. Rather, they focus on different things. The classical theory of measurement deals with the definition and detection of quantitative attribute structure. Representationalism handles the definition and representation of a more general class of attribute structures. Latent variable theory deals with the analysis of data that imperfectly reflect such structures. In practice, these theories could work in tandem. For instance, one could use the axioms of quantity to characterize an attribute structure. Then one could use results from representational theory to characterize idealized empirical relational systems that would allow for its representation with a certain uniqueness. Finally, one could specify corresponding latent variable models to test the resulting theory against actual data, which will invariably contain some noise. Such research strategies in fact exist (e.g., Doignon & Falmagne, 1999), although they are rare.

The place of psychometric modeling in this scheme perhaps deviates from the way it is routinely used in practice. Psychometric models have been developed to such an extent that they are available off-the-shelf, and are implemented in widely available computer programs. This is in principle a desirable situation as the development of a new psychometric model, optimally tailored to every new substantive situation, is probably too much to ask given the current state of psychological testing. However, it also leads to the risks inherent in any point-and-click implementation of statistical models: Researchers can be led to believe that the default options in computer programs exhaust the theoretical possibilities for modeling. In some cases they may start thinking that one particular model, like a factor model or a Rasch model, is invariably necessary for good test analysis. Especially with an eye on validation research, and the justification of test use generally, this can cloud the fact that the development of statistical models and software is often guided by pragmatic choices which need not comport with the substantive situation the researcher is working in. Theoretical justifications for measurement models, after all, cannot be expected to be defaulted in computer programs.

In accordance, while standard psychometric models may be fruitfully used to test specific measurement interpretations, the justification for such interpretations cannot rest on their application alone. For instance, the structure of the latent variable (e.g., continuous or categorical) in psychometric models figures as a very basic assumption in setting up the model. However, it is not explicitly or directly tested in fitting it to the data. The justification for choosing a given structure is likely to be grounded in different ways. For instance, it may be supported by considering substantive theory and prior research, and by working out and testing specific predictions that follow from it (e.g., bimodality in categorical models, double cancellation in quantitative models). When scores are put to use to make decisions about people, the importance of measurement models is further relativized to pragmatic, ethical, and social factors involving the consequences of test use (Messick, 1989). Thus, although measurement models and theories are indispensable in reasoning about tests and test scores, and specifically in deriving empirical predictions from theories about attribute structure, they address only a piece of the puzzle in the justification of test interpretation and use. The remainder of this book is devoted to investigating the role of two important other pieces of the validity puzzle, to wit, the causal background of test scores, and the meaning attached to them.

4.6. Further Reading

Borsboom, D. (2008). Latent variable theory. *Measurement*, 6, 25–53.

Fischer, G. (1995). Derivations of the Rasch model. In G. Fischer & I. W. Molenaar (Eds.), *Rasch models: Foundations, recent developments, and applications* (pp. 15–38). New York: Springer.

Kyngdon, A. (2008). The Rasch model from the perspective of the representational theory of measurement. *Theory & Psychology, 18*, 89–109.

Michell, J. (2008). Is psychometrics pathological science? *Measurement*, 6, 7–24.

Perline, R., Wright, B. D., & Wainer, H. (1979). The Rasch model as additive conjoint measurement. *Applied Psychological Measurement, 3*, 237–255.

Stenner, A. J., Burdick, H., Sanford, E. E. & Burdick, D. S. (2006). How accurate are Lexile text measures? *Journal of Applied Measurement, 7*, 307–322.

5 Test Scores as Samples
Behavior Domain Theory

Connections With Other Chapters

In chapter 3, generalizability theory was introduced. This theory interprets test scores as samples from a universe of observations. The corresponding conceptualization of the relation between test score and construct is given by behavior domain theory. This theory is interesting because it appears compatible with an approach to validity that makes no reference to causation. The present chapter develops such an interpretation and investigates its tenability. It is argued that behavior domain theory relies on implicit causal relationships, albeit minimal, to allow stable generalizations from test score to behavior domain. In addition, it is compatible with causal theories in three ways. First, one may take a causal structure as providing the basis for a homogeneous domain. Second, one can construct a homogeneous domain and then investigate whether a causal structure explains the homogeneity. Finally, one can take the domain score as linked to an existing attribute constrained by indirect measurement.

This chapter[1] explores the possibility of reconciling behavior domain theory (BDT) with a causal theory of measurement (CTM). In BDT, constructs are conceptualized in terms of domains of behavior, and item responses are considered samples from this domain. One can see BDT as the conceptual counterpart of generalizability theory, as discussed in chapter 3. As in generalizability theory, the relation between behaviors in the domain and item responses in the test is a sampling relation. This makes the inference from item scores to construct scores a generalization of the population-sample variety. In CTM, constructs refer to common causes (equivalently, *attributes*; Rozeboom, 1966) that underlie a set of item responses, so that people respond to items differently because they have a different construct score (Borsboom, 2008; Borsboom, Mellenbergh, & Van Heerden, 2004). In this case, conclusions about constructs, on the basis of item responses, require causal inference rather than generalization.

These theories suggest different conceptualizations of psychometric models used in factor analysis, Item Response Theory (IRT), and latent class analysis. The relevant differences in turn suggest different conceptualizations of test validity and, as a result, a different view of what constitutes evidence for validity. In BDT, the central tasks of test validation involve (a) fixing the identity of the behavior domain and (b) ensuring adequate sampling from that domain. Content validation is therefore primary, whereas other types of validation are secondary. In CTM, the central tasks of test validation involve (a) fixing the identity of the measured attribute, and (b) establishing a causal link between the attribute and the item responses. In this case, causal evidence is primary, and issues of content are secondary, relevant only insofar as they are needed to establish such evidence. This presents a case of syntactically equivalent models (Markus, 2002) in that evidence supporting one interpretation need not support the other interpretation of the same model.

The question arises of how psychometric theory more broadly should deal with these two theories of measurement. One option is to simply choose between the two and jettison one or the other from psychometric theory. A second option is to view them as dealing with different types of construct–observation relations, such that some tests should be validated according to one scheme and some to the other. A third possibility is to investigate the possibilities of reconciliation. If such reconciliation were possible, CTM and BDT could be used in tandem, each addressing different aspects of the validity problem, so that various types of validity evidence might work together in a less hierarchical fashion. Thoroughly exploring the possibilities for reconciliation before writing off one or the other theory or dividing tests between them thus seems like the optimal course of action.

The present chapter investigates whether BDT and CTM can be reconciled and, if so, what this reconciliation would look like. This is done largely within the context of standard *reflective* psychometric models, which decompose individual item scores into a common latent variable score and a unique score (Figure 5.1.). For example, the linear common factor model describes item scores as random continuous variables, distributed normally around a mean that is given by the product of the common factor value and the item's factor loading. Other examples of reflective models are IRT, latent class, and latent profile models. These contrast with *formative* measurement models, in which a composite variable is modeled as a weighted sum of the item scores (Figure 5.2.; Bollen & Lennox, 1991; Edwards & Bagozzi, 2000). Examples of formative models are models used in data reduction techniques like principal components

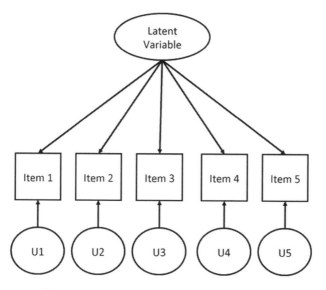

Figure 5.1 A Reflective Measurement Model. Variables labeled U1 to U5 represent sources of unique variance.

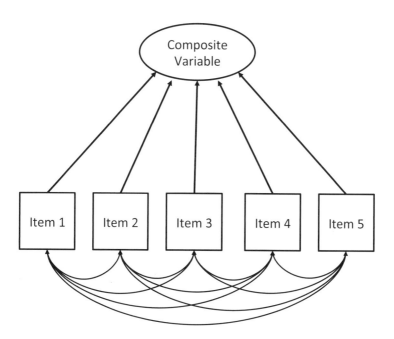

Figure 5.2 A Formative Measurement Model.

analysis and K-means clustering as well as cases in structural equation modeling where latent variables are determined by indicators.

Bollen and Lennox (1991) described reflective models as effect indicator models, interpreting the item scores as causal effects of the common factor. Edwards and Bagozzi (2000) introduced the term reflective measurement model to allow for both causal and non-causal interpretations, but also focused heavily on causal interpretations. The causal interpretation of reflective models comports with a causal theory of measurement that asserts that an item measures a particular attribute only if differences on the attribute cause differences in the item scores (Borsboom, 2008; Borsboom, Mellenbergh & van Heerden, 2004). Thus, along with further assumptions about the structure of the attribute and the form of the relation between attribute and item responses, measurement is analyzed in terms of a causal relation between what is measured (cause) and the measurement outcome (effect). Among researchers using structural equation models and similar techniques, such causal reasoning about the relation between measured attributes and item responses is commonplace.

In contrast, most of the literature on BDT proceeds with little attention to issues of causation (Holland, 1990; McDonald & Mulaik, 1979; Mulaik & McDonald, 1978; Nunnally & Bernstein, 1994). However, McDonald (1999, 2003) directly addressed the issue, providing two distinct arguments against causal interpretations of reflective measurement models. McDonald (2003) argued that a causal interpretation fails to accurately represent how items are written, and does not provide usable guidance for item writing. McDonald (1999) argued against such an interpretation on the grounds that the common factor is an abstraction over individual items and thus not distinct from them, while causes and effects should be distinct and separately identifiable. These two arguments raise important questions about the compatibility of BDT and CTM, suggesting that these theories may be at odds. Yet, BDT provides a basis for much psychometric theory taken for granted in test construction and use (McDonald, 2003; Holland, 1990) while CTM represents a widely accepted set of assumptions among researchers and within the literature on structural equation modeling (Bollen & Lennox, 1991; Edwards & Bagozzi, 2000).

In exploring the possibilities for reconciliation between BDT and CTM in light of McDonald's arguments, the specification of terms like causality, causation, and causal effects is of course important. However, any attempt to begin with a specific conception of causation would limit the results of the investigation to just that one conception. Following the same strategy as McDonald (1999, 2003), what follows is a discussion of causation in general terms and with minimal assumptions, seeking general results that apply across a range of specific analyses of causation. More specific accounts of causation will be reviewed in chapters 7 and 8.

The next section clarifies the notion of domain score in order to remove potential ambiguities and show that it is compatible with a reflective measurement model. The following two sections analyze two arguments from McDonald (2003) and McDonald (1999) against causal interpretations of the reflective measurement model. The final section discusses several ways of reconciling BDT and CTM.

Box 5.1. Behavior Domains and the LSAT

The Law School Admissions Test (LSAT) was introduced in 1948 and more or less took its current form in 1992. The testing program is maintained by the Law School Admissions Counsil, and new test forms are generated for each administration, four times a year. The test measures reading comprehension, analytical reasoning, logical reasoning, and writing with the intention of contributing incrementally to the prediction of performance in law school. The test is administered in six 35-minute sessions. The scored sessions comprise one reading comprehension, one logical reasoning, and two analytical reasoning sessions; and the remaining two non-scored sessions comprise one session of test items for future use and a writing sample that is sent to law schools along with the LSAT grades. The current test yields scores between 120 and 180 reflecting an unweighted sum of the first three constructs listed above equated across test forms, with a mean of about 150 and a standard deviation of about 10. Admitted students typically show means close to 155 and standard deviations slightly above 5 (Stilwell, Dalessandro and Reese, 2007).

The LSAT provides a useful example for behavior domain theory because new forms are generated for each new administration. As such, no fixed set of items defines the test, but rather a domain, or set of domains, from which new items are drawn. Although the Law School Admissions Council provides detailed reports on criterion-related validation research, they have reported less with respect to the item generation process (Erdmann, 1992). The LSAT preparation guide provides general descriptions of the three item types along with several examples (LSAC, n.d.). The three current item types represent the survivors from a larger domain of 41 different item types that LSAC has developed and investigated over the decades (Reese and Cotter, 1994). Plumer (2000) showed that the three current item types capture many but not all aspects of legal reasoning and suggested some possible new item types. Although technical reports do not describe exactly how LSAC assembles individual LSAT forms, a series of reports describe methods for assembling multiple forms simultaneously from a single pool in a manner that imposes several constraints based on test structure, item type, and item content, with the intent of holding equal the probability of selecting any one complete set of items composing a test form (Belov, 2005, 2006; van der Linden, 2006). It appears that test assembly remains an active area of research for LSAC.

5.1. Conceptualizing Domain Scores

It is useful to introduce some clear examples of the sorts of things that behavior domain theorists might have in mind when they discuss behavior domains. These will serve to test the abstract formulations against concrete examples of what the abstractions ought to capture. One example involves addition problems of the form "$m + n = ?$" with $9 < (m, n) < 100$. One can construct 8100 such items assuming that $m + n$ is not the same item as $n + m$. (Of course, allowing these as separate items would likely violate the assumption of a unidimensional domain because the ability to add $4 + 5$ would have more in common with the ability to add $5 + 4$ than, say, the ability to add $3 + 6$. In this case one could restrict the domain to the 4095 items in which $m \leq n$.) This set defines a behavior domain, where the relevant behavior consists of producing responses to the items in question. Nunnally and Bernstein (1994) presented a similar example with larger numbers.

It is assumed that a person has a response pattern over this domain which is comprised of that person's (hypothetical) responses to all of these items. A domain score is then a function over this response pattern. In this case, a sensible domain score would be the number of correct responses in the response pattern. Now suppose that a subset of items is given to a person, who then produces responses to this subset. The person's test score is a function over his or her response pattern, for instance the number of correctly answered items. Assuming that the person's responses are a sample from the behavior domain, one can use the person's test score to generalize to that person's domain score, just like one can infer population properties from samples of individuals in standard statistical theory. The idea of behavior domain theory is that this is what actually happens in psychometric testing.

The idea is readily generalized to other contexts. McDonald (2003) gave the example of a test that addresses knowledge of the key signatures of all 108 Haydn symphonies[2]. A more behaviorally inspired example might involve a word processing test in which test takers type a printed passage of text of a fixed length into a word processor, which is subsequently assessed for errors and/or timed for speed. In this case, if the passages contain 1000 words and the language contains, say, 40,000 words, the number of items in the domain would be less than roughly 10^{4602} (probably quite a bit less, but surely more than the number of items in the other two examples).

The examples provide increasing levels of finite approximation to the ideal of a countably infinite domain of items. Only in the Haydn example would completion of all the items in the domain by one test taker seem plausible except as a theoretical idealization. The infinite size of the domain is one of the essential factors that justifies BDT as an interpretation of commonly used psychometric practices (McDonald, 2003). In particular, for infinite domains, the domain scores may be thought of as unobservable variables which are estimated from the observable test scores. Hence, they lend themselves to identification with theoretical entities in psychometric models, such as true scores and latent variables (Ellis & Junker, 1997).

In keeping with this idea, McDonald (2003) describes the domain score as the limit of the mean item score as the number of items approaches infinity. This corresponds with what Cronbach, Gleser, Nanda, and Rajaratnam (1972) call a universe score. BDT typically assumes that the items in the domain adhere to certain conditions (one cannot use just any set of items to define a behavior domain). The condition that McDonald requires is *psychometric homogeneity*, which items satisfy if they "measure just one attribute in common" (McDonald, 1999, p. 78). Ellis & Junker (1997, Theorem 5) present necessary and sufficient manifest conditions for the required type of homogeneity; for behavior domain theory to sustain standard psychometric practice, as for instance required by McDonald (2003), these conditions imply that a unidimensional monotonic IRT model should exactly fit the infinite set of items. In the linear, continuous case this means that the infinite item domain exactly fits a unidimensional factor model with positive factor loadings. Ellis & Junker (1997) also present a more general conceptualization that allows composite scores of any form to be defined on an infinite domain of any form, but these generalizations do not comport with standard psychometric practice such as the use of reflective measurement models.

For readers accustomed to causally interpreted measurement models, a formative model may seem more naturally compatible with this definition of domain scores, because the mean item score is clearly a formative composite, constructed from the item scores. This intuition is correct for *finite* behavior domains: for such domains, item responses will not be conditionally independent given the domain score, just like observable variables are not conditionally independent given a formative construct. However, for infinite domains the formative composite takes on the properties of the latent variable in a reflective model, including properties like conditional independence (Ellis & Junker, 1997).

It is important to emphasize that, in the context of standard psychometric practice, these results only hold for behavior domains that contain items that are psychometrically homogeneous. So if (a) the behavior domain cannot be treated as infinite, or (b) the items in that domain do not themselves adhere to a undimensional reflective psychometric model, no equivalence follows. For infinite domains of unidmensional items, however, for a reasonably general class of IRT models, all empirical properties of the latent variable in a reflective model are met by the domain score (Ellis & Junker, 1997). For this reason, it is possible to justify common psychometric practices on the basis of the idea that such a latent variable *is* in fact the composite score on an infinite item domain. In addition, this equivalence does not require the assumption that the model is true for each individual (the *stochastic subject* interpretation; Holland, 1990); it can be derived from the weaker assumption that smallest subpopulations for which the model holds are subpopulations of people with the same domain scores (so-called *stochastic meta-subjects*; Ellis & Junker, 1997). This, in turn, allows one to interpret probabilities in IRT models in a purely between-subject sense (e.g., the probability of a correct item score given a position on latent variable is the limiting relative frequency of the correct item score in the subpopulation of individuals with exactly that position on the variable). Likewise, one may then interpret unique variance in the factor model simply as variance across people not shared among items in a test. Because there are no item-level true scores or errors in this approach, what is elsewhere often called item-level measurement error is treated as a person-by-item interaction (McDonald, 2003).

Conceptually, these technical properties suggest an opening to interpret such a latent variable as an abstraction created from the items in a domain, rather than as a common cause of the item responses. Such an abstraction, however, clearly cannot do causal work in producing item responses, as required by CTM. Therefore, BDT stands in a complicated relation to CTM, each seemingly implying a different interpretation of the reflective measurement model. The next section considers McDonald's (2003) item writing argument in this context.

Box 5.2. A More Detailed Look at Behavior Domain Theory and Formative Versus Reflective Measurement Models

We have chosen to discuss behavior domain theory in the section of the book on causation because it reflects a concerted effort to articulate a non-causal theory of measurement. This box considers how causal and non-causal interpretations might apply to formative and reflective models.

Consider the logical reasoning subdomain from the LSAT as a hypothetically unidimensional domain. For present purposes, let us restrict the discussion to notions of causation that assume that nothing ever causes something it has as a part or something that has it as a part. In at least one form, behavior domain theory rules out a causal relationship in either direction because it conceives of each LSAT item response as part of the behavior domain. As such, a causal relationship in either direction would involve the item response causing itself, because the behavior domain consists of the item response plus other item responses. Causal indicators would involve the item causing the item plus other items, and effect indicators would involve the item plus other items causing the item (McDonald, 2003).

Applying a reflective model to the LSAT logical reasoning items, one might interpret the domain score as the individual's ability to understand, analyze, criticize, and complete informal logical arguments (LSAC, n.d.). These items generally involve a brief passage of several sentences followed by a choice of conclusions that one might draw from the information in the passage, with only one correct conclusion and four incorrect. A one-factor reflective measurement model assumes that test takers vary along a single dimension of such skill and that this dimension fully accounts for the correlations among items (unless the model allows for correlated unique variances). The unique variances introduce sources of random error that sometimes cause individual item responses to deviate from providing exact reflections of the test taker's skill level, but these average out across items.

In contrast, a formative measurement model does not assume local independence. The associations between the items, which here serve as exogenous variables, remain unmodeled. Instead, the model reflects the construction of the domain score out of these items. The residual error on the domain score reflects items from the domain omitted from the particular model. A form of unidimensionality assumption remains in that the model includes only a single linear composite and identifies the domain score with this composite. In this case, however, the random component of item responses gets passed along into the domain score. So, here, one can better interpret the domain score as the typical item response rather than skill level. The typical item response involves all the factors that determine item responses, not just skill level.

Neither the formative LSAT model nor the reflective LSAT model require a causal interpretation, but both allow it, having causal indicators and effect indicators as respective special cases. One advantage of a causal interpretation is explanation, whereas a purely statistical model does not offer any form of explanation

unless one takes the statistical regularities themselves as explanatory laws of nature. This last possibility seems implausible when
explaining LSAT item responses. Behavior domain theory puts
some interpretive flesh on the statistical bones, but it is not clear
that sampling from a domain can offer an explanatory account
comparable to a causal account of LSAT item responses.

5.2. The Item Writing Argument for Behavior Domain Theory

In a first line of argument, McDonald (2003) argued that test developers
create new items on the basis of shared item characteristics that define a
behavior domain. Moreover, if forced to proceed on the basis of causal
intuitions about what other items share as a common cause, most would
find the task too difficult to proceed effectively. One can further flesh out
this argument by noting that test developers habitually write item specifications in terms of item characteristics rather than in terms of common
causes. As such, the practice of item writing appears more consistent with
a non-causal BDT than a CTM.

The force of the argument seems to depend upon an overly austere construal of causation and causal reasoning. Suppose that one takes causal
reasoning as resting on concomitant variation (Mill, 1874), primitive counterfactual laws, or any other form of causation that can only be discovered
through observed structural relationships. If so, then the test developer
would need to have some knowledge of causal regularities leading to item
responses. One imagines a vast catalog of such regularities for various test
items to which the test developer refers in selecting items. However, if the
items have yet to be written, let alone empirically studied, it seems entirely
implausible that their causal regularities could have yet made it into this
catalog for use in constructing tests. If one restricts the discussion to such
notions of causation, then the argument seems well founded.

In contrast, if one considers such structural relationships between variables as merely the nomothetic shadow of an underlying causal process
(Dowe, 2000; Salmon, 1998) or mechanism (Cartwright, 1999, 2007), then
this offers the test developer a richer trove of resources for causal reasoning
about possible new items. With such a notion of causation, it becomes possible to reason causally about items before they have been studied empirically. This becomes possible because one can have prior knowledge of the
item response processes elicited by new items. As such, the argument lacks
force with respect to such accounts of causal relationships.

Consider again the example of a test of knowledge of key signatures
for Haydn symphonies. If one simply followed a fixed item template,
filling in different numbers, one would produce only 108 items and no

more because that is all Haydn wrote in his lifetime. Although sharing a superficial common property, asking for the key signature of the 109th symphony would produce an entirely different kind of item with fundamentally different psychometric properties. However, if one works from a rudimentary causal account of how test takers answer the questions, more items may be possible. Suppose that the item response process comes down to two steps: (a) recognize the symphony, (b) recall the key signature. Based on this rudimentary causal process, one could then begin to think about alternative item formats that would still elicit the same causal process. For example, the 103rd symphony is also known as the Drumroll symphony. One might, then, write an item asking for the key signature of Haydn's Drumroll symphony. This would presumably allow a test taker conversant with the Haydn symphonies to first recognize the Drumroll symphony as the 103rd symphony, and then correctly recall the key signature as D major. Knowledge of the symphonies' key signatures, the focal construct, plays a causal role in determining the correct answer, just as with the original item for symphony 103, because both work though the same item response process. Moreover, such reasoning provides the test developer with an explanation of the folly of an item asking about the 109th symphony because it fails to elicit the desired response process beginning with the recognition of the symphony by the test taker. However, such a line of reasoning requires a richer notion of causation than mere concomitant variation or regularity of succession.

Now consider what happens if one subtracts the causal component of the above reasoning. One gets something reminiscent of Fodor's (1992, chapter 1) reconstruction of Sherlock Holmes's reasoning on an associationist account of mental process. Holmes correctly deduces that the doctor murdered the victim by setting loose a snake to climb down a faux bell rope hung from a vent over the victim's bed, which was bolted to the floor. Holmes gives an account of his reasoning to Watson that describes the ruling out of various alternatives (the door and windows were locked) and drawing on information such as the fact that the doctor owned a variety of poisonous snakes. This all depends on constructing a causal process leading to the death of the victim. In contrast, Fodor offers the following as a non-causal associationist account: "Bell-ropes always make me think of snakes, and snakes make me think of snake oil, and snake oil makes me think of doctors; so when I saw the bell-rope it popped into my head that the Doctor and the snake might have done it between them" (p. 21). Fodor remarks that such a chain of associations fails to resemble reasoning in any recognizable form. Certainly it should not convince anyone that the Doctor should be considered as a suspect.

Can one reconstruct the test developer's reasoning any more successfully using a fully non-causal account? This is doubtful. The problem is that there are very many shared properties of the test items, and most of these play no causal role in the item response process. Changing the font should make no difference. Changing the rendering of the numbers from numerals to words should not matter. Changing the grammar of the question from "The 103rd symphony has what key signature" to "What is the key signature of the 103rd symphony" should make no difference. These all relate to common properties of the items, but common properties that play no causal role in eliciting the appropriate response process. In contrast, the suggested new item stated in terms of the Drumroll symphony deviates from the other items in terms of a substantial shared characteristic, yet seems highly plausible as a new item that would retain the unidimensionality of the test on a causal account. It remains unclear how reasoning only on the basis of properties associated with the current set of items or the behavior domain could successfully pick out the important properties and abstract these to new item types without considering the causal role of the shared properties in the item response process. This suggests that the process of reasoning through new items sketched by McDonald (2003) in fact contains a hidden causal element if fully spelled out despite the attempt to offer it as an alternative to causal accounts.

If one assumes a simple regularity theory of causation, or indeed even a fairly sophisticated but purely nomological theory such as many counterfactual theories, it appears that McDonald's argument from test construction carries some weight in arguing that such an approach is inadequate to guide the generation of new items to measure a fixed construct. However, if one broadens the field to allow for a richer notion of causation, the resulting causal reasoning appears well suited to this task. Indeed, an attempt to flesh out McDonald's example suggests that it may be very difficult to account for item development without appeal to some sort of causal understanding of the item response process. Thus, the causal role of the important attributes common to the items in the domain may play a central role in distinguishing them from other unimportant common attributes of the items. The next section addresses a more technical argument offered by McDonald (1999).

5.3. The Distinctness Argument Against Domain Score Causation

McDonald (1999) states a second argument as follows: "The notion is that the variables are indicators, 'symptoms' or manifestations of the same state of affairs. For example, extraversion is an abstract concept whose instances are the recognized extravert behaviors, and it is therefore circular to say that extraversion 'causes' its manifestations[3]" (pp. 76–77). The evaluation of this argument begins with an examination of which elements of the situation produce the circularity in question.

The notion (or notions) of causation that underlies typical behavioral science research assumes that the cause is an entity distinct from the effect. Hume (1999/1772) described the distinctness of causes and effects as key to the fact that questions of cause and effect must be resolved empirically. If the effect were not distinct from the cause, one might be able to determine the effect of a cause by reason alone.

The assumption of distinctness arises as a corollary of the more basic assumption that causation must be an anti-reflexive relation between cause and effect (i.e., a relation R such that, for any x, xRx is necessarily false; in other words, nothing can cause itself). To make this concrete, consider an ordinary light bulb wired to a power source through a common dimmer switch. It seems reasonable to say that the setting of the switch causes the brightness of the bulb. It further seems reasonable to say that the switch setting causes the voltage of the electricity traveling through the bulb, and the voltage causes the brightness. It seems less reasonable to say that the brightness of the bulb is caused by the amount of light emitted from it, unless in saying this one means to distinguish apparent brightness from the physical qualities of the bulb that produce the appearance (which might offer a sound reductive explanation rather than a causal one). The distinctness assumption explains these intuitions: The switch setting and the voltage are *distinct* from the brightness of the bulb, and thus may stand in a causal relation to that brightness. However, the level of photon emission is either coextensive with the brightness or at least an integral part of the brightness (understood as a quality of the bulb) and therefore is not distinct from that brightness. As such, one finds a conclusion like *brightness is caused by magnitude of photon emissions* little more enlightening than saying that brightness causes brightness.

As a criterion for distinctness, assume that two things are distinct if and only if it is logically possible (imaginable without contradiction) to change one thing without changing the other. As a test case, consider a red glove. Now examine the properties *being red all over* and *having a red thumb*. Does the glove's being red all over cause it to have a red thumb, or vice versa? One cannot imagine, without self-contradiction, making the glove's thumb green while leaving the glove red all over, nor can one imagine making the glove red all over while leaving the thumb green. The two properties are not distinct because one is part of the other. Hence, they cannot stand in a causal relation.

For a finite item domain, this distinctness test shows that the domain score is not distinct from the item score. In particular, one cannot imagine changing the domain score without changing at least one item score. For instance, if one has a domain of ten binary items, one cannot change the domain score from five to six without changing at least one item score. Thus, item score differences are necessary for domain score differences (or, alternatively, domain score differences are sufficient for item score differences). In technical philosophical terms, the domain score *supervenes* on the item scores. This would seem to establish the distinctiveness argument.

However, things change for infinite domains. For instance, consider an infinite domain of binary items. Even if there is one item that a test taker always gets wrong (0), he or she can have a domain score of 100% correct (1) because $(n - 1)/n$ goes to 1 as n goes to positive infinity, as does $(n - 1000)/n$ for that matter. In general, the long-run properties of an infinite sequence need not depend on any finite subsequence. In fact, this property is the crucial element of Ellis and Junker's (1997) demonstration that tail measurable events on a behavior domain can provide an exhaustive empirical characterization of latent variables: "tail measurability is equivalent to the possibility of estimating [the latent variable] consistently (...) even though observations on an arbitrary finite number of the manifest variables may be missing" (p. 496).

Thus, the conclusion at this point is that the distinctness criterion for causes and effects is certainly violated for finite domains, but may not be violated for infinite domains. However, distinctness is a necessary but insufficient criterion for causation, and therefore this conclusion does not establish that, for infinite item domains, a causal relation between domain and item scores is feasible. In fact, this seems implausible. The following argument seems to get to the crux of this matter. Consider an infinite behavior domain. This domain may be divided into an infinite number of sets of k items, with whole-numbered $k \geq 1$. As the number of items approaches infinity, the impact of any one set of k items goes to zero, producing the seeming independence noted above. Knowing that the domain score is independent of the first k items, and also the second k items, one might then conclude that it is also independent of the first $2k$ items taken together. For any finite number j, one might then conclude similarly that the domain score is independent of the first jk items. As j approaches infinity, this inference rule seems to lead in the limit to the conclusion that the domain score is independent of all the items, but this is known to be false. The domain score is defined as the limit of the expectation of the mean of all the items. So, it appears that the domain score is distinct from every finite set of items individually but not distinct from all of them collectively (compare Ellis and Junker, 1997).

Granted the distinctness of infinite domains and finite subdomains, the domain score *can* figure in a causal explanation of every finite set of item scores, but *cannot* figure in a causal explanation of the infinite union of these finite sets because it is *defined* by that union. This deviates sufficiently much from a cause-and-effect relationship that the extension of McDonald's basic argument against the compatibility of BDT and CTM to infinite domains seems warranted. This yields the important conclusion that, even though BDT with infinite domains justifies psychometric representation of test scores with reflective latent variable models, if the latent variables in these models are interpreted as domain scores then they cannot also be interpreted as common causes. This only works for psychometrically homogeneous domains, but for such domains this seems to leave us with two incompatible interpretations of the reflective measurement model that must be held separate.

Box 5.3. LSAT Example: Behavior Domain Theory as an Alternative to a Causal Theory of Measurement

Assume a reflective measurement model correctly describes LSAT logical reasoning test item responses. The combination of a reflective measurement model with a causal theory of measurement results in the effect indicator model. Interpreted as a non-causal theory of measurement, behavior domain theories allow a reflective model but not an effect-indicator model. These two possibilities thus present competing interpretations of a reflective measurement model of LSAT responses.

On the causal interpretation, test takers have a certain level of ability in logical reasoning and this ability causes them to respond as they do to logical reasoning items. On balance, people with higher levels of logical reasoning ability answer more items correctly. The proper standardized test administration helps to guarantee that nothing disrupts this causal connection. For example, administering the test in a language not understood by the examinees would disrupt the causal connection and one would not necessarily expect the resulting scores to fit a reflective measurement model or otherwise show the same structure as properly administered items. As one moves from test takers with less ability to those with higher ability, the proportion of correct responses increases, and the probability of a correct answer to each question increases proportionately in accordance with the item response function.

In contrast, under the non-causal behavior domain interpretation, each individual has an average response across the entire domain of logical reasoning items. This in itself offers a contrast with the causal theory because under the causal theory the attribute of logical reasoning ability need not have any inherent connection to any method of measuring logical reasoning. On the behavior domain interpretation, however, the domain is defined by behavioral responses to a certain kind of stimulus, in this case a logical reasoning task which has logical reasoning items as either a proper or improper subset. The relationship between scored responses to any one item and the overall behavior domain score cannot be a causal connection in any sense of causation that assumes causes distinct from their effects, because the individual item responses make up the domain. The domain score contains the items scores, and the behavior domain contains the item response behaviors. If the size of the domain of logical reasoning items reaches infinity, then the domain score can reach independence from the items on any one version of the LSAT, or any finite number of versions, but the domain score remains connected to the full domain of item scores. In this case, the domain is defined by the common attribute shared by all items in the domain, which we might loosely characterize as logical reasoning. The test item specifications used by LSAT item writers would provide a more refined specification of the domain. In this case, changing the language would not disrupt a causal relationship required for proper measurement. Instead, it would sample items from outside the domain, disrupting the representation of the domain by the sampled items.

5.4. Reconciling Behavior Domains and Causal Theories of Measurement

This section considers the possibilities for applying both BDT and CTM to the same measurement model. The discussion here is restricted to the case of psychometric homogeneity, corresponding to a unidimensional reflective measurement model under both BDT and CTM. Three possibilities present themselves. First, one may put a definitional restriction on proper measurement domains, by requiring that such domains are not only psychometrically homogeneous, but must also be causally homogeneous, in the sense that a single attribute should cause differences on the item scores. Second, one may construct behavior domains from systematic item generation strategies such as the facet design, and leave the possibility of causal homogeneity open to empirical tests. A third possibility is that the item domain is psychometrically homogeneous without causal homogeneity. In this case there is no causal attribute, and BDT must stand on its own. In all three cases, the test total score estimates the domain score by item sampling. In the first two cases but not the third, the estimated domain score can be taken as a measure of the causal attribute. In the third case, the item domain seems to operationally define what is measured without any external measurement relation (Foster & Cone, 1995).

5.4.1. Causal Homogeneity as a Basis for BDT

The core assumption of BDT is that the items in a test can be considered samples from an infinite population of psychometrically homogeneous items. The required condition of psychometric homogeneity has been studied by Ellis and Junker (1997). They showed that necessary and sufficient conditions for the item domain to sustain BDT in standard psychometric practice are (a) positive conditional association and (b) vanishing conditional dependence. Positive conditional association roughly means that a positive function (e.g. the number of correctly answered items) on any two finite sets of items remains correlated when one conditions on a third finite set. For instance, under this condition the total scores on two subtests will remain positively correlated when controlling for a third subtest. Vanishing conditional dependence roughly means that the items are independent given the domain score, i.e., the mean score over the infinite set of items. So, taken together, these assumptions require that any two items are *dependent* conditional on any finite set of items, but that any two items are *independent* given the domain score over the infinite set. This means that the items will look just like they were generated by a unidimensional IRT or factor model. Unidimensionality follows from local independence conditional upon a single domain score (Box 5.4).

A simple way of reconciling BDT and CTM is by proceeding from CTM and defining behavior domains in terms of causally homogeneous sets of items. The domain score is then a measure of the causal attribute. CTM holds that items measure an attribute if and only if differences in that attribute cause differences in the item scores. Attributes that are measurable in this way are usually measurable through many items, possibly hypothetical. This domain of hypothetical items thus forms a behavior domain. The property that binds these items *as* members of the domain is precisely that they measure the same attribute. In this case, CTM thus restricts the proper basis of BDT: The items should have positive conditional association and vanishing conditional dependence precisely because they measure the same thing. A schematic representation of this reconciliation is given in Figure 5.3. The latent variable in the reflective measurement model causes the item score when interpreted as the attribute, but not when interpreted as the domain score that empirically characterizes that attribute.

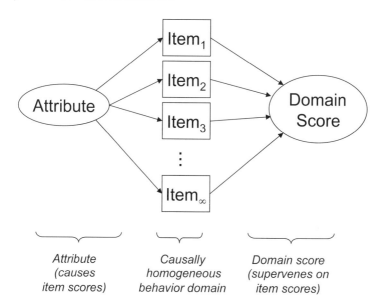

Figure 5.3 Reconciliation Through Causally Homogeneous Behavior Domains

---

Box 5.4. Tail Measurability and the LSAT

As described in the main text, tail measurability occurs when the expected value of the response across a domain of items becomes interchangeable with the latent variable as the number of items goes to infinity. The 'tail' in tail measurability therefore refers not to the lower tail of an axis indicating test length, where actual measurement takes place in finite tests, but rather to the upper tail where the test length approaches infinity. The score on any given LSAT form is not interchangeable with the latent variable underlying the item responses, but the score on an infinitely long LSAT would be. The three conditions given in the main text allow for a general assessment of the plausibility of this phenomenon in the case of the LSAT.

The first of the three conditions seems the most plausible: This requires that the probability of a correct response never decreases as the underlying latent variable increases. Violation would involve an LSAT item that became harder as ability increased. Let us assume the elimination of any such deviant items from the domain. Next, the LSAT would need to exhibit unidimensionality with respect to the underlying latent variable. Given a domain composed of three distinct item types covering a range of different content subdomains, this condition seems less plausible, and indeed the LSAT shows evidence of multidimensionality (De Champlain, 1995). Third, responses to individual LSAT items would need to exhibit local independence. In light of the presence of item sets with common stimulus material and other item clusters, it is not surprising to find some evidence against this requirement as well, at least in the form of mild local dependence (Reese, 1999). This demonstrates that the assumptions required for approaches considered in this chapter can run afoul of the complexity of practical applications. Nonetheless, it remains useful to consider the test validity concepts that these approaches help to illuminate, and to imagine their application to a slightly fictionalized LSAT that meets their assumptions, or else as a rough approximation to an actual test.

5.4.2. Causal Homogeneity as a Contingent Fact

The advocate of CTM is likely to argue that the causal homogeneous domain is not just a special case of BDT, but in fact the only case in which one can sensibly speak of *measuring* an attribute, because the main tenet of CTM is that the causal link between attribute and measures is what distinguishes measurement from mere registration of item responses. However, another position that one may take is that causal homogeneity, while not required for measurement, is a particularly useful thing to have, so that it makes sense to investigate whether this is so.

For instance, one may generate items through a facet design, in which case one has defined the item domain without reference to a causal attribute but rather by appealing to certain kind of item specification. Thus what defines the item domain is something different from a measured attribute. The investigation of the psychometric properties of the domain is then open, and it may be that the items in fact share the influence of a causal attribute. Mulaik (2009) for instance concludes that "Indicators of causal variables should have some set of attributes that suggest the attributes that are varied of the cause indicated. Other attributes of the indicator are the effects of the cause" (p. 192). One can understand this passage to mean that items have a variety of attributes. Some of these item attributes determine the identity of the measured person attribute. Other item attributes are caused by the measured attribute. In Mulaik's account, the items scores attained by a given person constitute such item attributes caused by the measured attribute. The distinction between these two sets of attributes may break the circularity about which McDonald (1999) expressed concern.

5.4.3. BDT Without a Causal Basis

Upon closer inspection, two distinct arguments emerge from within McDonald's circularity argument. First, domain scores are not distinct from item scores, and thus causation would be circular (distinctness argument). Second, domain scores are mathematical abstractions from item scores, not concrete, causally effective attributes of individual persons, so they are not the right kind of things to serve as causes of items scores (abstraction argument). Mulaik's proposal avoids the distinctness argument by rejecting the premise of the abstraction argument. The remainder of this section addresses the abstraction argument directly and relates that back to the distinctness argument.

Figure 5.4. presents a reflective measurement model with the addition of a separate ellipse representing the construct measured by the test. Here the construct represents a causally potent attribute of the test takers, as assumed in Mulaik's interpretation. The figure connects the construct to the domain score by indicating that the domain score measures the construct. However, what is the nature of this measurement relation that links the two? CTM seems to assume that it is one of identity. McDonald's view seems to reject this idea, suggesting instead that measurement is a matter of appropriately matching the items to the desired domain. Extrapolating from McDonald's descriptions, one can think of this in latent variable terms as choosing the items to properly align the domain score with the intended latent construct. On this view, measurement would involve either statistical association or causation between the

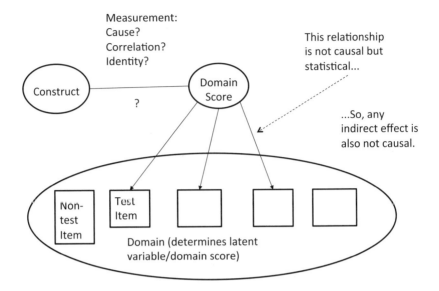

Figure 5.4 Measurement Relation Between Domain Scores and Constructs

construct and the domain score, but not identity. Alternatively, one might argue from a BDT perspective that the construct is superfluous and can be deleted from the figure without loss.

McDonald (1999, Ch. 10) appeals to a distinction between abstractive and existential concepts, citing Feigl (1950; compare MacCorquodale & Meehl, 1948, who attribute the term *abstractive* to Benjamin, 1937). McDonald describes abstractive concepts as "abstractions from what common sense would regard as observable" whereas existential concepts "have the status of postulated entities not (currently) observable" (p. 201). Suppose one were to find a positive correlation between the addition test scores and the word processing test scores from the previous examples. If one understands these as abstractive concepts, then saying that addition ability (i.e. the domain score) correlates with word processing ability (again, the domain score) simply provides a convenient shorthand for saying success at typing the words 'a . . . a' correlates with success at adding 10 + 10, typing the words 'a . . . aardvark' correlates with adding 10 + 10, . . . , typing the words 'a . . . a' correlates with adding 10 + 11, and so on for every combination of a set of 1000 words and a pair of two-digit numbers. The domains are real, the abilities to complete each item are real, but the domain score simply represents a convenient abstraction over the corresponding domain. McDonald (1999) surmised that most attributes measured by tests involve abstractive concepts. An abstraction cannot serve as a cause, so CTM seems out of order so long as it requires as much.

Feigl (1950) offered an argument that may contextualize the present issue. In this argument, Feigl assumes that (a) in scientific inquiry all knowledge comes from observation, be it direct or indirect, and (b) an observer cannot observe something that cannot have any causal effects on the observer (again, direct or indirect). Thus, an observer can have no scientific knowledge of something unless it can have a causal impact on the observer. By extrapolation from Feigl's argument, observers do have scientific knowledge of what they measure, and therefore whatever they measure must have a causal impact on the observer. CTM handles this by tracing an indirect causal effect from the latent variable (interpreted as the construct, i.e., the causal attribute) to the item scores to the observer. Non-causal BDT may handle it by allowing a causal effect of actual item responses on the observer, while viewing what is measured as an abstract property of a hypothetical behavior domain. Thus, consideration of this argument illuminates the present concern by showing that even non-causal BDTs involve causation. They are only non-causal in the sense that domain scores do not cause item scores.

Feigl's (1950) concern was to reconcile contrasting approaches to existential concepts (the paper does not contain the word *abstractive*) and his proposal suggests a means of reconciling BDT with CTM. McDonald's abstractive concepts correspond to Feigl's syntactical positivist approach to existential hypotheses and McDonald's existential concepts correspond to Feigl's semantical realist approach. Feigl noted that the above argument regarding causation and knowledge cuts against a more robust realism that posits entities that cannot be observed at all—neither directly nor indirectly. The argument thus restricts the positing of entities not directly observable to those that allow for indirect observation. This notion of an indirect observable comes very close to the modern notion of a latent variable.

Conversely, Feigl argues that the purely abstractive idea cannot work because in many circumstances the indirect observations exist at a different time or place than the posited entity, such as when current evidence is used to draw conclusions about past events. For example, strictly interpreted, one can only interpret a domain score in terms of test behaviors. Any inference from a word processing test score to word processing ability outside of the test situation, such as in the workplace, involves inference from the test domain to another domain, not a generalization within the same domain (Messick, 1989). In Feigl's terminology, one can confirm a hypothesis about word processing ability outside the test, but not verify it. This means that one can observe evidence that supports the hypothesis, but the hypothesis does not reduce to the observable evidence. This argument implies that measurement involves more than just abstractive concepts.

Combining these two arguments from Feigl, one comes to a compromise picture in which attributes have causal effects on their indicators, but the admissible attributes are restricted to those that can be tied to specific behavior domains. However, the ability to generalize from test behaviors to non-test behaviors reflects the surplus of the construct over the range of possible test behaviors. By making an existential hypothesis, one posits an attribute that has properties of its own, such as persistence through time.

It is not clear to what extent the above arguments would move a determined advocate of abstractive concepts. However, in the above light, the stalwart assertion that domain scores constitute abstractive concepts seems more like an axiomatic assumption than a theoretical inference drawn from empirical observation or prior facts about tests and test scores. Indeed, it becomes less clear whether a commitment to abstractive concepts motivates a rejection of CTM, or vice versa. These considerations invite further work clarifying the basis of a non-causal BDT.

Box 5.5. LSAT Example: A Compatibilist Approach

For present purposes, assume that LSAT logical reasoning items reflect an infinite and unidimensional domain and that unique variance behaves like random error. On a causal theory of measurement, each individual has a determinate level of ability for logical reasoning and this (partially) causally determines the LSAT logical reasoning score obtained by that person. The property might be very complex and realized very differently in different individuals, just as three containers might all contain one liter of water in very different ways and for very different reasons. This micro-level heterogeneity does not prevent the scalability of people along the dimension of logical reasoning ability, or the scalability of containers by capacity, so long as one does not misinterpret equal values as indicating homogeneous means of realizing that value. From the behavior domain perspective, the domain score represents the expected response to an item from the logical reasoning domain. One cannot take this overall behavior pattern as causing the individual test item responses using an anti-reflexive notion of causation because would-be effects collectively constitute the would-be cause. One cannot identify the domain score with the property described by the causal account. The property causes the item responses, and thus also causes the domain score. People have certain levels of ability that cause them to answer a certain proportion of logical reasoning items correctly both on the LSAT test and in the entire domain. For the full infinite domain, the domain score and the causal ability level will have a perfect correlation because both measurement error and stochastic elements of the causal process will average out over the infinite domain of items. As such, the two represent logically distinct but empirically concomitant quantities, one of which causes the item responses and the other of which summarizes them. This means that the corresponding reflective measurement model has two distinct interpretations, one identifying the latent variable as the domain score and the other as the causal ability level. Although empirically equivalent, these models differ with respect to the interpretation of the statistical relationships and the empirical predictions that follow from those interpretations. The reflective model has an anti-reflexive causal interpretation for the causal ability level but not the domain score. For example, training in logical reasoning would target the ability, not the domain score, and effective changes in the ability should then cause changes in item responses and thus the domain score.

5.5. Chapter Conclusion

This chapter has considered the relationship between behavior domain theories and causal theories of measurement with special attention to the defense of non-causal BDT offered by McDonald (1999; 2003), the theoretical exposition provided by Ellis and Junker (1997), and the contributions of Bollen and Lennox (1991) and Edwards and Bagozzi (2000). The fundamental difference between these two theories of measurement is that BDT situates what is measured in the behavior domain from which the items are drawn, whereas CTM situates what is measured in the latent variable that causes the item scores.

CTM and BDT hold appeal for contrasting reasons. A causal interpretation holds appeal because it provides an explanatory construct theory that allows strong predictions regarding the results of interventions on variables in the measurement model. This can offer a rich basis both for validation efforts based on manipulation (Messick, 1989; Zumbo, 2009) and also as a means of guiding item revision. A non-causal behavior domain theory has appeal because it avoids the metaphysical complexity of causation and provides a purely descriptive account based entirely on empirically demonstrable associations and basic sampling theory. Moreover, a behavior domain interpretation of a reflective measurement model avoids the stumbling blocks introduced by individual difference data from cross-sectional designs. In contrast, Simpson's paradox often gets in the way when individual-level causal interpretations are applied to individual differences data (Borsboom, Mellenbergh, & van Heerden, 2003).

Exploration of these issues offers several contributions to thinking about test validation. First, consideration of behavior domain theory has provided a very clear example of how basic philosophical issues impact practical activities like test development. A theory like behavior domain theory is much better suited to a more purely behavioral construct than one that requires abstracting a mental construct away from specific behavioral manifestations. As such, it is easier to develop the Haydn example in terms of behavior domain theory, if the domain is language specific, and harder if one abstracts knowledge of Haydn symphonies away from the language used in the test procedure. Identifying the 103rd symphony as being in *E flat* major in English may not depend on the same attribute as identifying it as *Es Dur* in Haydn's native language, and in this case these items cannot belong to the same behavior domain. An even stronger example comes from the relationship between the test developer's assumptions about causation and available item writing procedures. If one takes a strict stance against anything more than a nomothetic theory of causation, behavior domain theory offers some advice on writing new items, but one had best not attempt to reason in terms of a causal theory of measurement. The result would be to introduce contradictory assumptions into the construct theory guiding the test. In contrast, if one accepts a more robust theory of causation, coupling behavior domain theory with a causal theory of measurement can support a much richer account of item writing. This richer account might in turn better support validity inferences based on the test construction process.

Measurement provides an example of a context in which much depends upon the precise understanding of causation employed by researchers. Either a generic notion of causation or an agnostic attitude toward causation places important limits on the ability to flesh out the meaning of causal claims and the interpretation of causal measurement models. Ultimately, it may be only the test developer who can determine the most appropriate understanding of causation for a given focal construct. However, methodology can begin to flesh out alternatives and work out their methodological implications as a means of making that task easier for the test developer (Markus, 2004; 2008; 2010).

5.6. Further Reading

Ellis, J. L. & Junker, B. W. (1997). Tail-measurability in monotone latent variable models. *Psychometrika, 62,* 495–523.

Feigl, H. (1950). Existential hypotheses: realistic versus phenomenalistic interpretations. *Philosophy of Science, 17,* 35–62.

McDonald, R. P. (1999). *Test theory: a unified treatment.* Mahwah, NJ: Erlbaum.

McDonald, R. P. (2003). Behavior Domains in Theory and in Practice. *Alberta Journal of Educational Research, 49,* 212–230.

6   Causality in Measurement

Connections With Other Chapters

Chapter 3 introduced generalizability theory as a statistical model that views item scores as samples from a domain. In chapter 5, the associated conceptual model of domain scores was reviewed and analyzed. The chapter concluded that, despite appearances to the contrary, a minimal set of causal assumptions can hardly be avoided in the interpretation of the domain score model. In the present chapter, we discuss models that explicitly use causal relations between constructs and test scores. Two such models are of particular importance: the reflective model, in which test scores are modeled as effects of the construct, and the formative model, in which they are modeled as causes of the construct. These models are discussed in the light of validity theory. In addition we provide a brief review of alternative causal models.

In most cases of structured observation interpreted as measurement, there is an asymmetry between the measures and the attribute being measured. One uses a pointer reading of one's scale to measure weight, but one does not use one's weight to measure the pointer reading; one uses diagnostic interviews to assess psychiatric problems, not the other way around; and one uses personality test scores to assess personality dimensions, but personality dimensions never serve to assess test scores.

This asymmetry between the function of the measured attribute and that of the measure itself flows naturally from the function typically designated to measurement instruments. Measurement instruments serve to collect systematic observations that can be scored in a way that reliably separates test takers with respect to one or more aspects of individual difference. If we were granted the ability to directly observe the relevant attributes, we would have no use for the complicated apparatuses used in science, for the very function of these instruments is to assist us in doing this. It is thus natural to think of the differences between test takers that we study as somehow *determining* the observations that we obtain.

This interpretation squares with how test scores are interpreted in daily scientific work. One observes differences between two brain images and supposes that these must result from actual differences between the brains. One notes that a student has a very low IQ-score and concludes that there must be a problem in his cognitive functioning relative to normal development. One sees that one's client endorses depressed mood and lack of sleep items, and hypothesizes that the client is experiencing a cluster of symptoms elevated from normative levels in the population. One views an exceptionally high score on a neuroticism test as an indication of the person's characteristic mental and behavioral constitution relative to the norms of the population.

So far, the big word has not been used yet, but it is clear that in every such case one assumes that *something* about the test takers *causes* the deviations in the test scores. Further, if the measurement instrument works as it should, this something is precisely the something one *wanted* to assess. If one accepts this line of reasoning, then causality is not just central to the interpretation of test scores as measurements, but to the concept of validity itself. For if the attribute one wants to assess (say, extraversion) coincides with the causal determinant of the test scores (say, NEO-PI scores), then one measures what one was supposed to measure, and, at least according to one definition of validity (Borsboom, Mellenbergh, & Van Heerden, 2004), this means that the validity case is closed. More broadly, the causal theory of measurement is consistent with any validity theory that counts this as a necessary element of validity evidence that a test assesses a particular attribute, even if other elements are necessary as well.

Even if this picture may fit some cases of test use, however, it by no means fits all. Rather, the description above delineates a class of measurement theories; namely those that rely on a causal effect that flows from the measured attribute to the test scores. In several cases, however, this description does not accommodate accurately what researchers do, nor how theorists think about the relation between theoretical concepts and the observations gathered. The present chapter therefore explicates the different causal structures that have been proposed in the methodological literature, and serves to address the function of causal relations in them. As will become apparent, however, these structures work with causal relations, but leave the important question of what constitutes these relations unanswered; therefore the next chapter seeks to fill in this blank by applying different theories of causation to these cases. It is largely an open question how validity applies to each of these cases, so we discuss this matter in chapters 7 and 8.

The structure of this chapter is as follows. First, we spell out the relation between a wide class of measurement models and the common cause model. Second, we identify a class of models that is better described in terms of a common effect structure. Third, we discuss some cases that appear to be covered by neither of these models, namely theories that consider reciprocal relations between tests and attributes, theories that view test scores as influenced by large sets of partially overlapping attributes and processes, and theories that assume that homogeneity between test scores results from reciprocal effects between measured attributes.

Box 6.1. Do Personality Traits Cause Item Responses to Trait Adjectives?

The causal status of personality traits, such as those in the Five-Factor Model (FFM)—Extraversion, Neuroticism, Openness, Agreeableness, and Conscientiousness—has been much debated in personality psychology. On the one hand, the advocates of the FFM have taken the position that personality traits are biologically based tendencies that manifest themselves in a wide range of behaviors (McCrae et al., 2000). On the other hand, other personality researchers have resisted this interpretation, and have maintained that personality factors are categorization schemes that result from the activity of researchers, rather than being antecedent causes of behavior (e.g., Cervone, 2004).

The five factors originate from the analysis of trait adjectives as found in dictionaries. Presenting these adjectives to people, and letting them rate to what extent the adjective applies to them, then yields an association structure among the item responses. After many years of statistically analyzing such data sets, mostly through Principal Components Analysis (PCA), it was suggested that a five-factor solution provides the best balance with respect to completeness, fit, generalizability across samples, and stability of the solution (Digman, 1990; McCrae & Costa, 1987).

The PCA model is a formative model, so that the natural interpretation of the personality factors is that they are useful composites for describing variation in item responses to trait-adjective items. However, various findings have motivated theorists such as McCrae & Costa (2008) to adopt the stronger interpretation that the personality factors are real entities that cause behavior (i.e., that "E[xtraversion] causes party-going behavior," p. 288). Among these findings are (a) the reproducibility of PCA solutions in different cultures, (b) the high heritability coefficients commonly found for the five factors, (c) moderate to high test–retest correlations across the life span, and (d) the predictive utility of personality traits in forecasting a wide variety of outcome variables. Specifically, these researchers have proposed the view that the five factors map to a set of basic tendencies that are largely a function of genetic factors. As such they attempt to ground the reality of the personality factors in the biological constitution of human beings.

It would seem that the adequate model for testing such hypotheses is a reflective latent variable model, such as the Confirmatory Factor Analysis (CFA) model. In an early attempt to fit this model to personality data, however, McCrae et al. (1996) found that the CFA model corresponding to the Five-Factor Model did not adequately fit the data. Interestingly, this led them to reject CFA rather than the idea that the five factors are causal antecedents of item responses: "In actual analyses of personality data . . . structures that are known to be reliable [from principal components analyses] showed poor fits when evaluated by CFA techniques. We believe this points to serious problems with CFA itself when used to examine personality structure" (McCrae et al., 1996, p. 563).

It should be noted that CFA poses more restrictions on the data than the FFM latent variable hypothesis should be taken to imply (e.g., linearity, normality, etc.), so that the possibility should indeed be left open that McCrae et al.'s (1996) research rejected the CFA version of the FFM for the wrong reasons. However, an alternative interpretation of the situation is that the researchers have over-interpreted their principal components, endowing them with a latent variable status that was never warranted on the basis of the evidence. If this is correct, then what the FFM really captures is the fact that the association structure between item responses in personality questionnaires is relatively stable, and can be reasonably represented by five components. Compared to the hypothesis that the responses to personality items depend on five causally relevant latent variables, this hypothesis appears equally consistent with the evidence for the reality of the five factors provided by McCrae et al.

6.1. Causal Structures

In discussing measurement, researchers commonly divide the world into things to which we have access (test scores) and things that test scores measure, or that we infer from the test scores (latent attributes or constructs). An assumption that is common to all psychometric models of test theory is that, for such measurements or inferences to be possible, there must be an association between the attributes and the test scores. In criterion validity, as originally conceived, the focus is exclusively on the test scores and criteria (domain scores may be taken to be the attributes of interest such that the test domain score predicts the criterion domain score). In this case, validity reduces to the strength of this association, possibly extended with judgments of the representativeness of each test sample of the corresponding domain. More than this correlation is required for validity when one turns to more extensive theories of validity such as those that focus on the role of attributes in nomological networks (Cronbach & Mehl, 1955), the meaning of test scores (Messick, 1989), or explanatory relations between attributes and test scores (Zumbo, 2007). Several authors conceptualize the extra requirements for validity as the *causal* structure presumed to hold between measurements and attributes (Bollen, 1989; Bollen & Lennox, 1991; Edwards & Bagozzi, 2000; Borsboom, Mellenbergh, & Van Heerden, 2004).

If one limits one's consideration to the bivariate case, where there is only one attribute and only one test score, one may conceptualize the causal relation in two directions. Either the attribute causes the test score, or the test score causes the attribute. A model that supposes that the attribute causes the test score is often called an *effect indicator model*, represented statistically as a *reflective model*. In contrast, a model that supposes that the causal effect runs in the opposite direction is called a *causal indicator model*, represented statistically as a *formative model* (see Figure 6.1). One may attach various philosophical viewpoints to these different relations. For instance, it is natural to suppose that a causal effect of an attribute on the test scores requires some form of realism about the attribute in question (at least if one assumes that things that do not exist cannot have causal influences). On the other hand, if the causal relation is viewed in terms of a causal effect of the test scores on the attribute, one may think of this as being consistent with the view that researchers build up theoretical attributes from test scores (or observations); this is more consonant with empiricist views of science. The type of causation involved in these interpretations need not be the same; for instance, in Aristotelian terms, the reflective model may code for efficient causation (the attribute has a role in producing the test scores) while the formative model may code for formal causation (the attribute is made up of the test scores); this is an issue that we will take up in the next chapter.

6.1.1. The Reflective Model

Naturally, we cannot, from a single bivariate relationship, deduce the direction of causation. The theory is underdetermined by the data in this case. However, as Figure 6.1 illustrates, when the idea is extended to the multivariate case, testable predictions flow from the reflective model. Most importantly, if one has a number of test scores that depend on the same attribute, then the corresponding statistical model is a common cause model. A common cause model implies that the effect variables are independent conditional on the common cause. To see this, consider the famous correlation between the number of storks and the number of babies that are born in Macedonian villages; the more storks there are, the more babies are born. However, it is not the case that an increase in storks causes an increase in babies: both are the result of a third variable, namely the size of the villages. Larger villages have more residents who make more babies, and they have more chimneys that storks seek out to make nests in. However, conditional on a particular village size, the number of storks is independent of the number of babies born; all that remains is random differences between villages (error variance). In the philosophical literature, the condition that correlations between effects vanish upon conditioning on their common cause is known as 'screening off': the common cause screens off correlation between its effects (Reichenbach, 1956; Pearl, 2000).

In a measurement context, the situation often considered is one in which the researcher has a number of reflective test scores, each of which depends on the same attribute. In that case, the common cause is latent, and hence one needs more variables to render the predictions of the model testable. For instance, in factor analysis, where the functional form of the relation between test score and attribute is assumed to be known (i.e., linear), the model entails restrictions on the data when one has one latent variable and at least four observables (Mulaik, 2009). Thus, in that case, the model can be falsified.

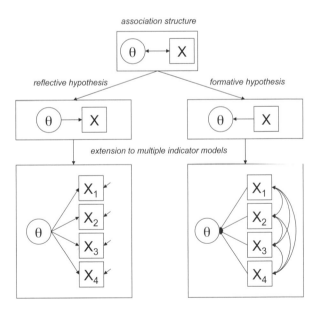

Figure 6.1 A Flow Chart to Outline How One Gets From a Pure Association Between an Attribute (q) and a Test Score (X) to Reflective and Formative Models. The reflective model implies local independence, which is not the case for the formative model.

If the common cause is latent, then the screening-off condition corresponds to the psychometric requirement of *local independence*: for every subpopulation of subjects with the same position on the latent variable, the association between the indicators vanishes. This hypothesis is common to many psychometric models, such as those covered by the monotone homogeneous item response model (Holland & Rosenbaum, 1986; Ellis & Van den Wollenberg, 1992), examples of which are the models of Rasch (1960) and Birnbaum (1968), as well as the 3-parameter logistic model (Hambleton & Swaminathan, 1985) and the single factor model with positive loadings (here the local independence hypothesis corresponds to the requirement that the covariance matrix of the error scores is diagonal). Models with nominal latent variables, such as the latent class model (Lazarsfeld, 1959) and the general mixture model (McLachlan & Peel, 2000) also have this property. The condition of local independence was in fact instrumental in shaping the origin of all latent variable models, namely Spearman's (1904) model of general intelligence, because it allowed him to deduce the condition of vanishing tetrads (see also Bollen & Ting, 1993).

If a number of indicators indeed depend on the same attribute, then this has implications for what one can do with the data gathered. For instance, in this case it makes sense to compute a composite score by summing the item scores, and to regard that composite score as an 'estimate' or 'measure' of the attribute. In many models, there are more precise ways of constructing the relation between summed item scores and latent attributes (e.g., Rasch, 1960; Grayson, 1988; Hemker, Sijtsma, Molenaar, & Junker, 1996, 1997), and sometimes weighted composites (latent trait estimates) outperform unweighted ones (although in many models the difference is slight; see also Grayson, 1988). We will not treat these issues in detail here, but rather note an aspect that is important in the context of validity: If a reflective latent variable model is true, then it makes sense to interpret the composite scores as measures of an underlying attribute. In fact, in this case the measurement errors average out as the number of test scores in the composite grows. Therefore, adding subtest or item scores is a good idea, because the unreliability of the composite will be smaller than that of its constituent variables. Thus, evidence that supports the truth of the reflective model can be adduced in support of this common practice.

6.1.2. The Formative Model

The set of test scores for which the reflective model assumption makes sense is only a subset of the set of test scores that are typically used in constructing composite scores. To give an example, newborn babies are, in many countries, standardly subjected to the Apgar (1953) test. This is a simple test designed to reach a quick decision on whether the newborn requires immediate medical attention. The test consists of just five criteria (one can think of these as items): The person administering the Apgar test checks the skin color, pulse rate, muscle tone, reflex irritability, and breathing of the infant. On each of these criteria, the newborn can receive a score of 0, 1, or 2 (for instance, for breathing, '0' means that breathing is absent, '1' that it is weak or irregular, and '2' that it is strong). After scoring each of the criteria, the scores are added to form a total score. A low score implies the decision that the infant needs immediate medical attention (naturally, the compensatory model implied by the use of a sum score only makes sense in certain ranges of these variables; e.g., if a child is not breathing, one would not postpone bringing the child to the hospital to wait until the results of the other indicators came in).

It would appear far-fetched to consider these criteria to be measures of the same attribute. Rather, they are measures of distinct attributes, each of which is important in deciding whether a newborn needs medical attention. In doing the Apgar test, and summing the item scores, one is in fact computing a unit weight regression for predictive or decision purposes, rather than computing an estimate of an underlying attribute for measurement purposes. Thus, even though the approach involves summing items—just like the reflective measurement model does—the justification for the summation rests on different grounds and has a different use.

The treatment of scores on measures like the Apgar test thus requires a different mode of thinking and different method of analysis. The question, in such cases, is not so much how to construct a composite that has optimal properties in terms of measurement (e.g., is unidimensional and has high reliability), but how to construct a composite that is most useful for the purpose at hand, where this purpose is usually not primarily one of measurement. In the methodological literature, it has been proposed to handle such cases through formative models (Edwards & Bagozzi, 2000). Specifically, causal indicator models treat the indicators as causes of the attribute under study, rather than as effects of that attribute (Bollen & Lennox, 1991). In this literature, the use of formative models has also been called *formative measurement*. This terminology is somewhat unfortunate, since what distinguishes formative from reflective models is precisely the fact that in the formative case the indicators are *not* interpreted as measures of the attributes under study, despite this conventional mode of speech.

In the formative model, one considers the attribute to be determined by the indicators rather than the other way around. This brings one to the right panel of Figure 6.1. When the formative hypothesis involves several indicators, then the resulting model is clearly different from the reflective case. For instance, instead of local independence (conditional on a position on the attribute, the test scores are independent) the model may imply local *dependence*: conditional on a position on a formatively modeled attribute, previously uncorrelated indicators will become correlated.

This latter property is related to the literature on causality, where the formative model corresponds to a common effect model. This model has played an important role in discussions of *overdetermination* (the situation where multiple causes contribute to a single effect). The classic case of overdetermination involves a firing squad, where soldiers A, B, and C are supposed to fire at a prisoner, but some of them may in fact refuse to fire. After the shooting, the prisoner may be dead or alive (this is the common effect variable, denoted D). Now, conditional on the state of the prisoner after the shooting, the cause variables (whether a given soldier has fired or not) are correlated. This happens because if the prisoner is dead, and we are given the information that soldier A did not fire, then the probability that B has fired increases and likewise for C. Thus, conditional on the value of D, the variables A, B, and C carry information about each other which means they are not independent. Hence, in a common effect model, previously uncorrelated variables will become correlated conditional on their common effect, whereas in a common cause model, variables must be uncorrelated conditional on a value of their common cause. In accordance, in a reflective model the indicators should be uncorrelated conditional on the measured attribute, whereas in a formative model they should be correlated conditional on the formative attribute. In the next chapter, we will see that this imposes limitations on which positive characterizations of causation could be used to flesh out the model.

It is important to stress that the reflective model imposes conditional independence constraints on the variables (as represented in Figure 6.1 through the omission of double-headed arrows between the indicators), whereas the formative model does not. In fact, the formative model as depicted in Figure 6.1 does not impose any restrictions on the data whatsoever. As may be expected from this, the formative model is not identified: given only a set of causal indicators, the parameters that relate these indicators to the formative attribute cannot be uniquely estimated from the data. Therefore, one must take some arbitrary weighting scheme (often unit weights, as in the construction of the Apgar score), and impose a heuristic constraint to optimize these parameters, or one has to expand the model with either a criterion to be predicted, or with indicators that function reflectively with respect to the attribute studied (i.e., that causally depend on it). These different courses of action are represented graphically in Figure 6.2.

Including pragmatically driven constraints is commonly done in techniques that are designed for data reduction, such as Principal Components Analysis (PCA) or K-means clustering. In a PCA model, for instance, the parameter estimates are optimized in such a way that the constructed composite variable explains as much as possible of the variance in the indicators. This is done through an Eigenvalue decomposition, which is similar to the way (exploratory) factor analysis is executed, and for this

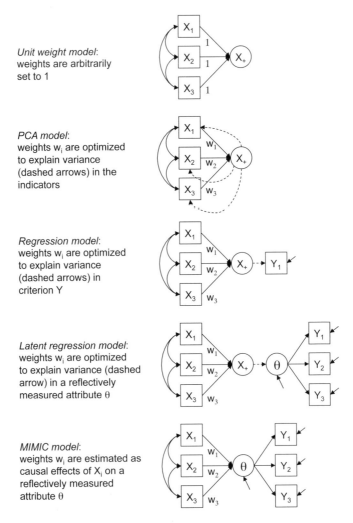

Figure 6.2 Courses of Action that Can Be Taken to Determine the Weights Used to Form the Composite. Causal relations are represented as continuous arrows, predictive relations as dashed arrows. It should be noted that the latent regression model and MIMIC model cannot be distinguished without experimental intervention that, for instance, directly manipulates the X-indicators; i.e., for a correlational dataset they are statistically equivalent.

reason the results of a PCA can in some cases align well with the results of factor analysis in practice. However, it is important to see that the causal status of principal components is not altered by this fact: they are, by definition, weighted sumscores (functions of the data) and not latent variables (which are hypothetical determinants of the data). The PCA variant of formative modeling is represented in Figure 6.3 together with a reflective model.

In addition, even in cases where PCA gives the same parameter values as factor analysis, principal component scores are equivalent to constructed factor score estimates, not to unobserved factor scores. This sometimes creates confusion, for instance when researchers think that, because factor score estimates are constructed from the data just like principal components are, the reflective hypothesis in the factor model is practically empty and principal components can be interpreted as being on the same psychometric footing as latent variables. This is not true because, even if there are cases where factor score estimates match nicely with principal component scores, the interpretation of these estimates as estimates *of* latent variable values depends on whether the latent variable model is correct, and not on the question of whether the PCA model is correct. Thus, interpretations of principal component scores as estimates of a latent variable cannot be made, *except* when one adds the additional hypothesis that the data were produced by a latent variable model. This is often done in psychology, but means that one adds the latent variable idea post hoc, and usually without testing it. Figure 6.3 lays out this difference between latent variable modeling and PCA schematically.

The addition of pragmatic constraints to the formative model is one way to optimize the weights attached to the indicators, which are used in the construction of the composite or formative attribute. Another way to optimize these parameters is by adding a criterion to the model, i.e., by adding a variable that one wants to predict from the composite. In this case, the weights used in the construction of the weighted sumscore are usually optimized according to a least squares principle (i.e., the parameters are chosen such that the squared deviation between the predicted criterion score and the observed criterion score is minimized). Thus, the composite is an optimal predictor. This model is represented as the regression model in Figure 6.2.

Finally, one can determine the composite weights by regressing a reflectively modeled attribute on the indicators. In this case, there are two possible interpretations of the model. First, the model can be interpreted as developing a composite that predicts as much variance in the reflective attribute as possible (the latent regression model in Figure 6.2). Second, the model can be interpreted as estimating the causal effects of the formative indicators on the latent variable (this is called a Multiple Indicators Multiple Causes or MIMIC model, also represented in Figure 6.2). These two interpretations lead to the same statistical model in a cross-sectional passive observation dataset, and are thus indistinguishable in this case. However, they are conceptually distinct, in that the causal interpretation predicts that the attribute will change if the cause indicators are subjected to experimental manipulation, whereas the predictive interpretation does not.

In contrast to a PCA model, a MIMIC model does impose restrictions

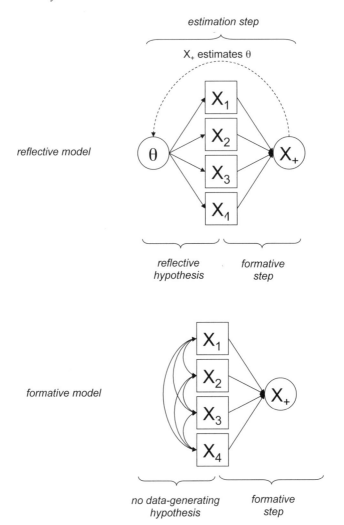

Figure 6.3 An Illustration of the Difference Between Formative and Reflective Modeling Strategies. Both models involve a formative step (the construction of a composite score, X+). However, the reflective model contains a data-generating hypothesis, and if that hypothesis is correct it makes sense to interpret the composite as an estimate of the attribute. The formative model contains no such hypothesis and essentially only consists of a formative step.

on the data. These restrictions come from two sources. First, some restrictions arise because of the fact that the reflective part of the model requires local independence, i.e., the reflective indicators should be independent conditional on the attribute measured. Second, the model involves a mediation hypothesis, in that all the effects that flow from the formative indicators are hypothesized to be mediated by the latent variable. That is, there are no direct arrows from the formative indicators to the reflective indicators. Statistically speaking, this means that the model implies proportionality constraints on the covariance matrix: the covariance between a formative and a reflective indicator must decompose into the product of the formative effect parameter and the reflective factor loading. This is a testable assumption given that one has sufficiently many effect indicators to identify the reflective part of the model.

6.2. Implications for Validity Theory

Reflective and formative models cover two widely used methods for the statistical analysis of test scores, and figure prominently in test construction methods. The reflective model is appropriate for cases in which one hypothesizes that the indicators, represented as items in a questionnaire, depend on the same latent variable. An example where this is often done is cognitive testing and intelligence research. For instance, researchers typically assume that individual differences in item responses depend on an attribute that functions as a common cause of these item responses. The formative model is appropriate for situations in which a common cause hypothesis is implausible, but one still wants to develop a composite score on the items for purposes other than measurement. An example where this is plausible is the assessment of life stress. In studies relating to this concept, researchers commonly assess the causal determinants of life stress (e.g., death of a spouse, birth of children, moving to a new house, etc.) rather than its effects, and hence a formative approach is reasonable.

A difference between the models that is important in the context of validity theory is their *referential stability*. The latent variable in a reflective model is referentially stable, in that the addition of new items to the model, or the deletion of existing ones, should not (if the model is correct) change the nature of the attribute measured. That is, the designation 'whatever this test measures' has the same referent independently of which particular items are used to assess it. This fact makes it possible to link different item sets to each other via one latent variable (a property that is used in test equating). Another advantage that follows from this is that one can choose items according to their appropriateness for a testee, without changing what one measures; this allows computerized adaptive testing (CAT; Van der Linden & Glas, 2000). Finally, the model buys one a way out of operationalism. One of the main charges against operationalism is that defining an attribute in terms of a measurement procedure leads to an undesirable multiplication of attributes (e.g., each newly constructed thermometer measures a new attribute because it defines a different measurement procedure). This problem is bypassed in a reflective model, because it by definition allows that different testing procedures measure the same latent variable.

To gain these advantages, however, one also has to make strong assumptions about the measurement properties of the items or subtests. In addition, it has been argued that, in the context of the causal theory of measurement, one has to commit to some form of realism about latent variables, however minimal (Borsboom, Mellenbergh, & Van Heerden, 2003). The reason for this is that the basic assumption of an effect indicators model, no matter the functional form, is that the attribute studied is causally responsible for the covariation between items and subtests, and therefore it must have some form of existence independently of its indicators. This also complies with the fact that reflectively measured attributes resist an interpretation as mere summaries of test scores: substituting a (weighted) sumscore for a latent variable (e.g., substituting a factor score estimate for a factor score) leads to inconsistencies; for instance, indicators are independent given the latent variable, but dependent given the sumscore.

The referential stability of formatively measured attributes is much more problematic. Because the formative indicators do not measure the same attribute, they are not exchangeable. Adding or removing formative indicators thus changes the composite—often in an unpredictable way. Therefore different formative measurement instruments may be considered to define distinct composite scores. There is, for a formative model, not even a guarantee that composite scores on distinct tests will correlate positively. As a result, different formative measurement instruments may be considered to define distinct composite scores that are not necessarily linked to each other via simple transformations (e.g., monotonic ones).

If the model is strengthened via the inclusion of predictive criteria, then the weights of the effects are defined with respect to these criteria, and the composite score is as well. This is not necessarily a problem (it is how the model is set up) but it may become one if researchers fail to consider that the weights used are specific to a particular criterion, and thus composites used in different studies may not be exchangeable in any way. That is, if one researcher uses a formative approach on, say, a number of socioeconomic status (SES) indicators (e.g., annual income, education level, etc.) to predict life expectancies, and another researcher uses it to predict happiness, there is no *a priori* reason that these researchers' composites will resemble each other, even though they use the same formative indicators. If researchers fail to realize this, then there is a risk that they will use the same name ('SES') for distinct composites. Howell, Breivik, & Wilcox (2007a) call this problem "interpretational confounding" (p. 239). The problem of interpretational confounding is schematically represented in Figure 6.4.

Bollen (2007) has argued that interpretational confounding is not a problem that is inherent in the model, because extending the model with distinct reflective indicators will reveal that there are multiple formative constructs, rather than a single one, that influence the distinct reflective indicators. Thus, interpretational confounding does not occur when one

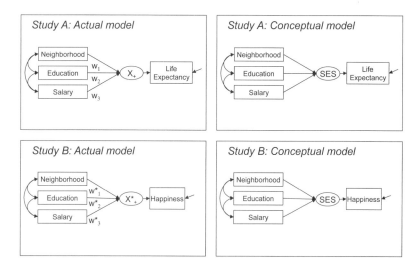

Figure 6.4 Interpretational Confounding. If researchers use the same indicators (here: Neighborhood, Education, and Salary), but a different criterion in distinct studies (Study A: Life expectancy; Study B: Happiness), the weights w and the composite X+ will be different (left panels). If the researchers nevertheless adhere to the same conceptual model (right panels), this may lead them to think that they are studying the same property (socioeconomic status—SES) which may not be the case.

incorporates the distinct reflective indicators in the same model. Howell, Breivik, & Wilcox (2007b) countered this argument by stating that, even though this is true, few researchers actually do take the distinct indicators into account. The reality of research, of course, is moreover that interpretational confounding is likely to occur *over* different studies rather than *within* a single study. That is, it is likely that scientists will interpret the formative composite SES as denoting the same attribute in studies where it is used to predict life expectancy *and* in studies where it is used to predict happiness, as illustrated in Figure 6.4. In such a case, interpretational confounding is a realistic possibility.

Edwards (2010) discusses this, and a number of other problems involved in the concept of formative measurement, to arrive at the conclusion that formative measurement is based on a fallacy. In short, Edwards uses problems like interpretational confounding and lack of identifiability to argue that formative models do not meet the requirements that can be reasonably imposed on a measurement model. Although many of the problems that Edwards discusses are indeed significant, we think they mainly result from the unfortunate marriage of the terms "formative" and "measurement." A formative model can be quite useful, and may adequately describe the relation between observables and construct. However, the formative model is not a measurement model, precisely because the notion of measurement presupposes that the measured attribute plays a causal role in the generation of test scores. Thus, the distinction between formative modeling and formative measurement is important. The terminology of formative measurement suggests that formative modeling can serve as a replacement of reflective models in a measurement framework, and we agree with Edwards (2010) that this is not the case. Measurement is always reflective. However, formative modeling can nevertheless play an important role in test analysis.

Above we noted that causally interpreted reflective models seem to entail ontological commitments to the reality of the attributes represented by the latent variable that serves as a common cause. This does not occur for formative models. In such models, one can take the latent variable as nothing more than a weighted sum score constructed from the observed indicators. However, the formative model does not rule out interpreting the latent variable as a real attribute that exists independently of the indicators within the constraints of interpretational confounding.

Box 6.2. Prediction, Measurement, and Referential Stability

Interpretational confounding is a term coined by Howell, Breivik, & Wilcox (2007), and applies to cases where researchers employ the same term (e.g., 'SES' in their example), but use differently weighted composites. In formative models, the composite formed usually depends on the criteria chosen for prediction, so that the latent variable in the model is referentially unstable; in such cases interpretational confounding is indeed a possibility.

The problem is broader, however. When one optimizes for measurement purposes (which normally involves fitting a reflective model), one is explicitly searching for referentially stable situations, because one attempts to select items that are unidimensional; i.e., items that measure the same thing in some sense. However, when one optimizes for prediction purposes, one is doing something very different, and referential instability is very likely to result.

As an example, consider the original Minnesota Multiphasic Personality Inventory (MMPI). This questionnaire was famously composed by selecting items that maximized the proportion of variance predicted in criteria (in this case, clinicians' ratings). It would seem, at first glance, that such a method would select items that measure the same attribute as the clinicians' ratings. However, the MMPI turned out to be a questionnaire with a quite unclear factor structure (Waller, 1999), which suggests that something different has happened.

The situation is not hard to understand once one considers how regression methods work. If one includes items in a test on the basis of the amount of variance they explain in a criterion, then one will not normally select items that form a unidimensional set (i.e., that measure the same attribute). The reason for this is that maximizing the amount of variance explained in the criterion comes down to selecting items that explain *unique* variance—and these are items that are highly correlated with the criterion, but show low intercorrelations among one another. Selecting items that measure the same attribute would actually be counterproductive in maximizing predictor–criterion regressions, because due to their intercorrelations they will not explain unique variance.

Thus, following this procedure, one is apt to select items that measure distinct attributes. Naturally, if one puts these into a single scale, they will not behave according to a reflective measurement model; the referential instability of the items is built into the item selection criteria. In all likelihood, therefore, the developers of the MMPI used item selection procedures that are most naturally interpreted in a formative modeling framework. Given that the factor model is reflective, it is no wonder that the factor structure of the test was unclear.

6.3. Direct, Indirect, and Mixed Models

In many cases, researchers are interested in attributes that are hypothesized to have indirect effects on the test scores. For instance, in intelligence testing, it is often supposed that general intelligence should be considered a second-order latent variable. In such research, data from a test battery are clearly multidimensional; for instance, the different testing procedures may depend on spatial, verbal, and numerical ability. These latent variables are positively correlated but cannot be identified with each other. However, one may hypothesize that the positive correlation between the primary latent variables are themselves caused by a higher-order latent variable; this latent variable is then considered to represent the so-called *g*-factor (Jensen, 1999). This model is represented in Figure 6.5.

A higher-order factor is a step further removed from the observational level than a first-order factor. This has consequences for the question of what validity evidence counts as support for such a factor. At the psychometric level, one cannot follow exactly the same procedures as one does when testing the hypothesis that a test is unidimensional, yields reliable scores, and behaves in the right way under experimental manipulations, for such procedures only serve to substantiate hypotheses that concern the first-order factor. In fact, it could be argued that hypotheses concerning, say, the *g*-factor, must assume that the validity of the first-order measurements is in order. This is because a second-order factor derives whatever

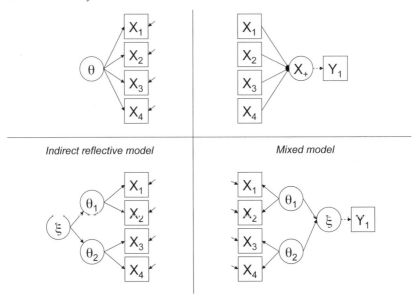

Figure 6.5 Direct and Indirect Models. Direct reflective and formative models are the same as previously introduced. Two extensions are represented in the lower panels. The left bottom panel gives the indirect reflective model. The right bottom panel represents a mixed model, in which the higher-order construct is a formative function of the lower-order reflective constructs.

explanatory value it has from the correlation structure of the first-order factors, i.e., that structure should itself conform to the hypothesis that a single continuous common cause underlies the correlations between these factors. Clearly, this only works if that correlation structure is estimated correctly, and this, in turn, assumes that the dimensionality and measurement properties of the observed scores have been adequately settled.

In the reflective case, the inferences being made regarding second-order factors are perhaps more problematic than those concerning first-order factors, but the structure of the model does not itself change upon invoking second-order factors. That is, the model says that the observations have a number of first-order common causes that explain their covariance; the additional hypothesis, in the second-order case, is that these first-order common causes themselves also depend on a common cause— the second-order factor. Although this hypothesis is indirect in that it concerns the explanation of a covariance structure between variables that are themselves not directly observable, the qualitative form of the hypothesis does not change—a common cause hypothesis governs each of the levels of the model.

In formative models, one may also invoke indirect paths in the model, but in this case the interpretation of the latent variables along the path changes substantially. For instance, when invoking indirect paths in the model, one may hypothesize that the observed variables themselves depend on a set of latent variables, and that the scores on this set of latent variables themselves determine the level of the formative attribute (i.e., the mixed model in Figure 6.5). When one has direct paths from the observables to the formative attribute, one may interpret the model causally in the sense that the scores on the observables determine, say, the PC-scores and they do so *via the computational procedures followed by the researcher*. That is, the researcher's operation of a program (e.g., SPSS) instantiates this causal process. Thus, one may consistently assume that the model codes a construction process (i.e., the process by which the PCs are constructed) and therefore one need not assign the formative attribute more ontological weight than that of being a construction of the researcher.

However, when the formative indicators are themselves latent, this is no longer the case. This is because, in this situation, the researcher does not have access to the latent variables that are hypothesized to cause the formative attribute. Thus, if one wants to think of these formative attributes as constructions, they can be no longer considered the *researcher's* constructions, because the researcher does not have access to the properties that should be used to construct the formative attribute. This means that, minimally, the construction process must be placed outside the researcher's actions.

Now this invites an interpretation of the model in a full-blown realist sense. That is, in this case it becomes sensible (or at least not plainly inconsistent with the model) to think of the formative attribute as being a real entity, that stands under the influence of the latent variables measured by the indicators. And, because the causal effects in this model are no longer those that the researcher brings to the scene, they must also refer to some process operating in the outside world. Note that, while such an interpretation is suggestive, it is not mandatory; for instance, one could hold the view that the formative attribute is a hypothetical construction out of the latent variables, even though the researcher does not have the latent variable scores to do the construction.

In the example of life stress, for instance, a realist interpretation of the formative attribute would be sensible. The questions asked in life stress questionnaires ('have you recently lost your job?', 'have you recently moved?') are thought to depend on distinct factors (whether a person has actually lost a job, whether a person has actually moved) and these factors are thought to influence life stress, which is assumed to exist independently of the researcher and to receive the causal effects of the latent variables that lie behind the indicators. That is, in this scenario, one assumes that the formative attribute of life stress is more than a construction of the researcher (i.e., a PC as constructed from the observations); one assumes that life stress exists independently of the researcher, and what one measures though the observations are the actual causes of life stress.

It is hoped, in this case, that by choosing an appropriate construction method (which may be a deliberately misspecified direct effects model, like a principal components model), the constructed formative attribute (i.e., the numbers assigned to people in the datafile) matches their scores on the actual, unobserved attribute of life stress.

What are the consequences for validating the claims based on either model? Clearly, the case that has to be built for the indirect reflective model is different from that which may bolster inference under the mixed model. In the case of the second-order factor model, for instance, one makes two claims that are of the same kind: the indicators are a function of a set of latent variables, and these latent variables are a function of a set of latent variables even more removed from the observed indicators—the second-order factors. As a result, the observed scores on the indicators may be interpreted (if the model is correct) as being indirectly caused by the second-order factors. Thus, if one allows that the term "measurement" need not stop at the first level of latent variables, one can claim that IQ-test scores measure the *g*-factor—albeit indirectly.

No such argument can be made for the mixed model case. In that situation, the variable that the researcher has actually constructed out of the indicator scores is assumed to be a proxy for the hypothesized common effect of the measured latent variables (e.g., the total score on a life stress questionnaire could be viewed as a proxy for life stress), but it is not clear that it should be viewed as a measurement of life stress from the perspective of a causal theory of measurement. The reason for this is that there is no causal pathway from life stress to the questionnaire item responses. What one measures are the attributes that underlie these item responses, and these are considered to be the causes of the variable one is interested in. The match between the constructed scores (i.e., the total scores) and the targeted attribute (life stress) depends not only on the adequacy of the measurement specification of the model, but also on the adequacy of the structural relations in the model (i.e., the representations of the effects of losing one's job and moving to a new house *on* life stress). This means that the model may be incorrect even if the measurement specifications are in order. One way in which this can occur, for instance, is when the effects of the measured factors on life stress are assumed to be independent (i.e., the specification of the model is additive) while in fact these effects interact (e.g., the effect of losing one's job is greater when one has just moved to a new house than when one has not moved). This possibility would not seem to exist for the indirect reflective model, as that model involves only measurement specifications (assuming, again, that the relation between the second-order factor and the indicator scores is a bona fide measurement relation).

On the other hand, the fact that validity depends on the adequacy of the structural specification of the model yields possibilities for research that scarcely exist for the indirect reflective model. For instance, one may undertake research in which the structural model is tested directly; e.g., a lot of research can be done specifically on whether and how life stress is produced by life events, like losing one's job. In addition, in some cases it is possible to experimentally manipulate the causal variables, and measure the effect of such manipulations on the attribute under study. The reason that this is relatively straightforward is that the manipulations in question can be devised to have an effect on variables that can be subjected to a first-order measurement model (i.e., the indicator variables in the formative model). This possibility hardly exists for a variable like the g-factor. Since the g-factor is more or less a second-order factor by definition, it has no direct indicators; therefore it is much harder to devise experimental manipulations that would affect it, without affecting the first-order factors directly. In addition, the rather structural latency of second-order factors like the g-factor makes it even harder to check whether one has succeeded in manipulating the right thing, i.e., it hampers establishing the validity of the experimental manipulation.

6.4. Other Structures

Reflective and formative models are the most often used methodologies to connect observations to theoretical attributes. Reflective modeling underlies a multitude of latent variable models (e.g., latent class, Item Response Theory, and common factor models). Formative modeling is the basis for a host of data-reductive models (e.g., various forms of direct formative modeling, such as PCA and clustering methods) as well as for indirect causal models that conceptualize focal attributes as common effects of the measured latent variables (most often seen in SEM applications). However, these canonical model forms are not the only way to specify relations between observations and attributes of interest. In this section we deal with a number of alternative structures that have been proposed in the literature.

6.4.1. Reactive Indicators

A first alternative that evades the reflective/formative modeling dichotomy is presented by Hayduk et al. (2007) in a paper on what they call *reactive indicators*. Reactive indicators are indicators that are both formative and reflective, in that the causal relation between observations and theoretical attribute is reciprocal. That is, the attribute has a causal effect on the measurements, as in reflective models, but the measurements have an effect on the attribute as well, as in (direct) formative models. Normally, such a model is not statistically identified, but Hayduk et al. (2007) give a number of situations in which its parameters could actually be uniquely estimated, thereby rendering the model potentially useful in practice.

The general idea that underlies reactive indicators may seem exotic to the reader accustomed with the standard views in psychometrics, but it is not as strange as it may initially seem to be. For instance, it is well known that one of the archetypical examples of measurement, namely the measurement of temperature, involves a reciprocal relation between the measurement instrument (a thermometer) and the measured property (ambient temperature). Take, for instance, the mercury thermometer, which consists of a volume of mercury in a fixed column. Because mercury expands when heated, and the column is fixed, the level of mercury will rise as a function of the ambient temperature in a room. The mechanism through which this occurs is that the particles in the room transfer kinetic energy to the mercury particles in the thermometer. Increases (decreases) in room temperatures thus cause increases (decreases) in the height of the mercury column.

However, the transfer of kinetic energy that lies at the basis of this mechanism is reciprocal. That is, the particles in the room transfer kinetic energy to the mercury particles, but the mercury particles transfer kinetic energy to those in the room as well. Hence, strictly speaking, this situation would be correctly represented as a case of reactive indicators. Normally, of course, the causal coupling between the systems will be highly asymmetric, because the room is much larger than the thermometer; hence the effect of the thermometer on the room will be negligible compared to the effect of the room on the thermometer. From a theoretical perspective, however, it is quite interesting that this archetypical example of measurement is, strictly speaking, causally reciprocal and hence a case of reactive indicators.

It is likely that in several cases involving psychological measurement, reciprocal effects exist. For instance, in research into attitudes towards the death penalty, it is customary to ask participants for evaluations of statements like "Do you feel that executing people who commit murder deters others from committing murder?" To the extent that a person does not yet have a fully crystallized attitude towards the death penalty, the presentation of such an item may, in itself, induce or modify a process of attitude formation. For instance, the person who is administered the above item may not have considered the effect of executions on future crimes yet, which means that the presentation of the item unwittingly presents a new argument for, or against, the death penalty; the person's attitude toward the death penalty may be modified accordingly. There is a wealth of experimental research into attitude formation that has shown even minor contextual variations to affect the resulting attitudes. Thus, a reactive indicator model for attitudes might seem exotic, but would in fact be quite consistent with current scientific knowledge of attitude formation. Indeed, the entire literature on unobtrusive measures in social and behavioral research could be read as an effort to reduce reactive measurement through research design. The reactive indicators model of Hayduk thus has initial plausibility, at least for some cases of measurement.

The reciprocal dynamics proposed in the model by Hayduk et al. (2007) are hypothesized to play a role during test administration; that is, the reciprocal effects are hypothesized to take place in-between item administration and item response. However, when contrasting the reactive indicators case with the reflective/formative model distinction that is central to this chapter, we may also consider longer timescales; in particular, reciprocal effects that take place after the measurement process. For instance, suppose that a person is administered a structured clinical interview, designed to assess whether the person suffers from a mental disorder. Assume the person is diagnosed with a personality disorder. It is quite likely that the diagnosis itself will have an impact on the person's life. For instance, the person may Google the prognosis and symptomatology of personality disorders, and unwittingly adapt his or her behavior to comply with the clinically typical case of the disorder. It is also likely that people in the person's social environment will modify their behavior in response to learning of the diagnosis. Likewise, the diagnosis could lead to treatment that alleviates the symptoms.

In this way, the diagnosis may feed back into the very same symptomatology that was originally used to furnish the diagnosis, thereby creating a reciprocal relation that lies outside the reflective/formative dichotomy. Thus, even though one may see the outcome of a diagnostic interview as a purely formative concept (in this case, a cutoff applied to a total score) that has no antecedent reality or causal status independent of the measurements, *after* the measurements have taken place, the diagnostic category—however arbitrary—may acquire a reality of its own through the behavior of the individual and its environment. Of course, the applicability of such a reactive model depends upon the precise interpretation of the attribute assessed by the diagnosis. If one understands it as a relatively stable trait, then the reactive model applies more naturally than if one understands the attribute as a temporary state. In the latter case, the diagnosis affects a later state.

In the philosophy of the social sciences, Hacking (1999) has discussed this phenomenon in some detail, including the example of diagnoses. Traditionally, natural sciences have been understood as striving to discover natural kinds, kinds that invariably remain the same, because such natural kinds were understood as the basis for natural laws that remain universal throughout time. Currently, biological, psychological, and social kinds are generally viewed as nonnatural kinds because they name sets of things that tend to change over time in their basic characteristics. For example, the basic characteristics of students with limited English proficiency, underemployed members of the labor force, or individuals diagnosed with neuroticism can change and evolve as social conditions change. Hacking characterizes the types of kinds studied in the social and behavioral sciences as interactive kinds. Unlike the natural sciences, these sciences study kinds that interact with their instances. Inanimate objects do not respond to having a certain label applied to them the way that animate beings do. Being labeled as having limited English proficiency, being underemployed, or neurotic affects how people think about themselves. This impact of labeling constitutes a form of reactive assessment to which a reactive measurement model could be applied.

As indicated above, the reactive measurement model applies only in cases in which the assessment contexts extends through time far enough to include the causal effects. In any event, in considering the validity of tests and test score interpretations, it is wise to keep in mind the extremely complicated ontology of psychological attributes. If the typical characteristics of individuals with a particular attribute change over the decades, then such changes will impact the inferences supported by test scores and the uses that the test scores can serve. If the process of assessing an attribute is apt to change the attribute itself, then the validity argument needs to provide a very clear description of how the attribute assessed should be understood. Assessing the level of an attribute after or during the assessment process may differ from assessing the level prior to the assessment process. Likewise, assessment may change the quality of an attribute from pre-reflective to reflective because the assessment itself causes the test taker to incorporate the attribute into his or her self-understanding. Moreover, the introduction of a particular theoretical attribute into public discourse can change the social environment of those to whom the theoretical attribute is applied, and the consequences may bear on decisions about the use of the test scores (chapter 9).

6.4.2. Bonds and Watersheds

Most of the standard measurement models in psychometrics attempt to represent a set of items by relating them to a *smaller* set of latent variables and a set of usually orthogonal random error terms for each item. This facilitates model identification and generally leads to parsimonious, testable models. However, when one considers the plausible causes of variation in item response patterns, then it is often easy to list dozens of distinct factors that may influence the item response process. For instance, solving a Raven item requires the ability to read and understand the instruction, accurate perception of the item, the formation of a mental representation of the figures in the item, performing various operations on that representation (e.g., concatenation, spatial rotation, contraction), the recognition of the correct answer once one has found it, and various motor skills that result in ticking the right box on the answer sheet. Clearly each of these processes may be subject to individual differences. If those differences affect the probability of various item responses, then the data will be inherently multidimensional.

The purpose of (unidimensional) test construction is to construct a set of items that, while individually perhaps multidimensional, as a group depend primarily on individual differences in one, or one group, of the processes involved. That is, one hopes that the intended ability causes the bulk of the (co)variance among the items, and that the other processes generate variance that behaves as random error (i.e., as transient influences not shared by different items). Naturally, this is a difficult task given the inherent complexity of item response processes, and in fact it may not be possible to construct strictly unidimensional tests in this strongly causal sense. In fact, for some groups of tests it may be impossible to construct distinct items that do not partly depend on individual differences in the same (sub)processes, thus creating a measurement problem.

This is the basis of the so-called *bonds model*, originally proposed by Thomson (1916) in reaction to Charles Spearman's general factor model of intelligence. Spearman (1904) had adduced the fact that all IQ-items correlate positively in the population (the *positive manifold of intelligence*) as evidence for the hypothesis that these items depend on the *same* latent variable (i.e., the g-factor). Thomson, instead, proposed that the positive manifold results from a measurement problem, because even highly distinct IQ-items (say, involving digit span and vocabulary) will always depend, to some extent, on the same basic processes. This is visually represented in Figure 6.6.

When there are individual differences in the basic processes that the items of subtests depend on, and all of the distinct tests depend partly on these processes, this will produce a positive manifold among the subtests. However, strictly speaking there is no general factor present in the antecedent causes of test score variation, even though the bonds model may

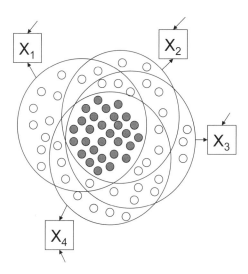

Figure 6.6 The Bonds Model. According to this model, each indicator is causally influenced by a large number of basic processes or "bonds." Indicators are associated to the degree that they share bonds.

produce formally identical covariances among the subtests, as Thomson showed in his classic 1916 paper. Largely neglected in the time since that publication, recently the bonds model has been revived in the intelligence literature by Bartholomew, Deary, and Lawn (2009). It should be noted, however, that its possible applications exceed the domain of intelligence testing. For instance, the idea of bonds of underlying processes can easily be generalized to attitude and personality research.

The bonds model is consistent with a conceptual model that represents the relation between genotype and phenotypes of various complexity that has been termed the *watershed model* and has been proposed in the literature by Cannon & Keller (2006; see also Penke, Denissen, & Miller, 2007, who use the model in the context of evolutionary psychology). The watershed model, graphically represented in Figure 6.7, incorporates the idea that variation in test scores results from the independent contribution of large numbers of antecedent factors that influence test scores. In the same way a river grows downstream as a result of the contribution of significant of numbers of streams that come to join it, abilities grow "downstream" by the contribution of lower-level processes and attributes. For instance, in psychometrics, one could view genetic differences as very far upstream, influencing the test scores via their contribution to more downstream cognitive and brain processes, which, with the additional input of education and experience, culminate in the ability to solve, say, an IQ-item correctly. Individual differences may then be interpreted to

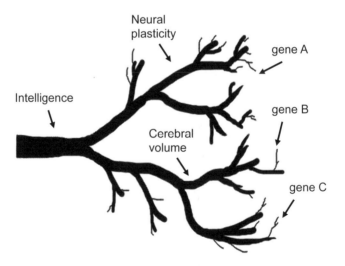

Figure 6.7 Watershed model of the Pathway Between Upstream Genes and Downstream Phenotypes. Substantial numbers of specific genes together influence variation in biological properties such as cerebral volume and neural plasticity. In turn, such properties contribute to variance in intelligence.

arise analogous to differences in the volumes of water in different rivers, resulting from myriads of differences in the antecedent processes.

The consequences of the bonds and watershed models for validity issues are significant. Should such a type of model be correct in a given domain of application, then it is by definition impossible to have causally unidimensional tests (naturally, test scores may still *seem* unidimensional, e.g., the data may statistically conform to a unidimensional model such as one depicting the items as being dependent on the same latent variable). The question of, say, "What does the extraversion scale of the NEO-PI measure?" then inherently has no single answer; rather the correct answer would be a long list of antecedent factors that induce (co)variation in item responses. Clearly, in such a case validation research would be extremely complicated; in fact, there currently does not exist a validation scheme or psychometric approach that allows for such a situation. However, perhaps the recent revival of the bonds model by Bartholomew, Deary, and Lawn (2009), as well as the attention to the watershed model in genetics, will change this situation.

6.4.3. Networks

If reflective latent variable models are interpreted as common cause models, then the unconditional associations between indicator variables are spurious, in the same sense as the correlation between the number of storks and the number of babies born in Macedonian villages is spurious. That is, the associations between observables result from their common dependence on the latent structure, rather than from direct relations between them.

This is not always equally plausible. For instance, consider the relation between symptoms for panic disorder. These include (a) the presence of panic attacks, (b) concern about having additional attacks, (c) worry about the attacks, and (d) a significant change in behavior associated with the attacks. One could model these relations as a function of a latent structure, but it is not clear that it is reasonable to do so, because it is likely that the relations between the indicator variables are not spurious at all. In particular, the presence of panic attacks has a central causal role in the system, as is indicated by the formulation of the symptoms (which refer back to the presence of panic attacks). One alternative for representing the relations between observables in such a case is by conceptualizing the variables as forming a causal network. An example of such a causal network is represented in Figure 6.8.

In general, causal systems can be analyzed by using techniques developed in causal modeling (Pearl, 2009; Spirtes, Glymour, & Scheines, 2000). For instance, if there are no feedback loops, a causal system is a Directed Acyclic Graph (DAG; Pearl, 2009) and entails conditional independence relations between the variables in the network (such relations

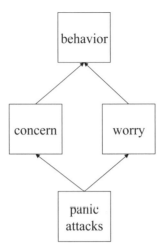

Figure 6.8 Network Model for Panic Disorder Symptoms (Borsboom, 2008b).

are not entailed by a latent variable model). Hence, in this case, a network model is testable and distinct from a latent variable system. However, in substantive research, it is often the case that reciprocal relations between variables are plausible. In this case, the difference between latent variable models and causal systems becomes less clear. For instance, if the network is fully connected (each node is connected to each other node) and all relations are reciprocal, the statistical predictions of a network model and a latent variable model may be equivalent.

An example of such a case that has been extensively discussed in a paper by Van der Maas et al. (2006) concerns the situation where the nodes in the network are continuous and the relations are mutualistic. In this case, increases in one variable promote increases in the other variables, and there are no inhibitory relations; the model is graphically represented in Figure 6.9. Van der Maas et al. (2006) showed that, in this case, the model is equivalent to a common factor model. In fact, they propose the mutualism model, as they call it, as a rival hypothesis to the *g*-factor in the explanation of the positive manifold in intelligence; the central idea is that, in development, cognitive systems such as working memory and processing speed co-evolve through mutualistic interactions. This leads to a positive manifold between measures of the performance of these subsystems (e.g., digit span and minimal inspection time). Cramer, Waldorp, Van der Maas, and Borsboom (2010) show how an analogous model may explain the excessive comorbidities often observed between psychopathological disorders.

Network models of psychological variables standing in reciprocal interactions have only just begun to be considered in psychometric theory; in the physical sciences, such models have been used more

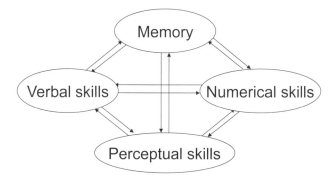

Figure 6.9 A Mutualistic Model of Intelligence. Van der Maas et al. (2006) propose that intelligence subtests have positive intercorrelations (form a positive manifold) because the skills they measure are reciprocally related during development, such that developing one skill is beneficial for the development of other skills.

frequently, for instance in modeling magnetic fields. The models are statistically complicated and present the modeler with significant problems, e.g., involving model fitting and parameter identification. Partly, such problems may be addressed through the use of dynamical systems models; however, it is too early to tell whether such approaches will be successful in psychology.

What we may address at this early stage, however, are consequences for thinking about constructs, observations, measurement and validity, assuming for the moment that there are cases in psychology, such as depression or intelligence research, where the network representation is broadly correct. These consequences are considerable. For instance, rather than the indicators being measures of a construct like depression, they should be considered a part of that construct—in this respect the relation between indicators and constructs is similar to that in the theory of behavioral domains. The problem of validity, viewed now as involving the correct representation of the construct–indicator relation, is no longer primarily one of establishing the right measurement relations, but of incorporating the right variables and establishing appropriate structural relations between them. Measurement problems are involved in relating the variables in the network to their real-world counterparts (e.g., relating the answer to the question "Are you tired?" to fatigue), but at the level that psychologists normally ask the validity question (how well does the item "Are you tired?" measure depression?), a conceptualization of the problem in terms of measurement may be fundamentally misguided. How one should go about in conducting validation research for test items that relate their constructs as nodes relate to networks is, at present, an open question.

Box 6.3. Alternative Conceptualizations of Personality

While there may still be disagreement on the number of factors that are necessary to adequately describe personality structure, there appears to be a relatively wide consensus on the appropriateness of factor analysis to analyze that structure. However, as has become clear in this chapter, reflective measurement models like the factor model are most appropriate when it is plausible that the item responses within a set of questions derive from a common cause (i.e., measure the same thing). It is not clear whether this conceptualization fits personality structure well; however, in the literature, few alternatives have been seriously considered. We shortly list a broad outline of such alternatives based on the models presented here.

Networks. Consider the conscientiousness items:

I don't seem to be completely successful at anything (SU)
Over the years I've done some pretty stupid things (ST)
Once I start a project, I almost always finish it (FI)
I have a clear set of goals and work toward them in an orderly fashion (OF)
I try to do jobs carefully, so they won't have to be done again (CF)
I never seem to be able to get organized (OR)

Such items may measure distinct characteristics that may relate logically and causally. For instance, if one does stupid things, then one will not be completely successful, ST → SU; if one is not able to get organized, one cannot work towards one's goals in an orderly fashion, OR → OF. A tentative causal model may look like this:

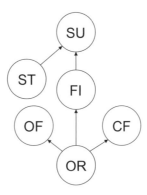

One can imagine building a network by working out similar chains for the entire space of personality items. If, in this network, the number of causal relations of factors within apparent traits is larger than between them, then one may expect a factor structure to emerge where the factors indicate dense causal systems, and between-factor correlations reflect sparser cross-trait relations (e.g., see Van der Maas et al, 2006).

Bonds. How do people answer personality test items? Consider the above examples from the conscientiousness domain. The participant has to indicate to what extent the statements mentioned applies to him or her. The response process plausibly involves the participant searching for evidence in favor of or against the hypothesis that a statement correctly describes him or her. Given the fair amount of semantic overlap between the items, it is likely that what counts as evidence for one item (say, when answering the item "I've done some pretty stupid things", the person recalls having messed up a project at work), also counts as evidence for another (say, "I don't seem to be completely successful"). In this case, item covariation may arise from the fact that the item response processes partially sample the same evidence, mainly across within-trait items; sets of such pieces of evidence may be considered bonds, since they influence distinct items in various constellations.

Reactive indicators. If pieces of evidence for statements function as bonds in a person's response process, then it is likely that retrieving a piece of evidence (e.g., the person remembers having messed up a project, as in the previous example) increases the availability, in memory, of that particular piece of evidence when another item is administered. If this happens, the item that is administered first functions as a prime for the evidence that affects the answer to the secondly administered item. Series of items may then be considered reactive.

Formative structure. Supposing that any one, or a mixture of, processes like the above are at play in determining the item covariation which serves as the empirical evidence for the Five Factors of personality, one may hesitate to infer from analyses of that covariation that it arises from the effect of five fundamental traits. Moreover, as has been indicated in Box 6.1, most analyses on personality data have been carried out using formative modeling techniques like PCA. One interpretation of the results of such analyses would be that five composites suffice to describe a sizeable portion of the covariance between personality items, but that the processes that generate the covariance structure of the items may be more in line with those described in the above alternative account.

If this analysis turns out correct, then the Five Factors should be interpreted as higher-level descriptive terms, rather than as underlying causes of item responses. In addition, the question of how, exactly, item covariation arises may be given more scientific attention than it has so far enjoyed.

6.5. Chapter Conclusion

An essential element of validity concerns the problem of finding an appropriate way to represent the relation between the theoretical attribute and the items or tests that are used to assess it. This chapter has discussed two ways of representing this relation as a causal one; in the reflective model, the theoretical attribute is represented as a hypothetical common cause of the item responses, whereas in the formative model it is represented as the common effect of the item responses. In addition, we highlighted other ways of thinking about the relation between test scores and attributes. The distinction between reflective and formative models represents an important idea in causal thinking about measurement. However, it only relates to the directionality of the causal relations in the models. That is, reflective and formative models do not specify what such causal relations are or how they are best interpreted. The next two chapters unpack this issue, by applying different theories of causation to interpret the causal pathways in reflective and formative models.

6.6. Further Reading

Bartholomew, D. J., Deary, I. J. and Lawn, M. (2009). A new lease of life for Thomson's bonds model for intelligence. *Psychological Review, 116,* 567–579.

Bollen, K. A., & Lennox, R. (1991). Conventional wisdom on measurement: A structural equation perspective. *Psychological Bulletin, 110,* 305–314.

Cannon, T. D., & Keller, M. C. (2006). Endophenotypes in genetic analyses of mental disorders. *Annual Review of Clinical Psychology, 2,* 267–290.

Cramer, A. O. J., Waldorp, L. J., van der Maas, H., & Borsboom, D. *(2010).* Comorbidity: A network perspective. *Behavioral and Brain Sciences, 33,* 137–193.

Edwards, J. R., & Bagozzi, R. P. (2000). On the nature and direction of relationships between constructs and measures. *Psychological Methods,5,* 155–174.

Van der Maas, H. L. J., Dolan, C. V., Grasman, R. P. P. P., Wicherts, J. M., Huizenga, H. M., & Raijmakers, M. E. J. (2006). A dynamical model of general intelligence: The positive manifold of intelligence by mutualism. *Psychological Review, 113,* 842–861.

7 Causation, Correlation, and Reflective Measurement Models

Connections With Other Chapters

Chapter 5 considered behavior domains as an alternative to causal measurement models. Chapter 6 considered various causal measurement models. A primary distinction from chapter 6 involves the distinction between reflective measurement models in which latent variables cause their indicators and formative measurement models in which indices cause their latent variables. The present chapter focuses primarily on the former, leaving formative measurement models and various alternatives to chapter 8. The present chapter also develops the distinction between statistically unidimensional models and causally unidimensional models mentioned in chapter 6. Statistical models need not be causally unidimensional. As noted in chapter 1, we adopt from the literature the term 'measurement model' but use this to describe assessment in general whether or not it involves the types of quantitative structure required by a strict sense of measurement (reviewed in chapter 2). Chapter 10 further develops the idea of interpretation and develops a rough criterion for deciding what interpretation to validate. Chapter 12 further applies material from this chapter to the process of test validation.

The methodological literature in the behavioral sciences generally discusses causation without broaching the issue that theories of causation attempt to answer. What do causal assertions mean when they refer to causation? Yet the answer to this question is crucial to understanding what a causal claim entails, and thus how one can test it empirically. The present chapter will consider some major approaches to understanding causation from the causation literature and relate them to issues of assessment. Different understandings of the term 'causation' differ from one another in at least two respects. They differ in terms of what they assume. They also differ in terms of what they deliver with respect to what causal assertions assert and what they entail. The basic strategy of the chapter will unfold as follows. First, a purely statistical, non-causal interpretation of measurement models provides a baseline for comparison. Then an evaluation of what a causal interpretation might add to a non-causal interpretation provides some sense of what one might want from a causal interpretation. What one might want then provides a framework for contrasting various causal interpretations.

Box 7.1. Measurement Invariance, DIF, and Bias

This chapter will make use of the measurement of competency to stand trial as a running example. The specifics reflect competency to stand trial as understood in the United States, but the general construct applies with variations to other legal systems. The broader validity issues readily translate to other legal systems and other constructs more generally. In the United States, the decision of Dusky v. United States (1960) resulted in the understanding of competency to stand trial in terms of three basic domains: (1) The ability to consult with one's lawyer, (2) the ability to factually understand court proceedings, and (3) the ability to rationally understand one's own court proceedings (Rogers, Jackson, Sewell, Tillbrook, & Martin, 2003).

The *Evaluation of Competency to Stand Trial—Revised* (ECST-R) assesses each of these three dimensions of competency to stand trial and malingering using a semi-structured interview format (Rogers, Tillbrook, and Sewell, 2004). Rogers et al. (2003) found that a three-factor model fit the data better than factor models derived from other theories of competence that postulated only one or two factors. Most items on the ECST-R involve multiple prompts, and the score for a given item typically equals the highest score among the prompts for that item. The *consult with counsel* scale and the *factual understanding* scale each contain 6 items, and the *rational understanding scale* contains 7. 28 additional items that measure four types of malingering: realistic, psychotic, non-psychotic, and impairment. The first three of these constitute non-overlapping scales, whereas the fourth includes some items from the first three. The competency items typically use a 0 to 4 coding whereas the malingering items use a 0 to 2 coding, except the impairment scale which uses 0 to 1.

For present purposes, consider a measure of the ability to factually understand court proceedings. Psychologists generally understand this to involve a basic knowledge of how the court works. For example, what the judge does, what the jury does, what the opposing lawyers do, and so on. According to a causal theory of measurement, the defendant's level of knowledge and understanding of these facts about courtrooms should cause the level of his or her test responses, and thus his or her score on the test. Such a test would then provide a useful source of information for psychologists tasked with assessing the competence to stand trial of defendants.

A theory of causal inference tells researchers how to collect and analyze data that will help determine the empirical support for this causal hypothesis. For example, known group studies administer tests to two groups of individuals known to differ on the variable assessed by the test, and compare their test scores. Stronger evidence might come from attempts to manipulate factual knowledge of court proceedings, or from the introduction of research design elements intended to rule out plausible rival hypotheses such as pretests, nonequivalent control groups, or statistical control for covariates.

In contrast, a theory of causation tells about the content of the hypothesis that knowledge and understanding cause test scores. The more fully one understands what such a hypothesis entails, the better position one is in to identify testable consequences of this hypothesis. Theories of causal inference generally begin with fairly vague notions of causation and draw out general implications that apply to any causal hypothesis. In many cases, fairly minimal assumptions about causation indeed produce fairly substantial and detailed implications about testable consequences. Nonetheless, these agnostic approaches can subsume distinct causal hypotheses that may have important consequences for measurement but no distinguishable empirical consequences under such vague terms of description.

For example, in the legal context, psychological assessment often involves a mixture of truthful responses to questions, and deceptive responses, described as *malingering*, in which the respondent attempts to fake a lower or higher score to obtain some legal advantage. In other words, the legal context involves very high-stakes testing, and invites uncooperative responses as a consequence. One could imagine a hypothetical situation in which test scores tend to covary with understanding of the legal system. However, attempts to manipulate understanding fail to influence test scores because the very attempt triggers malingering. In this example, as long as one does not intervene in the system, one gets a stable pattern of causal influence, but upon intervention the pattern is disrupted.

7.1. Reflective Measurement With and Without Causation

Throughout this chapter, as elsewhere, the term 'model' refers to the equations or path diagram. The interpretation of the model refers to the mapping of the elements of the model onto elements of the theory. Typically, variables in the model map onto variables in the theory. Coefficients in the model map on to specific interpretations of the type of relationship between variables that they represent. As such, one can interpret a reflective measurement model without any causal interpretation of the effect coefficients. Alternatively, one can enrich the model with a causal interpretation. The extent to which this interpretation enriches the model depends upon what and how much the causal interpretation adds over and above the non-causal interpretation. As such, the latter provides a baseline for comparison of causal interpretations.

7.1.1. Uses of Non-causal Interpretations

A non-causal interpretation comports well with the view that causation serves as a pre-scientific concept replaced by various statistical associations in a mature science (Hammond, 1996; Pearson, 1900, Russell, 1913). Understood this way, a reflective measurement model provides several useful things. It provides a parsimonious summary of a joint probability distribution for the items. Even without the inferred common cause, the model entails local independence, $P(x_i|F) = P(x_i|F, x_j)$, which is the same as to say that the items are stochastically independent conditioned on the latent variables $(x_i \perp x_j)|F$, where x_i and x_j are distinct items $(i \neq j)$ and F is the latent variable that accounts for their shared variance. The strength of the association between the latent variable and the items gives an indication of how much variance the items have in common, and thus how much information they provide about the latent variable. None of these uses requires a causal interpretation of the measurement model.

As an example, imagine an organization that provides a variety of services to new immigrants to help them adapt to their new country of residence. These might include providing direct assistance with immigration procedures, second-language instruction, providing assistance with employment, and assistance with community integration such as participation in schools, elections, and civic events. Suppose that the program offering these services constructs a survey for those using them asking for their degree of satisfaction with each of 15 services. Such a set of items sampled from the domain of services may or may not form a unidimensional scale. If it does, then we might expect a reflective measurement model with one latent variable to fit the items. For concreteness, suppose that the items use a 7-point Likert scale and that they fit a linear factor model with one common factor and 15 uncorrelated unique variances. Having fit this model, the program might conclude that the items measure a common dimension of satisfaction with the program services and that the sum score provides a useful overall measure of this level of satisfaction. To the extent that the proportion of item variance accounted for by the common factor remains high and consistent across items, the developers of the instrument might feel increasingly comfortable with the measurement properties of the scale.

Nothing of this use of the model requires a causal interpretation. The linear factor model functions like a predictive regression model, with the loadings estimating the optimal linear predictions of the item responses from the common factor. Indeed, to summarize the joint probability distribution, the test developers need not even infer the existence of an overall level of satisfaction represented by the common factor. They could instead simply interpret the factor analysis as an exercise in variance partitioning with the common factor a purely statistical representation of shared variance between the items. Alternatively, the test developers could adopt a behavioral domain interpretation where each satisfaction response to a specific service represents a sample response from an infinite domain. The program may not offer an infinite number of services, but one can understand that as a limit on the number of responses that one can conveniently sample from the domain rather than a limitation on the domain itself. For example, if the program offered dentist referrals, then the model would relate those responses to the behavioral domain in a similar manner to those services which were actually offered and sampled in the scale. However, the goal here is to consider how much of what one gets from a causal interpretation one can get from a non-causal interpretation. So, for present purposes, let us assume that the test developers interpret the common factor as representing an evaluative cognition of the service users. Even giving the common factor such an interpretation, the model has a purely predictive, statistical interpretation that does not rest on inference from local independence to a common cause (Haig, 2005).

7.1.2. General Causal Interpretation of a Reflective Measurement Model

Given the non-causal interpretation outlined in the previous section, one can next add a causal interpretation and ask what more one can get from a reflective measurement model that one cannot get from the non-causal interpretation of the same model. At present, let us consider a vague causal interpretation as commonly assumed in the methodological and measurement literatures of the behavioral sciences. One can take this vague notion of causation in one of two ways. One can take it as agnostic to the specifics about the exact details of the causal relation applied to measurement models. Alternatively, one can take it as incompletely specifying a specific understanding of causation as the appropriate understanding for measurement models. Nothing much turns on this distinction for present purposes.

At a very general level, however, behavioral sciences typically make a few basic assumptions about causation which often appear in introductory methodology texts. First, causation between variables has a specified direction: Saying that satisfaction causes satisfaction ratings differs from saying that satisfaction ratings cause satisfaction. Second, causes precede their effects, or at least do not follow them in time: Saying that satisfaction causes test scores entails that test takers have the satisfaction level at or before the time that they complete the test. Third, causation has transitivity. If satisfaction causes satisfaction ratings and satisfaction ratings cause funding decisions, then satisfaction causes funding decisions. Fourth, variables can correlate for reasons other than causation between them. However, if one variable causes another, absent balancing contrary causes of the same effect, then one can expect a correlation between the cause and effect. Fifth, observed changes in effects typically accompany manipulated changes in causes but not vice versa. Higher satisfaction increases satisfaction ratings. However, higher satisfaction ratings do not necessarily increase satisfaction. Finally, causes are distinct from their effects. Nothing causes itself or part of itself.

Given these basic assumptions, what value could a causal interpretation offer over and above a purely statistical interpretation of a measurement model? One can make this question more precise by asking what one can conclude from the assertion that the construct causes item scores that one cannot conclude from the assertion that the same scores fit a common factor model. The present chapter will explore three answers to this question. (1) The causal assertion provides greater reason to believe that interventions on the construct will affect the scores. (2) The causal assertion provides greater reason to believe that the probabilistic relationship will persist into the future. (3) The causal assertion provides greater reason to believe that the probabilistic relationship will remain robust to the right kinds of interventions. The three ideas amplify one another by working together to create greater possibilities for validation research and for stronger validity arguments.

7.1.3. Advantage 1: Interventions on the Construct

Consider the factual understanding subscale of the ECST-R. It seems plausible to suppose that if one began with individuals with little understanding of courtroom practices in the United States, but with the ability to understand the practices and no motivation to feign incompetence, that their scores would increase following instruction regarding courtroom practices. This result follows naturally from a causal measurement model. Suppose, instead, however that one begins with only the probabilistic model of test scores in relation to the common factor. If f_1 and f_2

represent levels of factual understanding such that $f_1 < f_2$, then $P(X|f_1)$ and $P(X|f_2)$ represent the probability distribution of item scores (X) conditioned on the given level of factual understanding. For example, an item scored <0, 1, 2, 3, 4> might have $P(X|f_1)$ = <.2, .3, .3, .1, .1> and $P(X|f_2)$ = <.1, .2, .2, .3, .2> indicating, for example, that full credit responses (scored as 4) occur 10 percent of the time before training and 20 percent of the time after training. Thus one could reason that, prior to training, if an individual has the level of understanding represented by f_1 then $P(X|f_1)$ gives the correct conditional probability distribution of the item scores. Contrariwise, if the person has the f_2 level, then $P(X|f_2)$ gives the correct conditional probability. Thus, if training changes the level of understanding from f_1 to f_2 then the probabilistic model would predict the corresponding change in item responses.

The difficulty with this line of reasoning involves the population characterized by the conditional probabilities. The probability estimates come from the observed populations with these levels of understanding. The inference requires a further assumption that the population of individuals manipulated to have a given level share the same conditional item probability distribution as those naturally observed with that level of understanding. This assumption may not hold. The spurious measurement model of Edwards and Bagozzi (2000) offers an example (discussed in chapter 6 as indirect). Suppose that the training targets specific procedural knowledge (f) but the items on the ECST-R respond to general semantic knowledge (g). However, g causes f instead of f causing g (Figure 7.1). In that case, the observed conditional probability distribution $P(X|f)$ holds because f and X share g as a common cause. However, interventions on f break the causal link between g and f and thus also disrupt the observed conditional

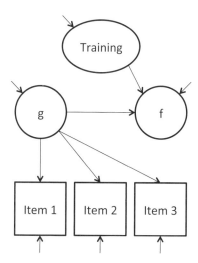

Figure 7.1 Spurious Measurement Model.

probability distributions. As such, if one only has a probabilistic model linking X to f, this does not offer as much support for the inference that f training will increase X responses. In contrast, if one has independent support for a causal interpretation of the reflective measurement model, then this allows one to reject alternative causal explanations such as that depicted by the spurious measurement model.

7.1.4. Advantage 2: Persistence of Probabilistic Relationships

Turning to the second advantage of causal models over non-causal models, consider the previously presented conditional probability distributions of item responses. Any estimates one has of these must come only from past cases because one cannot observe the future. So, in keeping with the classical riddle of induction, why should one expect future cases to follow the same pattern? For clarity, it helps to distinguish two interpretations of $P(X|f)$. One can interpret f as a direct reference to a latent variable that has its values independent of any observation of them, or one can interpret f as whatever common factor emerges from the factor analysis of ECST-R factual understanding scores. Now return to the spurious measurement model described above. Imagine something like the Flynn Effect producing a consistent rise in one type of knowledge while f refers to the other. Over time, this will result in a change in $P(X|f)$ with the items becoming either easier or more difficult over time depending upon which type of understanding increases and which kind f refers to. Either way, the probabilistic relationship between f and factual understanding item scores changes over time. One can construct a more dramatic example by replacing slow gradual change with a change associated with a particular historical event. For example, the probabilistic relationship $P(X|f)$ might remain relatively constant for decades, and then change abruptly due to increased popularity of courtroom procedural television shows during the first decade of the 21st century in the United States. Figure 7.2 illustrates the case for an item scored 0, 1 or 2. The conditional probabilities shift to the right on the f scale at time 2 but remain constant over time with respect to g. The vertical axis gives the probability of a given response. The f and g scales are given on the horizontal axis. The X > 0 curve is never below the X > 1 curve for a given f value. This holds because all responses above 1 also fall above 0 (i.e., responses coded 2). In contrast, responses of 1 are above zero but not above 1.

The second case involves taking f as referring to whatever common factor the factual understanding items share in common, allowing that this common factor might change. In other words, the same items might retain the same factor structure but the identity of the shared variance might change from one occasion to another. Consider two orthogonal factors f_a and f_b, perhaps representing semantic and procedural knowledge. Now, imagine writing a two-factor model with weights applied to

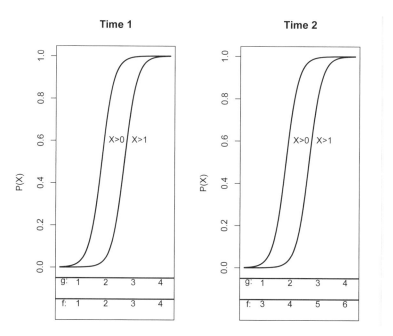

Figure 7.2 Conditional Probability of X given f and g at Two Times.

the product of each factor with its loading for a given item: $X = w_a(lf_a) + w_b(lf_b) + e$ where $w_a + w_b = 1$ and the factor loadings on each f factor are equal. The circumstances are quite unusual, but one could under such circumstances envision a shift, say in increase in w_a from time 1 to time 2, by which the identity of the common factor would shift from $w_af_a + w_bf_b$ to $(w_a + k)f_a + (w_b - k)f_b$ from the first time to the second, for some small constant k. Now, loosen the assumption that the loadings equal one another, such that $l_a \neq l_b$. Under this model, the loadings do not factor out, and thus the observed loadings will vary from time 1 to time 2 with the change in w_a and w_b when the single common factor model is applied to the factual understanding item scores.

The advantage of a causal measurement model in the above two cases depends upon how one introduces such a causal interpretation. If one simply estimates causal effects from past observations and seeks to generalize these to future instances based only on statistical induction, then one reproduces the same problem with slightly different labels. In both the non-causal and causal cases, one seems to need an unfounded assumption that the future will resemble the past. To obtain the advantage of a causal interpretation, one must give that interpretation some content beyond nomothetic causal effects represented by factor loadings or other effect coefficients in a structural model. One needs to link these causal effects to a causal process that underlies them (discussed in detail in sections 7.2.3 and 7.3.3). In the present example, the process would involve the cognitive processing. This processing begins from interpreting the assessor's question. It then involves recalling the required information from long-term memory and using the information to construct and answer. It ends with expressing the answer to the assessor. The process might also involve the interpersonal process of question and answer exchanges between the assessor and the respondent. Suitably elaborated, such a detailed causal account requires a much larger change to support a change in $P(X|f)$ than does an account based only on the non-causal statistical relationships. For example, suppose that $P(X|f)$ for some particular response on some particular item equals .30. If one takes this probability as a given law of nature, then one need only imagine that the law ceases to apply and a new one takes its place. If, on the other hand, one takes this probability as derivative of the process account of how respondents process ECST-R factual understanding items, then a change in probability entails further changes somewhere in the response process of a very specific type. Simply increasing the average knowledge level will not change the conditional probability for a fixed knowledge level. So, there would have to be an accompanying change in how respondents process the questions that resulted in a different probability for the response conditioned on the same fixed level of knowledge. Ancillary information about the responses processes provides further grounds to generalize from past to future.

7.1.5. Advantage 3: Robustness to Interventions

The third advantage of the causal measurement model involves greater reason to expect the probabilistic relationship to remain in place under a broader range of interventions than just manipulations of the focal construct as considered under the first advantage. One example of this involves typical measurement invariance type situations. For example, one might like to compare the factual understanding of defendants represented by public defenders to those represented by private counsel. Such group comparisons assume a fixed measurement model across comparison groups. Suppose that one were evaluating a program to provide private attorneys for defendants who would otherwise be represented by public defenders. Given only observed associations between factual understanding and the items that measure it, one has less of a basis to conclude that the intervention will not change these observed associations. For example, it may happen that the current public defender and private attorney populations each constitute a nearly equal mix of two causally heterogeneous subpopulations. Further, it may happen that the criteria for the program under evaluation result in selecting, from those with public defenders, individuals from one of these two subpopulations, changing the proportion of these in both the public defender and private attorney groups. As a result, the mixtures of the two subpopulations in the two populations change and so do the conditional probabilities for each population. If one begins with a causal measurement model, however, one has a stronger basis from which to infer stability under intervention. If the causal model with no subpopulations holds true, then the above phenomenon based on shifting mixtures cannot occur. If the causally heterogeneous subpopulations exist, then a correct causal measurement model would incorporate these differences and use separate measurement parameters rather than taking an average across a heterogeneous population. Either way, the parameters of a causally correct measurement model would not change as a result of the program to provide private attorney representation.

This last advantage of a causal measurement model, however, only applies to the right kinds of interventions. If one were to coach defendants on only the items covered in the ECST-R, then their responses might no longer reflect their actual overall factual understanding. In that case, defendants not competent to stand trial might be wrongly deemed competent because the relationship between the test scores and the focal construct had changed due to the intervention.

The illustrations of the three advantages in this section have each followed a common line of argument. Contrasting causal models were identified that produce the same conditional probability distributions under one condition, but differ under another condition. Because the non-causal measurement model remains consistent with either causal model, it does not provide a basis for inferences where the two causal models differ. However, if one begins with a causal measurement model, this removes the indeterminacy and provides a stronger basis for the desired conclusions. This line of reasoning assumes that causal structures produce statistical associations. One could counter that causal measurement models might not hold the three advantages over non-causal measurement models if the observed associations resulted from something other than underlying causal structures. The objection is sound, but not as ontologically innocent as it may sound. That causes produce associations remains the best available theory of how the socio-behavioral world works. Moreover, it seems unclear that any plausible alternative theory provides a picture of the world in which causal measurement models would fail to provide a stronger inferential base than non-causal measurement models.

Above, we have briefly explored three advantages to causally interpreting measurement models. In later sections we explore these in greater detail in relation to different specific notions of causation. Before moving on to that topic, however, in the next section we look at the distinction between probabilistic interpretations and causal interpretations of reflective models as they relate to the unidimensionality of tests.

7.2. Statistical Unidimensionality versus Causal Unidimensionality

Bollen and Lennox (1991) provided the following interesting argument against content domain sampling. Assume that the test conforms to a unidimensional reflective measurement model with independent unique variances for each item. The remainder of this section takes this as implicit in the term unidimensional because correlated errors introduce additional dimensions even if not explicitly represented in the model as common factors. Such a model entails exchangeability of equally reliable items in terms of test construction. Any subset of an equally reliable set of items provides the same quality of measurement of the construct. Thus domain sampling has no role to play. Conversely, if different items reflect different facets of the construct, then these introduce multidimensionality that violates the unidimensional model and the test should be modeled with an appropriately dimensioned measurement model. In terms of the competency test, Figure 7.3 depicts a reflective measurement model for eight competency items that models the items as both causally and statistically unidimensional. As the general level of competency rises or falls, the item responses (or probabilities of correct responses) rise and fall accordingly. If all the items have comparable reliability, then items 1 to 4 measure competency just as well as any other subset of four items. It makes no difference to which courtroom actors or tasks the items make reference. If the argument is correct, unidimensionality makes content domain sampling irrelevant to test validity.

The problematic step in the above argument involves the move from statistical unidimensionality to causal unidimensionality. The general theme of this chapter relates to the ways in which the content of causal measurement models exceed that of statistical measurement models. So

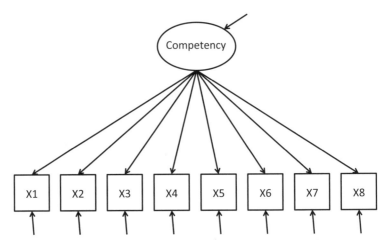

Figure 7.3 Causally Unidimensional Competency Model.

long as the content of the former exceeds the latter, one cannot infer causal unidimensionality from statistical unidimensionality. Causal unidimensionality constitutes a stronger claim than mere statistical unidimensionality. To illustrate this, consider Figure 7.4 which illustrates a statistically unidimensional but causally multidimensional reflective measurement model. The model assumes no malingering, contrary to the example in Box 7.1.

In the model depicted in Figure 7.4, the perfect correlations between the common factors combined with the orthogonal unique variances assure statistical unidimensionality. This follows a fairly standard approach to testing dimensional hypotheses (Hayashi, Bentler and Yuan, 2007). However, the causal explanation embodied in the model has four dimensions. From a purely statistical perspective, these are four names for the same statistical dimension. From a causal perspective, however, the models are not equivalent in content. To get a handle on this difference, it helps to think in terms of the range of cases for which statistical versus causal claims hold. Purely statistical claims refer to actual cases from an actual population only. In contrast, causal claims often refer to these and also to counterfactual cases that result from counter-to-fact modifications to the population as it actually, i.e., factually, exists (Markus, 2008a). This gives causal assertions surplus content over and above purely statistical assertions. According to the model depicted in Figure 7.4, it is possible, at least in theory, to manipulate someone's knowledge of a judge's role in

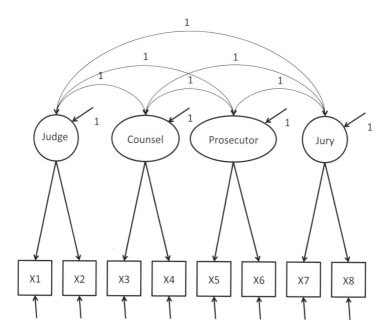

Figure 7.4 Statistically Unidimensional Competency Model.

the courtroom without comparable changes in his or her knowledge of the roles of defense counsel, the prosecutor, and the jury. Indeed, one can readily imagine doing this with a training program before the test. Let us assume for the moment that the impact of this intervention is linear on responses to the first two items (x_1 and x_2). In this case, the post-intervention scores would still fit the unidimensional model depicted in Figure 7.3 (and Figure 7.4), but the specific values of the item parameters would change. These changes would indicate that the judge items (the first two) became easier post-intervention. Nonetheless, despite still fitting a unidimensional model, such an intervention would provide evidence in favor of the model depicted in Figure 7.4 and against the model depicted in Figure 7.3. For the single-factor model (Figure 7.3), there is simply no causal mechanism by which the training could effect this change. A change to the common factor would affect all items, and parallel interventions via the unique factors of the first two items would violate orthogonality of the unique factors. Given that the same experimental evidence would confirm one model and disconfirm the other, they clearly differ in content. If one more realistically assumes a fan-curve growth model such that those who come to the training with more knowledge learn more, then the difference becomes even more dramatic. As a result of the nonlinear effect of the intervention, such that those with higher initial knowledge learn more, the linear correlations between the four causal factors depicted in Figure 7.4 will change and the test will cease to fit a unidimensional model. As an extreme example, if learning follows the function $J_{post} = 2 \wedge J_{pre}$ then the correlation between understanding of the judge's role and understanding of the defense counsel's role drops from r = 1.00 before training (J_{pre}) to r = .57 after training (J_{post}) if J_{pre} has a mean of 5 and a standard deviation of 2. By its very nature, the model depicted in Figure 7.3 cannot represent a causal intervention that would make the test multidimensional. Of course, the chances of perfectly correlated causal factors may appear vanishingly small but multicolinear causal factors might easily approach this extreme for all practical purposes in test development without population correlations of exactly one.

   Having established that the two models shown in the two figures represent statistically equivalent models with different causal content, let us return to the criticism offered by Bollen and Lennox. Despite fitting the unidimensional model, a test made up of the depicted items seems like a better measure of overall competence in factual understanding of courtroom procedures than a test made up of eight items about the role of the judge. For statistical purposes, the single-factor model depicted in Figure 7.3 offers a perfectly good psychometric model for estimating reliability and such. One need not model multiple dimensions for such purposes. Nonetheless, on any causal theory of measurement (which Bollen and Lennox gave every appearance of assuming in their discussion) or indeed any theory that makes measurement more than mere statistical association, the two models differ in content. If, as Guilford (1946) famously stated, a test is valid for anything with which it correlates, then item 1 (x_1) is as valid a measure of factual understanding of the role of the jury as of factual understanding of the role of the judge, even though the content of the item asks about the role of the judge. The model depicted in Figure 7.3 offers no basis to challenge this view. In contrast, on a causal theory of measurement, the model depicted in Figure 7.4 only allows that the first two items measure understanding of the judge's role, and that these two items only measure this construct. One can use understanding of the judge's role to very accurately predict understanding of the jury's role, but this differs from using a measure of the former to measure the latter. For this reason, contrary to Bollen and Lennox's conclusion, unidimensionality does not entail that interchangeability between the items. Sampling from the full item domain still improves the validity of the test as a measure of the full domain of factual understanding of courtroom procedures. Moreover, in the case of perfect colinearity, one need not introduce a statistically multidimensional model to model a causally multidimensional test. In this case, the breadth of the domain is introduced in possibility but not in actuality, as such possible multidimensionality need not entail actual multidimensionality. In other words, the deviations from statistical unidimensionality remain unactualized possibilities for an actually unidimensional test.

The argument against content sampling outlined above appears central to the support for a further criticism for which Bollen and Lennox provided little explicit argument. This further criticism rejects the idea that test developers should seek optimal levels of correlation between items on a test because overly high correlations indicate too much item overlap. It thus becomes interesting to reconstruct the support for the critique of optimal levels of correlation, especially in light of the cautions regarding the argument against content sampling just discussed. If the causal model depicted in Figure 7.3 underlies the generation of item scores, then the unique factors provide the only source of uncorrelated variance in the items. These factors, however, do not provide any reliable variance, they function like random number generators clouding the representation of the construct by the item scores. As a result, reduced correlations correspond exactly to increased unreliability, and in this case reduced validity in the sense that the items provide less information about the construct. As such, under this causal model, higher correlations correspond to better items. (Note that this argument requires that Figure 7.3 give the correct causal model and not just a correct statistical model—there can be no hidden causes in the unique variances.)

Faced with this argument, let us now consider the kind of context in which the advice against maximal inter-item correlations seems plausible. First, there are cases such as those considered by Bollen and Lennox in which the items fall into a small number of clusters that should be modeled as separate correlated constructs. For example, if our test included only the actor facet and only items about the judge, defense counsel, prosecutor and jury, then a four-factor model such as that shown in Figure 7.4 but with the covariance constraints relaxed might provide an appropriate measurement model. As Bollen and Lennox suggested, in this case the optimal level of correlation would be less than one and would be implied by the covariance structure of the model. However, there is a further case, which is really just a shading-off from the above case, that Bollen and Lennox did not consider. Suppose that we have six facets each with ten different values used to generate items. This would yield a measurement model with 60 common factors and a complex pattern of crossloading in which each item loads on six factors (one from each set of ten). One would sample items from a matrix with 10 ** 6 = 1,000,000 cells, requiring at least 30 items to provide three items loading on each factor. If, for simplicity, we assume a linear factor model, at seven measurement parameters per item, even a relatively short 30-item test would require the estimation of 210 item parameters and 1,770 factor covariances. This compares to 60 item parameters and 15 factor covariances for a simple six-factor model with no crossloadings. At some point, the sheer complexity of the model makes estimation impractical (indeed, without further constraints, one requires 67 items to achieve positive degrees of freedom). In such circumstances, one would expect items that share more facets to show higher correlations, but it still seems reasonable to approximate the measurement model with a single-factor model, particularly if the items were sampled from the 10**6 cells in such a way as to minimize the correlation of facet values across items. This latter case seems like a case where the unidimensional measurement model makes sense as an approximation, but one would still view a test with excessively high item correlations with suspicion.

As noted earlier in this section, the above considerations do not detract from Bollen and Lennox's basic message that the measurement model serves as the basis for practical decisions about the item construction, and rules of thumb about observed item statistics need to be evaluated in terms of the assumed measurement model. If anything, the above considerations extend this basic thesis further by considering the causal nature of the measurement model in more detail. Bollen and Lennox considered the statistical implications of a causal measurement model in some detail but did not fully work through the extra-statistical implications that play a crucial role in distinguishing causation from correlation. The considerations outlined in this section apply broadly to any notion of causation sufficiently strong to support counterfactual inferences from causal assertions. Indeed, even a relatively weak regularity theory (discussed below) would require something to distinguish causation from correlation. That something would most likely support the distinctions between causal unidimensionality and statistical unidimensionality elaborated above. As a result, consideration of the extra-statistical implications of the measurement model further refines the criticism of classical measurement premises offered by Bollen and Lennox some two decades ago.

In summary, one might modify the advice given to the developers of the hypothetical competency test as follows. First, even if the test fits a unidimensional statistical model, it makes sense to seek to achieve representativeness of the full construct domain if the underlying construct theory involves causal multidimensionality. Second, if the simple causal description of item responses represented by a single causal factor seems plausible, then maximizing inter-item correlations makes sense, but if the unidimensional model merely represents a useful approximation for a complex causal description, then a lower level of inter-item correlation may optimize the performance of the test. More broadly, these further considerations strengthen the advice to test developers to focus on an underlying measurement model before applying ad hoc principles in developing a test to confirm that the principles apply to the test in question. The present considerations extend this advice by emphasizing the need to distinguish causal from merely statistical measurement models, and attend to the implications that causal models have for counterfactual possibilities in excess of actual populations in their actual states. The idea that experimental manipulation has a role in test validation is nothing new (e.g., Messick, 1989) but the present considerations extend and broaden the underlying theory of the role played by such evidence in test development and validation.

7.3. Three General Theories of Causation

The present chapter considers three basic types of theories of causation: regularity theories, counterfactual theories, and process theories (Beebee, Hitchcock & Menzies, 2009; Markus, 2010; Psillos, 2002). The list is not exhaustive. Moreover, the chapter does not provide a comprehensive discussion of any of these, but does attempt to discuss each in sufficient detail to bring out some useful connections with measurement theory. Regularity theories are considered first because they are the oldest of the three approaches and attempt to explain causation with the fewest assumptions. Because of both their provenance and their parsimony, many consider regularity theories the standard against which to judge alternative theories.

As formulated here, counterfactual theories attempt to explain causation a little better by giving up a little in the form of further assumptions. The term is now widely familiar to behavioral scientists thanks to applications of counterfactual reasoning in the methodology literature (Morgan & Winship, 2007; Pearl, 2009; Rubin, 1974). Nonetheless, many such current approaches that incorporate counterfactuals do not strictly fall into this category. For example, Rubin's Causal Model provides a counterfactual analysis of causal effects, but does not attempt to provide a counterfactual analysis of causation itself (Rubin, 1974). Pearl's (2009) theory relates causation to closely related concepts, but does not attempt a reductive analysis (Woodward, 2003). It is not necessarily inconsistent to adopt a regularity approach to answering some questions about causation and a counterfactual approach to answering others. However, as narrowly formulated here, regularity and counterfactual theories present competing reductive accounts of causation. Each reduces causation to something different from the other. (Paul, 2009, provides a broader characterization that treats counterfactual approaches as compatible with regularity approaches.)

Finally, the chapter considers process theories. These enjoy neither the canonical status of regularity theories nor the current popularity of counterfactual theories. Moreover, readers primarily familiar with the statistical literature may find them less familiar because they do not translate causation into statistical terms as readily as regularity and counterfactual theories. They characteristically assume that causation must involve more than just associations and dependencies (Cartwright, 1989, 1999). As such, they have received less attention in statistics, measurement, and methodology literature. However, they approach the issue of causation in a dramatically different way that captures some central intuitions associated with everyday causal talk. They represent a longstanding tradition in the causation literature, and they have useful applications in measurement.

7.3.1. Regularity Theories of Causation

Regularity theories attempt to explain causation in terms of more basic regularities of nature. For example, assume a robust causal relationship in second language learning between interaction using the second language and performance in the course. By almost any lights, this relationship does not present a plausible candidate for a basic law. Instead, a regularity theory would seek to explain this causal relationship in terms of more basic regularities between classes of events. For example, a classical learning theorist might try to explain this relationship in terms of the reinforcement of correct second language use and the extinguishing of errors. A more cognitive approach might try to explain it in terms of more basic laws relating the depth of encoding to exposure to new and varied examples. For the reasons illustrated in these examples, regularity theories generally seek to explain causation in terms of special kinds of regularities. Not just any regularity will do.

Regularity theories of causation have their roots in empiricist thinking, in which sense data are the basic elements of cognition and the basic objects of knowledge and explanation. These sense data follow patterns, or regularities, which reflect underlying fundamental laws. A more contemporary formulation results from substituting events for sense data. This substitution makes regularity theory more easily adapted to a range of behavioral-science disciplines. The more traditional empiricist approach brings with it a fundamental distinction between sensory data about the physical world and introspective data about the mental world. In contrast, the more current approach more easily allows for a somewhat softer distinction between physical events and mental events both subsumed under a broader category of events, and thus treated similarly in at least some and perhaps many respects.

Regularity theories restrict the explanation of causal relationships to what actually comes to pass in the world. For example, the actual distribution of interaction and performance among second-language learners must suffice on such a theory to account for any causal relationship. Regularity theories seek to avoid any reference to non-actual states of affairs that are merely possible, or might have been. This represents a fundamental difference between regularity theories and counterfactual theories which take unactualized possibilities as their stock and trade. The attraction of regularity theories comes from the fact that, were such a theory to succeed, it would buy causation at a lower price than a counterfactual theory and thus provide a more parsimonious account of causation. The view that scientific discourse should refer only to actual states of affairs and not possibilities has a long tradition in empiricist thinking. Such thinking often holds things like unactualized possibilities as suspect because they are unobservable and speculative. In behavioral science methodology, contributions to regularity theory by Hume (1962/1739–1751), Mill (1874), and Mackie (1980) have substantially influenced the Campbellian tradition of causal inference (Cook & Campbell, 1979; Shadish, Cook & Campbell, 2002) which has in turn been very influential across a variety of disciplines. A good example of this influence is the widespread acceptance in behavioral science of the assumption that causation can only move forward through time. This represents an assumption that is key to regularity theories in their attempt to isolate lawful regularities but an assumption often weakened by competing theories. For example, this is sometimes done to avoid a circularity in defining the direction of causation in terms of the direction of time and the direction of time in terms of the direction of causation (Dowe, 2000; Reichenbach, 1956).

Perhaps the best-known modern version of regularity theory comes from Mackie (1980), although it is not clear that Mackie meant to endorse the regularity theory that he formulated for purposes of criticism. Mackie presented an *inus* condition as an insufficient but non-redundant part of an unnecessary but sufficient condition for something to occur. For example, suppose that students can pass a test either by reading the book and doing the homework or by attending class and studying their notes. In this case, reading the book is insufficient to pass the test, but is a non-redundant part of the first strategy because one cannot pass simply by doing the homework either. Finally, the first strategy is itself sufficient to pass but not necessary because of the second available strategy. Likewise, there are many possible causal routes to a particular item response. As such, Mackie's form of regularity theory allows for the fact that something can cause item responses but still allow for an imperfect association with item responses.

7.3.2. Counterfactual Theories of Causation

Counterfactual theories of causation concede a little in terms of parsimony in order to obtain a greater payoff in terms of accounting for causation (Markus, 2010). The defining characteristic for a counterfactual theory is that it attempts to reduce causation to counterfactuals. This contrasts with regularity theories, which attempt to reduce causation to fundamental regularities but also with non-reductive theories that make use of counterfactuals without attempting to reduce causation to them. Further attention to a number of the terms just introduced will follow shortly.

First, however, it may be useful to consider a concrete example. Imagine a stretch of train track that contains a single switch, at which point the single track divides into two parallel tracks (Collins, Hall and Paul, 2002). Consider that whenever the switch is set to the left position, trains proceed down the left track, and likewise for the right position and right track. Now, suppose that in addition to changing the direction of the switch, the motor also turns a sign that indicates which way the switch is set (Table 7.1). A counterfactual account would describe the causal relationship as follows. For any given train, the train proceeds down the track corresponding to the switch position, the actual state of affairs. Had the switch position been different the train would have proceeded differently, the unactualized possible state of affairs. Moreover, this relationship remains robust to a wide variety of minor changes in the situation such as the speed, length, weight and color of the train. Finally, cause and effect might be separated by a chain of counterfactual dependencies such as the one described, so an action taken at some distance by a switch yard operator may also count as a distal cause of the train taking the track that it does. In contrast, if the switch remained in the actual position but the indicator sign had pointed in the wrong direction, the train would still go in the direction of the switch. Thus, the direction of the train has the right kind of counterfactual dependence on the direction of the switch, but not

Table 7.1 Actual, Possible, and Impossible Happenings at the Train Switch

	Switch Direction	*Sign Direction*	*Train Direction*
What does happen	Left	Left	Left
	Right	Right	Right
What could happen	Left	Right	Left
	Right	Left	Right
What could not happen	Left	Right	Right
	Right	Left	Left

on the direction of the indicator, which is the desired result because the switch causes the path of the train, but the indicator sign does not.

This last point represents an important motivation for counterfactual theories because regularity theories often stumble on the distinction between accidental regularities and lawful regularities. In the above example, an accidental regularity holds between the sign position and the path of the train, and a lawful regularity holds between the switch position and the path of the train. The term counterfactual in this context refers to a state of affairs that stands counter to fact. If the train switch has the position leading the train to the left track, then one takes this as a fact. One then takes as counterfactual that the train switch has the position leading the train to the right track. If the switch changes position, then these two states of affairs reverse between fact and counterfactual. This use of the term differs from the also-common use of the same term to refer to a counterfactual conditional, which refers to an if-then structure with an if clause that is counterfactual in the above sense. As discussed here, both regularity theories and counterfactual theories fall under the rubric of reductionist theories in the sense that they attempt to reduce causation, as a poorly understood concept, to something better understood. Regularities seem better understood than counterfactuals, but counterfactuals still seem more intuitive and clear than the concept of causation itself.

One challenge for counterfactual theories comes from the property of transitivity. If review causes greater knowledge of addition, and greater knowledge causes more accurate answers, then one would typically like to conclude that review causes more accurate answers. However, counterfactual causation does not necessarily support this inference (Menzies, 2004; Hall, 2004). For example, if only those who do not take a review course need to take the examination, then review will not lead to more accurate answers on the test. Those who take review will not provide any answers to the test. This phenomenon occurs whenever the implicit contrast shifts from the first causal statement to the second. In this example, review causes knowledge for the combined population of test takers and non-takers. However, knowledge only causes more accurate answers for test takers, so the implicit contrast differs for the two causal statements. This blocks a valid inference to a causal effect of review on item responses in this context.

Perhaps the best-known and most influential counterfactual theory is that of David Lewis (Collins, Hall & Paul, 2004, especially chapters 1, 3 & 10). Lewis's mature theory defined causation as the ancestral of counterfactual dependence. In other words, c causes e if and only if c is connected to e by an unbroken chain of counterfactual dependencies. Event g counterfactually depends on event f if and only if g would not have occurred had f not occurred. This two-step reduction of causation allows Lewis' theory to account for cases in which c causes e but e does not directly counterfactually depend upon c. An example would be where students pass an exam because they were given the answers in advance, but, had they not been given the answers, they would have studied and passed anyway.

7.3.3. Process Theories of Causation

Both regularity theories and counterfactual theories share a general strategy of attempting to provide an account of causation that introduces as little as possible beyond the causes and the effects in question. Process theories go in the other direction by accepting a more robust explanatory base in order to provide a more successful account of causation (Markus, 2010). The present chapter uses the term 'process' to cover a range of theories that include processes (Dowe, 2007; Salmon, 1998), mechanisms (Bechtel & Richardson, 1993; Craver, 2007; Glennan, 2002), and natural or invented machines understood in a broad metaphorical sense (Cartwright, 1999). The critical element is that processes are understood as something more than just a chain of nomological connections between variables. Instead, processes exist independently and maintain such connections. Process theories take as their basic idea that the existence of a corresponding causal process separates causal regularities from non-causal regularities. For example, moving a light across the surface of a wall produces a regularity from illumination of one region to the next. Nonetheless, the illumination of the previous region does not cause the illumination of the next. Process theories explain this with the fact that no causal process follows the trajectory of the light along the wall (Salmon, 1998). However, a causal process does link the position of the light to the illumination, and this produces a genuine causal regularity.

Much writing on process theories has focused on physical processes. However, Cartwright (e.g., 1999) has also written extensively about economics and econometrics. For example, taxes have a capacity to causally affect prices. However, this causal influence does not reduce to general regularities or patterns of counterfactual dependence. The reason is that the capacity in question functions differently in different contexts. Cartwright fleshes out the idea of different contexts in terms of different relatively stable mechanisms (what she calls nomological machines) built up out of constituents with various capacities interacting with each other under relatively stable conditions. Thus, taxes levied on a product and used for unrelated services will likely increase the price of the product. Taxes levied on the same product but invested in funding research, development, and infrastructure might lead to advances that have the net effect of lowering prices for that product. The nomological relationships depend upon how the basic capacities are organized into underlying causal processes.

Modern cognitive modeling of test item responses fits very naturally with a process theory of causation (Embretson, 1983; 2010; Frederiksen,

Mislevy and Bejar, 1992; Mislevy, 2008). If one can offer a rich cognitive account of the steps of processing that link perception of a test item, to solving the problem, to selecting the correct answer, then one has a causal process linking knowledge to correctness of test item responses. In a given sample, it might also transpire that scores correlate with the last two digits of the test taker's phone number, but no such causal mechanism underlies this correlation. Similarly, if those who know more about addition also know more about multiplication, a regularity exists between knowledge of multiplication and correct responses to addition items. However, again, no causal process underlies this spurious correlation.

Process theories face several challenges (Beebee, Hitchcock & Menzies, 2009). One challenge for process theories is that processes sometimes connect things that are not causally related. So, it is a problem to pick out which processes underpin causal relationships. Another challenge involves apparent cases of causation by absences or omissions. These cannot be connected to anything via a causal process. A third challenge involves maintaining a reductive account of causation by articulating mechanisms in a way that does not itself rely on causal concepts, an effort that some process theorists have abandoned.

7.4. Reflective Measurement Models with Different Causal Interpretations

As discussed in chapter 6, causally interpreted reflective measurement models assume that the latent variables cause the observed indicators. The goal of this section is to consider what reflective measurement models require of a causal relationship and how various accounts of causation line up with these needs. The identification of the causal latent variable with the intended construct corresponds to a central issue of test validity. A test can fit a reflective measurement model but the latent variable can represent a common cause of the items other than the intended construct. Often times, the pattern of common causes across the items plays a central role in providing supporting evidence for the identification of the latent variable with the construct or constructs of interest. Table 7.2 summarizes the remainder of this section.

7.4.1. Regularity Theories and Reflective Measurement Models

A non-causal reflective measurement model, understood as described above, offers no basis for a distinction between accidental and lawful relationships between variables. It does offer statistical generalization from the sample to a population that it represents. On the basis of an inductive inference from sample to population, one could assert that the observed probabilistic relationships would hold in the population and thus for any representative sample from that population. With some

Table 7.2. Causal Interpretations of Reflective Models

	Approach to Causation		
	Regularity Theories	*Counterfactual Theories*	*Process Theories*
Future like past:	Persistence of regularities. Statistical induction.	Lawful counterfactual rests on something about the test and test takers.	Causal relationships maintained by underlying process.
Invariance under intervention:	Within the bounds of the regularity.	Within the bounds of the counterfactuals.	Within the bounds of the underlying process.
Proportional changes in indicators with change in latent variable:	If the latent variable change does not disturb the regularity.	If the change in latent variable does not disturb the counterfactual structure.	If the change in latent variable does not disturb the process.
Guidance for improving the performance of the items or test:	Very little.	Some understanding of causal structure, but black box. Properties that maintain counterfactuals are typically not well understood.	Greater understanding of anticipated results of various changes to the system.
Assumptions:	Little more than probability theory. Causation only involves regularities in actual events.	Facts about unrealized possibilities. Causation depends upon such facts.	More to causation than causal relationships. Causal processes sustain causal relationships.

further assumptions, one might include future administrations of the test in the population to which one generalizes. Of course, future administrations not available when the sample is drawn have a zero probability of being included in the sample. So, an inference to future administrations of the test requires support for the assumption that past samples represent a population that extends into the future. This is just the general problem of induction, justifying the assumption that the future will resemble the past, in a psychometric guise (Goodman, 1983). Having noted this complexity, let us assume that one can justify an inductive inference to future administrations based on the current sample(s) somehow representing a population that extends to future administrations of the test.

Assuming that inductive inference offers some grounds for belief that the observed statistical patterns will hold up in future samples, it still seems clear that one advantage to a causal interpretation involves a broadening and strengthening of this support. To make this concrete, consider some boundary examples. In the standard example of a test of addition of single-digit numbers, one expects that new students will continue to learn to add such numbers the same way in the future, with no transformational breakthroughs in either basic arithmetic theory or pedagogy on the horizon. As such, if a set of items fit a unidimensional reflective measurement model, then one might anticipate that future administrations of the test would also conform to such a model. In contrast, consider the frequently used example of the intelligence test item involving an ink drawing of a 1950s' era desk telephone without a cord accompanied by a prompt asking what was missing in the picture. With the advent of cordless phones, the item ceased to function as it had and past psychometric evidence did not support future use because the population had changed from the one represented by the past samples. The former example gives a paradigm case of statistical generalization into the future and the latter example gives the same for a case where such generalization fails.

What, then, does a causal interpretation buy the test developer or user beyond what a non-causal interpretation has to offer? The answer rests on the relative *fragility* of the statistical population in relation to the relative *robustness* of the causally homogeneous population. Recall that the non-causal interpretation asserts a certain set of probabilistic relationships but does not offer any explanation of why these relationships hold. The equations or path diagram associated with the measurement model do not represent any kind of explanatory model under this interpretation. Given that the model represents no explanatory factors, the relationships hold as a result of factors not represented in the model. Less trivially, they may hold as a result of variables and relationships not included in the model. For example, a unidimensional model might nicely summarize the probabilistic structure of a set of items with no common cause but bound up on a network of direct causation between the items (Borsboom, 2008). Likewise, a large set of highly intercorrelated common factor variables might be well approximated—beyond any reasonable threshold of model fit—by a unidimensional reflective measurement model. As a consequence, the non-causal measurement model might show considerable sensitivity to causal interventions in the system. It is in this sense that the population to which one can generalize the statistical results shows fragility: Minor changes can result in a change in population to which the result no longer generalizes. In contrast, a causal measurement model might remain much more robust to such changes. As a result, the generalizability of the results remains robust to a broader range of differences from the original sample.

Returning to the examples, consider the arithmetic test. If the unidimensional causal model is correct, then instruction aimed at improving single-digit addition should increase performance on all of the items proportionately to the size of the causal effect (e.g., factor loading or item discrimination parameter). If, on the other hand, the causal model underlying the non-causal unidimensional model is more complex, then this may not hold. For example, suppose that the larger of the two digits to be added always appears first in the addition problem (one might assume, for example, that students know the trick of reversing the numbers to solve the problem the easiest way). Allowing items that add a digit to itself, this constraint allows for 55 possible items. Suppose that each item loads on a general addition factor, a factor associated with the value of the sum (students differ in their ability to add numbers that sum to different values; one student might be particularly good at pairs that add to 10, another 5), and a factor reflecting the size of the smaller number (adding larger numbers is harder). An intervention might increase ability for different sums differentially, in which case the items would not improve proportionately in response to the intervention. Indeed, the intervention might even reduce some high correlation between specific factors, such that the test no longer fits a unidimensional model. As such, the causal unidimensional model provides more information about the persistence of the probabilistic relationships under intervention than does the non-causal unidimensional model. The causal unidimensional model defines a population that remains robust to such interventions whereas the non-causal model defines a population that may lack such robustness.

In the case of the causal unidimensional model, the probabilistic relationships between the items are lawful relationships determined by the causal structure. In the case of the non-causal unidimensional model generated by an underlying multidimensional causal structure, the unidimensional probabilistic relationships are accidental. In the same model, other aspects of the probabilistic relationships are lawful. These include the probabilities of the item responses conditional on their causal factors. Regularity theories of causation encounter difficulty in distinguishing between these sorts of lawful versus accidental patterns. One approach is to admit as lawful those that would fit into a final comprehensive theory (Psillos, 2002). However, it is hard to tell which those might be before such a theory is attained.

7.4.2. Counterfactual Theories and Reflective Measurement Models

As described above, counterfactual theories offer more than regularity theories because they cost more in assumptions. Applying a counterfactual approach to measurement models requires some care. Counterfactual theories account for claims of individual case causation (Amie passed the test yesterday because she studied) more naturally than general causal laws (students who study more pass tests). The difficulty comes from the assumption that facts hold about the present and past, but not necessarily the future. When one says that it is possible for Amie to pass the test tomorrow, one usually means more than that one does not yet know if she will pass the test. One assumes that it could happen that she passes or that she does not in a sense of genuine possibility that goes beyond simply not knowing which will transpire. Counterfactuals, tied as they are to fact, thus also relate primarily to past events rather than future ones. However, general laws extend into the future, and thus have an open quality to them that past facts lack. Saying that next year's class will not pass the test if they do not study differs from saying that last year's class would not have passed the test had they not studied. These assertions differ because last year's class passed as a matter of fact, whereas that fact remains open for next year's class.

Similarly, probabilistic causation plays a central role in measurement but can pose a challenge for counterfactual theories (Humphreys, 1989). The basic idea behind counterfactual theories involves the contrast between the effect occurring with the cause and the instance that it would not have occurred without the cause. The basic idea behind probabilistic causation, however, involves the idea that the effect may or may not occur with or without the cause. So, the element of chance poses a challenge for counterfactual accounts. The usual strategy for addressing both challenges involves adopting the standard formulation that causes don't cause their effects but rather cause the probability distributions of their effects. This formulation addresses the first problem because future events can have a determinate probability distribution as a matter of fact. It addresses the second problem because saying that the probability distribution would have differed had the causes differed does not stumble over the fact that particular effects can occur under different probability distributions. If next year's class does not study, they will be less likely to pass the test. As a matter of causal law, the conditional probabilities of passing given various levels of studying can exist as a matter of fact even before next year's class determines their level of studying. Likewise, the probabilistic formulation allows that some who study may nonetheless fail, and some who do not study may nonetheless pass.

If the causal law referred to in the above paragraph comes to nothing more than a regularity, then adopting a counterfactual theory seems to buy little advantage at the cost of all this additional talk of counterfactual possibilities and so on. However, the basic strategy of counterfactual theories goes beyond simply saying that as a matter of regularity students who study pass and those who do not study fail. Counterfactual theories go a step further in claiming that the same students who studied and passed would have failed had they not studied, all other things held equal. (Quite a lot turns on the exact understanding of 'all other things held equal' and the section on cross-sectional versus longitudinal models in chapter 8 considers this issue further.) Advocates of counterfactual theories, however, generally would not suggest that regularities in counterfactual states of affairs determine the truth or falsity of causal assertions in the actual state of affairs. Instead, such theories generally assume that something about the nature of things in the actual state of affairs determines how they would behave in counterfactual states of affairs. For example, the fact that Amie fails in a state of affairs where she did not study does not determine the truth value of the assertion that she passed because she studied. Instead, an intrinsic dependence of test-taking behavior on studying behavior makes it true that Amie would have failed had she not studied, and this in turn fixes the truth of the causal assertion. This idea of an inherent nature of things that determines their counterfactual behavior serves as the basis for the advantages of counterfactual theories over regularity theories purchased at the price of considering alternative states of affairs.

The exact spelling out of this intrinsic nature of things remains poorly understood. However, one can still draw some general conclusions about the application of counterfactual theories to reflective measurement models. Grounding observed regularities in inherent propensities to behave differently under different conditions offers greater reason to expect the future to resemble the past than does the brute-force induction relied upon by regularities theories. So long as the inherent nature of students and the learning process remains the same, one has some basis to expect the relationship between studying and passing to hold up. Likewise, one has more reason to expect student knowledge to continue to cause responses to individual items as characterized by the reflective measurement model.

Similarly, counterfactual theories begin to drive a wedge between prediction and explanation by providing an account of why effects follow their causes. Regularity theories cannot provide such an account because they typically equate prediction with explanation. This separation of prediction from explanation provides some traction for understanding the invariance of measurement relationships under intervention. If the interventions realize counterfactuals governed by the intrinsic propensities in question, then the counterfactual structure applies to the behavior under intervention. This contrasts with observed regularities where the very act of intervention produces a new population to which old inductive inferences may not generalize (Markus, 2008a). So, for example, one has no inductive base from which to draw conclusions about test-taking behavior following a new and untried pedagogy. However, if one has a counterfactual causal theory for which knowledge fully mediates the effect of pedagogy on test item responses, then such a theory provides a basis to expect the measurement relationships to remain invariant to the introduction of the new pedagogy. Note, however, that this requires a transitive counterfactual causal relationship such that pedagogy causes item responses indirectly through knowledge.

Suppose Amie knows 85% of the material. Plugging that number into a measurement model with known (or estimated) parameters yields predictions regarding the likely probability distributions of her responses to individual items. Perhaps she has a 75% chance of answering a particular item correctly and a 90% chance of answering another. Now, if one plugs in a lower level of knowledge, say 75%, then the measurement model predicts a proportional reduction (not necessarily linearly proportional, depending on the model) in the chance of answering each item correctly. The counterfactual structure posited by counterfactual causal theories, along with its basis in intrinsic propensities, provides a greater basis for anticipating such proportional changes in responses to latent variable changes than a regularity theory can provide.

For similar reasons, counterfactual approaches provide more guidance for test construction and item revision than do regularity theories. A counterfactual causal theory should be able to identify key properties of good items, and offer reasoned accounts of why certain item types would not work without requiring observational evidence of every causal regularity. For example, suppose that some students are more likely to answer an item incorrectly if it requires carrying a digit from one column of digits to the next because the digits in that column sum to a number greater than nine. Moreover suppose that the proportion of such questions has heretofore been fixed at 50 percent. If we change that proportion, all bets are off according to a regularity theory because we may have disrupted the stable pattern of regularities. However, on a counterfactual theory, one can reasonably assert that the causal relationship between digit-carrying and correct answering will remain stable for different proportions of such items because the proportion of items on the test does not alter the intrinsic properties of items and test takers that undergird the causal relationship. So, one can make reasonable inferences regarding the impact on test scores of changing the proportion of items that require carrying digits across columns. However, the guidance afforded by a counterfactual theory has limitations. The intrinsic properties that undergird counterfactual causal relationships generally remain poorly articulated and poorly understood.

7.4.3. Process Theories and Reflective Measurement Models

Process theories come at the greatest cost of metaphysical assumptions. What they lack in parsimony, they make up by providing a stronger basis for inferences. From the perspective of a process-type theory of causation, the reflective measurement model does not represent the causal process. Instead, it represents the nomothetic shadow of the underlying process. From this perspective, then, mediating variables do not represent processes that connect causes to effects. Rather, they merely add more nomothetic causal relationships, each of which requires an underlying process explanation. The processes support the arrows in the path diagram, but the arrows do not directly represent the processes. Rather, the processes imply the causal effects.

By this means, process theories provide the strongest support for inferences to future cases of the three types of causal theories. As long as the process supports the causal structure, and one can confirm that the process remains present in future cases, one has a strong prima facie basis to expect the causal structure to persist in future cases as well. Regularity theories can at best assume that future cases will resemble previous ones. Counterfactual theories can at best point to characteristics of the population involved as underwriting stable counterfactual laws. In contrast, process theories spell out the process that gives rise to the causal relationships modeled in path diagrams and systems of equations. If, for example, long-term memory stores the sums of individual digits, but sums of larger numbers are computed from simpler sums (Dinnel, Glover and Ronning, 1984), then one might expect test takers who have memorized more individual sums to complete addition problems more quickly and accurately. The cognitive processing model describes a process that has the causal relationship between the two variables as a consequence. In contrast, regularity theories take the causal relationship as a brute fact about how the world works, and counterfactual theories offer a less fully elaborated basis for the causal relationship than do process theories.

Similarly, an elaborated process theory provides a strong basis for expecting invariance of the causal process under intervention and proportional increases in item responses with increases in the latent variable. The causal process generates the causal structure, and the causal structure generates the joint probability distribution. So, as long as the intervention does not disturb the causal process, one can expect the causal relationships to remain in place. On the other hand, the process theory also provides a basis for making informed inferences about when an intervention will disrupt the causal process, and therefore the causal and probabilistic relationships. So, for example, more general practice may lead to proportionately better item responses. In contrast, practice focused only on addition problems that involve carrying digits might lead to disproportionate improvements in items involving such problems, but little improvement in responses to other items.

Finally, a well-developed cognitive model of item responses describes a process that, coupled with a process approach to causation, provides valuable guidance for item writing and revision. Discovery of classes of items that do not work well provides additional information for elaborating the process theory. The process theory approach provides detailed guidance for item writing and modification precisely because it does not take causal connections between variables as primitive, or as a black box, but rather attempts to spell out a causal process that explains the causal relationships. This process provides a detailed roadmap for building tests with the desired causal relationships (Embretson, 2010). Of course, none of this comes free. At a scientific level, development of accurate explanatory models of causal processes requires considerable research, and the most progress has come with the more straightforward cases of ability tests. One suspects that causal process models of personality tests may take more time to see comparable progress. At the philosophical level, process theories come at a greater metaphysical cost because they posit much more than do regularity or even counterfactual theories. This produces less parsimonious theories with more assumptions, some untestable, and more ways to go wrong.

Box 7.2. Effect Indicator Models and Factual Understanding

One possible model of ECST-R responses might have it that people learn a little at a time about what each person in the courtroom does. Depending upon how each question is asked, they may or may not have the information needed to answer a particular question about a particular role in the courtroom. However, as their overall understanding of the various roles accumulates, they become more and more likely to answer a randomly selected question correctly. On this model, respondents decode the question, call up the required piece of information (if they have it), and then encode a response that communicates the requested piece of information. Perhaps a more plausible model might have it that any one answer depends not on a single requested piece of information but instead that respondents construct answers using quite a large number of pieces of information (assuming that information is countable in pieces). Respondents with richer troves of information are able to construct better answers more reliably than are those with less information with which to work. Either way, the story makes a reflective measurement model a reasonable candidate for the factual understanding items. A causal interpretation of a reflective measurement model produces an effect indicator model, but the specific interpretation depends upon the implicit theory of causation.

On a regularity perspective, the causal connection between general factual understanding and individual item responses constitutes a lawful regularity. People who have greater factual understanding also tend to give higher-scored responses to, say, item 1. The causal interpretation does not require strict determinism, it can incorporate conditional probabilities. In this case, the value of the latent variable causes the specific conditional probability distribution of item responses. The strength of the regularity approach comes from the fact that it offers a causal interpretation with minimal further assumptions. The limitation of a regularity approach comes from the fact that regularities hold in actual populations. If we intervene, say with training, we change the population. Thus, without additional assumptions, a regularity theory does not allow us to predict the effect of training or any intervention that changes intact populations. That would require independent evidence that the regularity holds in the modified population. The regularity interpretation extends beyond the non-causal interpretation only in allowing a somewhat more robust basis for inference about observed cases within an intact population.

Where regularity approaches assume that actual cases suffice to fix the truth or falsity of causal assertions, counterfactual approaches instead assume that this depends upon possible cases as well as actual ones. Even if we could know that a regularity holds in an entire population, this does not entail a counterfactual–causal connection unless the regularity also supports counterfactual statements about non-actual possible cases. Thus, in the case of training, Kotone might have a factual understanding of f_1 and thus a conditional probability for item 1 of <.2, .3, .3, .1, .1>. However, with training, she might attain a factual understanding of f_2 and thus a probability distribution of <.1, .2, .3, .3, .2>. This later counterfactual has no bearing on a regularity interpretation of causation, but plays a critical role in determining the truth or falsity of a counterfactual interpretation. Conversely, then, a counterfactual interpretation of a reflective measurement model produces an effects indicator model that does allow one to infer the effects of training.

Counterfactual theories take the truth of counterfactual assertions as the basic foundation for the truth and falsity of causal assertions. Counterfactuals like Kotone's response pattern after training remain black boxes, brute facts on which other inferences rest. This makes it difficult to know when one may have intervened in such a way that might not simply disrupt actual regularities, but might also disrupt patterns of counterfactual dependence. An extreme example might involve training that had the unintended result of causing Kotone to become suspicious of the person doing the assessment and thus uncooperative. Under such circumstances, the previous counterfactual structure might cease to apply. A less extreme example might involve similar effects of fatigue resulting from the training and disrupting the measurement of Kotone's factual understanding. A limitation of counterfactual approaches involves the difficulty in recognizing such situations due to the black-box nature of counterfactuals.

Process approaches offer a means of addressing this limitation by grounding counterfactuals in independently observable or measurable processes. Suppose, hypothetically, that the response process for factual understanding items worked something like this: The respondent listens to the question and encodes the kinds of information relevant to answering the question. The respondent then recalls several pieces of information and evaluates whether they suffice to answer. If so, the respondent formulates an answer. If not, the respondent repeats the recall and evaluation step until either (a) he or she recalls sufficient information to answer or (b) he or she can recall no further relevant information. This no doubt reflects a gross oversimplification, but it offers a useful example. Imagine that as a result of nervousness or some other factor, Kotone consistently answers on the basis of the first few pieces of information that she can recall and this response process leads her to give answers that fail to represent her full level of factual understanding. In this case, she does not need training in courtroom facts to improve her scores, but rather training or feedback encouraging her to pause and recall more information before moving on to formulate her answer. A different set of counterfactual assertions will govern her actual and possible responses before and after such training. However, the concrete process theory makes it easier to conceptualize and monitor this response process. Indeed, a simple response time measure might provide valuable information in this context. Under this interpretation, factual understanding causes the distribution of item responses through the response process and the better one understands the response process, the better one understands the resulting score. The clear limitation to the process approach involves the introduction of many further assumptions and required knowledge about the item responses. To the extent that these exceed the available level of scientific evidence regarding the test, the process approach does not offer an advantage over simpler approaches to causal interpretation.

7.4.4. Reflective Measurement, Causation, and Validation

Table 7.2 summarized the comparison of approaches to causation based on regularities, counterfactuals, and processes in relation to reflective measurement models. Drawing together for comparison the material developed above, the table illustrates the trade-off between greater explanatory power purchased at the cost of more assumptions and metaphysical complexity. Regularity theories offer an austere approach requiring little more than a purely probabilistic interpretation of measurement models. Counterfactual theories purchase a little more at the cost of incorporating facts about unrealized possibilities. Process theories offer the richest explanatory base at the cost of the most elaborate metaphysical assumptions.

Regularity interpretations exact the smallest toll in terms of the evidence required to support them. Simply correlating item responses with measures of the explanatory variable, or simply fitting a latent variable model, will not suffice. The association could be spurious. However, establishing the association and ruling out plausible rival hypotheses can provide a strong foundation for inference to regularity causation. For instance, one might point to a well-fitting measurement model in a larger model that includes other constructs that offer rival explanations of the item responses. Alternatively, one might point to incremental prediction of item responses by the focal construct over and above rivals, but not vice versa, as is common in studies using hierarchical regression techniques. More detailed accounts of the right kind of regularity can yield more specific methodological prescriptions.

Counterfactual interpretations require additional evidence that the dependencies hold across possible cases and not just among the values passively observed in a population. Thus, counterfactual approaches depend encourage greater use of try-and-see methods rather than just look-and-see methods, although the latter still dominates much testing and validation practice. Interventions of various sorts provide the strongest evidence that dependencies hold counterfactually. Nonetheless, an extensive literature exists on inferring counterfactual dependencies from passive-observational data (Morgan & Winship, 2007). In essence, if one can indirectly manipulate item responses by directly manipulating another variable, then one has some basis to conclude that the item responses depend upon that variable.

Process interpretations require the most intensive validation research strategies. Here it does not suffice merely to show that item responses depend upon one variable or another. One must construct and support an explanation of this dependency that is not itself expressed merely in terms of mediating dependencies. One must develop a substantive causal model that describes how a causal process generates the item responses. The richness of this explanation opens the field to a broader array of rival hypotheses. In general, to take advantage of process interpretations, one needs a means of identifying the presence of the desired mechanism. It does not suffice to merely measure the values of antecedent variables. Instead, one needs to show that these variables are arranged within a process that will allow them to interact in the expected way. In many respects, this constitutes very familiar ground for those familiar with standardized testing. Standardized test administration involves precisely the effort to confirm that test administration practices in novel contexts conform in the relevant ways to the requirements of standardization. Some variables have no relevance because they do not affect the causal process that generates the item responses. Others have relevance because they do. The better one understands the item response process, the more effectively one can make such theory-based inferences. Such understanding comes from triangulating on item response processes from a diverse array of research strategies. Look-and-see methods alone will almost never suffice to support a process interpretation.

The greater generalizability of process accounts partly offsets the greater validation demands. For example, causal processes for item responses will typically involve more basic processes involved in sensation, perception, memory, decision-making, and other general forms of cognitive processing. As such, findings from one area can readily apply to another area involving the same basic processes in a different way. For example, dual processing theory most likely applies to many different types of attitude measures. If automatic processing and conscious deliberative processes both impact item responses, then it may make sense to consider multidimensional models that allow more than one latent variable to impact the item response. Alternatively, it may make sense to use latent mixture models to reflect the fact that one process dominates for some respondents and the other process dominates for others.

7.5. Chapter Conclusion

This chapter took up a seemingly simple question: What does a causal interpretation add to a measurement model over and above what one obtains from a purely statistical interpretation of the same model? Without claiming to have generated an exhaustive list, the chapter considered three basic answers: A causal interpretation can provide greater reason to expect future observations to resemble past observations. A causal interpretation can provide greater reason to expect the measurement model to remain invariant under certain kinds of interventions. A causal interpretation can provide greater reason to expect proportional increases in item scores following an increase in the variable that they measure.

However, the extent and manner in which a causal interpretation offers these advantages varies with the specific content of the causal interpretation. Some understandings of causation offer more than others. Conversely, understandings of causation that provide more also come at a greater cost. They require more evidence to support the causal inference, and they introduce more complexity into the substantive assumptions that underpin the research. In general, regularity theories cost the least and offer the least advantage in return. Counterfactual theories fall somewhere in the middle and process theories offer the most benefit at the most cost. Test validity theory has only just begun to explore these issues.

7.6. Further Reading

Cartwright, N. (1999). *The dappled world: A study of the boundaries of science.* Cambridge, UK: Cambridge University Press. (Chapter 3)
Dowe, P. (2000). *Physical causation.* Cambridge, UK: Cambridge University Press. (Chapter 5)

Embretson, S. E. (1998). A Cognitive Design System Approach to Generating Valid Tests: Application to Abstract Reasoning. *Psychological Methods, 3,* 380–396

Markus, K. A. (2010). Structural equations and causal explanations: Some challenges for causal SEM. *Structural Equation Modeling, 17,* 654–676.

Psillos, S. (2002). *Causation and Explanation.* Montreal, CA: McGill-Queens University Press. (Chapters 2–4)

8 Problems in Causation and Validity

Formative Measurement, Networks, and Individual Differences

Connections With Other Chapters

Chapter 6 distinguished formative from reflective measurement models as formal statistical models. Chapter 6 also discussed the idea of network measurement models. Chapter 7 discussed alternative non-causal and causal interpretations of reflective models in which constructs cause item responses (or their probability distributions). That chapter developed three advantages of a causal interpretation over a non-causal interpretation: reason to believe that changes in the construct will produce changes in the item responses, reason to believe that the patterns of statistical association will persist, and reason to believe that the measurement model will remain robust to certain forms of intervention on the population of interest. Chapter 7 also presented three broad approaches to causation: regularity theories, counterfactual theories, and causal process theories. As in chapter 7, these terms here refer to reductive theories of causation. Regularity theories reduce causation to patterns of succession in actual populations. Counterfactual theories reduce causation to counterfactual dependencies that hold across both actual and possible counterfactual populations. As noted in chapter 7, some well-known methodological approaches to causal inference make use of the concept of counterfactuals but do not provide a reductive account of causation. Process theories reduce causation to actual processes linking causes to effects. As elsewhere, the term 'measurement model' is adopted from the literature to apply broadly to all forms of assessment (chapter 1) and not just measures with quantitative structure (chapter 2). As discussed in chapter 1, the term 'indices' refers to observed variables in a formative model, in contrast to indicators in a reflective model.

The first half of the present chapter considers formative measurement models. Similar advantages to those found in reflective models also apply to formative models. However, formative models face two key challenges: causal misspecification and a seeming proliferation of causal composite variables. Different causal interpretations handle these challenges differently. A latter section briefly discusses a causal interpretation appropriate for network models. The last portion of the chapter focuses on causal interpretations appropriate to individual differences. Taken together, these topics canvass a number of open questions with respect to causation and assessment. Nonetheless, the chapter by no means exhausts the problems waiting to be solved. A box at the end summarizes some key open questions from the chapter.

8.1. Formative Measurement Models and Causation

The reader will recall that formative measurement models have the same basic profile as reflective measurement models but differ in the direction of the arrows (or asymmetrically interpreted equations). The latent variable depends upon the observed indicators rather than the other way around. As a result, in the reflective model the unique variances on the observed indicators constitute variance not explained by the latent variable. In contrast, in the formative model they constitute the entire variance of the observed variables. Conversely, the disturbance term on the latent variable represents a disturbance conditioned on the observed indicators for the formative model, although this was not the case for the reflective model. The formative model entails local independence of the latent variables conditioned on the observed variables whereas the reflective measurement model entails local independence of the observed variables conditional on the latent variables.

With one exception, the same general advantages to causal interpretations discussed with respect to reflective models also apply to formative models. Causal interpretations offer a theoretical basis to generalize to future observations and more reason to anticipate invariance of the probability structure under intervention. However, in the case of formative models, the causal interpretation entails proportional effects of manipulations of the observed indicators on variables that depend upon the latent variable. This runs opposite to the case with reflective measurement due to the reversal of the arrows. So, for example, if a_1 and a_2 causally indicate A, and A causes B, then a_1 and a_2 affect B proportionately to their effects on A. The present section will focus instead on two issues specific to reflective measurement models. The first issue involves causal misspecification and the second issue involves the identity of the latent variable.

The misspecification issue arises as a direct result of the direction of the arrows in formative models. One example of formative measurement discussed in the literature involves exposure to discrimination (latent variable) indicated by race, sex, age, and disabilities (observed variables; Blalock, 1964; Bollen, 1984; Bollen & Lennox, 1991). Figure 8.1 illustrates this model. The model gains intuitive plausibility from the idea that exposure to discrimination results from an individual's race, sex, age, disabilities and so on. However, the initial plausibility rests on a conflation of the actual race and the observed race, something encouraged by the relatively minimal measurement error one might expect. Nonetheless, no observed measure entirely escapes measurement error. The role of measurement error goes unmodeled in the formative model because the variance of the observed indicators incorporates both genuine variance and measurement error (Edwards, 2010). Figure 8.2 elaborates the model to partition out the measurement error. According to this model, the rela-

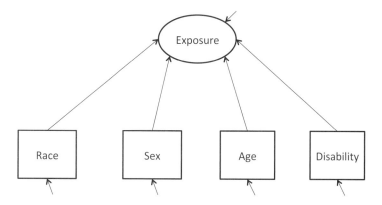

Figure 8.1 Formative Measurement Model.

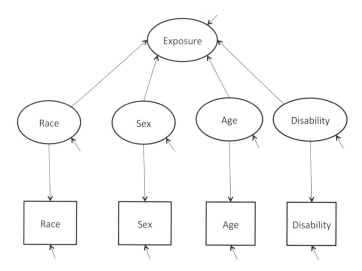

Figure 8.2 Spurious Measurement Model.

tionship between observed race and exposure to discrimination appears as a case of spurious measurement (Edwards and Bagozzi, 2000). The term spurious is familiar in the context of causal inference where it refers to a correlation between two variables attributable to a common cause. In this case, spuriousness describes the putative measurement relationships between the observed variables and exposure to discrimination that results from their sharing common causes as depicted in the model.

The diagram makes clear that in the context of the spurious model, one cannot expect proportional effects of the observed variables on effects of exposure to discrimination. The observed variables have no direct or indirect effects on exposure to discrimination in the spurious measurement model. Likewise, as a result of the measurement error, one cannot assume local independence of focal constructs (trivial in this example given only one focal construct) conditioned on the observed indicators. If the spurious measurement model correctly describes the situation, then the formative model involves causal misspecification because the spurious model has no effects corresponding to those in the formative model.

It becomes an interesting question, then, how far such examples might generalize. Can one conclude that formative measurement models for observed indicators generally misspecify the causal relationships by ignoring measurement error? A positive conclusion would not necessarily prove fatal to formative measurement models because they might nonetheless provide a useful simplification, especially with small sample sizes and minimal measurement errors. The remainder of this section will consider the question in relation to various causal interpretations of the formative measurement model.

The above example also serves to illustrate the second issue. Suppose that exposure to discrimination predicts an outcome variable as depicted in Figure 8.3. In this model, the exposure latent variable represents the optimal composite of the four observed variables for predicting the outcome. Change the outcome to a different variable, and a different com-

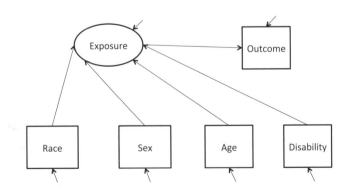

Figure 8.3 Formative Measure with Outcome Variable.

posite may optimally predict it. If one identifies the parameters in the model in Figure 8.3 by fixing the effects on the latent variable and the residual variance of the latent variable (Hayduk, 1987) then these fixed parameters also fix the composite up to the arbitrary mean. However, one can also identify the model by fixing only the residual variance of the outcome variable and the effect of the latent exposure variable on the outcome. This produces a nonsaturated model with zero degrees of freedom in that the fit varies with the choice of fixed parameter values. Even for correctly specified values, changes in the outcome variable will change the values of the effects of the observed indicators on the latent variable, and thus the latent variable itself.

The set of real numbers provides infinitely many linear combinations of the observed indicators to choose from. The causal interpretation of the formative measurement model interprets the latent variable as an effect of these observed indicators. Taken together, these two premises jointly entail that the set of observed indicators has infinitely many effects. Does the world we inhabit really contain such a profusion of effects? The answer may depend upon the details of the causal interpretation.

8.1.1. Regularity Theories and Formative Measures

Recall from chapter 7 that the primary attraction of regularity theories of causation comes from minimal assumptions. Of the three theories considered here, regularity theories offer the most austere approach, avoiding elaborate assumptions about the nature of reality or the object of measurement. This characteristic of regularity theories offers some advantage in addressing the issues considered in this section. Consider first the problem of observed causes. If one accepts the typical empiricist assumption that observational data provide the object of scientific explanation, causal hypotheses provide a tool for explaining regularities in observations. From this perspective, formative measurement models face no real problem with misspecification because causal regularities involve observed variables. Latent variables only serve to provide convenient summaries of patterns of regularities between observed variables.

Likewise, the second issue does not pose much of a problem for an austere regularity theory. If the latent variable only provides a convenient summary of the proportional causal impact of the observed indicators on the outcome, then one can multiply composite latent variables ad infinitum without cluttering the world with myriad variables. The latent variables merely provide convenient redescriptions of the fixed reality composed of observations. The basic elements of that reality do not multiply with the multiplication of linear composites in the measurement model.

Commitment to a regularity theory of causation, however, does not require that one accept the view that causation offers no useful content over and above empirical patterns in observed data. One can push regularity theory in the direction of distinguishing causal regularities as adding something to the world in excess of the observations that they subsume. Indeed, one can instead focus on regularities in events independent of whether any observation of those events takes place. For example, one could pursue the approach of taking true causal laws as those that figure into a complete final theory (Lewis, 1973; Ramsey, 1990). On this strategy, causal laws differ from other regularities as a matter of fact independent of our knowledge of them. Only the composite latent variables that figure into such causal laws, and not just mistakenly supposed causal laws, constitute genuine causes of other variables. So, even if one gives the positing of causal latent variables some content, regularity theories have strategies for avoiding the wanton proliferation of effects of observed indicators. The ultimate success of those strategies remains an open area of research.

8.1.2. *Counterfactual Theories*

As described earlier, counterfactual theories of causation concede a little in terms of assumptions in an attempt to address persistent difficulties with regularity theories. However, these additional assumptions may increase the difficulty with formative measurement models under counterfactual causal interpretations. It seems more difficult to avoid the criticism of misspecification under such an interpretation. It seems implausible, on the face of it, that the measurement error in the observed indicators should play any causal role. However, one needs to clearly specify the observer in situations where one seeks to measure a perceptual process. For example, mistaken identity could play a causal role in generating discriminatory behavior. However, the measurement model does not model measurement error in the perceptions of the individual actor but rather the researcher's measurement error in observing these features. Conventionally, the researcher does not play an active role in causing the outcome of the study, and as such, it seems implausible that measurement error in the researcher's observations plays such a causal role.

On a counterfactual account, causation derives from some elaboration of the basic idea that the outcome would have differed had the observed indicators of exposure to discrimination differed. However, the non-spurious formative measurement model implies that the researcher's measurement error in recording these indicators plays a causal role, and thus the outcome depends counterfactually on these measurements. This suggests a highly reactive measurement procedure that plays a causal role in determining the result of the observation. Given the effort generally put into avoiding such reactive measurement in research, it seems much more difficult to avoid the misspecification critique from a counterfactual perspective. It seems more plausible to use formative models as a convenient oversimplification in this context.

The issue of identifying the correct latent variable also seems more critical for a counterfactual causal interpretation than a regularity interpretation. A causal system might support many regularities at once in actual cases, but one would not expect most of these regularities to hold up counterfactually. For example, spurious correlations hold up in actual cases but not counterfactually: Having grandchildren might be correlated with exposure to discrimination as a result of age as a common cause but one would not expect that grandparents would experience less discrimination had they no grandchildren. As such, one may be able to construct many composite variables out of a set of observed indicators, but one would not expect every such composite to support counterfactual dependencies such that the outcome would have been different had the composite been different. So, a correctly specified causal model would need to use the observed indicators to model just the right composite variables out of all the plentitude of possible composite variables that one can form from them.

However, the counterfactual interpretation seems to enjoy much the same immunity to the concern that the multitude of possible composites clutters the world by assuming the existence of too many variables. Most of these composite variables constitute counterfactual dead ends. The latent composites counterfactually depend on the observed indicators but do not support any counterfactual dependencies upon the composite variables themselves. For example a variable formed as positively dependent upon minority race and sex but negatively dependent upon older age and more visible disability might demonstrate counterfactual dependence upon the four indices, but it seems unlikely that any outcome variables would demonstrate counterfactual dependence on such a composite variable.

8.1.3. Process Theories of Causation and Formative Models

Process theories of causation require a richer set of assumptions allowing for causal processes recognizable independently of nomothetic relationships be they actual or counterfactual. The misspecification issue looks much the same as it does for counterfactual theories applied to formative measurement models. Interpreting the models as correctly specified requires a causal role for measurement error which in turn suggests a highly reactive measurement process. Essentially, there must be some causal process linking the error-inclusive indicators to the latent variable. Given the difficulty of specifying causal processes between theoretical variables, the task of specifying a causal process from something that includes random measurement error seems exceedingly challenging. Some may rise to the challenge, but it seems more likely that formative measurement models represent a useful approximation rather than a correctly specified causal structure under a process theory interpretation.

A process theory approach to causally interpreting such measurement models also seems to bring more restrictions on the latent variable than the other two approaches. One can construct infinitely many composite variables out of the observed indicators, but specifying a causal process for just one of these poses a considerable theoretical challenge. It seems highly implausible that one could identify causal hypotheses to accompany very many, let alone all, such composite variables. The richer assumptions required for process theories bring a greater cost in admitting infinitely many effects of the causal indicators. However, they also suggest a counter to this excess of assumed variables. If one admits as genuine effects only those for which one can specify a causal process, then the infinite number of arithmetic composites reduces to the small number for which one can identify such processes. The others simply do not rise to the level of genuine causal processes. As such, they do not offer plausible rival hypotheses.

Box 8.1. Causal Indicators and Factual Understanding

For comparability, the present chapter continues the example of factual understanding as a component of competency to stand trial. Box 7.1 describes this example in detail.

In contrast to the reflective models considered in chapter 7, suppose instead that understanding of each discrete fact about courtroom procedures in fact represents a discrete piece of knowledge learned independently of the others. Different people might learn these in different orders. One person might learn a little bit at a time about each courtroom role, another person might learn all about what judges do, and then learn all about what lawyers do, and so on. One's factual understanding simply reflects the sum of this knowledge at any point in time. On this account, a formative measurement model makes more sense. One can then apply the various approaches to causation to the formative model in order to create contrasting effects indicator models that share the same statistical model and differ only by their causal interpretation (syntactically equivalent models; Markus, 2008).

Suppose Alexei has mastered two thirds of the domain of judge facts and one third of juror facts, whereas Bogdan has mastered just the opposite. First, consider various sum scores across these two sets of items. If the tests contains equal numbers of each type and the sum score weights these equally, then one expects Alexei and Bogdan to have roughly equal sum scores within sampling error and measurement error. This result reflects the fact that they have roughly equal stores of knowledge despite the different distributions across topics. Next suppose that we construct two additional sum scores: the judge-and-juror sum score weights judge items twice as heavily as juror items, and the juror-and-judge sum score does just the opposite. Here, one expects Alexei to score higher on the judge-and-juror score but Bogdan to score higher on the juror-and-judge score. However, one can go further by weighting the odd numbered items negatively, to produce an even-judge-and-juror-score and an even-juror-and-judge score. At this point, one has constructed five different effect variables all caused by the item responses. Next, consider the causal indicator model with the residual variance, reflecting the full domain of items, not just those included on the test. Once we add this in, it seems less likely that the happenstance odd/even regularities would hold up, and thus these would not likely rise to the level of causal relationships even on a regularity view. Nonetheless, even using the full domain to constrain the possible residual variation, one can construct various outcome variables by adjusting the item specifications that determine the domain. Limit the domain to items containing no more than 12 words and perhaps Alexei outscores Bogdan. Instead, limit the domain to items containing no words with more than three syllables and perhaps Bogdan outscores Alexei. Effects of the items proliferate with possible sets of item specifications. Even if every specification consistent with the items on the test had only two possible options, and the entire test could be specified with just 10 properties of items, this would produce $2^{10} = 1024$ causal outcomes of the items barring any further constraints. Moreover, introducing the residual also introduces concerns about misspecification. If the items contain measurement error, then the causal indicator model only holds in the population if those measurement errors play a causal role in determining the domain score.

Under a regularity approach, it suffices that actual cases follow regularities such as Alexei outscoring Bogdan on the judge-and-juror score and Bogdan outscoring Alexei on the juror-and-judge score. Under a counterfactual approach, causation requires something more. It requires that Bogdan would outscore Alexei on the judge-and-juror score if he had more knowledge in just the right way: primarily more knowledge about judges. It also requires that Alexei would conversely outscore Bogdan on the juror-and-judge score if he had more knowledge in just the right way: primarily about jurors. If the observed regularities held, but the counterfactual regularities failed to hold, then one would have a causal connection on a regularity approach but not a counterfactual approach. Such a situation might arise due to an interaction between test specifications. If a seemingly innocuous constraint on item content or presentation had the effect of disturbing the sampling from the content domain, then it might happen that learning more about judges does not improve Bogdan's judge-and-juror score because the newly learned facts do not appear on any possible test form as a result of other test specification constraints. Even with this added constraint on possible effects of item responses, however, the problems of proliferation of causes and of misspecification remain.

A process approach offers a curb on these two problems at the cost of a more complex set of suppositions about the phenomenon under study. If one assumes that only variables connected to the item responses by a causal process constitute true effects of the item responses, then one potentially greatly restricts the range of possible effects. The solution may be too strong, however, if one believes that such effects exist but cannot formulate a plausible mechanism by which a response containing measurement error causally affects another variable. For example, suppose that Alexei writes with his left hand and does better on tests when he takes them at a desk that accommodates this. What plausible interpretation of what the test measures includes a causal effect of this left-handed-writing element of the variation in test scores? Perhaps Alexei does better in the morning and Bogdan does better in the afternoon. How might that fit into the causal process linking item responses to the variable that the test measures? It may be that by making the causal process explicit, a process approach to causation brings into relief unwanted constraints on possible focal constructs in causal indicator models. A clever reader might produce a plausible example, but perhaps a safe conclusion would be that the process approach severely delimits the plausible application of causal indicator models.

8.1.4. Formative Model Summary

A causal interpretation of a formative measurement model potentially offers similar advantages over a non-causal interpretation as found for reflective models. However, formative models face at least two challenges that interact with causal interpretations. They must address the apparent causal misspecification that comes with ascribing to errorful observed variables causal influence on the latent construct. They must also avoid underwriting inferences to the existence of countless variables, in a sense of existence that makes such inferences prima facie implausible. The prospects for well-supported formative measurement models vary appreciably across different types of causal interpretations.

8.2. Network Measurement Models

Chapter 6 discussed the idea of network measurement models in which indicators have direct causal connections to one another but the focal construct nonetheless corresponds to a characteristic of the network of indicators as a whole (Borsboom, 2008b). Underlying theory for such measurement models remains sketchy, but it will be useful to consider how different notions of causation might apply, if only to underline the fact that reflective and formative measurement models do not present an exhaustive typology.

The interpretation of the causal connections between the indicators has at best an indirect bearing on measurement in the network model. These indicators do not measure one another. As such, the choice between a regularity, counterfactual or process interpretation of these constituent causal relations places no direct constraints on the interpretation of the relationship between the indicators and the focal construct. In contrast, none of these interpretations fit well with the relationship between the indicators and the focal construct under the network model. As discussed in chapter 5, efficient casual notions of causation assume distinctness of causes from effects, and in this case the focal construct subsumes the indicators. Were this not the case, one might simply superimpose the network model onto a formative or reflective measurement model for the focal construct and give it one of the interpretations discussed above.

As also discussed in chapter 5, one option involves seeking a notion of causation that does not presuppose the distinctness of causes and effects. One approach to developing such a notion of causation rests on the part–whole relationship (Markus, 2008). To return to the example of an arithmetic test, one might not consider the ability to add each pair of digits as distinct from the general ability to sum digits. Instead, one might consider the ability to sum each pair of digits as a part of the general ability. On this view, general ability with adding digits does not cause one to have the ability to add individual digit pairs. Instead, the specific abilities collectively constitute the general ability. One can conceptualize this relationship in terms of a mereological form of determination in which the state of the parts determines the state of the whole (Markus, 2008). In this case the specific ability levels determine the general ability level. Returning to the depression example from chapter 6, depression does not cause depressive symptoms. Instead, the levels of the individual depressive symptoms collectively determine the overall level of depression because the individual symptoms collectively constitute depression as parts of the whole.

Such a notion of causation differs in important ways from efficient notions of causation. In efficient causation, earlier events typically cause later events. In mereological causation, only the current state of the parts determines the current state of the whole. Efficient causation involves

changes over time and explains how things get into a certain state. Mereological causation involves static structures and explains relationships
between different aspects of a steady state. Efficient causation helps
answer questions about how best to accomplish an end. Mereological
causation helps answer questions about which ends it makes the best
sense to try to accomplish (Markus, 2008). As such, a mereological causal
connection between the parts and the whole need not conflict with efficient causal connections between the parts. The efficient causal connections govern the changes in the parts over time whereas the mereological
causal relation governs the states of the whole that change as the parts
change their states. The idea of network models as measurement models
remains largely unexplored, as do appropriate causal interpretations.

8.3. Causation and Individual Differences

Cross-sectional data across individuals can diverge in its patterns from
individual causal processes occurring within individuals (Hamaker, Nesselroade, and Molenaar, 2007; Molenaar, 2004). This represents a form
of Simpson's Paradox in which patterns can reverse when controlling for
a third variable, in this case, controlling for a person variable. Figure 8.4
illustrates this idea by plotting job satisfaction data for three individuals at three times. For each individual, job responsibility increases by 1
unit from time 1 to time 2 and from time 2 to time 3. Likewise, for each

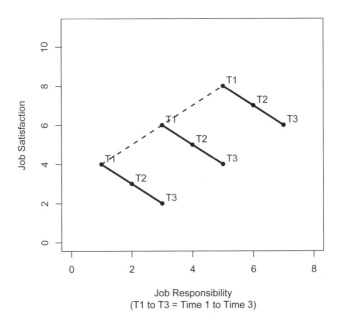

Figure 8.4 An Example of Simpson's Paradox.

individual job satisfaction correspondingly decreases by 1 unit for the same three time points. However, the individuals exhibit large individual differences in job responsibility and job satisfaction. If one looks only at the time 1 data points, one observes a positive correlation (dotted line) despite the fact that the two variables show a negative relationship for each individual taken in isolation (solid lines).

Perhaps the most common way to think about the above phenomenon construes the positive association in the cross-sectional data as an artifact of the true negative causal connection and some third variable. At a course level, one could take the individual case identifier as the third variable. More precisely, one might try to break that down in terms of a more substantive variable. For example, job level might have a positive effect on both job responsibilities and job satisfaction, explaining the positive association across individuals. Note that although described in terms of levels, this does not imply a multilevel model with random coefficients. The effect of job responsibilities on job satisfaction remains constant for all job levels (and all individuals) in this example. Moreover, for clarity, we present an example in which the direction of the effect changes. However, the same phenomenon can occur where the direction remains the same but the effect size differs between the within-person and between-person cases.

From the perspective of a causal theory of measurement, however, it holds interest to consider a different way of construing the situation. If we substitute the underlying job satisfaction construct for job responsibilities, the above example takes on the character of a reflective measurement model with the job satisfaction measure as an effect indicator. The remainder of this section explores the hypothesis that the cross-sectional pattern of individual-differences reflects a genuine causal relationship, but of a different order than the individual level causal relationship in the opposite direction. For ease of reference, and lack of a better term, we call this inter-individual causation. This contrasts with intra-individual causation as follows. Recall that Figure 8.4 shows a negative intra-individual causal effect, but a positive inter-individual causal effect. Consider the question (Q) Why did person p give answer a to item i? The question is ill formed and has no direct answer. Instead, let us distinguish the following three clarifications of the question. (Q1) Why did p give a to i given that p has probability distribution r for i? (A1) Because of pure chance, there is no further explanation (Humphreys, 1989). (Q2) Why did p give r for i as opposed to some other r' that p might have had? (A2) Because p was in state s as opposed to state s' that p would have been in if p had value v' of the variable being measured instead of v. (Q3) Why did p have r for i as opposed to some other r^* had by some other p^*? (A3) Because p was in s as opposed to the state s^* that p^* was in including having value v^* instead of v. The answer to Q2 involves intra-individual causation whereas the answer to Q3 involves inter-individual causation. The two causal processes do not introduce any explanatory redundancy because Q2 and Q3 pose distinct questions with different answers. Neither reduces to the other.

8.3.1. Regularity Approaches to Inter-individual Causation

Regularity theories do not offer a good fit with inter-individual causation. If one takes any stable regularity as causal, then one can take both the positive and negative associations in the above example as causal regularities. However, this approach runs afoul of the standard difficulties involved in distinguishing true causal regularities from accidental regularities from a regularity theory perspective. If one then strengthens the regularity approach by adopting the idea that causal laws are those that best systematize a general theory, then this seems to immediately rule out interpreting the cross-sectional regularity as causal. One can completely explain it in terms of the individual-level processes. As such, the cross-individual regularity reduces to the within-individual regularities and thus does not figure into the ideally systematized final theory.

8.3.2. Counterfactual Approaches to Inter-individual Causation

Standard counterfactual approaches make use of the wrong kinds of counterfactuals for inter-individual causation. They rest on the idea that if one changed an individual's job satisfaction, a corresponding change in that individual's job satisfaction indicator would result. For example, Pearl (2009) suggested a Do operator that formalizes casual counterfactuals on this basis. If we represent a causal system as a system of equations, then the Do operator replaces the equation for the counterfactually manipulated variable with a new equation setting it to a fixed value. The result of solving for the new value of the effect variable using the altered system of equations gives the counterfactual value of the effect variable for the same individual. As such, these approaches entail precisely what inter-individual causation should not.

However, one can produce an alternative counterfactual approach by modifying this basis. Instead of taking manipulation (real or ideal) as the basis for causal counterfactuals, one can instead construct them in terms of a different operation that involves swapping an individual with another individual from the same population. We dub this a Swap operator. If we take Person A and increase his or her level of job satisfaction, in the modification of the above example, he or she reports lower job satisfaction (perhaps because his or her standards go up). However, if we take Person A and swap him or her with an existing person who has a higher level of job satisfaction, then we would expect that person, Person B, say, to report a higher level of job satisfaction. Figure 8.5 illustrates this situation. If we begin with Person A having a latent job satisfaction score of 3 and an observed score of 5, Do(Person A = 4) yields an observed score

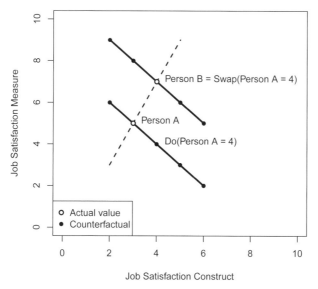

Figure 8.5 Do operation versus Swap operation.

of 4, but Swap (Person *A* = 4) yields an observed score of 7 by swapping Person *A* with Person *B* who has an actual latent score of 4. Thus the Do operator applies to causation within an individual, represented by the solid lines. The Swap operator applies to causation between people, represented by the dashed line.

The resulting notion of inter-individual causation supports the causal measurement model but does not conflict with the intra-individual causal process described by the Do operator. Thus the two forms of counter-factual causation do not contradict one another. They complement one another by describing different elements of the overall causal structure. As in the previous diagram, the negative intra-individual causal effect coexists with the positive inter-individual causal effect. Most well-known frameworks for causal inference assume intra-individual effects even when these are estimated using between-individual data (Morgan & Winship, 2007; Pearl, 2009; Rubin, 1974). This is evident from the way that they form the counterfactuals used to define causal effects, in terms of changes to individual cases. The approach outlined above uses a different kind of counterfactual to define a different kind of causal effect.

8.3.3. Process Approaches to Inter-individual Causation

If one can articulate a process account of the within-person causal process and this within-person process explains the between-person causal structure, then it would seem that one would also have a process account of the between-person causal structure. Suppose that the satisfying-ness of the job serves as the third variable that increases both latent job satisfaction and job satisfaction scores. Person B has a more satisfying job, and thus higher job satisfaction and higher scores than Person A. However, if one's satisfaction with the same job goes up, this involves a shift in how one evaluates job satisfaction, which also yields lower satisfaction scores because one interprets the questions differently. An elaboration of the processes just sketched would provide a process account of the intra-individual causal processes operating in the example. However, these also

---

Box 8.2. Doing and Swapping Factual Understanding

Let us return to the reflective measurement model considered in Box 7.2. Specifically, assume that factual understanding involves a richly interconnected inferential base from which respondents infer answers to specific items. Assume further a three-stage performance model. Individuals first decode the question and recall relevant facts in the first stage. They then deduce facts relevant to the answer in the second stage. Finally, they then use those facts to formulate an answer in the third stage. Factual understanding refers to the richness of the body of facts an individual can produce, an interaction between the number of facts that they can recall and the inference rules that they can apply.

Imagine that Ximena has a strong factual understanding and also has strong verbal fluency. Yuliana has less factual understanding and also has a serious verbal fluency impediment that interferes with the third stage. For concreteness, suppose we are interested in the causal effect of factual understanding on an item related to the role of the prosecutor. Ximena scores better on this item than does Yuliana. So, if one swaps Ximena for Yuliana, then one expects a higher score than was earned by Yuliana. This provides a causal connection at the individual differences level. However, if one intervenes to change Yuliana's factual understanding to equal Ximena's factual understanding, Yuliana's verbal disfluency still results in a lower score. So, one does not find the same causal connection at the individual level following this sort of counterfactual approach. If we imagine a general positive correlation between verbal fluency and factual understanding, then we might expect the individual-differences causal relationship to hold in the population even if a corresponding within-individual causal connection does not hold in any individual.

Given that verbal fluency does not constitute part of factual understanding, one might appeal to the competence-performance distinction to suggest that the test confounds competency to stand trial with verbal fluency. Under this interpretation, then, one would not take the individual-differences-level causal connection as a causal connection between factual understanding and correct item responses, but rather as an artifact of the verbal fluency confound that blocks some competent individuals from performing at a passing level on the test. This contrasts with the following case.

Assume Zarita has a rich store of facts about roles in the courtroom. However, she has very weak inference skills which lead to lower scores. For example, she knows that the judge decides whether to accept or reject objections made by the prosecutor but does not naturally make inferences from this to the role of the prosecutor unless someone leads her through the inference explicitly. Once pointed out to her, however, she recognizes that the conclusion of the inference is consistent with what she already understood. As with Yuliana, Zarita scores lower than Ximena. Swapping Zarita with Ximena leads to higher scores. However, in this case, we can consider two forms of intervention. Intervening to set Zarita's store of knowledge equal to that of Zimena, as a training program might, would not produce scores comparable to those of Ximena. This result obtains because Ximena still has superior inference skills when drawing on the same body of factual knowledge. Thus, the causal connection between the store of knowledge and correct item responses does not hold at the individual level on this approach to causation. However, an intervention that builds both Zarita's knowledge store and inference skills to be comparable to Ximena's would produce comparable item responses. Thus the causal connection between factual understanding and item responses would hold at the individual level if understood this way.

Indeed, one might go further to apply the sorts of cognitive task analysis developed as a method of construct validation of cognitive ability tests (Embretson, 1998; Embretson and Gorin, 2001). Items that require more independent facts may prove harder for test takers to answer, as might items that require a larger number of distinct inferences, or greater verbal fluency. One could even imagine a situation in which the causal relationship between factual understanding and correct item responses operates in a different direction between people than within people. Imagine very large individual differences in factual understanding. In addition, imagine a very small effect within individuals such that training to improve their factual understanding causes a reduction in motivation that in turn reduces their probability of correct responses more than the increase in factual understanding increases the probability. This effect occurs as a result of changing a person's level of factual understanding, but the direction of the effect of factual understanding on correct item responses remains opposite in the general population. This situation means that factual understanding has a positive overall causal effect on item responses at the individual difference level (in the Swap sense of cause), but a negative overall causal effect within individuals (in the Do sense of cause).

account for the inter-individual causal structure. So, it appears that the same process account can underpin both causal structures. As such, they do not appear to conflict with one another on this approach.

8.4. Validating Causal Measurement Models

Chapter 6 discussed the ways that different causal measurement models have different implications for validation evidence. It should be clear from the above discussion that the same holds for different causal interpretations of the same measurement model. For simplicity, let us focus on measurement models with effect indicators under various causal interpretations. This is a book on test validity theory, not research design. So, the remainder of this chapter does not attempt to provide an encyclopedic treatment. Instead, the more modest goal is to connect the dots between the test validity theory developed here and familiar research methodology from the literature. However, the general idea of causally interpreting measurement models brings a much broader range of research methods to bear on test validity issues than has been fully explored in the literature to date.

Several choices facing the test developer involve the desired strength of the causal interpretation to be validated. The first choice facing the test developer involves the need for an inter-individual causal effect. Validation of only inter-individual causation requires less validation evidence than does validation of a causal effect that holds both within and between individuals. In some instances, it may be worth the extra effort to validate inferences about within-person differences in addition to between-person differences. This essentially comes down to demonstrating that one obtains the same results sampling across individuals on the same occasion as one gets sampling across occasions for the same individual (Molenaar, 2004). However, in many cases such empirical support may be impossible because the intra-individual causal relationship simply does not hold or the effect differs from the inter-individual causal effect. In some cases, a purely inter-individual notion of causation may suffice for the test developer's needs. In which case, it is only necessary to provide empirical support for the between-person causal relationship. In such cases, it is important to recognize that between-person methods based on within-person counterfactuals test intra-individual causation, not inter-individual causation. For example, an experiment testing that people randomly assigned to construct-related training do better on a test than those assigned to construct-unrelated training tests an intra-individual causal relationship. The method rests on same-person counterfactuals. In contrast, a study testing for differences in test scores between experts and novices that cannot be explained by covariates provides evidence of inter-individual causal effects. An experiment manipulating item format to confirm hypotheses based on a hypothetical mechanism linking expertise to test item performance might offer stronger evidence in support of inter-individual causation (perhaps on a process theory interpretation). For example, such a study might show that items with certain characteristics are more sensitive, say, to cognitive processing strategies typical of experts. As a general rule, of course, the best validity evidence comes from a variety of different studies bringing different types of evidence to bear on the same interpretation.

Having made the above decision, the test developer next faces a decision about how best to interpret the intra-individual or inter-individual notion of causation. The above discussion suggested five out of six viable options, eliminating the regularity approach for inter-individual causation. Where a regularity approach applies, evidence based on conditional probability relationships takes precedence (e.g., Granger, 1969). One cannot simply read causal relationships off of observed associations, as the case of spurious measurement demonstrates. However, one can, on this approach, read causal relationships off of sufficiently multivariate patterns of association that demonstrate the right kind of robustness to control for other variables.

If the test developer instead wishes to pursue a counterfactual interpretation, then passive observational data generally will not suffice. (Sufficiently strong assumptions can make it possible to estimate counterfactual-causal effects from passive observational data: Morgan & Winship, 2007; Pearl, 2009. However, passive observational data does not make it possible to distinguish counterfactual-causal effects from merely regularity-causal effects.) For the counterfactual approach, it is precisely the difference between observed and counterfactual patterns that distinguishes causal relationships from non-causal associations. However, this does not necessarily restrict the relevant evidence to randomized experimental data. Natural experiments based on passive observation data from naturally occurring stochastic processes can also provide useful validity evidence. Similarly, quasi-experimental data, particularly longitudinal data, can also provide useful validation evidence to support counterfactual causal relationships between the latent variable and the observed indicators. In the above example, one might predict that efforts at job enrichment might make jobs more satisfying and lead to higher satisfaction ratings whereas efforts to induce cognitive restructuring with respect to the same job might yield lower job satisfaction ratings (even if latent job satisfaction increases).

If the test developer wants to validate a process interpretation, then this requires looking beyond nomothetic relationships. By definition, regularity and counterfactual approaches describe causation in terms of nomothetic relationships whereas process theories require an account of an underlying causal process that maintains these nomothetic relationships. In both the intra-individual and inter-individual cases, this involves spelling out a cognitive, behavioral, or social structure that functions in a certain way that results in the observed nomothetic relationships. Validation then involves providing empirical evidence to support this causal process as an accurate description of how the system works. In the job satisfaction example, a purely cognitive process, by which job holders represent the levels of various facets of their jobs and compare these to how much they want of each facet, will lead to one set of empirical predictions (Locke, 1969). An affective process by which individual differences in the expression of negative affect swamp cognitive differences will lead to a different set of predictions (Weiss, Nicholas and Daus, 1999). In both cases, simply estimating causal effects does not suffice to support a process interpretation. One must instead develop a means of assessing the functioning of the process independent of the nomothetic causal effect linking the two variables. An example would be research showing that various interventions impact the process leading from the construct to the item response in predictable ways. For Locke's theory, this might involve contextual information intended to change the respondent's frame of reference, such as comparison groups, in a way that alters expectations, and thus satisfaction ratings. For a dual process theory, this might involve interventions intended to encourage either a more emotional pre-cognitive response or a more deliberative cognitive response. If neither intervention affects the construct measured, these can provide evidence of the hypothesized mechanism linking the construct to the item response.

In all cases, the interpretation and thus the validation strategy depend upon the intended use of the test. A test used for low-stakes selection in a relatively fixed population may not require a causal interpretation of the measurement model at all. One merely predicts based on statistical induction. If the test is only used for within-person comparisons, then only intra-individual causation has relevance. If the test is only used to compare individual differences, then only inter-individual causation has relevance. The same test may have high validity for one use but have low validity for the other. If the test scores will be used in highly variable circumstances or with highly variable populations, then a process based interpretation offers the strongest grounds for generalizing validity to new populations and contexts.

8.5. Chapter Conclusion

In the present chapter, we have built on the material from the previous two chapters, applying contrasting types of causation to formative measurement models and network measurement models. We have considered the methodological challenges related to individual differences and causal research as they relate to test validation. Finally, we have briefly explored methodological options for test validation in the above contexts. These extend beyond traditional fitting of psychometric models to data drawn from passive-observation designs. Taken together, the four chapters that comprise this section of the book suggest a variety of avenues for further work developing and refining validation strategies for specific causal inferences and addressing the many open questions in this area (Box 8.3). In the next section, we turn to issues of interpretation and meaning as they bear on test validity.

Box 8.3. Open Research Questions Related to Causation and Validity

Perhaps the most fundamental open question regarding causation and validity asks whether or not measurement involves a causal relationship between constructs and indicators. If not, then neither formative nor reflective measurement models have a correct interpretation as cause or effect indicator models. Measurement models either have only a statistical interpretation, or some other interpretation that is more than statistical but not causal in nature.

A closely related question asks whether, given such a causal relationship, the causal relationship plays an essential role in assessment. In other words, granted that some assessment involves causation, does assessment require a causal relationship, or do assessment and causation sometimes but not always coincide? Establishing the causal connection plays an essential role in test validation given an affirmative answer, but may not play any essential role given a negative answer.

Intertwined with each of the above questions, two additional basic questions ask (1) what kind of causal connection do the above questions involve and (2) do the questions have the same answer for all tests, or different answers for different tests? The latter question does not require a yes or no answer but might instead shade off between the two alternatives by defining broader or narrower classes of tests that share common answers to the above questions.

The answers to these foundational questions lead to a series of more pragmatic questions. How central a role does evidence of causal relationships play in a validity argument? How can one best design validation studies to provide the best evidence? With respect to the latter question, advances in modeling the cognitive processes behind item responses suggest that item responses coupled with variables coding item properties can provide a strong basis for causal inference when interpreted as a within-subject design, even without randomization of item order. The relatively large number of conditions (item types) coupled with highly specific causal models help facilitate such inferences.

Another area that remains under-developed involves the use of causal models to improve test items, particular for tests other than ability tests. Models that merely posit a relationship between the construct and the item responses offer very crude causal models because they treat the specifics of the causal relationship as unexamined constants estimated from the data. Models that seek to explain the specifics of the causal relationship, however parameterized given the choice of measurement model (e.g., factor loadings, Item Response Theory parameters), in terms of item characteristics provide a richer causal model. A richer causal model provides more guidance for item writing and improvement. However, pending firmer answers to the questions canvassed above, even this avenue of research remains in its infancy despite the steady progress that has been made. If some assessment does not involve causation, then causal models are not useful in such instances and validation requires other forms of explanatory theories. If different forms of causation apply to different contexts of assessment, then specifying the appropriate form of causation can help focus research and avoid wasted effort. Working out the application of specific forms of causation can also provide templates for use in the constructions of specific types of tests. Application of such templates would always require critical evaluation, but would still offer an advantage over starting each new validation project from scratch, or with minimal guidance regarding the form of the causal explanation of item responses.

The questions outlined in this box span a broad range in terms of specificity and the appropriate research methodology for addressing them. They run the gamut from philosophical questions of ontology to scientific questions regarding theories of specific constructs. Nonetheless, it proves helpful to bring them together under one tent in order to better understand how they fit together and how progress in one area connects with progress in another.

8.6. Further Reading

Bollen, K. A., & Lennox, R. (1991). Conventional wisdom on measurement: A structural equation perspective. *Psychological Bulletin, 110,* 305–314.

Edwards, J. R. (2010). The fallacy of formative measurement. *Organizational Research Methods.* DOI 10.1177/1094428110378369.

Edwards, J. R. & Bagozzi, R. P. (2000). On the nature and direction of the relationships between constructs and measures. *Psychological Methods, 5,* 155–174.

Molenaar, P. C. M. (2004). A manifesto on psychology as idiographic science: Bringing the person back into scientific psychology, this time forever. *Measurement: Interdisciplinary Research and Perspectives, 2,* 201–218.

9 Interpreting Test Responses
Validity, Values, and Evaluation

Connections With Other Chapters

In chapter 1, we canvassed various perspectives on test validity. In subsequent chapters, we presented various approaches to thinking about and empirically modeling test scores and item responses. Material in those chapters illustrated how specific validation strategies can depend on the assumptions about measurement and the assumptions about causation that underlie a given test interpretation. The present chapter explores literature bearing on the breadth of test validity theory and specifically the role of values in test validity theory. Chapter 10 then turns specifically to the topic of test score interpretation.

It does not take professional training to produce interpretations of test scores. Human beings have a remarkable capacity for spotting patterns and assigning meaning even where they do not exist. Effective testing, however, requires justification of interpretations of tests scores. Untutored interpretations will not consistently meet this standard. As such, justifications of interpretations of tests scores play a central role in test validity and test validation.

If a test measures suitability for forestry work but nobody can justify this interpretation of the test scores, does the test have validity? The question points out the fundamental schism between two aspects of test validity (developed further in chapter 12). At one level, one might like to think of validity as an attribute of a test inherent in the test and waiting for researchers to discover it like a law of nature. At another level, however, testing involves meta-cognition. Interpreting a test score as indicative of some quality or quantity involves a knowledge claim. Because one knows the test score, one knows something further about the individual tested. However, knowledge traditionally involves three things: that a fact holds true, that one believes that fact, and that one has some basis to justify belief in that fact (Shope, 1983). Thus, for a test to provide scores validly interpretable in some way requires not just that the scores correspond to what they measure in the appropriate way, but also that the interpreter has some justification for believing that they do.

We have just distinguished that which the test measures from that for which one can justify belief that the test measures it. This distinction connects with the complex issue of what has validity. The traditional view that a test has validity corresponds quite closely to what the test measures because it excludes the user. However, the second aspect of validity, what beliefs about the test the user can justify, relativises validity to the test user. If validity requires justification and Jack can justify his belief in the validity of the water purity test but Jill cannot, then the test has validity for Jack that it lacks for Jill (until Jack shares his justification with Jill).

Finally, each of these distinctions interrelate with a basic distinction between fact and value also related to test validity. If one thinks of validity only in terms of the question whether, or the degree to which, a test measures something then one might take this as a purely factual matter. On the other hand, if one takes the justification for interpreting a test's scores in some fashion as an evaluation of the test as a means to measure something, then one might view test validity as involving values or value judgments.

The present chapter develops these issues further by examining some exemplary arguments. The chapter begins with Messick's (1989) validity chapter summarizing the attempt to synthesize a comprehensive notion of validity and looking at both the antecedents and responses to the incorporation of values into this synthesis. The chapter then considers criticisms of this idea from Shadish, Cook and Campbell (2002) and Scriven (2002). Lastly, the chapter considers contributions from Searle (1969) and Putnam (2002) relating to the fact/value distinction and relates these back to test validity. The chapter assumes no prior familiarity with these contributions. Also, rather than attempting to adjudicate the differences of opinion, the chapter focuses on evaluating specific arguments toward the broader end of providing a richer contextualization of the general issues involved.

9.1. Messick's Unified View of Validity

> Validity is an integrated evaluative judgment of the degree to which empirical evidence and theoretical rationales support the adequacy and appropriateness of inferences and actions based on test scores. As such, validity is an inductive summary of both the existing evidence for and the potential consequences of test interpretation and use. (Messick, 1989, p. 13)

To date, Messick (1989) provided the most systematic and most influential advocacy of a comprehensive view of test validity as including all lines of evidence bearing on a decision to use or interpret a test in a given way. To keep the issues involved straight, it helps to distinguish three separate aspects of Messick's validity synthesis. The first involves formulating a unified notion of validity. The second involves equating this unified notion with the total justification for using or interpreting a test a given way. The third involves recognizing and attempting to provide a theoretical basis for the role of values in test validity.

To understand the motivation behind the first of these, it helps to place Messick's work in the context of validity theory at the time he developed his synthesis. At the time, most test theory viewed constructs as a special sort of variable that only come into play when one attempted to measure something not directly observable. The normal circumstance involved measuring an observable variable in which case construct validity had no role and either content or criterion validation designs offered the appropriate validity evidence. Landy (1986) indicates that as a result, court cases challenging testing procedures as discriminatory often turned on the classification of the test as measuring a construct or not. The effort to unify test validity, primarily under the rubric of constructs, responded to this context by asserting that all variables involve theoretical aspects and thus fit under the rubric of constructs (Loevinger, 1957). This constituted an attempt to reconnect test development and test theory with the full range of skills and expertise that psychologists typically bring to hypothesis testing and theory development. However, the unified approach to test validity differs from a unitary approach in that it continues to recognize different kinds of validity evidence or validation designs. This constitutes the least contentious aspect of Messick's synthesis and the arguments considered below will generally hold this aspect in common with Messick's work. Even this aspect, however, is not uncontentious. As discussed below, one might hold the view, for example, that showing that a test effectively predicts an outcome does not relate to validity and should not be considered test validation.

The second aspect of Messick's synthesis involves the articulation of test validity as the total justification for a particular test use or interpretation. This aspect also stems from the test theory context preceding Messick's work. As noted in the book chapter by Scriven (2002) discussed below, the classical definition of test validity equates it with the degree to which a test measures what it purports to measure. At the same time, the dominant context of test validation involved doing a validation study that would justify the intended use of the test. These combine to form the untenable view that merely measuring what it purports to measure provides a sufficient total justification for the use of a test. Messick responded to this untenable conclusion by giving up the classical definition in order to retain the total justification aspect of test validity. As discussed below, Scriven chose the opposite strategy, as have others (Borsboom, 2005; Shadish, Cook & Campbell, 2002).

Finally, the third aspect involves direct attention to the role of values in test validation (Markus, 1998a; 1998b). This has emerged as the most controversial aspect of Messick's validity synthesis. It flies in the face of the traditional distinction between facts and values and the traditional notion of science as value free. Messick acknowledged a role for values through a consequential basis of validity, though he rejected the notion of consequential validity which, if nothing else, conflicts with the unifying aspect of his program. Much of this chapter will concern clarifying the central issues related to this aspect of Messick's work. It will be helpful to trace some historical antecedents and also to consider some reactions to Messick's attempt to find a place for values in validity.

9.2. Historical Context and Recent Literature

David Hume's influence is probably best known to behavioral scientists through his skeptical theory of causation and causal inference. However, Hume (1896) also introduced a skeptical view of values that continues to influence many behavioral sciences today, although with less recognition. Hume responded to violent conflicts over moral and political views of his day by analyzing human knowledge into two types: rational knowledge demonstrating the inherent relationships between ideas, such as geometric proofs; and factual knowledge derived from observation. In both cases, a statement holds true because it correctly describes some relation between ideas or some fact. Values, however, constitute original facts in and of themselves; they do not correspond to any merely descriptive facts. Instead, values reflect human passions that cause people to act as they do, something not uniquely determined by the facts of their environment. Arguing along these lines, Hume introduced the strict dichotomy between facts and values that occupies the present chapter. This dichotomy was warmly embraced by logical positivists during the early 20th century (Ayer, 1952; 1959) who viewed values as based only in emotions. This view of science and reason as separate from value permeated thought during the formative years of test theory. On this view, science and reason serve only an instrumental function, identifying the best means to ends determined extraneously by values.

The primary challenge to such thinking within the context of behavioral sciences comes from the field of program evaluation where evaluation based on data forms the central purpose to which measurement and research contribute. Here, some theorists maintain the instrumental view of science as value neutral (e.g., Campbell, 1982) but Scriven (2001) and others have argued strongly for an alternative view, that evaluators gather data to inform value choices. At the same time, trends in the philosophy of science have backed away from logical positivism toward more open recognition of the role of values in science. Values play a role in determining what questions get asked, what data gets collected, and how the data gets used and interpreted. However, these ideas have not generally filtered down into introductory research methods or measurement textbooks.

Within the above historical context, it is perhaps not surprising that the idea of incorporating consequences, and thus values, into test validation has served as something of a lightning rod issue. Nichols and Williams (2009) and Kane (2001, 2006) offer helpful reviews of the literature on consequences and validity, including a series of papers that appeared in *Educational Measurement: Issues and Practice* in 1997 and 1998. Sheppard (1997) argued that concern with consequences had always been implicit in discussion of validity, although explicit discussion of the issue has emerged more recently. Kane (2006) notes that Messick (1989) advanced a more moderate view of the role of consequences than did Cronbach (1971, 1988) in that Messick presented consequences as drawing attention to sources of invalidity attributable to construct underrepresentation or construct-irrelevant variance, whereas Cronbach viewed negative consequences as a form of invalidity. Much criticism of the inclusion of consequences in validation appeals to a fact/value dichotomy and an attempt to insulate the rationality of science from the politics of values (e.g., Green, 1998; Lissitz and Samuelsen, 2007; Mehrens, 1997; Popham, 1997, Reckase, 1998; Shadish, Cook & Campbell, 2002). Even where such criticism accepts a role for consequences in evaluating tests, it often seeks to separate this from validity on the basis of something like the fact/value dichotomy. The next sections turn to examining arguments drawn from two recent critiques.

9.3. Shadish, Cook, and Campbell's Critique

> We use the term validity to refer to the approximate truth of an inference. (Shadish, Cook, & Campbell, 2002, p. 33)

> However, if validity is to retain its primary association with the truth of knowledge claims, then it is fundamentally impossible to validate an action because actions are not knowledge claims. (Shadish, Cook & Campbell, 2002, p. 476)

Shadish, Cook, & Campbell (SC&C, 2002) present a narrower construal of validity in the context of testing than that presented by Messick (1989). Their book evaluates the strengths and weaknesses of a range of research designs primarily in the context of field research aimed at supporting causal inferences. Their comments on test validity arise in that context and reflect Campbell's view of science as an instrumental technology that identifies effective means to attaining ends selected outside of science. To better understand SC&C's argument, it will help to first review some basic concepts from informal logic. An inference involves a movement from some premises to a conclusion. Logic assumes that any given premise or conclusion either holds true or false. A deductively valid argument preserves truth in the movement of inference such that if the premises hold true the conclusion must also hold true but if one or more premises fails to hold true, all bets are off. As a result of this definition, a valid deductive argument can nonetheless have a false conclusion and an invalid deductive argument can nonetheless have a true conclusion. A sound argument has both validity and true premises and thus, unlike a merely valid argument, must have a true conclusion. Inductive inferences differ from deductive arguments, and are always deductively invalid. One measure of the quality of an inductive argument is that the more confident we feel about the truth of the premises the more confident we feel about the truth of the conclusion. Even though an inductive argument can have true premises and a false conclusion but still be a good argument (note that Messick described the validity argument as inductive), the quality of an inductive argument is sometimes called inductive validity. To illustrate these ideas consider the following argument.

(9.3.1)   All tests with red covers are valid.
(9.3.2)   This test has a red cover.
(9.3.3)   This test is valid.

Statements 9.3.1 and 9.3.2 constitute the premises and 9.3.3 the conclusion. The inference takes us from 9.3.1 and 9.3.2 to 9.3.3. In this case the inference is deductively valid because the truth of 9.3.1 and 9.3.2 would ensure the truth of 9.3.3. However, the falsity of 9.3.1 opens the door for the falsity of 9.3.3, illustrating a valid but unsound argument. If it turned out that as an empirical regularity, most tests with red covers are valid, and one has no further information pursuant to the validity of this test, then the argument might nonetheless offer a good inductive argument. Of course, the example is fanciful in that inductive support for 9.3.1 is highly implausible.

SC&C, however, use the term 'inference' in a slightly different way, to refer to the conclusion itself (as clarified in a footnote on their page 33). This allows them to define validity as the approximate truth of the inference (i.e., conclusion). For consistency of expression, the present chapter will use the term 'inference' only in the first sense to refer to the movement from premises to conclusion and use the term 'conclusion' to mean what SC&C mean by 'inference.' Where Messick speaks of a total validity judgment combining all the evidence for a given test interpretation or use, SC&C identify this instead with evaluation. They view validity more narrowly based on an argument summarized just below (see SC&C 2002, pp. 475–478). Box 9.1 applies this argument to the TOEFL examination.

(9.3.4)   Only knowledge claims hold true or false. (premise)
(9.3.5)   Actions are not knowledge claims. (premise)
(9.3.6)   Actions do not hold true or false. (9.3.4, 9.3.5)

(9.3.7)   Validity of a conclusion refers to the approximate truth of the conclusion. (premise)

(9.3.8)   Validity only applies to things that hold true or false. (9.3.7)

(9.3.9)   Validity does not apply to actions. (9.3.6, 9.3.8)

The argument clearly assumes that one restricts actions to actions other than interpretations. This assumption begs no questions and greatly simplifies expression and can thus be granted without harm.

A proper evaluation of the argument requires that one separate two distinct issues. First, the previous argument (9.3.1–9.3.3) illustrated that a valid argument can have a false conclusion. As such, SC&C's use of the term 'validity' differs from the standard sense canvassed above. However, this does not affect the validity of SC&C's argument because one can replace 'validity' with 'truth' of the conclusion throughout 9.3.4–9.3.9 and evaluate the argument in that form. If an action cannot have a true or false conclusion, then it cannot have a valid or invalid argument for inference to a true or false conclusion. The deviant use of the term 'validity', then, represents a completely separable issue from the validity of the argument in support of the conclusion that validation does not apply to actions. The validity of the argument against applying test validity to actions based on test scores stands or falls independent of the above issue.

One might object to the validity of the argument by pointing out that a statement about an action can hold true or false. SC&C (2002) recognize this objection. However, they argue that this makes the inclusion of actions in the form of test use in the definition of validity superfluous. The validity of a test use reduces to the validity of an inference about test use. Their dismissal of this objection seems too quick because such a criterion for superfluity would render many a statistical and mathematical proof superfluous. As deductive arguments, mathematical proofs always produce conclusions that reduce to their premises. However, they nonetheless serve a purpose by demonstrating that the premises do in fact yield the conclusion. Likewise, it may be non-superfluous to include actions in the definition of validity simply because failure to state this will leave the impression that inference validity excludes action validity.

Despite this weakness in their argument, SC&C draw attention to an important distinction. The distinction separates validity arguments for interpretations from validity arguments for actions. This distinction bears a connection to the distinction drawn earlier between what a test measures and what one can justify believing that the test measures. With respect to validation of inferences, the validity argument serves as a meta-linguistic argument for the validity of an inference from test scores. With respect to validation of actions, the action itself does not have validity in the sense discussed here. The validity argument is a first-order argument in support of the action in question. As such, SC&C correctly perceive that validity arguments for actions differ importantly in kind from validity arguments for interpretations and that the inclusion of the former in test validity extends the use of the term 'test validity' in important ways. Even a statement about an action involving test scores relates to testing very differently than an inference from test scores. Test scores serve as premises in an interpretation but not in an action.

SC&C also recognize that one has to evaluate test use. However, they argue that evaluation differs from validation roughly as follows.

(9.3.10)   Evaluation requires (a) evaluation criteria, (b) a performance standard on those criteria, (c) data regarding performance, and (d) a procedure for combining information about performance on various criteria into a summary judgment. (premise)
(9.3.11)   Validity offers only one criterion. (premise)
(9.3.12)   Other criteria for tests include good manuals, cost-effectiveness, and just outcomes. (premise)
(9.3.13)   Validity theory does not tell us how to evaluate criteria other than validity or how to combine information regarding various criteria but evaluation theory does.
(9.3.14)   Evaluation exceeds validation. (9.3.11, 9.3.12, 9.3.13)

The argument succeeds more at focusing the issue than at deciding it. The crucial premise, of course, is 9.3.13. Messick could readily have agreed with premises 9.3.10 through 9.3.12 but rejected 9.3.13 by instead claiming that validity theory should do precisely what this premise describes. One can read Messick's (1989) chapter as an effort to provide a systematic approach to combing various strands of validity evidence. In some sense, premise 9.3.13 begs the question by presupposing a preference for a more circumscribed notion of test validity. Later sections of this chapter will consider one likely motivation for preferring a more circumscribed notion of validity. First, let us turn to criticism of the expansive notion from another source.

Box 9.1. Applying SC&C's Argument to the TOEFL Examination

The Educational Testing Service (ETS) currently offers its Test of English as a Foreign Language (TOEFL) in Internet-based (iBT) and paper-based (PBT) formats. The two formats have different structures but ETS designed both to measure the ability to use English as spoken and written in North America. Many universities in the USA and Canada use TOEFL scores in admissions decisions for foreign students. Funding agencies outside the US also use the TOEFL as part of funding decisions for projects involving research or study in the USA or Canada.

Following the argument of SC&C, validation of the TOEFL can provide evidence in support of the interpretation of scores and indicative of facility with North American English. Validation cannot provide evidence in support of the use of TOEFL scores to make decisions related to such facility. That task belongs instead to test evaluation. Specifically, the interpretation of an applicant's TOEFL score as indicating adequate facility with English language constitutes a knowledge claim. For a given student, such a claim holds true or holds false, depending upon his or her facility with English. The admission decision constitutes an action and as such cannot hold true or false. If one accepts the SC&C definition of validity as applying only to things that hold true or false, then it follows naturally that validity does not apply to the admission decision.

Likewise, if one accepts SC&C's assertion that validity theory cannot tell us how to incorporate into our decisions criteria other than the validity of the test score interpretations, then it follows that validation of the TOEFL can only tell us about the validity of interpreting TOEFL scores as measures of facility with English and not about other considerations such as the quality of the TOEFL manual, the cost of using the TOEFL, or justness of decisions based on the TOEFL. Conversely, if one remains open to a broader notion of test validation, this conclusion fails to follow. In both instances, the arguments do more to clarify the view of validity advocated by SC&C than to justify it.

In practice, these theoretical issues can take on new wrinkles. For instance, one criticism of the TOEFL is that students can learn superficial orthographic patterns that allow them to correctly answer test items without understanding the underlying grammatical issues. This fact may introduce bias in the form of construct-irrelevant variance into the test scores. While it may be true that a given student with a high TOEFL score has correspondingly high facility with English grammar, the above source of bias could introduce some systematic discrepancy between the score and the level of facility. Thus too strict an interpretation of the test scores may hold false but a sufficiently guarded interpretation might hold true. As such, validity can depend upon the specific knowledge claim made by the test interpreter within the framework advocated by SC&C and these validity assessments may play differently into evaluations of test use.

9.4. Scriven's Critique

Scriven (2002) also argued for a more restricted notion of test validity than Messick's view. Whereas Messick took test validity as a misnomer and emphasized the validity of inferences from test scores and the use to which one puts them, Scriven seeks to restore the emphasis on test validity in contradistinction to the validity of inferences. Scriven is well known for advocating empirical bases for value judgments in the context of evaluation as it intersects a wide range of other disciplines (Scriven 1991). His argument for a narrower view of test validity runs roughly thus.

(9.4.1) Test validity refers to the extent to which a test measures what it purports to directly measure. (Definition)

(9.4.2) Test utility refers to the degree of support for more tenuous inference from test scores that those to what the test directly measures. (Definition)

(9.4.3) Test validity is based on logical analysis of the test and not on empirical relationships. (Premise)

(9.4.4) Test utility is based in part on empirical relationships. (Premise)

(9.4.5) Test validation involves a relatively circumscribed task. (9.4.3)

(9.4.6) Assessment of test utility involves a much larger and more complex task. (9.4.3, 9.4.4)

(9.4.7) Test validity and test utility are disjoint. (9.4.3, 9.4.4)

(9.4.8) One can establish test utility without establishing test validity. (9.4.7)

(9.4.9) Calling test utility validity cheapens the notion of validity (9.4.8)

(9.4.10) One does not want to cheapen the notion of validity. (Premise)

(9.4.11) One should distinguish test validity from test utility. (9.4.10, 9.4.11)

As illustrated in Figure 9.1, Scriven does not disagree with Messick about what is required to justify a given test interpretation or use. The two authors differ in that Messick identifies this total justification with the validity argument whereas Scriven views it as just one specialized aspect of the total justification. Scriven (2002) illustrates his view of test validity with several examples. For instance, he interprets projective tests as tests of responses to ambiguous stimuli and personality tests such as the MMPI as measures of agreement with sets of statements. Further inferences to psychodynamic states or personality move beyond validity to utility. However, thermometers measure temperature not just mercury expansion because good empirical evidence has established a direct connection between the two.

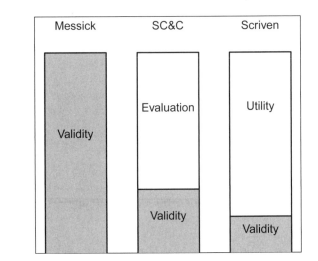

Figure 9.1 Three Notions of Validity.

Note that Messick and Scriven agree that some weakening of the traditional view of test validity is required. On that view, test validity involves only a test measuring what it purports to measure and test validity provides sufficient justification for testing applications. In Messick's view, one does one's best to weaken the traditional view by expanding test validity beyond the first criterion to meet the second criterion. Scriven prefers to weaken the traditional view by abandoning the second criterion in favor of retaining the first. Either way, one weakens the traditional view of test validity in a way that avoids the indefensible consequence of the traditional view that a test measuring what it purports to measure provides a sufficient justification for test use.

By beginning with a stipulative definition of test validity, Scriven's argument opens itself to a charge of question-begging similar to that of SC&C. One could, however, modify the argument to begin with a definition of *smalidity* in 9.4.1 and then continue on to argue in favor of identifying validity with smalidity later in the argument. This would avoid the charge of question-begging. Nonetheless, the pattern of beginning criticisms of one view of test validity with a contrasting definition warrants attention because it speaks to a lack of systematic method for constructing such arguments in the field.

On one reading, both SC&C and Scriven seek to purify test validity of the aspects of Messick's unified view tainted with value, restricting test validity to purely factual aspects of the total justification of a test interpretation or use. (SC&C and Scriven clearly disagree about the role of values outside of test validity.) Is this tenable? To develop our consideration of this question, we next turn to two philosophers critical of the division between facts and values.

9.5. Searl's Naturalistic-Fallacy Fallacy

> The first fallacy I shall call the *naturalistic-fallacy fallacy*. It is the fallacy of supposing that it is logically impossible for any set of statements of the kind usually called descriptive to entail a statement of the kind usually called evaluative. (Searle, 1969, p. 132)

> [T]o call an argument valid is already to evaluate it and yet the statement that it is valid follows from certain 'descriptive' statements about it. (Searl, 1969, p. 175)

As noted above, one reading of both the SC&C critique and Scriven's critique takes as a basic aim of both critiques to extricate values and valuation from test validity. Both SC&C and Scriven affirmed the role of values in science more broadly (cf. Scriven, 1991). However, SC&C contrasted the factuality of knowledge claims with the evaluation of actions and Scriven contrasted validity as a logical attribute of a test with utility as a matter of empirically derived valuation. Both evaluation and utility have clear and unmistakable ties to value. Although the authors may or may not have intended this reading, it certainly offers a plausible reading of their criticism worthy of attention in its own right. Is such a separation of validity and value possible? The present section considers Searle's (1969) critique of the Naturalistic Fallacy in relation to this latter hypothesis. Searle is a philosopher who has contributed to the philosophy of language in the area of speech act theory, philosophy of mind in the area of consciousness, and social philosophy in areas such as social construction and rationality.

The Naturalistic Fallacy (Moore, 1903) rests on a distinction between descriptive and evaluative statements and the fallacy states that no argument can validly derive an evaluative conclusion from purely descriptive premises. An example will help draw out the plausibility of this idea. One can take as premises a variety of facts about standardized testing: It helps provide information relevant to decision-making, it helps ensure that the same decisions are made the same way for different people, and it helps institutions that use it function more efficiently. From these descriptive premises, however, one cannot validly conclude that standardized testing is good. This requires a further evaluative premise that all of these facts about standardized testing are themselves good. Someone who did not consider these facts good might reasonably not consider standardized testing good. So, the basic idea is that the evaluative conclusion requires some form of evaluative premise. (For the purpose of this simple illustration, we overlook other positive and negative consequences.)

Searle (1969) criticized the Naturalistic Fallacy by providing examples of evaluative conclusions that follow validly from descriptive premises.

Interestingly enough, he took deductive validity as one of his examples. Searle here criticizes an example introduced by an advocate of the Naturalistic Fallacy and thus may not himself accept some of the premises of the argument he builds. Nonetheless, the argument runs roughly thus (cf. Searle's section 6.1, Scriven, 1991, offers a similar example of a ballpoint pen with a factual proper function).

(9.5.1) Categorization of an argument as valid differs, for example, from purely descriptive classification as an instance of a certain argument form. (premise)

(9.5.2) Statement that an argument is valid constitutes a form of endorsement, that it is a good argument. (premise)

(9.5.3) Statement that an argument is invalid constitutes a form of criticism, that it is a poor argument. (premise)

(9.5.4) 'This argument is valid' is an evaluative statement. (9.5.1, 9.5.2, 9.5.3)

(9.5.5) A valid argument is one in which the premises entail the conclusion. (definition)

(9.5.6) That an argument's premises entail its conclusion is a descriptive statement. (premise)

(9.5.7) It follows from 9.5.5. that the fact, that an argument's premises entail its conclusion, itself entails the validity of the argument.

(9.5.8) At least one evaluative conclusion follows validly from descriptive premises. (9.5.4, 9.5.6, 9.5.7)

(9.5.9) The Naturalistic Fallacy is not a true fallacy. (9.5.8, definition of Naturalistic Fallacy)

The argument involves some important subtleties but sheds some interesting light on test validity. Genova (1970) argues that the conclusion (9.5.9) contains an ambiguity. Searle has shown that one sort of value, what Genova calls an institutional value, derives from descriptive statements or what Genova calls institutional facts. In this case, the normative rules of argumentation make it a matter of definition that valid arguments constitute good arguments. However, Searle does not show that another sort of value, what Genova calls brute values, can derive from descriptive statements. As such, Searle's conclusion shows the fallaciousness of the Naturalistic Fallacy if applied universally to all evaluative statements but does not show the fallaciousness of the Naturalistic Fallacy as it may well still apply, non-fallaciously, to brute values. To the best of our knowledge, this issue remains unresolved today and has largely transformed into the issue of cognitivism about ethics: Can values constitute a form of knowledge? Box 9.2 applies Searle's argument to the TOEFL.

In Searle's example, the evaluation of a valid argument as a good argument constitutes an institutional value because the institution of argumentation creates that value as part of its rules. However, the value of participation in the institution of argument in its present form constitutes a brute value, not fixed by the institution itself. Searle shows the derivability of the first but not the second. Likewise, the evaluation of a valid test as, all else held equal, better than an invalid test follows the same pattern. Within the institution of testing as it exists, the evaluation follows from the description of a test as valid. However, the basis for valuing the institution of testing itself remains outside the bounds of Searle's conclusion.

If the foregoing has not very badly misconstrued things, then the very act of describing the validity of a test involves participating in an institutionalized activity that attaches value to validity in tests. As such, describing a test as valid inherently carries with it an evaluative aspect as part of the rules governing the use of the term 'valid' as applied to tests. In the view put forth by SC&C (2002), validity constitutes one desiderata among others used to evaluate a test. In the view put forth by Scriven (2002), validity constitutes a valued quality of a test along with, and possibly basic to, the test's utility. As such, one cannot properly or plausibly interpret either view as separating validity from valuation. The next section turns to a very different sort of argument that does not rest on a distinction between brute and institutional values.

Box 9.2. Applying Searle's Argument to the TOEFL

Searle's argument suggests that one consider the TOEFL in the context of socially institutionalized sets of practices in which it plays a part. In this instance, let us turn to the use of the TOEFL in evaluating grant applications for scholarly work by non-native English speakers in English-speaking countries. Application review committees play a specified role in a set of institutional practices that involves selecting grantees who are most likely to make successful use of the funding agencies grants. In this context, decisions that maximize this likelihood constitute better decisions. Moreover, the connection between greater facility with English and greater likelihood of success offers a reasonably strong link between screening out applicants with poor facility with English and making decisions that maximize likely success. From this it follows that rejection decisions based on a valid knowledge claim that someone lacks facility with English constitute good decisions. In this context, validity evidence that TOEFL scores offer a valid basis for inferring facility with English also provides evidence that using the TOEFL in funding decisions in the specified manner will, on balance, yield better decisions than will using no measure of facility with English.

It would appear that the very same test validity information inherently supports both a factual and a value claim.

Genova's criticism asks us to look beyond the institutional value of funding decisions based on the current institutional practices and ask about the value of the entire institution of such grant funding decisions. Within the institution as we practice it, validity evidence may support the institutional value of using TOEFL scores. From outside the institution, Searle's argument does not necessarily demonstrate that factual evidence can support the brute value of the institution itself. This application of Genova's criticism to the TOEFL assumes that brute values exist and that the value of the institution constitutes such a value. One response to the criticism might be to deny one of these assumptions. Either way, the abstract theory developed by Searle and Genova helps to frame the discussion of concrete questions about testing practice.

9.6. Putnam's Critique of the Fact/Value Dichotomy

> Knowledge of facts presupposes knowledge of values. This is the position I defend. It might be broken down into two separate claims: (i) that the activity of justifying factual claims presupposes value judgments, and (ii) that we must regard those value judgments as capable of being *right* (as 'objective' in philosophical jargon), if we are not to fall into subjectivism with respect to the factual claims themselves. (Putnam, 2002, p. 137)

The previous section looked at Searle's argument to the effect that at least some value statements can derive from fact statements, and drew out some implications for test validity. Putnam (2002) reverses the issue and argues that knowledge of facts derives from, and depends upon, knowledge of values. Putnam is a philosopher who has contributed to the philosophy of mind through the idea that mental states are individuated by their functions and that many brain states can realize the same mental state. He has also contributed to the philosophy of language by sharing in the development of the causal theory of reference, and also by developing arguments in favor of the idea that meanings of mental states such as thoughts or beliefs depend upon the physical context of the individual and not just other mental states.

A familiar picture gives rise to the project of removing values from validity. First one collects the relevant facts. One does this in as objective and dispassionate a manner as possible. Once one has collected the relevant facts, one then sets down to evaluate options against this basis in facts. In the case of testing, the proposals canvassed above each seek to limit test validity to the former step. One collects factual information about the test, more in SC&C's proposal, less in Scriven's proposal, summarized under the rubric of test validity. This factual validity information then plays into a larger evaluation of the utility or otherwise construed value of the use of the test in a given context.

Drawing heavily on Dewey (1926, 1938), Putnam (2002) rested his critique of the fact/value dichotomy on a critique of this familiar picture. He suggested that values imbue any inquiry, no matter how basic. Before inquiry even begins, every person is situated in multiple contexts of critique and problem-solving. The basic argument runs roughly as follows.

(9.6.1)   Concepts remain open to criticism. (premise)
(9.6.2)   Criticism involves valuation. (premise)
(9.6.3)   Adoption of certain concepts depends on values. (9.6.1, 9.6.2)
(9.6.4)   Concepts shape perception. (premise)
(9.6.5)   Factual inquiry rests on perception. (premise)
(9.6.6)   Factual inquiry rests on values. (9.6.3, 9.6.4, 9.6.5)
(9.6.7)   People can and do distinguish warranted and unwarranted judgments of value. (premise)
(9.6.8)   What can be warranted or unwarranted can be known. (premise)
(9.6.9)   Knowledge of facts rests on knowledge of values. (9.6.7, 9.6.8)
(9.6.10) Skepticism about values entails skepticism about facts. (9.6.9)

The relation between values and critique plays an important role in Putnam's argument. The two do not admit of any linear hierarchy in which one grounds the other. Instead, the two form a mutually constitutive pair. Critique makes valued things into knowable values capable of truth and falsity. At the same time, values guide critique, distinguishing it from description. This mutually constitutive pair then provides a basis for conceptualization, perception, and factual inquiry.

The argument that values and critique play this basic role in factual inquiry has particular pertinence for the issue of conceptualizing test validity. Looking at the literature, one sees that the field has developed some facility at describing alternative conceptualizations. However, expositions present these as merely factual, emphasizing the correct description of the facts of testing and test validation. The elective aspect of the description generally does not receive acknowledgement and the possibility of contrasting accurate descriptions goes unconsidered. The literature demonstrates far less facility in the field with evaluating competing conceptualizations and justifying choices between them. The lack of a well-developed methodology for this task presents a significant opportunity for further research and theoretical work in test validity.

Putnam's argument offers a noteworthy counter to an argument advanced by SC&C (2002). SC&C argued that an inclusive notion of validity runs the risk of leaving what counts as valid to the preferences of the powerful. They support this conclusion with the argument that the dominant sociopolitical system will primarily determine what counts as just. As such, conceptualizing validity as dependent upon just consequences of test use places validity in the hands of the dominant sociopolitical system, and hence the powerful. Putnam's argument that criticism renders value claims capable of truth or falsity undermines the central premise of this argument. If a power elite imposes a value system in a way that precludes critical dialog, it loses its status as either correct or even capable of truth or falsity. This does not mitigate the legitimate concern about values imposed by a power elite. However, it does make clear that this concern does not weigh against an expanded notion of validity. The expanded notion of validity can put into place safeguards against such concerns in the form of positive criteria for what counts as value knowledge. The narrow notion of validity directs responsibility for such concerns away from validity theory and places it in the lap of evaluation theory which would ultimately need to introduce the same sorts of safeguards as the expanded notion of test validity to address the same concern.

A dispute between Putnam and Habermas (2003) revolves around an aspect of the issue central to testing human test takers (Box 9.3 applies these issues to the TOEFL). Habermas is a philosopher and sociologist who has contributed to ethics and the philosophy of law through the development of discourse ethics, and social theory through the development of ideas such as communicative reason, the public sphere, and deliberative democracy. Contrary to the conventional view, both agree that value statements belong to a class of statements to which speakers correctly attribute truth or falsity, for which speakers require justification in terms of reasons, and about which individuals and groups can hold mistaken beliefs. Statements about the value of testing, a particular testing practice, or a particular test would all fall into this category as value statements. Habermas contrasts a mindset associated with action and daily practice that accepts such statements as unproblematically true as a basis for taking action and completing practical tasks with a mindset associated with meta-theoretical reflection that retains a fallibilist perspective recognizing that one can draw a false conclusion even in the face of the best available evidence. Habermas and Putnam diverge in their conception of the manner in which values resemble facts. Putnam, recall, views facts and values as lying along a continuum with no line dividing them. Habermas, in contrast, describes an essential distinction along the following lines. If it is a fact that water is heavier than oxygen, then the property of the physical world that makes this statement a fact holds independently of the existence or distinctive characteristics of sapient beings who use language to express this fact. These factors may shape the expression of the fact but not the feature of the physical world that makes the expression true. Values differ in that they hold true or false precisely because they correspond to what members of a community would agree to if they were able to talk through the issue under ideal conditions in which biases due to power differentials and practical limitations did not intervene. As such, facts have an independence from the knowers who know them that values do not fully share.

The distinction takes on a more subtle form when we move from water and oxygen to examples closer to testing human test takers. Unlike the weight of physical substances, measurement of properties of human beings such as personality, knowledge, or beliefs depends entirely on the existence of human beings who have such properties. In some sense, then, neither factual truths nor valuation truths hold independently of human beings within the domain of test validity theory applied to humans. Nonetheless, the distinction drawn by Habermas survives in a less obvious form. The facts that a given test taker falls within the competency range of a given construct, that a certain item has greater difficulty than another in a given population, or that a given test has greater reliability in one population than another, all hold true of the specific test taker, items, or populations in question. One expects values of variables to vary across people and one expects item difficulties and test reliabilities to vary across populations. To treat values in a parallel fashion, however, would collapse them back into a form of subjective relativism that both Putnam and Habermas argue against. An impartial observer can assert that a given individual values educational testing as a tool of improving education but an impartial observer cannot assert that educational testing is good for the given individual without entering into the very valuing discourse on a par with the individual described. Value assertions do not hold true for one person but not another, but only for the entire community of discussants capable of bridging differences of perspective through mutually informative dialog. A bit of science fiction may help bring this into focus: An alien anthropologist can describe facts about human psychology that he or she (or it) does not share. As such, the truth of the factual assertion holds independent of the alien observer. In contrast, as soon as the alien anthropologist makes a value assertion, he, she, or it steps into the community of discussants that determines the truth of the value assertion. As such, while the truth of value assertions remains independent of any one speaker, it does not share the same independence of the broader community of speakers that the truth of factual assertions does if Habermas is correct in his assessment. Nonetheless, Putnam and Habermas would agree, for different reasons, that value statements can be true or false. As such, question the assumptions that go into any attempt to render test validation value neutral or exclude evidence for value judgments from the domain of scientific inquiry.

Box 9.3. Objectivity, Values and the TOEFL

One could plausibly imagine a situation in which a North American university wishes to attract foreign students and considers using the TOEFL as part of its admissions selection criteria. The program faculty may face the concern that the cost of the TOEFL will screen out low-income students who might otherwise apply as foreign students. If the faculty adopts a broad notion of validity, then they will address this issue as part of the consequential basis for test validity. If the faculty adopts a narrow view of validity, then they will address the issue as one of test evaluation outside the narrower confines of the validity argument (although in a strict sense if construct-irrelevant factors deter some test takers from taking the test then the test quite literally does not measure what the test users intend it to measure for those individuals). Either way, the faculty faces an issue of test use that involves assessing the use of the test against value concerns.

Before relating this example to the views of Putnam and Habermas, it may prove useful to first develop the example in relation to a representative of the kind of view with which both contrast. Campbell (1982) advances the view that whereas values can indeed influence science, science remains value neutral in the sense that it cannot establish values. Instead, certain ultimate values (e.g., survival of the species) force themselves upon any human beings and form the justificatory basis for all value judgments without themselves having a justification. Science then justifies all other values as instrumental to advancing these ultimate values. Campbell recognizes, however, that mere survival cannot suffice to ground and fully distinguish between all instrumental values. However, as one begins to elaborate on ultimate values, one encounters fewer and fewer obvious choices forced upon humans in general and more and more alternatives about which one does not find agreement in an increasingly diverse and globalized world. Indeed, the absence of such a bedrock of consensus constitutes one of the core elements characterizing post-globalization social thought. In the absence of a core of universal values, one has two options: the kind of relativist ethical subjectivism that Campbell was reacting against or the kind of ethical objectivism advanced by Putnam and Habermas in response to positions similar to that of Campbell.

Indeed, it seems difficult to imagine demonstrating that the adoption of the TOEFL by the program in this example will have a demonstrable effect, one way or the other, on the survival of the human species. However, it seems equally difficult to specify a core set of ultimate values that would both suffice to settle the question of the use of TOEFL scores in this instance and also receive universal agreement. In Putnam's view, the justification of one or the other choice comes from a source much closer to the problem in question. In facing the problem of selecting students for admissions, the faculty members are struggling with a problem that involves facets of the world around them that can either work out well for them or work out less well. Certain features of the world make factual assertions (e.g., the TOEFL measures facility with North American English) true or false and likewise certain features of the world make value assertions true or false (e.g., it is best to use the TOEFL in admissions decisions). Habermas questions whether values have the same pre-existing universal truth as facts and instead views a sense of shared community as a precondition for a shared correct answer to value questions associated with the conclusion reached under idealized conditions of discussion.

If one supposes that a certain community of potential applicants belongs to a separate community from the faculty in the program, one can imagine a situation where Putnam and Habermas might disagree. For Putnam, the correct value choice holds independent of community. The shared commitment to finding the correct answer should lead members of both communities to a process of inquiry that yields the same results. In contrast, Habermas questions the existence of a shared correct answer unless the applicant community and program community come to see one another as part of a common larger community. Only at that point does the end of ideal discussion constitute a correct answer for all involved. In practice, one could see both Putnam's view and Habermas' view as converging on the standard practice in program evaluation of identifying different stakeholder groups and incorporating their perspectives into the process of evaluation. In either case, one could imagine the applicant group raising criticisms of the selection process because it excludes certain low-income applicants and imagine the program feeling compelled to address this concern. Both Putnam and Habermas might agree that a good response would be to form a working group with members from both communities to address the issue. However, they get there by different routes and justify this strategy for addressing the problem in different ways. Putnam might view it as a means of pooling resources to conduct an inquiry of common interest. He would view the assumption of a universal correct answer as a precondition of the collaborative inquiry. Habermas would view the formation of a broader sense of community as a precondition for a correct answer to the question common to both groups. Both agree in rejecting the view that such questions have no correct answer.

9.7. Conceptualizing Test Validity and its Consequences

Theories of test validity attempt to describe one aspect of tests and testing. One can distinguish between strong and weak underdetermination of descriptions by what they describe. Strong underdetermination entails that the choice has no important consequences and anything goes. Weak underdetermination entails that although the contrasting descriptions both hold true of their subject matter, the choice between them nevertheless has consequences of importance. The contrasting views of test validity explored in this chapter illustrate weak underdetermination. The choice has consequences of importance to the field.

For example, the choice between an inclusive and restricted characterization of test validity might have, perhaps unpredictable, implications for legal dimensions of testing. It could affect what aspects of the total justification for test use admit legal challenge. For example, in the United States, job applicants can challenge an employer's use of tests in selection on the basis of racial or gender discrimination. Such challenges can turn on validity evidence for the use of the test. An inclusive characterization of test validity clearly includes discrimination issues whereas the more restrictive characterizations considered here would exclude it. The direct legal implications of the characterizations, however, seem difficult to predict. One could argue that a more inclusive characterization places a greater burden on validation and thus increases the opportunities for legal challenge. Alternatively, one could argue that a more restrictive characterization will force legal issues to extend beyond the validity argument and thus potentially extend the opportunities of legal challenge beyond what an inclusive characterization allows for.

The choice between an inclusive and restricted construal of test validity could also affect the division of labor between testing specialists and administrators or managers. An inclusive notion of test validity clearly demarcates the total justification for a testing program as within the purview of testing specialists. A more restricted view of test validity, however, views test validity as just one component of the total justification and experts in management, administration, operations research, or other areas might easily lay claim to other components of the total justification. For example, many other fields might offer more experience in computing the return on investment for a testing program than would testing specialists. The desirability of such shifts in the division of labor requires further investigation.

The construal of test validity may also have implications for the relationships between validity issues and ethical issues in testing. Ethical values constitute only a proper subset of values. Clearly, the values involved in one's tastes in clothes, food, or entertainment need not involve ethical values. A failure to appreciate the music of Stravinsky does not constitute an ethical failing. However, the distinction cuts even closer to the sorts of values that guide interpersonal interaction. Searle (1969) gives the example of promising to attend a party (see his p. 188) and then deciding not to go. Many would consider the act remiss but few would consider it unethical. The arguments considered earlier establish that values infuse test validity in an indelible way. They do not touch on the role of specifically ethical values in testing. However, testing clearly does involve ethical issues and so the question arises how these interrelate.

Lefkowitz (2003) illustrates these issues with an example in which a state agency has an established history of discriminatory hiring (cf. pp. 322–326). The issue involves a test for a job category for which those currently holding the job in question would apply in addition to others not currently holding the job. The agency proposes a selection test that measures the job skills developed by those currently performing the job which would serve to reinforce the effects of past discriminatory hiring because those on the job have had preferential opportunity to develop the tested skills. Lefkowitz concludes that the overall justification of the test exceeds narrow validity issues in this example because everyone agrees that the test validly measures the job skills. The example clearly illustrates that ethical issues, in this case fairness, can weigh on test use. The precise relationships between validity issues and the ethical values seem more complex.

To partially unravel some of this complexity, consider how one might spell out the separation between validity issues and ethical issues in this example. It seems fairly clear, as Lefkowitz describes, that Messick's inclusive notion of test validity would incorporate the ethical issues due to the adverse consequences of the proposed test use. Would a more restricted notion of test validity serve to separate these two sets of issues? One can approach the question from either the validity or ethical direction. Let us begin with the latter because this approach seems the less complex of the two.

On a restricted view of test validity, do validity issues play a role in ethical issues? This seems clearly the case. Unequal but inconsequential treatment raises no ethical concerns. If the test simply assigned random numbers to applicants, then it would not introduce any bias—or at least no differential unfairness—into the hiring process. The ethical issues involved rest quite directly on the fact that the test does validly measure a construct sensitive to the prior differential treatment of the two groups of applicants. Thus the validity issue, however narrowly construed, plays a central role in the broader ethical issue in this example. The point readily generalizes.

Conversely, then, on a restricted view of test validity, do ethical issues play a role in validity issues? To make the issue concrete, imagine hiring typists for an agency that uses a proprietary arrangement of keys on a keyboard that reduces those familiar with the standard QWERTY system to hunting and pecking but with a few hours of proprietary training allows typists to type faster than with a standard keyboard. The criterion construct in this instance corresponds to job performance after training, not before. Certainly, a proprietary typing test cannot predict this equivalently both before and after training. If one restricts one's view of validity to just the direct relationship between the test and the construct that it most immediately measures, one could make the argument that the ethical issues in this case—fairness, nondiscrimination—involve only the extraneous issues of prediction of future job performance. One could argue that the measurement of job skills remains the same and equally valid in both groups independent of the broader issues related to prediction of job performance and selection for hiring. One might then further argue, on the basis of this conclusion, that the interrelations between validity issues and ethical issues do indeed depend upon the broad or narrow construal of test validity. Can one make this line of reasoning work?

One line of argument against this conclusion might focus on the bases of the narrow validity argument and the broader justificatory argument. To fully separate these, one needs to break the justificatory argument into two modular steps. First, the narrow validity argument focuses only on establishing that the test measures the job skills. Second, the justificatory argument needs to take the conclusion regarding validity and combine it with other premises related to the purpose of predicting future job performance for selection of new hires. By hypothesis, the validity argument holds independently of the extent of training or work experience that the test takers have. Clearly, however, the justificatory argument does not have this property. In short, by conceptualizing the validity argument in terms of measuring job skills only, the same validity argument fits into a justificatory argument for using the test to predict future performance from post-training job skills and also into an argument against any sound justification for predicting the same from pre-training job skills. To some, such a narrow view of validity may seem to render validity a trivial component of any real-world testing decision. Nonetheless, the validity argument does play an essential role in the larger justificatory argument and this approach does separate the validity argument from the ethical issues involved in Lefkowitz's example.

Putnam's argument regarding conceptualization, however, makes it clear that the above approach fails to separate the validity argument, even in this restricted form, from all value concerns. One must choose between the conceptualization of the construct of interest as either job skills irrespective of pre-training or else post-training job skills (or something else). This choice involves a value judgment to prefer one conceptualization to another and this value judgment becomes correct or incorrect through a process of critical discussion. This application of Putnam's argument clinches the argument that narrowing the notion of test validity cannot separate it from issues of values.

This argument leaves open, however, the possibility that the values inherent in test validity stand distinct from ethical values and involve only values of a different sort. If so, then the restricted approach to validity would succeed in the more limited task of separating validity from ethical values. However, Lefkowitz's example seems to demonstrate the difficulty in achieving even this more limited separation. In the example, the ethical considerations involving test fairness and prior discrimination bear directly on the choice to conceptualize the purpose of the test in terms of job skills irrespective of training versus post-training job skills. In some instances, of course, ethical concerns may not bear directly on the conceptualization of the construct measured. In general, however, these considerations demonstrate that narrowing the construal of test validity will not uniformly succeed in insulating test validity from ethical considerations. In other words, narrowing test validity does not provide an effective procedure for achieving this separation. Similar arguments apply to scientific values that guide choices between good and bad evidence and good and bad theory construction.

In summary, the choice of conceptualization of test validity will affect the interrelations between validity issues and ethical issues. It will not fully separate validity issues from value issues. However, it can have an impact on the manner in which broader ethical issues interconnect with test validity issues in the broader justificatory argument. Despite these differences in how the different elements interlock, however, the overall ethical issues remain essentially isomorphic across different conceptualizations of test validity. The differences primarily involve the role of test validity—which of course differs across conceptualizations thereof—in the broader ethical issues.

9.8. Chapter Conclusion

If a test measures what one interprets it as measuring, test scores can still remain sensitive to other factors as well. If a test only measures what one interprets it as measuring, then it still may fail to measure it as effectively as it could. Even if a test measures only what one interprets it to measure and does so highly effectively, the broader system of decision-making or resource allocation in which the one embeds the use of the test may have drawbacks or admit preferable alternatives. For these reasons, decisions about testing require more information than a narrow construal of test validity provides. Advocates of a narrow interpretation generally do not dispute this point.

Given the untenability of the traditional view that test validity is both restricted and sufficient for justification, the concept of test validity needs weakening in one of these two respects. One can approach insufficiency as a problem and seek to address it with a broader theory or else take insufficiency as a virtue of a clear and simple theory of validity and seek

220 Interpreting Test Responses: Validity, Values, and Evaluation

to supplement validity with other information required to make testing decisions. Various authors have explored alternatives in varying degrees of detail. Messick sought to retain sufficiency for justification whereas SC&C and Scriven sought instead to retain a narrower construal of test validity. However, the literature lacks detailed or conclusive argument in favor of taking one approach or the other to weakening the concept of test validity. Resolution of the issue requires further research into the entailments and consequences of the various options. The present chapter does not seek to resolve this issue but the foregoing discussion does begin to explore the theoretical context of the issue. In that context, the general agreement about the nature of the argument required to justify a test interpretation or use seems much more important than the specific distribution of terminology on which the field ultimately decides.

9.9. Further Reading

Messick, S. (1989). Validity. In R. L. Linn (Ed.), *Educational measurement* (3rd ed., pp. 13–103). New York: Macmillan.

Putnam, H. (2002). *The collapse of the fact/value dichotomy and other essays.* Cambridge, MA: Harvard University Press. (especially chapters 6 and 8)

Scriven, M. (2002). Assessing six assumptions about assessment. In H. I. Braun, D. N. Jackson, & D. E. Wiley (Eds.), *The role of constructs in psychological and educational measurement* (pp. 255–275). Mahwah, NJ: Erlbaum.

Searle, J. R. (1969). *Speech acts: An essay in the philosophy of language.* Cambridge, UK: Cambridge University Press. (Chapters 6 and 8)

Shadish, W. R., Cook, T. D., & Campbell, D. T. (2002). *Experimental and quasi-experimental designs for generalized causal inference.* Boston: Houghton Mifflin. (Chapter 14)

10 A Model of Test Score Interpretation

Connections With Other Chapters

The familiar idea of a test score interpretation was introduced in chapter 1. Chapter 9 considered the basic tenets that (a) validity is sufficient for test interpretation and use and (b) validity involves only a restricted range of evidence and found them jointly inadequate. A theory of validity can embrace either of these tenets, but not both. Moreover, careful unpacking of a number of relevant arguments suggests that values are deeply embedded and fundamental to the validation process. Validation involves evaluating tests according to some normative standard, and any such scientific judgment involves implicit values. Validity and valuation are joined at the hip. Finally, the implications of these considerations for the role of consequences in test validity were explored. Chapter 11 considers open questions in test score interpretation and meaning.

This chapter and the next build on the foundation laid in the previous chapter by exploring the contribution that various forms of evidence can make toward supporting a conclusion regarding the meaning or interpretation of test scores. The issue of score meaning connects with the measurement section in that assumptions about the nature of measurement fit into the interpretation of test scores as outlined in this chapter. The issue also connects to the middle section of the book because in order to establish a causal assertion that a given construct causes a given set of test scores, one first needs to fix the reference of the terms used in the causal assertion. The present chapter develops a general theoretical framework. The next canvasses open questions related to the meaning of test scores. Chapter 11 will survey various types of evidence relevant to test validation research and explore how it bears on test score interpretations in light of the model and questions presented in this chapter.

The next two sections introduce a focal example used to carve out a basic understanding of the issues at hand and then develop some key concepts and a basic picture of test score interpretation. The section that follows these presents the basic picture in more detail and considers potential criticisms.

Consider a very simple test that many of us use on a regular basis: knocking on someone's door. The test is intended to indicate whether the person is inside. An answer or an opening of the door, or more or less any response, counts as a positive response (keyed response). Non-response counts as a negative response. Like all real tests, this one involves some measurement error. Non-response could occur because the person is otherwise occupied (on the phone perhaps) and thus unable to respond. A misleading response could occur, say, if one heard the occupant's voice on an answering machine that just happened to activate after the knock. By and large, however, the test is widely used because it tends to be quite reliable and more practical than available alternatives (e.g., X-rays, breaking down the door, slipping a spy camera under the door).

Consider three users of this test: Aleena, Brandi, and Jan. Aleena habitually assumes that the test is inconclusive. She often attempts to open doors after receiving no response, or simply walks away after receiving an invitation to enter. Brandi habitually assumes that the person is available if she receives a response and not otherwise. Jan habitually assumes that no response indicates that the person must be dead. He then immediately deletes the person from his smartphone. Intuitively, one might naturally describe Aleena as making inadequate interpretations of the test scores, Brandi as making useful, appropriate, and justified interpretations, and Jan as over-interpreting the test scores. The goal of the present chapter is to flesh out this intuitive description in a way that sheds light on test interpretation and use, and their validity.

An alternative to the above description might deny that it makes sense to talk about interpretations of test scores. Such a description might take the relationship between the construct being assessed (availability of the person behind the door) and the test scores (response or non-response to a knock) as an entirely natural phenomenon subject to scientific description and explanation, but not interpretation. From such a perspective, interpretations might only apply to linguistic entities such as utterances, written sentences, and perhaps pictures. On this description, Aleena has an inadequate theory of knock responses, Brandi has a good theory, and Jan has a strong but incorrect theory. One can interpret statements of the theory, but not the object of explanation itself. Thus, from this view, familiar and intuitive talk about interpretation of test scores is simply mistaken or confused. Such a view might become attractive if all attempts to make sense of test score interpretation fail but, as a general rule, a theory that makes sense of common practice offers something preferable to a theory that fails in this attempt. Iconoclasm is generally not the option of first preference.

To gain some purchase on the intuitive description of test score interpretation, it helps to think in terms of the process of sensemaking (Weick, 1979; 1995), the process through which people make sense of and assign meaning to their environment. In some cases, sensemaking involves ascribing an intended meaning to a linguistic message, such as in interpreting a note from a colleague as meant literally or ironically. In some cases, sensemaking involves ascribing an intention to a non-linguistic action or event, such as interpreting one's colleague's closing his or her door as either indicating a need for quiet or a desire not to be interrupted, and possibly basing one's decision whether or not to knock on the door on this interpretation. In some cases, sensemaking involves ascribing meaning to objects for which no author's intention has any bearing, such as interpreting uniform work stations as a symbol of regimentation (or egalitarianism), reinterpreting a broken pencil sharpener as a potential paperweight, or retaining a nameplate or other small object as a memento of a previous place of employment. In all three cases, the interpretation is not fixed by the object or an author, but instead depends upon the context (Derrida, 1988; Wieck, 1995). All three examples could take on different meanings in different contexts. However, in all three examples the ascription of meaning affects the truth or falsity of various sentences (such as one's answer to the question "Do you have a paperweight in your office?").

One thing that can make the anti-interpretation view appealing is the traditional model of language as a means by which a sender encodes a mental representation of objects in the world and transmits it to a recipient, and by which the recipient decodes the representation. One way to see how this model can be overly restrictive is to consider that natural languages contain words for things that do not exist. Standard examples include unicorns and minotaurs, and psychometric examples might include feeblemindedness and the ability to detect unobserved gaze (Colwell, Schröder & Sladen, 2000). Conversely, cognitive science has increasingly come to recognize that minds developed as parts of bodies operating in the world and this aspect of minds plays an important role in their constitution and functioning (Dennett, 1991; Varela, Thompson & Rosch, 1991). For example, minds process procedural knowledge that involves no representation of the outside world such as the phenomenon of muscle memory where repetition and practice allows a person to master and remember a task too complex to be described to another person. Similarly, interpretation of test scores does not follow the model of encoding, transmitting, and decoding a mental representation of the outside world. However, in light of other exceptions to the model, this lack of fit does not give us reason to reject the idea of test score interpretation.

Consider how the reading on a thermometer, perhaps the canonical example of a physical measurement of a natural phenomenon, can have different interpretations. The same reading could be interpreted as a measure of temperature, of heat (as for a body of known mass and uniform temperature), of localized temperature (as for a meat thermometer in a roasting chicken), or even pressure (as for a body of gas with a known volume). In another context, one might interpret it as indicative of the successful repair of a heating system. In the case of a score on an achievement test, the meaning is unlikely to be related to the test taker's intention, whereas in the case of a score on an attitude survey, it might bear a much closer connection. The remainder of the chapter will flesh out this picture in greater detail.

10.1. Focal Example: Tuna Cleaner Work Sample

Envision a tuna canning facility with a large number of employees working as tuna cleaners, a job that involves separating tuna white meat and dark meat from the bones and each other after other tuna skinners skin the tuna, remove the head and tail, and quarter the resulting tuna loins (Garson, 1994, chapter 1). Suppose that the personnel office of the canning company wants to develop a selection test for this job category. The job has two main criteria of successful performance: speed and accuracy. The personnel office develops a job simulation procedure which instructs applicants in proper slicing procedures and then asks them to slice tuna for a fixed period of time with the further instruction that they are to slice as quickly as they can without sacrificing accuracy. Scorers then evaluate the product in terms of the quantity of tuna sliced and the quantity of misplaced white and dark meat—either placed with the wrong kind of meat or with the bones. These two quantities respectively yield speed and accuracy scores. The example raises broader organizational issues of work design and work conditions, but in the present context the purpose is only to provide a concrete example of a specialized work sample used as a selection test. Where a unidimensional example is needed, one can imagine modifying the tuna cleaning test, as might be done with a typing test, to require complete accuracy and then assessing speed for completely accurate tuna cleaning work samples.

The selection process eliminates applicants below a minimum cut-score on accuracy, and then selects from the remaining applicants in order of speed. The personnel office wishes to interpret the test scores as valid indicators of tuna slicing ability, justifying their use as a selection tool for tuna slicers. Critics could conceivably challenge this interpretation on a number of grounds. For instance, the ordering of applicants in terms of ability may change if they are given more practice between instruction and testing. Moreover, the ordering of ability might change if speed and accuracy are measured over a long period, more typical of a work day, than a shorter period typical of only the start of a work day. Before one can begin to consider these issues, however, one needs a clear understanding of how various types of evidence can bear on the interpretation of the test scores. Before one can begin to develop a clear description of such relationships, however, one needs to back up still further and consider what test score interpretations amount to and how test scores take on meaning, the central concern of this section of the book.

10.2. Interpretation and Entailment: Construct Theories as Inference Engines

Before entering further into a discussion of the interpretation of test scores, it is important to clearly identify the intended object of interpretation. Figure 10.1 distinguishes the test scores from both the construct and the construct label. For a tuna cleaner, his or her speed serves as the construct, a phrase such as 'tuna cleaning speed' serves as the construct label, and the estimated value of the construct given by the test serves as the test score. Moreover, one can express the same value on a linear or logarithmic scale, or perhaps in binary or hexadecimal format, without changing the score itself. So, the score is the actual value not its representation in digits or some other form.

The basic idea developed in this chapter is that two interpretations differ if one can draw different conclusions from them. If one makes more fine-grained distinctions, the converse does not hold: two interpretations supporting the same conclusions can still differ. However, such differences are presumably differences that do not make a difference in practice. So, we focus on the differences that affect conclusions. The construct theory provides the engine for such inferences by providing a clear statement of the interpretation and how one can draw conclusions from it. Two interpretations that produce the same inferences constitute distinct expressions of the same interpretation.

For example, '$x > 1$' and '$x \geq 1$' have different meanings because one entails that '$x \neq 1$' whereas the other does not. By analogy, we can gain some purchase on the meaning of test scores under a given interpretation by comparing what follows from them. Interpreting a measure of

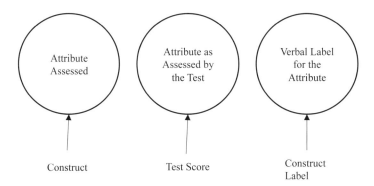

Figure 10.1 What the Test Score Is and Is Not.

an individual's weight in an absolute sense entails that wherever they may be, they will exert roughly the same amount of force on the surface beneath them when at rest. Interpreting the same scores as measures of mass allows that weight itself is relative to the proximity to a gravitational source. This difference has important practical implications if one is designing a vehicle for space travel. The score interpretations differ in meaning because they differ in their entailments with respect to the force an individual can be expected to exert. Likewise, interpreting admissions test scores as measures of aptitude entails that learning opportunity and exposure have minimal effects on the construct measured by the admissions test. In contrast, interpreting the scores as measures of achievement acknowledges the impact of opportunity and exposure on the construct measured by the test. The interpretations have different entailments, and these are empirically distinguishable. Moreover, the different interpretations have different implications for the use of the scores in practice.

In practice, most construct theories and test score interpretations will make use of natural language descriptions and thus involve informal arguments and inferences. Nonetheless, it can be helpful for test validity theory to consider formal representations as a means to better explicating the nature of the informal inferences. Such formalizations encourage a distinction between two elements of an inference engine, axioms and inference rules, and this distinction is useful for informal construct theories as well. Suppose that one applies some basic test theory to estimate a standard error of measurement for the tuna cleaning speed score (or a conditional standard error of measurement function from observed test scores to standard errors). That the test score estimates the construct functions like an axiom of the construct theory for the test. That one can infer from a test score that the construct value probably lies within certain bounds is an inference rule. These combine with the test score to allow an inference from the test score to the interval estimate of the construct. It follows directly, then, that differences in interpretation result not only from different presumed facts (like formal axioms) about a construct but also from different inferential practices (like formal inference rules). The presumed facts about the construct do not exclusively determine the allowable inferences.

Moreover, to the extent that the inference rules allow inputs from outside the construct theory, new information from outside the theory can add new conclusions. For example, suppose someone invented a new tuna cleaning tool such that those who could clean tuna well with the current tools also do well with the new tool. However, some proportion of people who cannot clean tuna effectively with the existing tool can with the new tool. Based on this knowledge and the construct theory, one can draw further inferences from the test scores. For example, one can infer that high-scoring individuals will also clean tuna effectively with the new tool. Conversely, the interpretation of low scores is modified because some low scorers could clean effectively if they had access to the new tool. This makes test score interpretations very sensitive to contextual information, but this seems the desired result. One advantage of a highly elaborated construct theory is that it makes test scores more informative and the above phenomenon accurately reflects that.

Before moving further, this is perhaps a suitable point to address some sources of discomfort with the idea that test scores have interpretations. Bernstein (1983) identified a Cartesian anxiety pervasive through a number of contemporary debates rooted in various forms of an assumption that scientific knowledge is universal and timeless, and must be based on universal principles to avoid falling into an anything-goes form of relativism in which any method is as good as any other and choices between conclusions have no basis in facts or evidence. In the context of test validity, this either/or thinking can manifest itself in an implicit assumption that test validation must rest on a unitary methodology that produces universal timeless knowledge about test scores or all testing rests on arbitrary subjective opinions. Bernstein describes an incipient dissolution of this either/or thinking through shift toward greater appreciation of the interpretive aspects of scientific practice. The role of interpretation in test score use does not mean that test scores can mean anything anyone wants them to. It does mean, however, that the justification of test score interpretation is a conversation in which two or more parties need to work to agree upon a shared approach of resolving disputes. Test validation cannot effectively proceed by one party stipulating to the other the criteria for justifying a test score interpretation. According to Bernstein, it is precisely this communal collaborative effort that promises to move us past the paradoxes of the Cartesian either/or thinking. This shift is implicit in the pragmatic elements of the theory of validity arguments (Kane, 2006) and the idea of validation as explanation (Zumbo, 2009).

With this intuitive notion of interpretation in mind, let us return to the focal example in order to further evaluate the hypothesis that scores take meaning through the process of measurement. If a given employee slices five kilograms of tuna in the allotted time, and does so within the allowed level of accuracy, then he or she has a speed score of five according to the testing procedure. A minimal interpretation of the score of five contains no content in excess of this particular individual having a score of five on this job sample. By using a number of formal rules of logic, one may derive infinitely many conclusions from this: The employee exists, the employee's score is either five or six, either the employee's score is five or pigs fly, the employee's score is five and either pigs fly or they do not, and so on. These multifarious deductions share the feature of not providing much interesting information. They seem far removed from the sorts of practical inferences that surround test use in practice.

If we interpret the test score a little further, however, interesting conclusions begin to fall out. For instance, if we interpret the score to mean that the employee has a score of five and this score represents the individual's true ability plus random error, then we can begin to draw conclusions like the fact that the score is the maximum likelihood estimate of the person's true ability, and if the employee repeated the job sample, we would expect increasingly dissimilar scores with decreasing probability. In contrast, if a critic is correct to interpret the score as a score of five representing the employee's true ability, random error, and a practice effect subtracted out, then different conclusions follow. One would expect, on average, that the next score for the same employee on the same job sample would exceed the previous score by the practice effect. So, already the two interpretations have empirically divergent consequences that the personnel office might use to choose between them.

Box 10.1. The WAIS-III Digit Span Subtest: Overcautious, Cautious, and Insufficiently Cautious Interpretations

The Digit Span subtest of the WAIS-III involves repeating a sequence of digits in reverse order. The administration of the test involves one-on-one assessment of a single examinee. The Digit Span subtest constitutes one of seven verbal subtests, and one of 14 total subtests. Verbal subtests involve language, in contrast to the seven performance subtests which involve physical manipulation rather than verbal communication.

Suppose that a particular examinee earned a digit span score of 6. An extremely overcautious interpreter of this score may take it to mean only that the person doing the assessment assigned a score of 6 to the examinee. Such an overcautious interpretation does not provide much usable information or support interesting inferences. It does support uninteresting inferences, like the fact that tomorrow it will remain the case that a score of 6 was assigned to this examinee, and so on. This interpretation does not support many natural inferences that one might ordinarily make from the test score. For instance, it does not support the inference that one might expect a score close to 6 on a second administration. It does not support the inference that the person performed better than a typical person with a score of 4. It certainly does not support any inference whatsoever about the person's abilities or performance. For all one knows, it may simply reflect a random number assigned to the person upon completion of the digit span subtest.

This absurd paucity of inferential value reflects the fact that the above overcautious interpretation leaves out information that a test user would ordinarily take for granted. As such, one would want to augment the interpretation to include some of this information in order to improve the usefulness of the score. If one includes information about the proper administration and scoring of the digit span subtest, and the fact that these were followed for this score, along with some basic test theory regarding the stochastic relationship between individual scores and the underlying ability to remember, reorder, and repeat digits, the score reaches a level of meaning that supports more useful inferences. For instance, from the score of 6 one might reasonably infer a lack of any serious cognitive deficits related to the digit span task.

It would not be difficult, however, to expand the interpretation further to something insufficiently cautious. A clumsy example might involve incorporating some incorrect information into the interpretation. For instance, one might incorporate the non-fact that 2 represents an average score, or that the digit span subtest has perfect reliability and no error variance. From such false assumptions, many further incorrect and misleading inferences would flow, such as that the person's ability was far above average, and that if the person took the test again it would yield a score of exactly 6.

A more subtle example might involve plausible assumptions that nonetheless lack adequate support. One example might be the common assumption that the digit span, letter-number sequencing, and arithmetic subtests collectively measure working memory, providing a basis for a working memory index formed from these three sub-scores. This assumption might lead a test user to misinterpret a poor arithmetic score as indicative of a working memory deficit, when in fact it might instead represent a deficit in verbal comprehension (Kane & Krenzer, 2006; McGrew, 1997). This over-interpretation of the arithmetic score might encourage the use of the arithmetic subtest in isolation, without the full administration of the other subtests in order to reduce the assessment time and the burden on the examinee (the full administration takes between 60 and 90 minutes). However, such a shortening of the test protocol might eliminate the sources of information most likely to raise questions about the questionable assumption. High digit span and letter-number sequencing scores might suggest another reason for a low arithmetic score, but not if the working-memory interpretation encourages the test user to skip the other two subtests to avoid redundancy.

10.3. Interpretations of Test Scores

One can encapsulate the picture developed in the present chapter in terms of the following six claims. The claims are stated together here, but elaborated more fully through the remainder of the chapter.

Claim 1. Item response behaviors are coded and used to produce test scores. Individuals take values (e.g., magnitudes, ordinals, class memberships) as test scores, not words or numerals, not necessarily the correct result of the testing process, and not necessarily the correct value of the construct being measured.

Claim 2. Values take on interpretations as scores when interpreted by test users as part of the communicative processes in and through which testing takes place.

Claim 3. Interpretations of an individual test score can be modeled as a set of propositions which must at minimum include the proposition that the individual has the magnitude in question as his or her test score. Assumptions about the nature of measurement also enter the picture at this point (the kinds of assumptions discussed in chapters 2 to 4).

Claim 4. Differences in entailments signal differences in interpretation. Thus, test score interpretations differ when they differ in what one can conclude from them. However two different interpretations can have the same implications.

Claim 5. The strongest evidence for deciding between rival interpretations involves observations that involve maximal differences in entailments between the two interpretations. Informal assessment of such comparative judgments suffices in routine practice, but when disagreements challenge these judgments a theory such as the above has utility in clarifying and working through such disagreements.

Claim 6. Good interpretations have the strength to support useful inferences without overstepping evidential support. This bears on the practice of validation which should seek to validate good interpretations.

This picture provides in rough outline an explanation of how empirical evidence can bear on the interpretation of test scores. For ease of reference, we dub this picture the Goldilocks Model because it advises seeking an interpretation that finds a balance between hardness and softness (Ober, 1981). One does not want a Momma Bear interpretation, too soft to support workaday inferences but one also does not want a Papa Bear interpretation, so hard that it exceeds reasonable evidential support and thus also fails to support workaday inferences. Instead, one seeks a Baby Bear interpretation that gets this balance just right. The interpretation should be strong enough to support the required inferences, but also sufficiently supported by evidence that the evidence supports the inferences as well.

This model integrates neatly with Kane's (2006) ideas of interpretive arguments and validity arguments. As shown in Figure 10.2, to this list we add the interpretive inferences described above. All three are related in a chain. The validity argument draws on various premises (P_v) to support conclusions (C_v) to the effect that, in general, the scores from the test indicate a particular construct. These conclusions, C_v, provide some of the premises in the interpretive argument (P_i) supporting conclusions about specific test takers on the basis of their scores (C_i). Likewise, these latter conclusions, C_i, then serve as some of the premises (P_t) in the interpretation of the test scores and these, in turn, yield a set of conclusions extending beyond the scope of the interpretive argument (C_t). The conclusion of the interpretive argument, C_i, constitutes the denotation of the test score, whereas the conclusions drawn from interpretive inferences, C_t, constitute its full interpretation. As such, different interpretations differ because they hold different entailments. We refer to this as an interpretation rather than the meaning of the test scores because interpretations are expressible in language and thinkable whereas meanings outnumber these. Lewis (1973) notes that the set of sentences of finite length in a finite language will have the same size (cardinality) as the set of real numbers (aka $\beth_1$) whereas the set of possible worlds is larger (as large as the set of subsets of real numbers, $\beth_2$). Lewis (1986) posits that the set of propositions understood as sets of possible worlds would then be yet larger (at least as large as the set of subsets of the set of subsets of real numbers, $\beth_3$). The upshot of all of this is that there are propositions that cannot be thought or expressed in language. If we understand meanings in relation to propositions, this means that the meaning of tests scores exceeds their interpretation because the interpretation is expressible in language but the meaning is not fully so. Indeed, if Lewis is correct, the meaning of a test score might not even be fully thinkable.

As does Kane (2006), we envision the actual work of test validation as involving informal expressions of such arguments and inferences. However, we also see a place for at least partial formalization to clarify and resolve disputes where they occur or to advance test validity theory outside of the context of workaday inferences used in test development or test use. Citing Toulmin (2003), Kane seems to envision a strict distinction of kind between formal and informal arguments. We do not find in Toulmin's work a reason to believe that arguments naturally divide into inherently informal and inherently formal arguments, or that these mark a fundamental difference in kind. Toulmin's focus seems to lie more

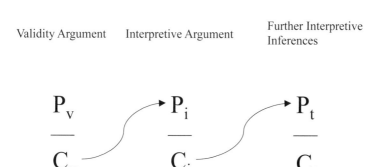

Validity Argument   Interpretive Argument   Further Interpretive Inferences

Figure 10.2 Two Arguments and an Inference

directly with the distinction between analytic arguments (e.g., mathematical proofs) and substantive arguments (e.g., inductive inferences). While we agree that test validation does not reduce to a formal calculus, it is not clear that the statements we treat as analytic differ inherently from those we do not (Quine, 1980) or that the distinction between analytic and substantive arguments drawn by Toulmin necessarily gets to the heart of the matter dividing formal logic from applied logic (Cowan, 1964). Moreover, we agree with Pollock (1990) that formalization is often an effective tool in advancing the study of a particular topic. In short, we see a place for the occasional formalization of validity arguments treated informally in the validation process.

To illustrate, let us return to the tuna cleaning work sample. Suppose the employer wants to use the test scores to make inferences about who will be the most skilled employees (C_i). The observed test scores combine with a host of assumptions about the testing process—no interference with optimal performance, the test takers understand the task, the scores are recorded properly, the work sample conditions are similar to actual work conditions, and so on—to support this inference (P_i). The inference from P_i to C_i constitutes the interpretive argument in this case. An inference from work sample scores to work performance could go wrong due to any of the additional premises in the interpretive argument. For example, the task may not have been adequately explained in which case prior job knowledge might interject a form of construct-irrelevant variance. The validity argument musters support (P_v) for these various additional premises of the interpretive argument (C_v). What we are calling interpretive inferences differ from the interpretive argument in that they go beyond the immediate inference identified as the intended purpose of the test. Validation involves providing support for the interpretive argument, but not every additional interpretive inference. The additional interpretive inferences, however, flesh out the meaning of the scores in ways that may or may not directly relate to the intended purpose of the test scores. It seems clear that one can construct more than one correct path from P_v to C_t for any given case. The choice between these may simply come down to convenience for a specific application. As such, the illustration developed here provides just one example of how one can flesh out these three elements.

For example, let us suppose that the target construct is tuna slicing ability assumed to remain constant during the first year of employment. If research supported the theory that tuna cleaning ability is relatively fixed, then the test scores would support additional interpretive inferences to the effect that employees' cleaning ability would remain close to that indicated by their current scores for the foreseeable future. In contrast, if research supported the theory that tuna cleaning ability follows a fan curve over the period of employment, then the scores would instead support interpretive inferences to the effect that employees' relative ranking in ability would remain the same, but that the gaps between employees would grow over time. These further inferences are not crucial to the interpretive argument if the purpose is to choose applicants who will have the most tuna cleaning ability during the first year. However, they may have further implications for the employer in terms of how many tuna cleaners he or she wants to hire in a given year, the design of productivity incentives, or decisions about designing opportunities for lateral transfer into the factory's job structure.

The above framework applies to various forms of models relating items on a test to a construct. The tuna example most naturally corresponds to a reflective model, although not necessarily measurement in the strong sense of the term. One could also apply the framework to a set of items used in a formative model where the items cause the construct. In this case, the validity argument might include evidence that the items do in fact cause the intended construct. Moreover, the argument might include evidence that the causal effects weight the items appropriately for the desired composite variable and that the residual variance is within a range consistent with the intended construct.

The distinction between the interpretive argument and these ancillary interpretive inferences helps clarify the sense in which test validation is continuous with scientific research into the construct, but nonetheless not identical with it. The interpretive inferences are similar in kind to the inference embodied in the interpretive argument. However, validation focuses on the interpretive argument whereas scientific research into the construct may extend beyond this to the various interpretive inferences. Validation focuses on one circumscribed set of inferences whereas scientific research casts a wider net. However, there is no fundamental difference in kind between the inferences included in the interpretive argument and those relegated to interpretive inferences outside of that argument. The inference from test scores to long-term development of tuna cleaning skill might be considered external to the identity of the tuna cleaning construct during early stages, but then become more central to distinguishing the construct from rival hypotheses about what the test assesses in later stages. In such a case, the inference would function as an interpretive inference early on, and then transform into part of the interpretive argument as the construct theory became more sophisticated. The distinction is context dependent.

Before moving on, it may be useful to comment further on the application of Toulmin's model to inferences involved in testing. Toulmin (2003) argues that treating all premises of an argument as of one kind obscures important functional differences. Taking classical Aristotelian syllogisms as its starting point, Toulmin distinguishes data and warrants as two kinds of premises. For example, that Cheng-gong has a score of 21 on a given test provides data, whereas other elements of the interpretive argument provide warrants to infer from that score something about

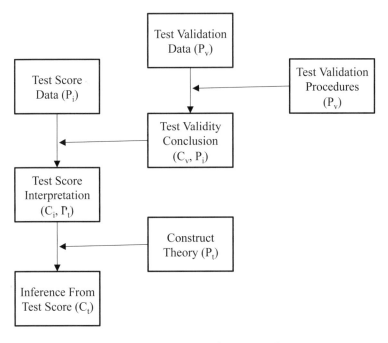

Figure 10.3 Toulmin Model of Test Score Inferences and Arguments

Cheng-gong's level on the construct measured by the test, or that a certain action can or should be taken with respect to Cheng-gong on the basis of this score. The conclusions of the validity argument (C_v) provide warrants for the interpretive argument (P_i) and the premises of the validity argument provide what Toulmin calls backing for these warrants (P_v). Likewise, the conclusion of the interpretive argument, C_i, provides the data for interpretive inferences that invoke warrant drawn from the construct theory (Figure 10.3). The remainder of this chapter develops the various elements of the picture spelled out in the previous numbered claims, and considers foreseeable objections.

10.3.1. *Claim 1: Test Scores as Values*

The key term in Claim 1 is 'value'. Claim 1 applies this term to both magnitudes and properties that individuals take on values as test scores. The previous examples involved quantitative measurements for which the corresponding values take the form of magnitudes or quantities. However, it has become customary, following Stevens (1946), to apply the term 'value' as well to nominal or ordinal measurements where the corresponding values take the form of names or positions in an ordering rather than magnitudes. This use of the term 'value' of course contrasts with the use in the previous chapter to refer to normative value in the sense of merit or worth (although the shared etymology is clear enough). One normally prefers to avoid using one term in two distinct senses. Given the entrenched use of the term in each of these senses, this seems unavoidable, but the context should nonetheless serve to make clear which sense of 'value' applies. Whereas the previous chapter primarily addressed values in the normative sense applied in ethics and evaluation, this chapter and the next primarily address values in the descriptive sense applied in measurement and statistical analysis.

10.3.2. Claim 2: Test Scores Interpreted

Claim 2 attributes interpretations directly to scores and this warrants some comment. One normally speaks of interpreting things said or written but not of interpreting trees or shoes. What makes test scores more like things said or written than like trees or shoes in this context? The message encoding–decoding model of communication discussed at the start of the chapter produces conflicting intuitions here. In one sense, one encodes information into test scores that test score users decode, but this is not the relevant sense here. As discussed above, in the present context, we refer to properties, ordinal positions, counts, or magnitudes as test scores. We do not refer to the symbols that encode these as test scores. So, the interpretation of the symbols as encoding one of the above sorts of values is not at issue in Claim 2. For example, that '101' encodes an IQ score one point above the mean is not at issue. The present concern rests with the fact that one interprets the score of 101 as indicating that the person tested at a certain location on the norm referenced IQ scale and that one draws certain conclusions from this. Such interpretation does not involve decoding a message encoded by a sender. So, it is not really that test scores are more like things said or written than like trees and shoes. Instead, it is that test scores are observations and test score users interpret and use those observations in much the same way as people do with other less formal types of observations.

Nonetheless, test scores are more similar to things said and written than to words and sentences in one important respect. The structural approach to language considers word and sentence meanings as fixed universal attributes of an abstract language (Cann, 1993; Radford, 1988). The discourse approach to language considers utterance meanings as specific to the context of use and as part of concrete patterns of discourse practices unique to contexts and specific sets of individuals (Bakhtin 1986; Brown & Yule, 1983). So, it is not highly abstract universal test score interpretations that interest test users so much as specific context-dependent interpretations. The focus of test validation follows the interests and activities of test users.

Test score interpretations, as understood here, involve the nexus at which test scores enter into semantic relationships such as entailment, contradiction, or providing support for conclusions in informal arguments. Chloé's IQ score of 94 entails that she scored below the mean. Enzo's score of 110 contradicts that he scored 111. Océane's score of 168 supports her petition for admission to a gifted education program. It is in this sense that we speak of test scores as having interpretations.

10.3.3. Claim 3: Modeling Interpretations as Premises

Claim 3 asserts that one can model a test score interpretation as a set of premises from which one may then draw further inferences. This approach carries a number of important implications. First, it indicates that test score interpretations function as more than merely labels attached to familiar and unambiguous objects. Throughout the chapter we will refer to this overly simple picture as the *price tag theory* of constructs because it presents an image of test developers uniquely identifying variables with little more than a casual inspection and then attaching the appropriate label from a fixed inventory list. Upon entering a typical department store for the first time, a complete novice could attain near perfect reliability at identifying when two randomly selected products constitute two of the same product as opposed to two different products. Identifying constructs does not normally work that way. Presented with an abstract construct such as personality or intelligence, figuring out how best to differentiate the construct from related entities and how best to characterize it as part of that process prove more challenging than in the case of the department store items. These tasks become a significant portion of the theoretical and empirical work involved in researching the construct. At an even more basic level, however, this price tag theory of constructs fails to account for the tremendous amount of information about the origin of the scores implicit in the testing process and about the characteristics of variables implicit in the measurement model. Yet, these sources of information play crucial roles in drawing inferences from test scores in even the most mundane testing practices. In the next chapter, discussion of open questions will bring out further objections to assuming a simple and unproblematic naming process as an adequate characterization of test score interpretation. For present purposes, recall from chapter 1 that we use the term construct to refer to the magnitude or property either assessed or intended for assessment depending upon the context (Wiley, 2002). We never use it to refer to the word or term used to refer to this magnitude or property. The main point for present purposes is that the possible constructs that a test could measure are not laid out for us beforehand in a discrete, accessible, and unambiguous manner such that we can simply point to the one we have in mind to select it from the others. Instead, identifying a construct as what a test measures involves a complex, creative, messy, and difficult task of conceptualizing that magnitude (Sechrest, 2005) and working out a theory of it that distinguishes it from rival hypotheses while explaining the bulk of the existing empirical data that bears on it (Messick, 1989). This does not rule out the idea that constructs subject to assessment with tests can sometimes involve natural kinds in the sense of types that exist as types independently of human conceptualization (Mill, 1874; Quine, 1969). Natural kinds are types that are discovered rather than invented. Nonetheless, nature does not lay out a list of natural kinds from which one can choose in so obvious a manner as in the department store example given above. Discovery of such kinds involves hypothesis formation and revision of the same messy and complicated sort that we find elsewhere in empirical sciences. For example, it may be easy to recognize silver and gold as natural kinds of mineral, but it may take some empirical trial and error to distinguish between gold and iron pyrite as distinct minerals. Such processes extend beyond a simple price tag theory of constructs, one that envisions constructs presenting themselves transparently to researchers, requiring only that a name be bestowed upon them.

A second implication is that the approach recognizes that language use is tied to knowledge of the world (Davidson, 2005). During the first half of the twentieth century, empiricist views of language construed it as an arbitrary set of rules or norms for symbol use (Ayer, 1946). This view accepted but also gave unprecedented force to the still older idea of a dichotomy between two kinds of assertions (Kant, 1929/1787). The dichotomy contrasts analytic assertions, true simply by fiat of the norms of language, with synthetic assertions which have empirical content. On this view, constructs are defined analytically in terms of what certain items or tests measure. For example, the work sample measures tuna cleaning ability because the norms of the English language define 'tuna cleaning' in this way (Maraun, 1997, 1998; and Maraun and Peters, 2005, have offered a spirited defense of such a view). Such a view implies that empirical evidence would never encourage a change of definition because we impose the definitions as a matter of convention in order to provide a means of describing the empirical evidence. In other words, no empirical evidence can overturn an analytic definition of a construct in terms of certain test procedures. However, Quine (1980, chapter 2) offered persuasive arguments that such a distinction cannot hold. Empirical evidence does not test individual assertions in isolation, but rather depends on a network of interdependent assertions, and the joint constraints of meaning and fact spread across this network in a way that does not allow the isolation of certain assertions as purely analytic, or true by definition. The successive renaming of the SAT from scholastic aptitude to scholastic assessment, and more recently to scholastic reasoning and scholastic achievement, reflects just such a change in interpretation motivated by empirical and substantive theoretical advances. Moreover, a price tag theory of constructs could at best apply to the construct intended but not to the construct actually measured (Wiley, 2002). A definition might determine the use of a word, but not the use of a test. Perhaps the most devastating criticism of the view of language as a shared set of normative conventions comes from the empirical fact that ordinary language use commonly involves interpreting novel or mistaken uses of language that violate such conventions but nonetheless yield successful communication (Davidson, 2005, chapter 7; also chapter 8 and 1984, chapter 18). As Davidson argues in some detail, shared norms or conventions cannot possibly explain such commonplace occurrences. An understanding of the world around them shared by the parties to the linguistic exchange plays an essential role in such communication. For example, the tuna cleaner interviewed by Garson (1994) refers to dark tuna meat as cat food. Both Garson and the reader immediately understand the reference. This does not occur because of any prior norm governing the use of the term 'cat food'. Instead, it occurs because others are able to grasp that she means that the dark meat becomes cat food—an empirical fact about the world. Modeling test interpretations in terms of sets of premises and conclusions drawn from them recognizes that knowledge from related domains has an impact on the interpretation of test scores. The exact details of this influence remain a work in progress both in the context of test validity theory and in the theory of language use from which we have drawn. However, the basic idea that empirical evidence impacts test score interpretation, that this is not a matter of arbitrary convention, seems well supported by a range of considerations. The idea of test validation as an empirical enterprise rests on this basic idea, and the Goldilocks Model helps to illuminate it.

As a third implication, it follows fairly directly from the above that the Goldilocks Model draws the line between interpretation and theory more liberally than would the price tag theory. The proposed model points up the inferential weakness of minimal interpretations and thus encourages robust interpretations as far as the evidence will support them. At the very least, useful interpretations incorporate the assumed measurement model and what it entails about the relationships between items, test scores, and the construct measured. Such relationships play a crucial role in supporting inferences from test scores. Evidence permitting, however, the model does not rule out including premises about the empirical relationships between the construct, and thus the test scores, and additional external variables. In keeping with the continuity between test validation research and substantive research in general (Messick, 1989), the present model views test score interpretation as the kernel of a construct theory that may eventually extend to a network of related constructs and their interrelations.

We offer one further caution regarding Claim 3: The claim states that one can model test score interpretation in this way. It does not claim that test users necessarily have a list of premises held in consciousness, or encoded in their memories, or even that they could necessarily report on if called upon. The Goldilocks Model does not provide a psychological model of cognitive processing involved in test interpretation. Instead, it provides a model in the sense that if one accurately models the interpretation, the list of premises will produce the same inferences as a test user operating pre-reflectively. This approach to modeling interpretations has the advantage of making the inferences and their bases explicit and open to public scrutiny. As such, it provides a useful tool for focusing discussion of test score interpretation. It does not attempt to provide a theory of the tacit cognitive operations that it models. Test use does not seem to require a theory of that nature and it may be some time before cognitive psychology advances to the point that it could reasonably provide one.

Box 10.2. Applying Claim 3 to the WAIS-III Digit Span Subtest

Returning to the interpretation of the WAIS-III digit span subtest, this box will apply the model to an interpretation that is intended as neither overcautious nor insufficiently cautious. In accordance with the first claim of the model, it is the score values on the digit span test that serve as the object of interpretation. In keeping with the second claim, these take on meaning as part of a set of communicative practices surrounding the use of the test. In this case, the test manual encourages that the scores be used in the context both of other subtest scores and also scores on other assessment instruments to provide an overall assessment of cognitive functioning. Results of assessment might impact decisions about individual diagnoses, treatment for disorders, competency with respect to various legal proceedings, employment, or provision of special services. In each case, the score is interpreted as indicating an underlying quality of the person that bears on his or her mental functioning, competence, ability, or qualification for services.

In keeping with Claim 3, in theory one can spell out the intended interpretation (but not the full meaning) in terms of a set of propositions from which further inferences follow. In practice, such a spelling-out may always remain partial or approximate. The following list of propositions might represent one such interpretation. Unlike previous examples, this example attempts to provide a general interpretation schema that abstracts over specific score values. The interpretation gives an example, not a uniquely correct interpretation of the test scores. One would expect the details of the interpretation to vary with the purpose, both in detail and emphasis.

(1) Each individual tested receives his or her score, x, in accordance with the standardized administration procedure described in the manual, or a reasonable approximation thereof.

(2) Under ideal conditions, the score reflects the ability to remember orally presented digits and repeat them back in reverse order and random measurement error.

(3) Standardized administration conditions seek to minimize the effect of additional factors such as fatigue, stress, and distraction on the score assigned to a particular examinee.

(4) Measurement error in the population to which the examinee belongs is normally distributed with a mean of zero and a known variance.

(5) Scores in the population to which the examinee belongs have a known mean and standard deviation.

(6) Digit span ability, and working memory more broadly, remain relatively stable in adults except when illness or injury induces a deficit.

From this sort of set of premises, test users can draw various conclusions. From premise 1 one can conclude that Giuseppina's and Giovanna's scores are comparable to one another. From the first two premises, one might conclude that Antonio's higher score and Mario's lower score suggest that Antonio has more ability to repeat back strings of numbers. Later premises could be used to support conclusions about whether or not Maria's ability is above or below average. More powerful premises could support more powerful conclusions, such as conclusions extending the interpretation to more abstract constructs such as working memory.

10.3.4. Claim 4: Differences in Interpretation

Claim 4 asserts that a difference in entailments indicates a difference in interpretation. The asymmetry of the relationship between the two types of differences warrants comment, as does the reference to entailments and its entanglements with hypothetico-deductive hypothesis testing.

As noted earlier, an asymmetry obtains between two claims: (a) Differences in entailments indicate differences in interpretation and (b) Differences in interpretation indicate differences in entailments. Claim *a* constitutes a fundamental element of the Goldilocks Model. Claim *b*, in contrast, constitutes an optional further assumption. If one has no theory of test score interpretation, one lacks a principled means of determining when two statements of test score interpretations express the same interpretation and when they express distinct interpretations. In other words, one lacks a means to individuate test score interpretations. Consequently, one also lacks a means to count them. Accepting both Claim *a* and Claim *b* offers an attractive initial approach to individuating test score interpretations. Differences in entailments provide a necessary and sufficient condition for differences in interpretation with both assumptions. For example, suppose that an ability interpretation entails that additional exposure will not produce additional learning and an achievement interpretation entails that it will. Claim *a* tells us that the ability and achievement interpretations constitute distinct interpretations of the test scores. Suppose that a third interpretation shares all the same entailments as the achievement interpretation. In that case, Claim *b* tells us that these express one and the same interpretation.

If future theoretical developments suggest other criteria for distinguishing interpretations, then one can drop Claim *b* and still retain the Goldilocks Model. For example, consider a job knowledge test. One way of developing the underlying construct theory might take content validity evidence as more fundamental, and a single factor as a derived assumption of the theory. A second way of developing the theory might take the single factor model as fundamental and the content validity evidence as derived in part from this assumption. Both approaches share the same entailments because they arrive at the same assumptions; they simply arrive at them by different means. However, in the face of disconfirming evidence, the first approach might lead researchers to question the single-factor model whereas the second approach might lead researchers to question the content validity evidence. Under such circumstances, one might want to distinguish these as two different interpretations that share the same entailments, but differ structurally. In such an instance, Claim *a* would still apply, but Claim *b* would not. In most areas of testing, a level of theoretical sophistication that would encourage dropping Claim *b* remains an aspiration.

The notion of entailment plays a central role in the Goldilocks Model. As used in the canonical hypothetico-deductive model of hypothesis testing, the notion of entailment is often associated with the idea that all sciences function as axiomatic deductive systems of postulates and with the idea that one can test individual entailments in isolation from others. Nonetheless, the relevant notion of entailment need not imply that scientific theories take the form of axiomatic deductive systems. The entailments will most likely take the form of informal inferences in practice until and unless criticism or technical problems in the testing program force closer examination, and even then an elaborated informal theory seems more plausible than an axiomatic system (Toulmin, 2003). Moreover, distinguishing meaning on the basis of entailments does not require that one can test any one entailment individually. Testability bears more directly on Claim 5 discussed below. Finally, differences in meaning between two interpretations does not depend upon the accuracy or truth of either. One can apply Claim 4 to difference in meaning between two false assertions. As such, inferences from the truth of the entailments to the truth of the assertions that entail them play no role in this procedure for distinguishing meaning.

At this point, it may help to note that Claim 4 does not imply a verificationist theory of meaning. It states that interpretations differ if their implications differ from one another. It does not restrict such implications to empirically testable implications. The final claim turns the focus to such implications for practical concerns of empirical test validation. This emphasis does not imply any simple equating of interpretation with empirical implications. Moreover, broadly understood, meaning exceeds interpretation understood narrowly in terms of implications.

Box 10.3. Applying Claim 4 to the WAIS-III Digit Span Test

In keeping with Claim 4, a number of inferences follow naturally from the interpretation in Box 10.2. Some of these are relatively simple, such as the inference that examinees with higher scores on average also have higher digit span ability. Even such a limited inference, however, would not be possible without the inferential basis of the test score interpretation. This inference does not follow merely from the fact of examinees receiving higher and lower scores. If one might characterize such a limited inference as clinging to the edge of the pool, then an inference that moves away from the edge might involve calculating the standard error of the estimate and inferring the range within which the score for the same examinee on a second testing would likely fall. A bolder inference, heading confidently into the deep end of the pool, might go further to infer the relationship between digit span and particular cognitive deficits. An inference such as this last one would go beyond the above premises, perhaps by combining them with outside information to derive further consequences.

10.3.5. Claim 5: Guiding Validation Research

Claim 5 directs test validation efforts toward testing assertions that maximally distinguish between interpretations in the sense of spawning the inferences that show the greatest divergence between rival interpretations. Practical import may offer the most useful guide to the degree of divergence. The degree of difference in practice entailed by the two rival interpretations bears most significantly on the choice between them. Two interpretations that converge in every way with respect to practical decisions offer very little urgency with regard to choosing between them.

As noted above, it may seem tempting to test each premise of an interpretation separately as a systematic means of validation. However, science simply does not work that way. A test of any one premise requires a host of auxiliary assumptions. In test validation, these will often include other premises from the interpretation. However, even in a seemingly ideal situation in which one can express two rival interpretations as nested sets of premises, one exceeding the other by a single premise, one cannot test this decisive premise in isolation. The auxiliary premises to the test merely lie outside of the interpretations under such circumstances. For example, consider research designed to distinguish between the interpretation of the work sample as a measure of tuna cleaning ability over an eight-hour shift and as a measure of ability over the short time span of the work sample. Such research would depend upon a host of other assumptions that link the observations to the theoretical claim that the researchers wish to test. The absence of a fatigue effect might constitute such an assumption. In practice, then, one ideally triangulates on divergent implications of rival interpretations with studies employing a variety of methods (Campbell, 1986; Cook & Campbell, 1979).

The wording of Claim 5 carefully allows for varieties of evidence. Much evidence in test validation takes the form of empirical research findings. However, test validation, like empirical research, also rests on a field of plausibility judgments. It always remains possible, for example, that a mischievous poltergeist intervenes supernaturally at precisely all the necessary moments in the validation process to create the illusion of validity for a poorly performing test. However, test developers rarely keep Ghostbusters in their Rolodex because a general consensus assigns a relatively low plausibility to this explanation of validation results. Often, such judgments rest less on empirical data than reasoning from general principles about the types of entities involved. For example, one might reason that a chair will support one's weight either from repeated empirical tests or from general principles about what makes a well-constructed chair along with the construction of the chair in question (Pepper, 1942, chapter 3). Likewise, inferences of this latter type probably play a pervasive role in plausibility judgments involved in test validation. The intended notion of evidence has sufficient generality to include such reasoning.

Box 10.4. Applying Claim 5 to the WAIS-III Digit Span Test

Claim 5 deploys the analysis of rival interpretations as a means to select the most useful validation evidence to decide between them. For example, a rival interpretation to that in Box 10.2 might question the assumed error structure and instead posit that easier items have more error variability than hard ones, making it possible to measure examinees with high ability more precisely than those with low ability. Such an interpretation would differ in its premises, particularly, it would need to replace premise 4 with something more appropriate to the alternative error model. One might then fit a 1-parameter and 2-parameter Item Response Theory model to show that the easier items in fact have less item discrimination than do the hard ones, that the item information function is lower at the lower end of the ability spectrum, and that ability estimates have larger standard errors for response patterns that correspond to lower item total scores.

In contrast, validation work that focused on the role of biases due to test fatigue or stress would not provide such useful information in this context because it does not focus on the premises that distinguish the two rival interpretations. Such work might be valuable for other purposes, but it does not focus on the differences between the competing interpretations and thus does not help decide between them. As such, spelling out the rival interpretations in terms of their premises offers one tool for guiding the choice of validation questions.

One might ask how the above procedure squares with Kane's (2006) advice to focus validation on the most controversial assumptions of the validity argument. If one construes controversy over assumptions in terms of rival hypotheses, then the approaches coincide (Messick, 1989). If one imagines situations in which critics merely question an assumption without offering an explicit alternative, then focusing on rival hypotheses offers only a special case of Kane's broader procedure. In either case, however, spelling out the interpretation(s) in question along the lines of the Goldilocks Model helps to clarify the nature of the controversy.

10.3.6. *Claim 6: The Goldilocks Criterion for Good Interpretations*

Claim 6 asserts that an optimal interpretation of a test's scores gets just right the balance between supporting practical inferences and staying within the evidence. The claim does not go so far as to suggest that this balance has a uniquely correct solution. In practice, a range of interpretations will most likely meet this criterion adequately well. The Goldilocks criterion supports criticism from either direction, too soft or too hard, but does not entail that the two meet at a single point in the center. In practice, the criterion probably leaves a good degree of latitude for test users between interpretations open to well-founded criticism of either type. Within this zone of acceptable interpretations, the choices depend on practical matters of what inferences interest the test user given his or her specific application of the test. It also seems worth noting that the acceptable zone will generally extend further than the test validation data. Scientific inference involves generalization from data, and inferences that go beyond the data. These sorts of routine inferences will carry the acceptable zone of test score interpretations beyond the strict limits of the data.

The zone ends where inferences from the data extend beyond what the relevant norms of scientific inference deem justified by the evidence.

The interesting region for test validation involves the frontier between the acceptable zone and the slightly-too-strong zone. One might consider this the zone of proximal development for the test interpretation (Vygotsky, 1978). Within this zone lie the opportunities for test validation research to strengthen the supportable interpretations of the test scores. For example, if existing research cannot rule out the possibility that poor scorers on the work sample will perform better with practice, or perhaps outperform high scorers over the long haul, then the available evidence does not support an interpretation strong enough to justify the use of the work sample as a selection tool. However, it may be that a few additional studies would clear this up and provide adequate support for an interpretation that in turn supports this use of the test. As such, validation research extends interpretations into this frontier guided both by practical concerns and Claim 5 of the model.

Box 10.5. Applying Claim 6 to the WAIS-III Digit Span Test

Claim 6 advises seeking an interpretation that gets the balance between strength and caution just right. For the sake of keeping the illustration relatively simple, the interpretation developed in the previous boxes probably errs on the side of caution. However, even this relatively cautious interpretation exceeds merely recognizing scores as values assigned to individuals, and suffices to support many useful inferences. Overly weak and overly strong interpretations were given in the first box.

10.4. Chapter Conclusion

This chapter has presented a general model for test score interpretation and meaning called the Goldilocks Model. The model rests on six claims and integrates with current descriptions of validity arguments and interpretive arguments. The model also helps to guide validation research and to distinguish the scope of validation from the scope of general scientific research into a construct. Guidance for validation is important because the move away from ad hoc validation strategies based on types of validity toward an integrated theory of test validity brought with it a degree of generality and abstraction that offered less concrete direction for test developers seeking to validate their tests. Clarification of the scope of test validation is important because the continuity between validation research and scientific research on a construct has led to a degree of confusion about the scope of validation research.

10.5. Further Reading

Campbell, D. T. (1986). Relabeling internal and external validity for applied social scientists. *New Directions for Evaluation*, 31, 67–77.

Cowan, J. L. (1964). The uses of argument—An apology for logic. *Mind, 73,* 27–45.

Kane, M. T. (2006). Validation. In R. L. Brennan (Ed.), *Educational Measurement* (4th ed., pp 17–64). Westport, CT: Praeger.

Markus, K. A. (2008). Constructs, concepts and the worlds of possibility: Connecting the measurement, manipulation, and meaning of variables. *Measurement, 6,* 54–77.

Sechrest, L. (2005). Validity of measures is no simple matter. *Health Services Research, 40,* 1584–1604.

11 Open Questions About Test Score Meaning

Connections With Other Chapters

Chapter 1 described meaning as the least well-understood aspect of test validity in comparison to measurement and causation. Chapter 9 explored the relationship between test validity and values. Chapter 10 developed a model of test score interpretation dubbed the Goldilocks Model. Taking that approach, test score interpretations can be modeled as a series of premises and these can be used to individuate and compare different test score interpretations. Like chapters 4 and 8, the present chapter is devoted largely to open and unresolved issues.

Having developed a theory of test score interpretation in the previous chapter, the present chapter will delve into unresolved problems in test score interpretation based primarily on work drawn from various literatures outside of test validity. Specifically, we first turn to the early psychologist William James regarding the meaning of test items and other stimuli. We then turn to philosopher Hilary Putnam for the questions his work raises about the idea that meaning can reside in the heads of test takers. We next turn to the Slavic literary theorist and philosopher Mikhail Bakhtin for insight into the dynamics of meaning produced when competing modes of speech interact within a given utterance, or test item. Fourth, we turn to philosopher Saul Kripke to consider how his puzzle about belief applies to the psychology and measurement of beliefs, attitudes, and other intentional states. Together, the work of these four authors challenges some conventional assumptions about testing and test validity as it relates to meaning. The chapter concludes with a brief look at issues of indeterminacy of meaning as they relate to test validity.

11.1. The Psychologist's Fallacy and Test Score Interpretation

William James was a psychologist-turned-philosopher. His work on psychological theory remains influential today, but he is perhaps best known as one of three philosophers who helped form pragmatism as a school of philosophical thought. In a chapter surveying various methods of research available to psychology, and various sources of error in making use of those methods, James (1950/1890, chapter 7) introduced what he termed the *psychologist's fallacy*. According to James, this fallacy occurs when the psychologist confuses his or her perspective with that of the object of study. In the context of testing, this occurs when the test user too casually projects his or her understanding of the test responses into the test taker. If it was once fair to describe this as the unique affliction of psychologists, it seems safe to say that they have generously shared the affliction during the century that has passed since the James named the fallacy. Even if we focus just on the variety of the fallacy that applies to test score interpretation, any field that tests mental properties bears the risk of falling prey to the psychologist's fallacy.

An example involves Luria's early 20th-century research on Uzbekis, who clearly did not understand syllogisms in the way intended by test developers. For instance, they were presented with the syllogism "In the far north, where there is snow, all bears are white. Nova Zembla is in the far north. What color are the bears in Nova Zembla?" (Luria, 1976, p. 109). The responses Luria describes are remarkable. One respondent answers: "We always speak only of what we see; we don't talk about what we haven't seen" (p. 109). When Luria repeats the syllogism, the respondent says "Well, it's like this: our Tsar isn't like yours, and yours isn't like ours. Your words can be answered only by someone who was there, and if a person wasn't there he can't say anything on the basis of your words" (p. 109). Standard coding instructions would render these responses incorrect; however, to do so uncritically would be to project one's own understanding of the syllogism into the mind of the respondent. In our view, this is a likely case of the psychologist's fallacy.

The psychologist's fallacy is also a potential problem in the analysis of response processes in testing. For instance, in order to assess validity, Scriven (2002) describes a process of inspecting the testing procedure and making a logical analysis of what it involves on part of the test taker. Such a procedure succumbs to the psychologist's fallacy if it assumes that the testing materials or responses have the same meaning to the test taker as presumed by the person doing the logical analysis. More broadly, various procedures for providing content-related validity evidence succumb to the fallacy if they assume (rather than assess) the equivalence between the meaning of the testing materials to the test taker and to the subject matter expert. In general, armchair analyses of how respondents interpret and answer items are vulnerable to the psychologist's fallacy.

To avoid the psychologist's fallacy, one should at least recognize the potential for a difference between how the test users understand test items and how test takers understand them. Some familiar psychometric technology can be deployed toward this end. Differential item functioning analyses (with known groups) or mixture modeling (with unknown groups) can help identify subsets of test takers who may respond differently to the same stimulus materials, provided that the subgroups are sufficiently large and not too numerous. Multiple indicators can help to identify items that do not behave like other items, and this can indicate differences between items in how test takers interpret them. Modeling the nomological network can help identify when a measure does not behave in a way consistent with the construct theory, possibly because it fails to measure the intended construct in the population under study. Likewise, modeling Item Response Theory parameters as a function of item characteristics can help identify heterogeneous subgroups of either items or test takers. All such methods, however, tend to break down if the range of interpretations becomes too diverse, at which point statistical power plummets, and statistical analyses tend toward estimating average behavior across heterogeneous populations.

In some respects, then, James' psychologist's fallacy gets at a broader concern. James emphasizes two features of this situation. First, the test taker and the test user bring different background knowledge and perspectives to bear on the test stimulus. Second, the test user sees the test stimulus and test response together, and also within a broader context, whereas the test taker need not share either the same degree of reflective awareness of the response, beyond that required to actually perform the response, or awareness of the same broader context. Such differences apply most apparently in the context of tests of attitudes, beliefs, or other such cognitive or affective states. An example of the first type might occur if a test used an agree/disagree format to ask about satisfaction with a variety of aspects of a training program as a measure of overall satisfaction. The test user might interpret consistently low responses as a negative evaluation of the training. However, a test taker might respond with disagreement because he or she interpreted mere satisfaction as too low a standard, mis-describing his or her enthusiasm about the training as less than it was. An example of the second type might occur if the test taker sought to assess how systematic the training participants perceived the training to be. The test users might view the training with an eye to systematic learning principles opaque to the training participants. The participants may judge the training as systematic but instead base their judgment on the sequence of topics. If this difference escaped the test user in the interpretation of the responses, it would involve the psychologist's fallacy. The test user wrongly assumes that the test taker perceives the object of perception the same way that the test user does.

Applications of the psychologist's fallacy to test interpretation extend beyond self-report data for mental states. Returning to the work sample test from chapter 10, one could imagine a situation in which the canning company intends for use certain portions of fatty tissue that the local fishing community, from which many workers come, does not recognize as part of the white meat (or vice versa). In such a case, the sorting of this material with the bones and other refuse might be scored and interpreted as an inability to correctly identify and separate white meat. However, the workers who lower scores may in fact have the ability—they just perceive and categorize the parts of the tuna differently. A first problem in test score interpretation, then, involves how to gather evidence that bears on interpretation, while recognizing that test takers need not (and in some respects *cannot*) share the test user's perspective on the test stimuli.

At a basic level, James' concern with the psychologist's fallacy speaks to a contrast between two fundamentally different metaphors for the testing process: testing-as-observation and testing-as-conversation. The testing-as-observation metaphor treats the test taker as relatively non-reactive to the testing process. This allows the testing process to read off some pre-existing property of the test taker. The testing-as-conversation metaphor takes the testing process as more interactive, involving communication between the test taker and test user. Passive behavioral observation in a natural setting might provide the prototype for testing-as-observation, whereas an opinion poll interview might provide the prototype for testing-as-conversation. In many respects, James's notion of the psychologist's fallacy highlights the importance of the second metaphor in thinking about testing. This perspective on the testing process emphasizes the interpretive process involved in completing tests. The greater the divergence in the backgrounds that test user and test taker bring to the test, the greater the room for divergence in the meaning of the test materials or responses. This issue is perhaps most explicitly addressed in the area of cultural competence in assessment (APA, 2003).

The testing-as-conversation metaphor helps to illuminate how the psychologist's fallacy applies to performance tests. The fallacy involves conflating the information in the item as understood by the test user or test developer with the information in the item as perceived by the test taker. Consider that completion of a performance item involves more than just reasoning from the information given in the item to the best answer. It involves at least a two-stage process of first encoding the information in the item and then reasoning to the best answer (Bejar, 2010). The encoding step, however, involves an interpretive element through which the test taker comes to understand the test item, ideally in much the same way that the test developer understood it. Such encoding is not analogous to simply copying a list of numbers from one place to another, or even analogous to simply transcribing a list of Roman numerals to Arabic numerals. Instead, it involves a more complex task of creating an understanding of what the test developer intended to communicate, and choosing a response consistent with that understanding of the test developer's expectations. Background knowledge and assumptions bear on this interpretive process and differences in background open one door to divergence between the test developer's intentions and the test taker's interpretation of the item. Perhaps the most famous example is the application of Piaget's water conservation task in which the same amount of water is poured from one shape of container to another. A frequently told story has it that when this task was applied to desert-dwelling children, at least one responded that the quantity of water was not the same. This was not because the child lacked the concept of conservation of quantity, but instead because the child noticed a drop of water that ran to the bottom of the original container rather than transferring to the new container. More mundane examples might include confusion between alternate uses of the same formal notation in mathematics problems, such as a single quote meaning either a prime or the matrix transpose function, horizontal line brackets meaning either absolute value or matrix determinant, or parenthesis meaning either multiplication or the application of a function to an argument.

Box 11.1. Illustrating the Psychologists' Fallacy with the National College Entrance Exam

Several million high school seniors in the People's Republic of China (PRC) take the National College Entrance Exam (Quánguó gāokǎo, 全国高考), seeking admission to one of several hundred public colleges and universities within the PRC. The examination was created in 1952 and is administered by the National Education Examinations Authority under the Ministry of Education (Davey, Lian & Higgins, 2007). The number of test takers has increased steadily, nearly reaching 10 million in 2010 (*Global Times*, 2010). The exam is administered once a year (in June) over two days, and contains both multiple-choice and constructed-response items. Every student must take the Chinese, English, and mathematics portions of the test. A fourth section offers alternative topics from which the applicant can select (Davey, Lian & Higgins, 2007). The following two items are typical multiple-choice English items (downloaded 28 July 2010 from http://shiti.edu.sina.com.cn/paper/52/20/32052/account.php).

2. Many lifestyle patterns do such _____ great harm to health that they actually speed up _____ weakening of the human body.

A. a; /   B. / ; the   C. a; the   D. / ; /

11. Do you think shopping online will _____ take the place of shopping in stores?

A. especially   B. frequently   C. merely   D. finally

Item 2 is clearly intended to test the grammatical use of articles. The options for the definite ('the') and indefinite ('a') article seem self-evident, but the representation of no article using a slash ('/') introduces a convention that may not be self-evident, but instead requires some interpretive effort on the part of the test taker to understand the intent behind the question. If a test taker misunderstood the slash to mean both 'a' and 'the', then he or she might choose option C as the correct answer instead of the intended answer, B. This example would illustrate a discrepancy between the content intended by the test developer and the content perceived by the test taker.

Item 11 is more typical of English items in that it involves correct word choices from a broader range of general vocabulary rather than focusing on a narrower grammatical category such as the articles in item 2. A striking feature of the item for at least one native speaker of North American English is that the words that most naturally come to mind to fill the blank do not appear among the available response options (e.g., 'eventually', 'completely'). This illustrates the impact of background on test item perception. The only option that seems obviously wrong from this perspective is option B, because the term 'frequently' does not make sense for a long-term historical trend and one does not normally apply the phrase 'take the place' to case-by-case choices. One could imagine specific discursive contexts in which answers A or C provide correct sentences (online shopping will replace many things, but especially shopping in stores; online shopping will merely replace in-store shopping, it will not create more shopping than already exists). However, only the keyed answer, D, offers a sentence completion that would seem natural as a means of introducing the topic, absent such an assumed prior context of discussion. Thus, successful completion of the performance task requires not just a knowledge of English grammar but also an intuitive understanding of how the test items are intended. This illustrates the interpretive aspect of performance tests highlighted by the test as conversation metaphor. Successful completion of the performance task (not based on luck) requires an interpretive step of grasping how the test developer intended the item and what he or she meant to ask.

11.2. Meaning's in the Heads of Test Takers?

In order to make any use of test scores, one must interpret them. Test score interpretation involves assigning meaning to test scores. Hilary Putnam is an American analytic philosopher who is perhaps best known for his contributions to philosophical theories of mind and of language. In "The meaning of 'meaning'" Putnam (1975) introduced some now classic thought experiments on meaning. These thought experiments can be extended to the case of test scores, in order to illuminate the way in which test scores acquire meaning. To introduce Putnam's ideas in the context of testing, imagine a behavioral checklist that measures behaviors related to physical exercise. Test scores do not get much more concrete than that. The more items a respondent checks, the greater his or her range of exercise behaviors. Clearly, meaning is assigned to the test scores even at this concrete level; namely, they are interpreted in terms of exercise, and they are supposed to order people from non-exercisers via moderate exercisers to extreme exercisers. How does this meaning arise?

We might intuitively consider a two-part theory. First, meaning is assigned to test scores according to some criterion that a test interpreter has learned. For instance, a test user has learned to interpret these particular scores as self-reported exercise behaviors, because they arise from the application of a test that asks for such behaviors. This is a criterion that regulates the interpretation of the test scores. The criterion is something that resides entirely in the head of the test user. Second, by application of this criterion, the test user picks out the things in the world to which the test scores apply. In the above example, the test user expects self-reported exercise behaviors to pick out exercise-behavior self-reporters of degree 0, 1, 2, on up to the maximum score on the test. So, by applying a learned criterion (which is *in the head*, in Putnam's terminology) to the test scores, they acquire meaning; and through this meaning, the interpreted test scores designate external objects (which are not in the head). Intuitively, the meaning of the test scores depends on how the test user interprets them; that is, it is entirely determined by the way the user applies the criterion.

Putnam's classic paper seeks to undermine this account. In particular, Putnam argues that meaning is *not* solely fixed by the criterion in the head of the interpreter. Instead, meaning is partly determined by (a) the structure of the world itself, and (b) the linguistic conventions of a social community. Toward this end, Putnam introduces the twin-earth story. In the story, two perfectly identical twins exist, identical right down to the neural and molecular state of their brains. As such they cannot differ in terms of what is in their heads, so to speak. However, one lives on earth where water has the chemical formula H_2O and the other on twin-earth where water has a complex chemical formula abbreviated XYZ. The twins do not differ in their understanding of the word 'water' because they are identical, but the word refers to something different for each of them. Putnam argues that the word 'water' means something different for each twin even though the twins are completely identical. The twin-earth story suggests an essential role for the physical environment in fixing the meaning of the term. Thus, meaning is not entirely in the head. Putnam introduces similar stories about aluminum and oak trees that suggest an essential role for the linguistic community. Extending these arguments to our example, the meaning of the test score of zero on the exercise check-list depends on both the physical context of test interpretation and the linguistic community of the test interpreter. The same applies to other scores.

To simplify matters, let us set aside the full set of test scores and focus on just one possible test score: zero. What does a score of zero mean? Straightforwardly, a score of zero indicates a non-exerciser or at least a no-exercise reporter. As such, the class of zero-scorers corresponds to a class of individuals indicated as non-exercisers by the checklist (which need not correspond directly to non-exercisers for a variety of reasons including measurement error, bias, construct instability, and the like). We have a universe of individuals containing a subpopulation of non-exercisers. In theory, an omniscient observer could pick out exactly those members of the universe who belong to the subpopulation of non-exercisers at any given point in time. The checklist presumably does this imperfectly, providing an imperfect indicator of non-exerciser-hood. To get a better grip on the workings of the test, let us first consider the term *non-exerciser*.

The term *non-exerciser-at-time-t* picks out exactly those individuals existing at time *t* who do not exercise prior to time *t*. It makes no difference whether we can, cannot, or cannot-even-in-theory successfully determine exactly who falls into this category. One might sit right next to a non-exerciser without realizing it but still understand the term. Only the fact that one can use this term to successfully refer to this class matters to the meaning of the term. (The above distinction implicitly rejects the verification theory of meaning in its more vulgar forms.) One can thus communicate with others about this class without having the ability to actually determine which individuals do not exercise. So, for instance, one can understand the sentence 'non-exercisers tend to take escalators rather than stairs' perfectly clearly without the ability to pick out the non-exercisers.

Similar considerations presumably apply to the checklist. One can understand the test scores as imperfect indicators of non-exerciser-hood without the ability to identify them any better than can the test. Were this not the case, one could only interpret test scores in situations that rendered the tests superfluous. At best, one could only interpret tests in instances where imperfect tests offer cost savings over some other method available to measure the same attribute or attributes without measurement error. Such a state of affairs would no doubt send home feeling a little grumpy a good number of test developers and test users. Fortunately for all, every indication suggests that one can indeed assess with error what one cannot assess without error. The absence of the ability to assess without error, however, leaves us with a question. If the test user cannot actually delineate the non-exercisers from the exercisers without error, then in what sense can meaning in fact be in the head.

To complicate matters further, imagine, just by happenstance, that we find a diary from 1810 in which the owner recorded exactly the sentences that later turned up on the exercise checklist along with his or her assent or dissent to each. Interestingly enough, the journal keeper dissented to each and every one. Does this provide a documented case of a self-reported non-exerciser? According to part (a) of the above account, it may not, simply because the way the world worked in 1810 might not link checklist scores to non-exerciser-hood the way it does today. Let us assume it does. According to part (b), the term will still do the same work of linking the test scores to the class of non-exercisers. Does it? According to Putnam, it may not. First, the stereotypical characteristics that nonspecialists use to identify non-exercisers may not match up with non-exerciser-hood in 1810 the same way that they do today. As a result, the term might not pick out the same set of people even if its use remains phenomenologically similar across time periods. For instance, people may get a lot more physical exercise as part of their daily routine in 1810 than in 2010. Perhaps even more significantly for testing, the meaning of the term *non-exerciser* probably depends in part on a linguistic division of labor, and thus on the linguistic community of the user of the term. Appreciating the import of this part of Putnam's discussion involves disentangling some closely intertwined points.

Most test users today will recognize that test validity depends upon the population. A verbal test may measure a personality trait for a literate population but not for an illiterate population of test takers. The trick, of course, lies with learning to delineate the relevant populations without reducing each individual test taker to a population of one. In the above example, the sentences from the checklist may simply mean something different in 1810 than in 2010. This difference in meaning illustrates nothing terribly new to test users. Likewise, it matters little that the term *non-exerciser* might mean something different in 1810 than it means in 2010, because the interpretation of the scores found in the journal by a reader in 2010 holds interest in 2010, not the interpretation of a reader in 1810. Neither of these sources of variation in meaning has theoretically interesting implications for test score interpretation. Both seem well understood.

The linguistic division of labor presses a more interesting point. Most of us, very possibly including somebody who might develop an exercise checklist and very likely including many if not most users of such a checklist, rely on exercise experts to tell us what does and does not count as exercise. As a result, our grasp of the term *non-exerciser* does not fix the membership of the category of non-exercisers. We rely on experts for that. Now, it might well come to pass that different theories of exercise hold sway at the same time in the US and in the Netherlands. U.S. experts may demarcate non-exerciser-hood differently than Dutch experts. If so, the meaning of the test scores for the same test takers, say a population of English respondents, differs along with the linguistic community of the test interpreter or test user. The zero-score of a zero-scoring English respondent may simply mean something different to a Dutch interpreter of the test score than a U.S. interpreter.

Suppose one of the behaviors on the checklist counts as exercise in the US but not in the Netherlands. In that case, a zero score suggests a necessary condition for non-exerciser-hood in the US (not sufficient because the checklist may omit some other forms of exercise behavior) but neither a sufficient nor necessary condition in the Netherlands where a score of 1 earned on the relevant item does not count against non-exerciser-hood. Suppose a Dutch and U.S. insurance firm each adopt the same checklist on applications filled out identically by the same English applicant. The same answers might mean something different to each according to Putnam's argument. Test developers comfortably think of test validity as relative to a population of test takers, less so as relative to a population of test users. The above considerations provide an illuminating example of how the abstract idea that theories color data can play out in testing practice. As indicated above, the same test score from the same test taker can have different meanings depending upon the test user.

The above considerations also bear on the two contrasting metaphors that guide thinking about psychological measurement introduced earlier: the metaphor of physical measurement (testing-as-observation) and the metaphor of an interview (testing-as-conversation). The above considerations help cleave apart the differing implications of these two metaphors. On the first metaphor, it makes no difference how the test takers understand the questions, so long as their answers conform to the requisite statistical and causal regularities. On the second metaphor, the success of the interlocution between the tester and test taker depends upon a common understanding of the questions asked and answered.

In the above example, the test taker presumably can respond to the items on the basis of only one understanding of them. Perhaps a given test taker participates in two different language communities and can understand the items as two different test users do (Orom & Cervone, 2009), say the Dutch and American test users described above. Nonetheless, the test taker must choose one or the other understanding to guide his or her responses. If the understandings of the Dutch and American test users differ, the test taker's understanding can at best correspond to one of them. On the first metaphor, it would seem that the test might remain valid for both users (albeit perhaps valid for different things and to different degrees). On the second metaphor, it would seem that the test can have validity for at best one of the two test users. On the face of it, both metaphors seem to have a certain plausibility. We take up these metaphors further in the next section.

Box 11.2. Internalism and Variability: The Social Aspect of Test Score Meaning

For a further example of the dependence upon social context explored by Putnam, let us first consider a general issue related to math items and then return to the English items discussed above. One particularly elegant way to develop algebraic operations on the basis of a simple set of basic axioms is to begin with a sequence of numbers and a successor function that returns the next number in the sequence after the number to which the function is applied. For example, in the usual sequence 1 is the successor of 0, and x + 1 equals the successor of x (Quine, 1981). If we start with different orderings, we get different algebras. For example, if we start with 0, 1, 2, 3, 4, 5, 6, 7... then 2 + 2 = 4 but if we start with 0, 1, 2, 3, 5, 4, 6, 7, 8... then 2 + 2 = 5. In both cases, the answer is the successor of the successor of 2. The meanings of the digits remain the same in both algebras. In both cases '4' and '5' represent the same respective quantities. If we suppose that the second ordering represents, say, someone's order of preference for numbers, 1 being his or her favorite, then in both cases '4' represents the fifth favorite number and '5' represents the fourth. The meanings of algebraic operations, however, differ between the algebras. These two algebras share many theorems (e.g., x + 1 = x + 2 - 1) but differ in other instances (e.g., $4x > 5x$). One could create two algebras sharing the same theorems by ordering the numbers the same way for different reasons. The key point is that most people learn algebraic operations without learning their basis in assumed orderings and successor functions. People depend upon experts for that. The result is that the meaning of mathematical statements depends upon the social context. Two test takers could be psychologically and physically identical, and answer all the same questions the same way, based on the same cognitive operations, but the same items could mean different things for each test taker due to different social contexts. This would happen in the case of two algebras with the same theorems where one test taker relied on experts who ordered the numbers in the usual way for the usual reason and the other relied on experts who ordered the number in the usual way for different reasons (e.g., preference).

Burge (1979) gives the example of arthritis in which people depend upon doctors as experts to fix the meaning of the term. Burge discusses a patient who uses the term to refer to symptoms in the thigh whereas normally it applies only to inflammation in the joints. Imagine an English question on the National College Entrance Exam that uses the stem "It is not _____ to have arthritis in the thigh" and response options that include p*ossible* and *common*. The correct choice between these might depend upon whether arthritis is understood in the narrow or broad sense, and that in turn might depend upon experts other than the test taker and test developer. Such a case would illustrate the idea of the meaning of the test item and the resulting scores depending upon social context beyond those directly involved with the test.

11.3. Heteroglossia: Speaking in Diverse Tongues

James' focus lay with differences between conscious perceptions of the psychologist and the research participant, while Putnam's lay with the role of the world and linguistic community in making meaning. Mikhail Bakhtin was a Slovic literary theorist and philosopher who evolved from an early Kantian influence to develop a unique and original theory of language use. Bakhtin provides us with a still different focus, namely on the role of speech and language use in creating context-specific, competing sources of meaning. The present focus, of course, rests with the applications of Bakhtin's work to test validity, which deepen and broaden the issues raised in the section based on Putnam's work.

Most statistical models of tests scores or item responses take a decidedly behaviorist slant, in the sense that they do not attempt to incorporate the item content into the model. Nonetheless, very few test developers would consent to work on the development or validation of a test under the condition that they would not be granted access to the test items, and would instead work only from the data recording item responses. This hesitation demonstrates that, while item wording and content may not have made it into the most commonly used statistical models, the field nonetheless considers such information critical in interpreting and working with such models. Indeed, one would be hard pressed to revise items for a particular purpose based on only their item statistics. Likewise, it has been standard practice for many decades to interpret exploratory factor analysis solutions in terms of the interpretations of the individual items that load on each factor. Cognitive modeling of test items offers the strongest advance in the area of incorporating attention to item content and features more formally (Bejar, 2010; Embretson, 2010), but generally focuses on abstract features of items rather than specific content.

Significant progress in incorporating the interpretation of verbal items into test development and validation methods, by either formal or informal means, would be a great stride forward in psychometrics. Such advances would, however, need to tackle issues central to Bakhtin's work.

Speakers of a common language often use individual terms differently from one another. Such differences constitute an uncontroversial phenomenon for which any approach to language must account. Structural linguistics typically attempts to downplay the phenomenon as a local imperfection in a linguistic system. The imperfection involves a dual mapping of the same term onto two or more meanings. The term thus takes on multiple meanings, referred to as polysemy. The general strategy of distinguishing these meanings, and enumerating them as distinct senses of the term, comprises a familiar feature of any dictionary. From a test validity perspective, one might address this by identifying ambiguous items (usually based on the test developer's linguistic intuitions) and rewriting them to remove the ambiguity.

Bakhtin's work, however, suggests a different understanding of this phenomenon. Whereas the polysemy approach takes variation in use as an unexplained flaw, to be corrected in a language, Bakhtin (1986) instead takes it as central to the normal functioning of language. Bakhtin begins with the notion that specific patterns of language use develop around specific speech contexts and practical activities. Because the context of language use varies both within and between people, differences in the use of terms emerge as a commonplace feature of language. Bakhtin refers to this as speaking in diverse tongues, or *heteroglossia*.

This explanation has immediate ramifications for thinking about ambiguous items. The heteroglossia idea suggests that ambiguity depends upon the concrete linguistic practices of the test takers, which is determined by their specific contexts of language use. As such, valid item writing requires not just linguistic competence in an abstract language but cultural competence in the specific practices of the test-taking population's daily life. Knowledge of the dictionary definitions of words in a language does not suffice to avoid writing items using terms that vary in meaning either across test takers or between test takers and test users. The previous example involving variation in application of the term 'white meat' to various parts of a tuna would illustrate this phenomenon if the variation in use reflected the different practical concerns of the fishing community and the fish canning industry.

Another key theoretical concept in Bakhtin's work involves the notion of dialog. Because the same people participate in different speech contexts, and because people familiar with different speech contexts communicate with one another, variations in the meaning of terms eventually come into contact with one another. When users of the terms become aware that their intended meaning cannot be taken for granted and that it competes with other patterns of use, the heteroglossia (diverse tongues) becomes *dialogized*. In Bakhtin's (1981/1975) phrase, use of the term becomes engaged with other uses, transforming it into speech with a sideward glance toward other contexts of use.

A very common phenomenon illustrates this process of dialogized heteroglossia. People commonly assert completely obvious and uncontroversial facts as a means of fixing a certain use of the terms used to express such facts. Consider a market research survey with ten sequentially numbered checklists with instructions that the respondent check all that apply. The marketing researcher who wrote the survey might refer to each of these ten checklists as a test item, whereas the marketing researcher responsible for analyzing the data might instead refer to each individually checkable element of a list as an item. In such a context, the first researcher might assert that the survey has ten items in order to implicitly assert the former use of the term 'item' and deny the second use. The second researcher might instead assert that the survey has one hundred items to achieve the opposite.

The researchers have no disagreement about the make-up of the survey, but instead use this shared understanding to fix one or the other manner of speaking as the accepted one in the present context. The assertion of one manner of speaking to the exclusion of the other constitutes a form of dialogized heteroglossia in that different uses of the term arise in survey writing and data analysis, but the two researchers need to communicate with each other and become aware of the different uses of the term in that process. As a consequence, an assertion that a complete checklist constitutes an item becomes an implicit assertion that individual list elements do not constitute items, and thus the meaning of the assertion in part hinges on and reflects meanings not just of the language user but also other language users with whom the speech enters into dialog (even if they are not present).

Returning to the hypothetical satisfaction scale, one can easily imagine that various terms used in the scale items involve contested meanings wrapped up in dialogized heteroglossia due to diverse uses in diverse contexts. This situation seems particularly ripe for occurrence in a training context where new concepts and vocabulary very likely constitute part of the training content. For example, with an eye toward transfer of the training to work activity outside the training context, the trainers might ask about opportunities to practice the trained skills. They may intend to refer to on-the-job practice. The training participants, in contrast, might view the term 'practice' as connoting something that is not real, and thus take offence at the idea of applying the term to their work. As such, they might deliberately answer the item exclusive of on-the-job practice even though they understand the intended interpretation, precisely because they reject the intended characterization of their work as practice. Such a deliberate assertion of their interpretation of the term 'practice' would reflect dialogized heteroglossia in the terminology used in the satisfaction measure.

Structural linguistics tends to assume a common language with individual variations in competence and performance. Post-structural linguistics recognizes subgroup variation within a language. Bourdieu (1984, 1994) has developed the idea that different social strata of a society have different levels of access to linguistic resources. He called these resources symbolic capital. By and large, it seems safe to characterize psychometric theory as structuralist in character, in the sense that psychometric models do not accommodate for individual differences in item interpretation. The notion of heteroglossia suggests a greater need for attention to individual heterogeneity models in item response theory. Respondents likely vary not only on the variable measured by the test but also in terms of their relation to various linguistic resources used to measure the variable. As a consequence of this variation, the relation between the variable and the test scores may well vary across individual respondents in complex ways. Error terms in stochastic models can easily mask such inter-individual variation. Post-structural linguistic theory provides a substantive theory for beginning to think about such variation.

Response processes such as the one just described have two important and immediate implications for test theory and the way that it discusses item responses. Traditionally, the psychometrics literature has implicitly treated equations describing test responses as external representations of the testing process, untarnished by item ambiguity or related issues. However, applying equations to substantive phenomena requires interpretation (Markus, 2002; 2008). Whereas traditional treatments do not always make such interpretation explicit, the approach presented in the previous chapter for modeling test score interpretations provides a means of making interpretations of psychometric models more explicit. It should be clear that nothing insulates the test developer's language, whether expressed in words or other symbols, from the fray of heteroglossia. The linguistic behavior of test developers does not take place on a linguistic plane above the fray of test takers' linguistic behavior, but in fact exists as part of the same network of speech communities, overlapping, interacting, and creating dialogized heteroglossia throughout the common language that they share. A second major question regarding test score interpretation, then, involves asking how best to incorporate the phenomenon of heteroglossia into our models of item responses and into our test validation work.

Heteroglossia also affects the language of test theory itself. For instance, test specialists have very specific notions of test validity and reliability. For lay people, reliability, analogous to a reliable witness or reliable source, tends to mean what test specialists mean by validity. In contrast, analogous to a valid driver's license or valid password, validity tends to mean a stamp of legitimacy or approval, a meaning distinct from either reliability or validity in the parlance of test specialists. (Likewise, the term psychometrics can mean fortune telling to the lay person in both English and Dutch.) These phenomena constitute heteroglossia. The heteroglossia becomes dialogized when two groups become aware that the words mean something different for one another and use the words with this awareness so as to assert one meaning over the other. This occurs when a psychometrics instructor asserts the technical meaning over the lay meaning of the above terms. It also occurs when stakeholders in testing infuse official terminology with irony or simply re-assert a heterodox meaning in order to better express their concerns.

This second implication cuts more deeply by making problematic the basic assumptions underlying traditional psychometric and statistical representations in the social and behavioral sciences. Statistical language, like formal logic, begins by assuming a fixed set of property bearers with a determinate set of properties. Thus, a logical predicate 'CAT' might characterize the set of objects such that object x is a cat because $CAT(x)$ holds true if and only if x is a cat. Likewise, the statistical variable *cat* might range over cats and non-cats alike, taking the value 1 for cats and 0 for non-cats. Both formal procedures assume a fixed set of objects over which the predicate or variable ranges and that the value of the predicate function or statistical variable has a determinate value for any given object (i.e., every x is either a cat or a non-cat). The manner of proceeding reflects the history of science rooted in natural theology in which nature was conceptualized as a book written by a single and unique God. As such the language of the book was fixed by its author, and the correct interpretation was fixed by the intent of the author (Harrison, 2001; Mason, 2000). Indeed, Galileo Galilei famously stated that the book of nature was written in the language of mathematics.

The notion of heteroglossia grows out of attempts to make sense of a world that lacks a unique language fixed from the outside, from a God's-eye perspective, in which the ultimate truths of the universe are expressed. If two manners of speech differ in whether they consider something a cat, we not only lack a clear undisputed procedure for choosing between them, but also lack a clear basis to assume that one or the other must be uniquely correct. More specifically to testing, different test developers conceptualize and theorize the same phenomena in different ways without one of them necessarily resulting in error. Even more fundamentally, however, the test taker's properties in his or her own understanding depend to some degree on social context. They depend upon who the test taker's speech addresses, and what other speech it interacts with.

For example, suppose one wanted to test attitudes toward cats. One would presumably proceed by constructing a test in which the test taker expresses agreement or disagreement with various statements about cats. One might then take these item responses as indicative of the beliefs and attitudes toward cats held by the test taker. However, the meaning of these statements, both on the test and in the mind of the test taker, use words susceptible to heteroglossia. Consider the common platitude that cats are people too. The purpose of this platitude is precisely to stretch the use of the term person to apply to more than just humans. It thus represents an example of dialogized heteroglossia in which a manner of speech that includes cats as persons is cast into dialog with an opposed manner of speech that restricts personhood to humans. The platitude reflects an attempt to promote the idea that cats should be treated with dignity and respect, and this only makes sense in the presence of competing manners of speech that do not promote this attitude. In the absence of such competing forms of discourse, the platitude would have a different meaning. Yet, acceptance of the platitude is part of the property of the test taker that the test user seeks to test. As such, reinforcing the lessons from the previous section, the property in question depends not just on the internal state of the individual but also on the broader social context of the speech used by the individual to communicate with others, as part of his or her internal self-talk, and to complete the test. The next section turns to further complexities in the role of talk about beliefs in testing.

Box 11.3. Dialogized Heteroglossia and Item Responses

As a further illustration of heteroglossia as applied to testing, let us return to the National College Entrance Exam question about shopping online taking the place of shopping in stores. This test item clearly reflects processes of social change experienced in China at the time that the item was written. Without researching the issue in ethnographic detail, one can easily imagine ways in which this might become caught up in dialogized heteroglossia, and such a fictionalized embellishment suffices to illustrate the basic concepts.

Let us focus on the word 'shopping.' Clearly, online retailers compete with stores for at least some of the same customers. These competing interests provide fertile ground for dialogized heteroglossia as each group creates forms of discourse that reflect its interests. For example, online retailers may find it advantageous to emphasize the continuity and similarity between the two forms of shopping, as well as the convenience or other advantages of shopping online. In contrast, stores may find it advantageous to maximally contrast the two forms of shopping, emphasizing the aspects of shopping in stores not duplicated by online shopping. For example, store owners might emphasize the ready availability of sales clerks who can offer expert advice about products, and the opportunity to maintain long-term social relationships with various shopkeepers in your neighborhood. Thus, in the speech of online retailers, shopping may come to have a narrower meaning (finding products and purchasing them) whereas in the speech of shop owners, shopping may take on a broader meaning (human interaction, shopping as a social activity and form of recreation, shopping as building long-term relationships with retailers, the physical space of shopping places as public places). In such a context, the use of the term 'shopping' in either sense refers implicitly to the other sense, and often the affirmation of one implicitly asserts the negation of the other. (In the United States, this is currently illustrated by the political slogan that 'Marriage is between a man and a woman' which clearly negates a broader understanding of marriage.) Such difference in meaning can in turn affect the grammar by which one combines 'shopping' with other words to form English sentences. For example, saying that shopping online will merely replace shopping in stores makes better grammatical sense if one understands the two forms of shopping as largely equivalent and interchangeable. It makes less grammatical sense if one considers shopping online as fulfilling only one of many purposes of shopping in stores.

11.4. Test Takers and Their Beliefs

Saul Kripke is an American philosopher and logician best known for his contributions to the logic of possibility and necessity, and his contributions to the philosophy of language. As a final open issue in thinking about test score meaning, consider the following story, introduced by Kripke (1979). Pierre speaks normal French and no English, living in France and never having visited London. Through pictures or some other indirect means, he comes to believe that "Londres est jolie," that the city he knows as Londres is pretty. However, later in life Pierre moves to an ugly part of London, picks up some rudimentary English, and comes also to believe that "London is not pretty." Now, Pierre will assent to "Londres est jolie" but not to "London is pretty." So, what are we to make of the assertion that Pierre believes that London is pretty? It seemed fairly well founded until Pierre moved to London and learned some English. This puzzle challenges the disquotation principle that if a speaker of normal English assents to "p" then the speaker believes p, something widely taken for granted and directly relevant to test validity.

Imagine test developers facing the task of designing a test to measure attitudes toward London. "London is beautiful" presents itself as a sensible item stem for use in the test. Kripke's puzzle questions the apparent simplicity of making inferences from agreement with this item stem to what the respondent believes. To develop a validity argument in favor of the proposed interpretation and use of the test scores, a developer first needs to define the construct that the test measures as clearly as possible (AERA, APA and NCME, 1999). For simplicity, put aside other attitudes about London and focus on the belief that London is pretty. Kripke's puzzle suggests that test developers will find themselves hard pressed to come up with a clear explanation of what they mean by stating that a given respondent believes London is pretty. Imagine Kripke's Pierre completing the test, indicating disagreement with the item in question. Kripke canvassed four possible interpretations of Pierre's response in combination with the knowledge that Pierre would agree with the translation of the item into French. One could deny that Pierre ever believed (in French) that London is pretty, posit that Pierre changed his belief after learning English, deny that Pierre currently believes that London is pretty, or posit that Pierre holds contradictory beliefs about London being pretty. Upon reflection, none of these options holds up, yet they appear to offer an exhaustive set of options. As such, our usual practices of belief ascription seem to falter when applied under such circumstances.

Test developers, of course, represent a pragmatic lot. Kripke allows that one can set aside talk of belief and adequately describe the situation in other terms. Might this let the test developer off the hook? Could we have an adequate description of the construct in other terms? Not if the construct remains belief that London is pretty. As Kripke points out, the puzzle remains because people take such talk as so central to their usual ways of describing things. Attempting to redirect the client away from measures of belief will not likely land the contract, or lead to a test that serves the desired purpose.

Suppose that one ignores the problem of translation and develops the test for unilingual English-speaking tourists only. (Test developers in the US have access to a sufficient population of these.) Does this restriction of the population for which the test measures belief that London is pretty solve the problem? No. As Kripke showed, the same problem can occur within a single language. Nonetheless, the puzzle rests on a single seemingly intuitive principle: Assent to 'p' corresponds to belief that p (allowing for proper interpretation of pronouns and such). An English-speaking Pierre might well believe that The Big Smoke[1] is pretty but not that London is pretty where these names co-refer to the same city but Pierre does not know that they do. (Implausible? How many beliefs does a well-read graduate student acquire about Michael Scriven or David Kaplan before learning that Michael Scriven [2002] is the same Michael Scriven [1962] but that David Kaplan [2008] is not the same David Kaplan [2005]?) This might easily lead to an unusual item response pattern consistently agreeing with The Big Smoke items but disagreeing with London items. Still, Kripke's puzzle remains. We cannot easily interpret the responses to mean that Pierre believes London pretty or that Pierre does not believe London pretty. We can say that Pierre tends to agree with The Big Smoke items and disagree with London items. If we interpret this pattern of agreement in terms of the corresponding beliefs, however, trouble arises. *The Big Smoke is pretty* expresses the same belief as *London is pretty*. So, what construct does the test measure?

Again, test developers constitute a pragmatic lot. Perhaps our test developer can simply indicate in the test manual that response patterns such as that of Pierre reflect an artifact that arises in certain cases and that the test user should not interpret the scores as valid measures in such cases. Again, Kripke shows that this leads to difficulty. Suppose Pierre answers the first question "London is pretty" without ever having before seen the term The Big Smoke. Suppose Petra does likewise, providing the same answer. Pierre goes on to learn the term The Big Smoke without associating it with London whereas Petra learns The Big Smoke as another name for London. At the time that they answered the first item, Pierre and Petra shared the same belief (not yet having diverged in their learning of The Big Smoke). So, if our test developer lacks a clear interpretation of Pierre's answer, he or she also lacks a clear interpretation of Petra's. That is, the interpretation of a test item cannot depend on what happens to the test taker in the future. Pierre and Petra only differ in terms of their life course after they answer the question. So, the puzzle about Pierre's answer extends to that of Petra as well even though she understands London and The Big Smoke as referring to the same city.

Stepping back from the minutia, let us take stock of the big picture. If one thinks of the proposition p as what the sentence 'p' expresses, then this leads naturally to thinking of belief as one attitude one might take toward the proposition. Other such propositional attitudes include knowing, hoping, or fearing. Kripke's puzzle suggests a problem for the assessment or even assertion of any such attitudes. This poses an immediate problem for construct descriptions for attitude measures. If one considers knowing that p, it also creates a problem for knowledge tests where the knowledge involves propositions. Skill tests seem to dodge the bullet because they involve procedural knowledge but even in this case one has to tiptoe carefully around any propositional representation of procedural knowledge. One might, in Scrivenesque fashion (cf. Scriven, 2002), wryly conclude the invalidity of all such measures. More cautiously, one might conclude that test developers and substantive researchers have some theoretical work to do before they can offer a cogent account of what such tests measure.

One option involves giving up the notion of a proposition. The idea that people use sentences to express propositions has some appeal for exactly the reason that such propositions seem to offer a means of translation between languages. Nonetheless, many have found this notion of language-independent meaning problematic (Derrida, 1978; Bakhtin, 1986) because they see meaning as grounded in the specific linguistic practices associated with a particular language and group of language users. Kripke (1980) argues along similar lines, linking the meaning of names to their causal history within a language community although he does not outright reject the notion of universal propositions. If the notion of a proposition itself rests on a confusion, this would undermine Kripke's seemingly intuitive disquotation principle and perhaps dissolve the puzzle. It would also require considerable rethinking of the basis of much psychological theory and psychological testing. Test equating across languages would take on a whole new substantive dimension under such an approach.

Another option involves giving up, or at least de-emphasizing, the notion of belief (e.g., Stitch, 1985). As touched on above, however, this stings test developers particularly hard. Tests only have value if they address some instrumental purpose embedded within some matrix of social practices. For the present at least, those social practices incorporate the notion of belief at a very deep level. As discussed in Box 9.5, even performance and achievement tests involve the notion of belief. One might articulate a clear construct theory and corresponding test specification based on a vocabulary that eliminates the notion of belief. One would encounter great difficulty, however, in explaining it to everyday test users.

A third option would involve scrapping the idea of a substantive construct theory and basing judgments of test validity entirely on statistical criteria. One could, in essence, conclude that all constructs measured by tests involve no more than convenient summaries of the behavior of the items or perhaps of infinite populations of items that the scale items sample (intervening variables rather than hypothetical constructs in the terminology of MacCorquodale & Meehl, 1948). The notion of measurement that relates a set of item scores to a construct, then, would reduce to the satisfaction of certain constraints on the joint probability distribution. This program has received considerable attention in the history of psychology and has yet to prove that it can provide enough substance to the interpretation of test scores to keep a science based upon it from falling apart at the seams (or at least fragmenting into micro-theories).

In the end, then, Kripke's puzzle poses a challenge to test theory that will not go away easily. If the construct theory of a test rests on a propositional attitude, it would seem to require some form of disquotational principle: A respondent holds the appropriate attitude toward '*p*' (thinks, believes, knows, fears, fantasizes, ...) only if he or she thinks, believes, knows, fears, fantasizes, or ... that *p*. Nonetheless, the same test taker can hold different attitudes toward co-referring expressions of the same proposition (London is pretty, The Big Smoke is pretty). This poses a serious stumbling block for the exposition of any construct theory in terms of attitudes toward propositions.

The above puzzle, however, represents the very best test theory has to offer the various substantive disciplines in which testing plays a role. By rendering abstract concepts concrete, testing forces researchers to clarify those concepts. The need for a clear construct theory to articulate the validity of a test forces issues with respect to the substantive theory surrounding the test. In this case, Kripke-inspired reflection on the general requirements of a clear construct theory for tests of propositional attitudes brings to the fore a deep-rooted and significant problem for substantive theory. Whenever the process of test validation can bring into focus significant substantive issues for basic research, the discipline in question can count that as progress.

Box 11.4. Belief, Test Translation and Adaptation, and the National College Entrance Exam

The fact that the National College Entrance Exam is a performance examination does not insulate it from Kripke's puzzle about belief. Selecting the correct answer on a performance examination involves belief as much as does selecting an answer on an attitude measure. Normally, it involves belief in the correctness of the answer. However, if one grew up learning the standard geometry but believing that it was false, one could still pass a standard geometry examination, such as the math test on the National College Entrance Exam, by correctly identifying what one believed to be wrong but expected answers based on the standard geometry. So, the puzzle applies to performance and achievement examinations as well as to tests of attitudes.

In this context, it is interesting to compare some of the forgoing considerations to current approaches to test translation and adaptation for use in other cultures than that for which the test was developed (Hambleton, Merend & Spielberger, 2005). Much work on cultural adaptation of tests has focused on the static, stable aspects of culture. Dynamic processes within cultures can also affect test validity, as discussed throughout this chapter. This provides one explanation for the fact that validated tests do not necessarily remain valid over time. Effectively addressing such cultural effects requires a clear and consistent theoretical vocabulary for discussing beliefs of test takers.

Of course, it is precisely such a vocabulary that Kripke shows to be absent. We can imagine translating mathematics items from the National College Entrance Exam into English. For example, consider an item asking the test taker to compute the length of the hypotenuse (xié biān, 斜边 or 斜邊). The disquotational principle would suggest that if a test taker assents to "The hypotenuse is of length 5" then the test taker believes that the hypotenuse is of length 5. However we could imagine a test taker who assents that the xié biān is of length 5 but misunderstands the English word 'hypotenuse' in such a way that he or she would not assent that the hypotenuse is of length 5. Does the test taker believe that the hypotenuse is of length 5? The problem is that we understand the word 'hypotenuse' and use it to refer to the xié biān, but the test taker does not understand the English word in the same way. In such situations, we lack a clear and coherent way of describing beliefs. Yet, the central goal of test adaptation is to construct an English language test that assesses the same beliefs (and abilities to derive such beliefs from information given in a problem) in both languages.

11.5. Validity Without Determinate Meaning

A number of authors working in different traditions have questioned the determinacy of linguistic and thus symbolic meaning in ways that open a set of challenging questions for test validity theory and test validation practice. Perhaps the most entrenched and best-developed approach to understanding meaning links meaning to variations in truth value. For example, one would not interpret a passing score on a certification exam as meaning that the test taker had attained competency because such an interpretation would hold only if it were always and only true that the test taker had attained competency if the test taker passed the test. One can assume that measurement error and other factors preclude such a strong interpretation. So, instead, one adopts a more cautious interpretation, say that the test taker has attained a level of competence within certain probabilistic bounds of the desired level. A change in meaning accompanies any change in the desired level of competence because the truth of such assertions differs for some test takers depending upon the desired level of competence. The basic idea is that meaning and truth of sentences vary together in a determinate manner, and thus the latter sheds light on the former.

Quine (1960) stirred the pot by suggesting that agreement on truth conditions cannot suffice to fix the reference of terms. Quine gave the colorful example of a novel word 'gavagai' which we agree with native speakers applies when we point to rabbits. Nonetheless, does the term really mean the same as the English word 'rabbit'? Or might it instead mean something like 'undetached rabbit parts'? It is not clear that truth conditions for sentences using the word can tease out such differences. Putnam (1981) developed this line of thought further and more mathematically by showing that for first-order languages (talk about things excluding talk about talk) one can always permute the reference of the terms while keeping the truth conditions for all sentences constant. Hale and Wright (1998) extended this result beyond first-order languages. Davidson (1984) developed Quine's ideas to argue for a general indeterminacy of interpretation. Working in a different tradition, Derrida (1978, 1988) also developed the idea that meaning always remains open and is never fixed or determinate. A detailed exposition and exploration of this body of work would require a book in itself. Our goal in the space we have left is merely to offer some constructive suggestions about how test validity theory might incorporate and accommodate some of the basic developments in what remains an active and dynamic area of research.

In many ways, test validation has traditionally begun with the assumption that test scores have a determinate meaning out there to be found and validation is the process of finding it and demonstrating it to a sufficient degree of satisfaction to justify the use and interpretation of the test scores. If meaning is fundamentally indeterminate, then this suggests a careful rethinking of this basic premise of test validation. To illustrate, let us return to the hypothetical certification test. Suppose that the construct in question is certification to repair personal computers using a particular operating system. Quine's idea is that there is no amount of empirical evidence that can settle the question of whether the operating system manufacturer and the test developer mean the same thing when they refer to such competence. Likewise, no empirical evidence can establish that test takers understand the terms used in the test the same way as do the test developers or test users. Putnam's idea is that even if we take into consideration the truth and falsity of every possible sentence on which two individuals can hold a belief, it is possible that two individuals can understand key terms differently and still agree on all empirical evidence. Hale and Wright (1998) showed that this extends to two individuals' beliefs about language and meaning itself. Validation cannot begin by categorically establishing agreement on the meaning of a construct to be measured, because no means exists to categorically demonstrate such agreement. Instead, agreement can at best be established provisionally as an empirically plausible hypothesis open to revision in the face of further data. The meaning of the construct can never be bracketed off as something fixed and certain, providing a fixed foundation for empirical validation research.

Viewed from the traditional perspective, such a line of thought might seem to lead to subjectivism, nihilism, or just a conceptual dead end providing no basis for language use. However, none of the above authors questioned our ability to use language or advocated capitulation to insoluble problems. Instead, an alternative picture emerges from this and related work (e.g., Wittgenstein, 1958). The traditional picture assumes that communicative actions have fixed and determinate meaning and people communicate by encoding and decoding messages expressing these meanings. The alternative picture instead understands communication as a more dynamic juggling act, a process that people engage in over time without a fixed foundation. So, from the traditional perspective, one might assume that competence simply and inherently consists of something-or-other and that validation is a matter of showing that the test assesses just the right something-or-other. From the alternative perspective, such competence does not have a fixed identity independent of how people conceptualize, theorize, and talk about it. On this view, agreeing on a construct is not a matter of selecting a precut slice of the world and then finding a test that assesses it. Rather, agreeing on a construct is a matter of triangulating different vocabularies that slice up the world differently, bringing the goals and objectives for testing into alignment across various involved parties, and providing evidence that makes sense to various parties and allows them to agree on the reasonableness of the testing procedure. Validation, from this perspective, is less like a tower built on a fixed foundation than it is like a dynamic network built between several independent nodes.

Far from being nihilistic, this alternative view is arguably much better suited to test validation in an increasingly global environment familiar to many test developers and users. Indeed, one way to sum up the picture is to say that there exists no foundation of truths expressed or expressible in a uniquely determined language on which test validation can build (Derrida, 1989). Instead, to the extent that validation may rest on anything like a foundation, it rests on a dynamic interplay between languages or vocabularies adopted by different languages users. Unlike a fixed foundation of determinate meanings and identities, the alignment of various vocabularies and modes of speech remains open to revision in light of new data and information (Quine, 1980). The enterprise of evaluation bears a greater resemblance to a ship floating on the sea than a tower built on stone. Much like a ship, a poorly designed, poorly maintained, or just unlucky testing program risks sinking. One area of continuing debate involves the extent to which such contrasting vocabularies can differ in how they understand the world (Davidson, 1984, chapter 13).

None of the above considerations require beginning with a fresh slate. Just as cognitive science approaches to test validation have adopted and redeployed concepts from behaviorist approaches (Messick, 1989), so test validation methods developed under an anti-pluralist foundational view of

---

Box 11.5. Open Questions Related to Meaning

1. What safeguards can be built into the validation process to guard against conflating the test taker's perspective with that of the test developer or test user?
2. How can test validation recognize and incorporate aspects of meaning that are not determined inside the cognitive agent?
3. How can models of test responses address heteroglossia more effectively than by treating it as ambiguity or random error?
4. How can test theory speak non-paradoxically about belief, given that belief plays such a central role in test theory? Are coherent construct theories possible? If so, how so?
5. If meaning is never fixed, what impact does that have on testing and test validation?

language and meaning can find applications with an anti-foundational plu-
ralist view. Nonetheless, rethinking the foundations of test validity theory
in these terms remains an open, vast, and potentially fruitful endeavor.

11.6. Chapter Conclusion

Kane (2009) suggested that "validity is simple; validation can be difficult" (p. 49). His main point was that agreeing on a construct to assess
and collecting evidence to show that one has assessed it need not be an
insurmountable task, and indeed presents a circumscribed and manageable task in many testing situations. However, validation requires thinking through the goals, inferences, and support for those inferences to a
greater degree than may be customary among test developers and test
users at present. We do not disagree, but the considerations in the present
chapter suggest that Kane's basic point might just as readily have been
expressed by asserting the opposite: Validity is difficult, validation can
be simple. In other words, the basic practices of test validation might
be well understood and readily implemented in a particular application.
Nonetheless, the underlying theory that clarifies and justifies those practices might at the same time remain sorely underdeveloped. In the present
chapter we have surveyed several core theoretical issues that seem to have
a profound bearing on the basic theory of test validity and yet remain
poorly understood and barely acknowledged. We see each of these as an
invitation and a demand for further research on test validity theory.

11.7. Further Reading

Bakhtin, M. M. (1981). *The dialogic imagination: Four essays* (C. Emerson &
    M. Holquist, Trans.). Austin, TX: University of Texas Press. (Russian text
    published 1975; essay four: Discourse in the novel.)
James, W. (1950). *The principles of Psychology* (Vol. 1). New York: Dover.
    (Originally published 1890; Chapter VII: The methods and snares of
    psychology.)
Kripke, S. A. (1979). A puzzle about belief. In A. Margalit (Ed.), *Meaning and use*
    (pp. 239–283). Dordrecht, Netherlands: Kluwer.
Putnam, H. (1975). The meaning of "meaning". In K. Gunderson (Ed.), *Minnesota
    Studies in the Philosophy of Science, VII*, (pp. 131–193). Minneapolis, MN:
    University of Minnesota Press.
Quine, W. V. O. (1969). *Ontological relativity and other essays*. New York:
    Columbia University Press. (Chapter 1: Speaking of objects.)[2]

12 An Integrative View of Test Validity

Connections With Other Chapters

The previous chapters have analyzed three important concepts in validity theory: measurement, causation, and meaning. This chapter presents an integrative model of validation, and ties together the concepts by showing how they play out in the larger scheme of validity theory and validation research.

One can summarize the arc of the previous chapters as follows: Measurement involves an inference from observable response behavior to the property measured (chapter 2). The same holds true for almost all cases of assessment and testing. In psychometric models, such inferences are commonly cast as inferences from observable to latent variables (chapter 3). To support such inferences, item responses must carry information about the measured property. This means that these responses either depend on that property (reflective model; chapter 6), or determine it (formative model, chapter 6), or are part of an estimate of it (behavior domain theory; chapter 5). The inference from observation to property thus requires a dependence relation. We understand this relation as either being causal (chapter 6), or as resting on other causal assumptions (chapter 5) but leave the door open for a fully non-causal account of assessment should one emerge. Within the causal interpretation, the nature of the causal relation is not fixed. Several ways of constructing that relation are open to the researcher (chapters 7 and 8).

The question of whether or not differences in the assessed property cause variation in test scores is itself factual. However, decisions about testing cannot avoid evaluative concerns. Examples are concerns involved in the decision of what to measure in the first place, or in evaluating what counts as a good measure (chapter 9). Making applied decisions on the basis of test scores requires one to interpret them. The adequacy of that interpretation rests on (a) a validity argument to support the validity of the test in general (b) an interpretative argument that supports the interpretation of test scores as administered in a concrete setting to a given person (chapter 10). In addition, further interpretive inferences lead to hypotheses tested in the validation process or extensions of the underlying construct theory as part of basic research. The interpretive aspect of measurement and assessment figures centrally in item writing, in item revision, and in making inferences from test scores. However, the underlying theory remains less well developed than either that for measurement or causation (chapter 11).

The current chapter seeks to tie together threads from the previous chapters and to provide an integrative account of the place of measurement, causation, and meaning in the larger scheme of testing and test validation. In the next section we present a detailed schematic model of the test validation process. Sections that follow unpack the implications of aspects of validity theory developed in previous chapters for the process of validation depicted in the model. These several small connections form a seam, stitching together the fabric of test validity theory with that of test validation practice. The resulting picture of test validation presses test validation further away from simple checklists. At the same time, it also moves test validation further in the direction of offering test developers clear direction for validation without a simple checklist. The key concept in this regard is that of alignment, through which test developers can select validation strategies most appropriate to the intended interpretation and use of the test scores.

12.1. An Integrative Model of Test Validation

Tests and test functioning play an important role in scientific research, but also in society at large. Scientific and societal applications of psychological tests are not always characterized by the same concerns. Likewise, they do not necessarily require the same evidential standards. For instance, for scientific research designed to assess whether the correlation between two constructs is positive or negative, one does not need highly advanced instrumentation. However, in an application where decisions about individuals are made on the basis of test scores, higher standards apply. Scientific and societal concerns may also work against each other. For example, from a scientific point of view it is often advisable to use multiple measures per construct. However, in a given application, time limitations, resource limitations, or the burden of testing on the test taker often limit the number of measures that can be used. In medical contexts decisions may need to be made quickly. In individual psychological assessment, the burden of testing can outweigh the value of additional test information.

Thus, there may often exist a tension between scientific and societal concerns, including pragmatic issues of time and money. However, insofar as societal test applications have a scientific basis, the presence of scientific methodology should always be considered an essential core aspect of test development and validation. For, as Cronbach and Meehl (1955) noted, the proposition that a test can be used to assess or measure a given attribute is never devoid of theory. In fact, it is itself a hypothesis that requires testing. This means that, normally, there should be an empirical moment of hypothesis testing or model checking in the procedure that leads to test use. This even holds in the extreme case of operationally defined behavioral observation measures: Even if the property measured is defined by fiat in terms of observable behavior, empirical tests are needed to show the correspondence of the intended behavior to the scores generated by the measure (Foster & Cone, 1995). Such empirical checks make the difference between building confidence in a measure through validation research and simply taking a leap of faith in accepting a measure. Such checks also connect test development research with substantive research.

If empirical checks are indeed in place, the process of test development and use has a scientific core, and may be represented as in Figure 12.1.

As depicted in Figure 12.1, test construction and validation involves a number of contextual factors such as existing data, accepted theory, and

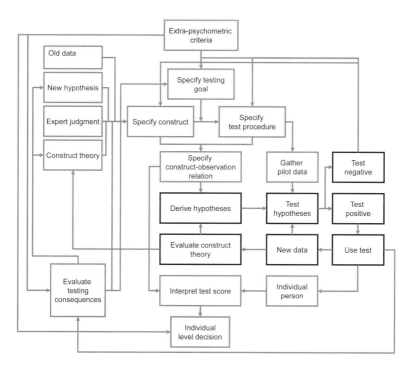

Figure 12.1 A Flowchart that Describes the Process of Test Construction and Validation and Emphasizes the Scientific Core of the Process in Boldface.

the purposes of testing. These shape the scientific research that goes into test validation. The results of the research along with the results of the applied testing program feed back into the process, possibly leading to revisions in the construct theory or the purpose of the testing program. Testing is justified before validation ends because the choice to use the test scores can be justified based on existing information, but further research and test use can provide new information that suggests reassessment of test validity and possibly revision of the test or changes in its use.

The model laid out in Figure 12.1 emphasizes the iterative nature of validation research (and science general); hence, one could enter the process at any point. For purposes of exposition, however, we will start at the top level and walk though the various processes in a single run. Suppose we start with the box *extra-psychometric criteria*. This involves the larger context in which testing takes place. For instance, a testing procedure for cognitive ability may be part of a larger research program on personnel selection; or an educational test for arithmetic may be part of a state- or nationwide examination program. When a testing procedure is part of a larger scheme, this generally implies restrictions; for instance, test development may be budgeted, or the goals of the larger program may emphasize some aspects of validation particularly strongly. These issues are largely fixed from outside, i.e., are rarely under full control of the test developer or user. In fact, a test developer may be faced with extra-psychometric criteria that conflict with his or her expert knowledge, or with what is known from scientific research. For instance, a governmental institution may ask a test developer to construct a measurement instrument to test the linguistic abilities of four-year-olds to identify who is at risk for developing, say, dyslexia. The test developer may consider such a goal infeasible due to the difficulties involved in testing very small children who cannot yet read. In these cases, the results of research may themselves inform extra-psychometric criteria, as when the test developer attempts to change the goals set by the organization that asks for a measurement instrument to be developed. In this example, the test developer may attempt to argue for testing older children. In the negotiation process that follows, the test developer and other stakeholders *specify a testing goal*. For instance, the goal of a test procedure may be to identify eight-year old children with dyslexia to select them for a remedial teaching program.

Here, it is useful to emphasize that the specification of a construct is rarely a simple matter. For example, searching for "dyslexia" in a database for scientific publications easily returns 100,000 hits, so one is likely to require expert knowledge in delineating exactly what the modern understanding of a construct comes down to. In addition, scientific theories on psychological constructs are often in a state of constant flux, so one usually has to decide whether to follow an accepted understanding of a construct or to introduce a novel theory. Different experts may decide differently from one another in this respect, with some favoring one theory and some another. The importance of devoting sufficient time to studying the construct literature is often underappreciated. However, mistakes made in this phase are extremely hard to correct later in the process of test development. In addition, if too little time is devoted to this issue, one runs the risk of duplicating earlier efforts, or pursuing research avenues that have been taken before and found to be blind alleys.

When a construct is specified, this often naturally suggests a test procedure, or sets limitations on which test procedure are feasible. For instance, in the case of dyslexia it is natural that some form of written text should play a role in the test. In addition, there are often practical concerns that dictate what the form of the test ought to be. In this case, practical concerns may suggest, say, the development of a paper-and-pencil test that can be administered by a nonspecialist in a classroom in less than 30 minutes. This sets limitations on what is and is not possible. By narrowing down these possibilities, one eventually arrives at a *specification of the testing procedure*. For instance, the test may become a paper and pencil test that requires eight-year-old children to identify spelling errors typically overlooked by dyslectic children.

The specification of the test procedure then continues with the process of test construction and administration of preliminary tests. This is an iterative process, often with a strong qualitative component, in which pilot data can already be used to test some basic hypotheses, e.g., to check if the test is working at all (i.e., do children understand the instructions; do they interpret the item format properly; etc.). As with the specification of the construct, this is a process that should be adequately budgeted; errors made in the test construction process can be extremely expensive. For instance, if the test is not adequately set up, this can corrupt the results of large-scale validation research later on, effectively making that research useless.

When both the intended construct and the testing procedure are identified, the test developer can begin to fix a relation between the specified theoretical construct (i.e., dyslexia) and the observations anticipated from the test administration (i.e., a set of item responses scored as correct–incorrect). This is the *specification of the construct–observation* relation. Here, we are entering the empirical core of the validation process, because in this phase we are starting to connect the theoretical construct to empirical data. The issues discussed in chapters 2 and 3 of this book now become increasingly relevant. For instance, what is the notion of measurement involved in the testing process, if there is one at all? Should we utilize a causal measurement model or should we rather treat the issue as a prediction problem? If we specify a measurement model, how exactly do we expect the relation between test scores and construct to pan out? Is dyslexia better modeled as a categorical variable (i.e., specifying dyslexia to be a discrete state) or as the low end of a continuum? By which cognitive processes does dyslexia affect the item responses? These issues all bear on the specification of the construct–observation relation, and force the researcher to develop precise ideas on the behavior of observations as a function of the construct, or the other way around (see also chapters 6–8).

When the construct–observation relation is specified, then one can start *deriving hypotheses* from that relation. For instance, if one has settled on the conceptualization of dyslexia as a single continuous variable that causes the item responses (chapters 6 and 7), then the dichotomous nature of the item responses suggests that the items should minimally conform to a nonparametric Item Response Theory (IRT) model, and possibly to a more restricted model. However, if one thinks that dyslexia is a multidimensional or discontinuous construct, then this implication does not necessarily follow. Importantly, if one has taken the perspective that the item responses (or subtest scores) are mere *predictors* of dyslexia, or measure its *causes* rather than dyslexia itself, then the psychometric models suggested are of an altogether different nature (chapters 6 and 8). Many of the possible conceptualizations have testable empirical predictions, because they imply restrictions on the probability distribution of the item responses. Hence, these form the first testable implications of the construct theory joined with the test procedure specified.

We then enter the phase of *testing hypotheses*. If the test is new, one does one's best to begin such tests in a somewhat larger sample in research that still has the status of a pilot. The reason is that, very often, psychometric research will indicate defective items that need to be culled from the test or revised; it is very hard to construct an adequate set of items in a single effort. It may not be possible to fit a full-blown psychometric model to the sample, for instance because it is too small, but often the simpler statistical procedures of classical test theory can be used to spot weak items, as can qualitative techniques such as interviews and think-aloud protocols. In addition, simply making univariate graphs of item response distributions can help in identifying problematic items. Thus, *gathering pilot data* is an essential step in validation.

When this process works out as expected, and the test begins to approach the status of a well-understood assessment device, one can begin to set up larger studies. In this phase, *test use* enters the picture, because for the first time the test is being put to work in research that involves costly input—not only of a financial nature, but also with regard to participants' efforts. In addition larger studies often involve the investigation of substantive relations between the focal construct and other variables that typically lead to scientific publications in which the test functions as an operationalization.

Also, such research allows for testing external relations between the test score and other variables, and thus makes it possible to assess whether the test conforms to what is already known about the construct. For instance, if a test for dyslexia showed a negative relation with age, that would signal a serious problem, while finding a slight sex difference with girls scoring a little higher would be in line with some of the previous research. In addition, one can begin to investigate multitrait multimethod hypotheses, expecting the latent variable assessed by the test to correlate highly with that assessed by teacher's ratings of reading ability, but being less strongly associated with paper-and-pencil test scores on mathematical ability. These investigations incorporate the classical idea of construct validation as originally proposed by Cronbach and Meehl (1955). It is worth noting that most theories of psychological constructs are not matured to a point that they can function as indisputable benchmarks for test functioning; thus, when test scores do not behave as expected, it is often hard to decide whether the problem lies with the theory, with the test, or with both.

Thus, *new data* do not only fuel independent tests of hypotheses that pertain to test functioning, but may also lead one to *evaluate the construct theory*. If the test works out as hypothesized, then that is a good sign for the test developer, because at least the basic theoretical idea of how the test is supposed to function is supported. A minimal scientific justification for using the test to make decisions about an individual person is then available. In that process, the test user often comes to be a different entity from the person or organization that developed the test. For instance, a test may be developed by a team of researchers or by a test publisher, but when it is put to use in selecting students, or diagnosing clients, it is typically put on the market and used by a wide variety of organizations. In this process, tests can become over-interpreted or misused; hence it is important to monitor and *evaluate testing consequences*, to establish that they do not run counter to the psychometric and extra-psychometric criteria that motivated test development. For instance, when a dyslexia test is inadequately used or interpreted, the testing procedure can have unintended adverse consequences; one can imagine that test users start interpreting the test scores as carrying implications that are not supported (e.g., that the test measures an unchangeable property) and that have adverse consequences (e.g., to no longer try to improve situation, because the test user thinks that dyslexia cannot be changed). In this case, researchers and psychometricians have the obligation to warn against misuse of tests and against the over-interpretation of test scores.

Because psychological tests are prone to over-interpretation, and because the test user is a different person or organization from the test developer, it becomes very important to convey sufficient information for the test user to adequately *interpret the test score*. Here, the empirical research discussed above furnishes the material for a validity and interpretative argument as discussed in chapter 11. Test manuals have traditionally become main sources of information in this respect, although the fact that they are often published by commercial entities, which profit from test use, suggests that independent critical evaluation also serves an important purpose. In several countries, there are organizations who publish such independent assessments of commonly used tests. These include the Buros Institute of Mental Measurements in the United States and the Committee on Test Affairs Netherlands in the Netherlands.

When a sufficiently strong argument can be made for interpretation of test scores in terms of a specified construct at the level of the individual person tested, then there are grounds for making *individual-level decisions*. It is here that the extra-psychometric criteria that originally motivated testing start to finally be evaluated. For instance, when schools start using a dyslexia test to select children for remedial teaching, this is the moment at which the test starts fulfilling its original goal. The question whether the use of the test in this way indeed satisfies the goals set provides input for new research questions and new testing schemes. Together with the data gathered in the studies executed, these results become input for the development of novel tests. In this way, the process of validation research proceeds in an iterative fashion.

12.2. Truth, Justification, Knowledge, and Action

We now zoom in on the scientific heart of validation research, noting some important aspects involving the relation between empirical and normative claims. First note that, if science is indeed involved in test development, then there is always a *factual* element to the justification for test score use. For instance, in a given setting, test score variance may or may not causally depend on variance in the attribute of interest. Whether it does or not is an important, if not decisive, factor with respect to the validity of the test as an assessment instrument. We may construe this issue as matter of truth, if we accept that the sentence "attribute Y causes test scores X" expresses a fact. If so, it must have truth conditions—states of affairs in the world that make the sentence true. This means that, for the sentence to be true, the world must be structured in a certain way. To the extent that the truth conditions of the sentence require detailed analyses of what terms like 'assesses', 'measures', 'attribute Y' and 'causes' mean, chapters 2–8 have explored various ways that sentences like these can be interpreted. Such interpretations furnish the *empirical claim of test validity*. Observable or testable implications of such interpretations guide the collection of test validity evidence. Greater testability of the empirical claim yields greater amenability to validation and thus the support that comes from it.

If the test has validity in this sense, i.e., if the empirical claim is in fact true, this does not entail that a researcher or test user *knows* that this is so. Knowledge is an epistemic concept and therefore requires that, in addition to the world being structured in a certain way, the knower also has the *proper grounds* for believing this to be the case. Test validity is concerned with the relation between indicators and theoretical attributes.

Therefore, the grounds for concluding the validity of a test usually, if not always, involve the acceptance of a theory, however minimal that theory may be. The *justification* for accepting test validity involves the construction of a validity argument. This argument legitimizes *interpreting* test scores in a particular way. This requires one to argue not only for the plausibility of the *empirical claim of test validity*, but also to clarify why one is *justified* in accepting this claim. Such justifications are relative to the audience of the validity argument, the evidential standards in place, and the available alternative courses of action.

Call the claim, that one is justified in believing the empirical claim, the *epistemic claim of test validity*. Table 12.1. lays out the incremental nature of justification claims over simple empirical claims. The empirical claim of test validity is a simple proposition p (e.g., "test X assesses cognitive ability"). However, the epistemic claim is of the very different form "Z justifiably accepts p" (e.g., "we are justified in accepting the statement 'test X assesses ability' as true"). One can see the incremental nature of this claim in the fact that nested quotes appear in the example; this indicates that we are dealing with a claim about a claim. The higher order epistemic claim involves a notion of justification. Therefore it is not purely empirical: It also has a normative component. Because the epistemic claim involves an actor Z (i.e., the person or community doing the accepting) the claim is to some extent relative to human standards and cognitions. These issues were taken up in chapters 8–11.

Of course, even if the researcher has good grounds for believing that a test measures a given attribute, this need not entail that others believe it as well. They will also want to see the evidence, and will need to be persuaded. Different researchers may have different standards of justification, adhere to different methodological norms, or belong to different paradigms of thought. This holds to an even stronger extent when consid-

Table 12.1 Empirical, Epistemic, and Action Claims Relevant to Test Validity.

Type of claim	General form	Example
Empirical claim	p	Cognitive ability tests measure cognitive abilities.
Epistemic claim	X justifiably accepts p as true (relative to X's evidential standards)	We have good reason to conclude that cognitive ability tests measure cognitive abilities (relative to our evidential standards).
Action claim	If X accepts p as true, then (relative to X's concerns) X should do Y	If we have good reason to conclude that cognitive ability tests measure cognitive abilities and such tests offer the all-around best available alternative, then (relative to our concerns and those of relevant stakeholder groups) we should use the relevant cognitive ability tests for personnel selection.

ering people outside the research community (policymakers, stakeholders, lawyers, politicians). The implementation of tests in society thus, to some extent, depends on the formation of *consensus* with respect to the empirical and epistemic claims of test validity.

The role of scientific researchers in that process is to make as clear as possible (a) exactly what they claim when proposing that a test assesses a given attribute, (b) what the evidence for and against that claim is, and (c) why they think that the empirical claim of validity should be accepted. Scientific researchers are usually experts in (a) and (b), but can claim no special expertise in (c). This is because, in arguing for (c), scientists implicitly argue for a set of methodological standards, which brings them outside their specialisation and inside the territory of methodology and philosophy of science. This territory is to some extent the specialisation of methodologists, but also to some extent part of the public domain.

Even when a community reaches consensus to conclude that we can justifiably assume that a test is valid, the *use* of that test is *not* thereby legitimized. One may have a perfect test, but decide that its use has consequences that one judges as adverse. For instance, MRI scanners are perfectly valid for detecting whether you have your keys in your pocket or not, because the magnetic field generated is so strong that your keys will be violently attracted to the machine. However, using MRI scanners to this end is not advisable in the interest of safety, because if the keys are indeed in your pocket, you will be violently attracted to the machine as well.

Conversely, if a test is not valid, there may nevertheless be good reasons for using it. Using lotteries for college admissions is an example of the intentional use of a purposefully invalid test (its outcome causally depends on *no* properties of the individual whatsoever). Even though lotteries do not have validity for any attribute, their use can be sensible nevertheless. For instance, in a sense lotteries are intrinsically fair: because the outcome is random, it cannot be systematically biased for or against any individual.

Thus, the relationship between empirical evidence and normative issues is complex. One must take the idea that it is always better to use a valid test as a simplification. The question here is a partly normative one that involves the question to what extent the end justifies the means. Thus, there is never a direct line from *evidence* to *action*. Action requires a contextually driven rationale in addition to evidence. Providing such a rationale is not the privileged task of scientific researchers. While a scientific researcher may be in a privileged position when it comes to understanding what is involved in the empirical claim of test validity, and may also have some advantage in appreciating the epistemic claim involved, he or she has no special status with respect to the action claim.

12.3. Kinds of Causality and Types of Evidence

There is thus a route from facts to knowledge (via evidence and justification), and a route from knowledge to action (via values and normative beliefs). As we have stressed throughout this book, causal thinking about test scores usually has a central place in bolstering validity arguments that may justify test use. Based on the material developed in chapter 7, Table 12.2. illustrates a number of ways in which causal relations in measurement may be conceptualized. The interpretations are progressive in strength. Hence they require incremental scientific support for their adequacy. Each of the four types of interpretations provides a potentially sound interpretation of a measurement model. As such, they reflect syntactically equivalent models in the sense that the statistical model remains identical but the interpretation and thus the supported inferences differ (Markus, 2002; 2004; 2008).

12.3.1. No Causation

Without a causal relation between construct and indicators, modeling offers little beyond generalization of statistical relations of the specific variables studied to a specific population. Generalizability requires only that the statistical relations between these variables do not change from one application to the next. Suppose it has been found that the score on a given set of items (say, Raven items) predicts success in a given job (say, mechanic). Then the stability required to justify the use of that relation in testing policies is just that this specific correlation between these specific measures in this specific population remains stable. Apart from this stability claim, the only evidence required to support generalizability is that the sample adequately represents the population, i.e., that standard assumptions of statistical theory are broadly correct.

This is a metaphysically lean position, and for this reason it may appear that this is a favorable situation in which one makes as few assumptions as possible. This is true, but as discussed in chapter 7, there are several reasons why one normally wants to go beyond this interpretation. Perhaps most importantly, the fact that one has no specified causal link between items and construct means that one has no way of telling whether a given change in the research setting will or will not affect generalizability. This means that one claims too little to defend the inference that, say, changing a questionnaire's font type from Times to Arial will not affect its psychometric properties. After all, this requires one to claim that a change in fonts has no causal effect on test functioning. And this is clearly a causal statement. In addition, a fully non-causal account cannot carry the transfer of statistical relations to novel populations. That is, if the relevant statistical relations have been established among North Americans, then there will be no reason to expect the same relations to hold

Table 12.2 Causal Interpretations in Measurement Models.

Type of causation	Robustness to change of situation	Model interpretation	Required evidence
No causation	Items will show similar covariances with each other and other measures in samples from the same population (as long as the world does not change).	Measurement models as merely descriptive of statistical associations.	Sampling of persons and indicators is adequate; backup for stability assumption.
Regularity causation	Causal models will remain robust to causally inert control variables. Psychometric models will therefore generalize to various subpopulations. Manipulation of constructs will impact items (reflective) or vice versa (formative) so long as intervention does not disrupt causal regularities.	Measurement models with generalization over inert variables based on statistical induction.	As in (a), plus support for transfer over inert variables (replication of results in new populations and situations) and support for a causal link through model fitting or experimentation.
Counterfactual causation	Causal models will remain robust to interventions that change the values of control variables outside the measurement model, so long as the values remain in keeping with the scope of the counterfactuals.	Measurement models with more readily generalizable causal links, but purely nomothetic.	As in (a) and (b), plus support for a causal link that is robust against changing control variables (e.g., measurement invariance over their levels).
Process causation	Causal models will remain robust to any intervention that does not alter the response process. This response process can be determined independently of the item responses.	Measurement models with elaborated causal mechanisms that explain nomothetic relationships and aid generalization.	As in (a), (b), and (c), plus evidence that the proposed process indeed establishes the relevant causal link.

among English-speaking Europeans. Thus, for every category of person not already in a population covered by existing findings, a new research project should be started (Figure 12.2).

12.3.2. Regularity Causation

Clearly, a fully non-causal account supports much less than we would normally assume unproblematically about test scores. Hence it would seem that, typically, test scores are taken to support much more robust inferences. This requires some kind of causal structure to be in place.

We would normally want to claim that the color of a test's cover page does not alter it sufficiently to threaten its validity. Similarly, we would want to maintain that testers need not keep track of what color shoes respondents are wearing, when testing for their intelligence. Such ordinary statements are extremely important. The reason is that they introduce the idea of some item characteristics (such as cover page color) and some person characteristics (such as shoe color) being *causally inert*. This means that they these factors do not matter for the way the responses come about.

The idea of causally inert factors specifies conditions under which the statistical relations required for generalization are invariant. This invari-

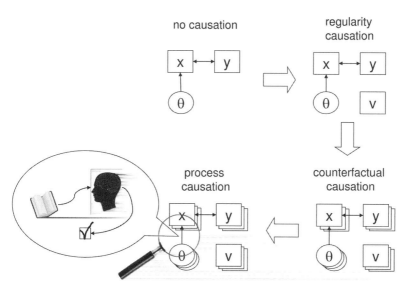

Figure 12.2 A Graphical Representation of Progressively Stronger Causal Claims in Validity Theory. Theta is the focal construct; X is the focal test score; Y is an external variable (e.g., a criterion); V is a causally inert control variable. A single box or circle represents a variable across actual cases, whereas stacked boxes or circles vary over possible cases as well.

ance exists because the response process will not change as a function of such factors. This conclusion is important, because such a specification, if successful, entails that the statistical relations established in a given research setting may be safely taken to transfer to a new setting in which the test is being used. This generalization will work over all levels of causally inert factors. This same basic principle makes it possible to compare scores across different test takers.

Under regularity causation, such inferences across inert factors can be justified without saying anything specific about a causal link between the construct of interest and the indicators. Of course, the notion of causally inert factors contrasts with factors that are not causally inert (factors that cause differences in test scores), but one need not specify or name these to establish generalizability across inert factors.

Evidence for regularity causation typically arises from studies that establish generalizability of main results to novel populations (e.g., inhabitants of different countries), or to different testing contexts (e.g., computerized assessment). The concept of causally inert factors also helps bridge the gap from passive observation to intervention. Suppose that an intervention is hypothesized to affect the focal construct but not to affect the test scores directly. For example, consider an after-school enrichment program that addresses the full mathematics curriculum for a given grade and does not merely teach to the test. Further, assume that the construct is sufficiently delineated to be manipulated in (quasi-) experimental research. Under these circumstances, regularity causation implies that manipulation of the construct should be followed by changes in the test scores (reflective model) or the other way around (formative model). Establishing this effect is the goal of several standard validation research procedures (Borsboom & Mellenbergh, 2007).

12.3.3. Counterfactual Causation

Regularity causation allows one to list a set of inert variables over which generalizations hold. Thus, it would typically identify the factors that do make a difference negatively (i.e., as not occurring in the list). Among the factors that do make a difference, one may or may not find the focal construct one intended to assess. If one does, one knows one is on the right track. However, each new context, distinguished by a change in background variables, or an intervention in variables previously studied through passive observation, requires extensive new empirical study to support the generalization of the regularities to the new context. This limits the usefulness of regularity causation in facilitating applied testing programs.

A counterfactual model strengthens the claims that may be inferred. It does so by bolstering the measurement system by adding a primarily positive account that specifies the counterfactual dependence of the test score on the measured construct (or vice versa, in a formative context). Hence, a counterfactual account implicitly defines causally inert factors as factors on which neither actual test scores nor possible (would-be) test scores depend. As with non-causal and regularity interpretations, the measurement model represents the relationship between the construct of interest (represented by θ in IRT, ξ or η in LISREL SEM notation) and the test scores or item scores. The difference is that each variable in the model now represents not just actual values in a specified population, but also possible values for the individuals in the population that differ from their actual values. This expanded interpretation allows counterfactual causation to support would-be inferences.

Validation strategies differ between regularity and counterfactual approaches. Counterfactual approaches attempt to support stronger theory in order to support broader inferences. In other words, a greater validation investment yields a larger return. One gains the ability of the construct theory to support interpretive inferences and interpretive arguments (as presented in chapter 9). Validation research attempts to provide support for a set of causal relationships that hold counterfactually, supporting inference to counterfactual conditions. This support, however, stops short of universally generalizing causal connections. Counterfactual approaches still incorporate boundary conditions on generalization. For example, the causal relationship in reflective models will hold up under training on the construct of interest, but can still be short-circuited by teaching to the test.

One important technique for establishing invariant test functioning over populations, which is consistent with the counterfactual causation model, is by checking whether the measurement model is invariant over the right types of populations. One can think of distinct populations as instantiating different levels of control variables. Invariance of the model under these changes of levels for control variables implies that the focal test score is conditionally independent of these variables, given the latent variable that represents the focal construct. This is a standard implication from counterfactual causation. Thus, measurement invariance research can be used to offer evidential support for the counterfactual model. Regularity approaches can support invariance in a piecewise manner. Counterfactual approaches can interpret measurement invariance evidence in terms of what would be the case if members of one population belonged instead to another population. This requires populations distinguished in ways that make such cross-population counterfactuals plausible. For example, measurement invariance across treatments and locations supports counterfactual inferences more readily than measurement invariance across genders or cultures. Just the same as single-group measurement models, multi-group measurement invariance models allow for syntactically equivalent models. Such models differ in the interpretation of the causal effects in the model but share the same statistical model.

12.3.4. Process Causation

Process causation is the strongest of the three forms of causal theory in measurement models considered here. One can think of the counterfactual model as representing the network of causal relationships, but leaving the causal arrows in the model as black boxes. That is, an arrow from θ to X says how the distribution of X changes over levels of θ, but it does not say what processes instantiate the causal effect. It could also be said that the counterfactual model fails to specify how the cause is *productive* of its effect; a process causation account can be used to specify a mechanism that characteristically yields the effect variable as output when fed the cause variable as input. For instance, a counterfactual account of the relation between smoking and cancer could state that the prevalence of lung cancer today would have been lower if fewer people had smoked. A process account would instead detail the mechanism by means of which smoke (the cause) carries tar into the lungs which through a sequence of molecular effects typically leads to cancerous mutations (the effect).

Thinking this through for typical psychological or educational tests, one could for instance take item administration to be the causal factor and item response to be the effect. Now consider a counterfactual claim that may be involved in test validity: The proportion of affirmative responses to the question "Do you make friends easily?" would have been lower had there been fewer extraverted subjects in the sample. If in a process model the causal factor is item administration, and the effect is the item response, the differential response of extraverted as opposed to introverted individuals must stem from (a) a different process taking place in these individuals, or (b) the same process taking place with different parameters. That is, in a process model that accompanies a counterfactual measurement claim, the measured attribute must moderate (option a) or mediate (option b) the response process.

This is essentially continuous with paradigmatic measurement cases in physics. For instance, an object's mass is a parameter in the process taking place between putting it in the pan balance—the cause—and reading off the scale value—the effect. Therefore mass mediates the effect of submitting the object to the measurement instrument on the value read off from the scale. However, it remains essential to the process approach that one does not reduce the process to a set of nomothetic relationships (moderation, mediation) between variables. The central tenet of the process approach is that the process explains and maintains the nomothetic relationships between variables. These relationships, in turn, are just the statistical manifestation of the process that maintains them. To reduce a process to a nomothetic model introduces an infinite regress, requiring more mediators to explain every new mediator. Explaining relations between variables in qualitatively different terms allows a means of escaping such regress.

12.4. Justification Through Alignment

As discussed in chapter 1, we see recent developments in test validity theory as follows. A number of very clever but broadly ad hoc procedures were developed as specific solutions to specific practical problems, producing a fragmented field. Increasingly, the lack of underlying test validity theory made it difficult to systematically address accumulated technical problems and paradoxes. The unifying theoretical efforts of Loevinger, Cronbach, Messick and others successfully overcame these difficulties by providing a unified (albeit not unitary) theory of test validity. However, this contribution had the unforeseen consequence of leaving test developers with too little specific direction for validation efforts. The very source of the breadth and flexibility of the unified approach brought with it a lack of clarity about how best to proceed with validation and to evaluate the merit and adequacy of validation evidence.

As an outgrowth of the construct validity approach, Kane's argument-based approach to validation moved the field back in the direction of specific detailed guidance for validation efforts, without regressing to a simple checklist approach. In our view, the idea of a validity argument organized around an interpretive argument allows for the flexibility to allow validation efforts to support different kinds of conclusions (the test measures X, the test assesses X without strict quantitative structure, the test predicts X without bias, the test adequately operationalizes X) from different kinds of evidence. However, it also places sufficient constraints on the process to provide more concrete guidance and criteria for evaluating the adequacy of validation evidence. We have tried to further extend and develop this basic approach through careful attention to unresolved problems and unanswered questions in test validity theory related to measurement, causation, and meaning. Toward this end, the present section elaborates a notion of test validation alignment that helps clarify and concretize the process of validation through the construction of a validity argument.

As we have hopefully shown in this book, there are varied legitimate uses of test scores. These uses differ with respect to the interpretation of the scores: as measures, as assessments, as predictors, as operationalizations, and so on. In the case of measurement and assessment, validation interest rests primarily with the construct measured or assessed. In the case of prediction, interest rests more with the predicted criterion construct and with the absence of inappropriate causal influences on test scores. In behavioral observation, interest rests with the operationalization of the domain and the validity of the observation process. This diversity of uses and interpretations of test scores suggests that the task for the test developer is to seek the test score interpretation that optimally aligns with the intended use of the test scores, the test construction method, and with the available validity evidence. For instance, test items that have been selected to jointly predict a criterion variable as well as possible are not expected to assess a single attribute in accordance with a reflective model, but rather to measure distinct (sets of) attributes that explain unique variance in the criterion variable.

Thus, in the case of optimal prediction, there is little value in seeking evidence of a common factor or latent variable, or evidence of internal consistency within the predictor variables. Rather one would want to seek evidence of non-redundancy, strong prediction, and an absence of biasing factors. Similarly, it makes little sense to seek to maximize the variance of a certification test, or to show good discrimination in the tails of the distribution. Instead, one wants to show good discrimination around the cut point, and to justify the cut point in terms of the absolute level of competence being certified. The same evidence that offers valuable validity evidence when well aligned with the test can offer little value or even become counterproductive when out of alignment with the test (including its intended use and interpretation). Likewise, as has been well understood for some decades, strong validity evidence can support one use and interpretation of a test but not another. Even the best tests have no validity for most uses and interpretations. The point is to align the validity evidence to the appropriate uses and interpretations.

Rather than a linear process of defining a construct and developing a test to measure it, the alignment concept allows for a more dynamic, non-linear process. As validation evidence accumulates, two things happen. First, the evidence firms up support for the initial interpretation and use. At the same time however, the improved knowledge and understanding of the test makes it possible for test developers to raise their aspirations for the test. The field has long recognized that contrary evidence can lead to the revision of a construct theory. The alignment concept also highlights the way that confirming evidence can shift the intended use and interpretation of a test by bringing additional goals into reach. Additional validation research can help transform a purely norm-referenced test in a criterion-referenced test. Such research can allow a test designed to measure individual differences to take on additional uses supporting counterfactual inferences. Also, research can result in improving the measurement properties of a test, possibly refining the level of measurement from ordinal to interval, or ratio. Additional research might similarly make it possible for a test designed to track changes in a single group over time to also provide information about group comparisons. In all of these examples and others like them, validation involves a process of seeking an *equilibrium* between test score interpretations on the one hand, and evidence on the other. According to the Goldilocks Model of test score interpretation presented in chapter 9, one seeks an interpretation that is in optimal alignment when it provides the most useful justifiable interpretation in light of existing evidence, accepted theory, and the context of use. When any of these change, the equilibrium may shift. The various feedback loops in Figure 12.1 reflect this equilibrium process.

This alignment idea can be helpful to test developers because it moves the discussion of validation beyond discussing how to construct a validity argument toward discussing how to decide which validation argument to construct. Essentially, test developers should seek to construct the most useful validity argument that the available evidence and evidence that can feasibly be collected can support. Seeking to develop too strong a validity argument (too soon) can be counterproductive if it delays development of a weaker validity argument that suffices to support a given application. Seeking to develop too weak a validity argument can be counterproductive if it fails to adequately support a test application that could have been supported had the same validation resources been devoted to validating a stronger argument. This further clarifies the mechanism by which testing can be justified before validation reaches its conclusion.

12.5. Knowledge, Value, and Action

Testing serves as an applied technology and as such one typically performs test construction and validation as part of a broader effort to take some action and achieve some purpose. Reasonable people can disagree about whether facts can ever suffice to justify a course of action. However, even someone who believes that facts can do this will be hard pressed to provide an account of this that does not in some way involve values. If facts can justify action, they do so by means of justifying values that play an essential role in justifying action. So, in large part, the question of whether facts can justify action reduces to the question of whether values are discovered (cognitivism) or invented (non-cognitivism), and thus justified by facts or not.

To make this concrete, consider an example from selection testing. One way of looking at fairness in selection involves equal probabilities of selection errors where individuals are categorized into those who should be selected and those who should not based on some cut score along the continuum of scores (Cole, 1973). Another involves measurement invariance such that individual scores bear the same psychometric relationship either to criterion scores (Cleary, 1968) or latent variables (Mellenbergh, 1989; Meredith, 1993) across groups. These two basic approaches will typically produce conflicting results when groups differ in their means (Borsboom, Romeijn & Wicherts, 2008; Millsap, 1997; 2007). Similarly, the first approach alone can produce conflicting results depending upon whether one looks at the probability of selection or the probability of non-selection (i.e., screening out; Petersen & Novick, 1976). One approach to the latter problem has been for testing specialists to leave it to others to specify the values in the form of utilities of outcomes and for testing specialists to focus on how to best achieve the stipulated outcomes (Petersen, 1976). A more recent approach has been to shift the emphasis to focus on stakeholder perceptions of fairness (Chan et al., 1998) and thus to incorporate stakeholder values into decisions about selection systems. Such practices stretch the limits of the traditional approach to validity as providing a justification on the basis of universal principles that everyone should accept. The discussion in chapter 9 extends the validity argument model in a way that helps it to accommodate these developments in testing practice. This extension also helps illuminate and clarify the role of values in validation and the justification of actions that make use of tests.

The underlying theoretical shift involves moving away from the view that everyone should accept the premises of a validity argument because they represent acceptable basic assumptions. Instead, the starting point is that something counts as an acceptable basic assumption because agreement has been reached on it. This does not simply reflect a matter of majority rule, but rather a deliberative process that leads to a broadening of perspectives as all parties to the discussion move toward a consensus view (Habermas, 1990; House & Howe, 1999). Moreover, empirical evidence can play a central role in developing value judgments (Scriven, 1991) and thus constrain the range of defensible value judgments. Understood this way, the validity argument is not something that can be created by test developers working in isolation. Instead, a validity argument intended to persuade stakeholders must be developed through a process that involves stakeholders at least enough to justify the underlying value choices that justify actions taken on the basis of test scores. As such, the validity argument cannot function as a tool to stifle dissent, but only as a tool to pursue mutual agreement and acceptance of the assumptions that justify action based on test validity evidence.

One can incorporate all of this process into the validation process (e.g., Messick, 1989; Markus, 1998a) or one can attempt to partition some aspects of the process as validation and label the others as test evaluation (e.g., Borsboom, Mellenbergh & Van Heerden, 2004; Shadish, Cook & Campbell, 2002). Either way, value decisions are required to bridge the gap from psychometric facts to justification of actions based on test scores. Whether one considers it part of test validity or not, the validity argument approach, extended to view the development of the argument as a deliberative process between stakeholder groups, provides a theoretical underpinning for the justification of action based on test scores (Kane, 2006). Such a justification is not forthcoming without some such extension of the idea of validation beyond that of an activity carried out in isolation by test developers.

12.6. Chapter Conclusion

Any decision that is made on the basis of test scores is situated in a complex space of factual, evidential, and normative concerns. This space is large and complex and this makes the issue of test validity somewhat like a Russian nesting doll, where every answer to a question reveals a new question, so that one may progress ever deeper to arrive at some of the fundamental questions of human inquiry: How does scientific theory relate to the world? What is the referential status of psychological concepts? What is meaning? Regardless of this, we think that the current work makes clear that the main factors to structure this space are measurement (because assessment and measurement are what we aim to do), causation (because this determines the origin of variation in test scores), and meaning (because interpretation is the assignment of meaning to scores).

In addition, the interplay between these factors is largely what structures dynamics of validity theory itself, with different positions arising naturally from accepting different answers to the questions of how measurement, causation, and meaning should be conceptualized and of what their relative importance is. The present chapter has provided a succinct walk-through of the major issues that we encounter when reasoning back from an observation to its putative causes. In doing so, it provides a bird's-eye view of the major themes of discussion in this book. Hopefully, this will be of use to researchers, test developers, and policy makers in evaluating test score interpretations.

Perhaps one of the most revealing aspects of the current work is how much territory remains to be explored. However far we have taken our attempt to provide a deeper treatment of some basic issues in test validity, we have only discussed broad currents in approaches to measurement, causation, and meaning. These topics have each led to the production of thousands of books in disciplines such as statistics, cognitive science, philosophy, and psychology. Certainly there are many shaded positions in between these prototypical approaches. We realized from the start that a complete treatment was out of the question. However, despite this realization, the sheer magnitude of the topic has impressed us greatly. Despite this, we hope that we have succeeded in mapping out the dimensions and structure of the major issues in test validity.

13 Epilogue as Dialog
The Future of Test Validity Theory

In this chapter we look back at the material from the previous 12 chapters and consider it in a broader context. We have chosen to break from speaking in a shared authorial voice in order to facilitate a more free-ranging exchange of perspectives between the two authors. In our view, this approach also reflects the current state of a field characterized by open questions and contrasting perspectives. In some sense, a dialog also reflects the process of theory development. Each of us provided three of the six topics of discussion that comprise the chapter. By mutual agreement, turns do not exceed 500 words.

13.1. Test Validation Methods

KM: It was not possible and would not have been desirable to embed text books on standard psychometric theory and research methods inside a book-length treatment of test validity theory. However, one result is that we discuss the pros and cons of things like a causal interpretation of measurement models without giving a lot of concrete advice about how to empirically support such interpretations. Clearly, simply fitting a model to passively observed cross-sectional data and stipulating a causal interpretation of the parameters does not offer much of an advance over a non-causal interpretation of the same model. Indeed, in some respects it may be a step backward. The Goldilocks Model from chapter 10 offers some general guidance: Push your interpretation as far as you can within the bounds of what evidence will support. We have also written about a general shift from look-and-see test development to try-and-see test development that incorporates evidence based on manipulations, experimental or otherwise. Perhaps we could briefly offer some more concrete thoughts on designing validation studies to test causal theories of measurement. Perhaps we could highlight some key connections between standard research methods literature and test validation in this context.

DB: The classic psychometric modus operandi is tightly tailored to fitting a single model to a single dataset and then deciding whether that model fits the data. Almost all psychometric work of the past decades is directed towards the optimization of this process. If one wants to make a case for a causal interpretation of measurement models, as I would indeed think is generally required, then one needs more. But what? One important ingredient is to develop a reasonable process model for the causal effects that are presumed in the model. This amounts to developing a process-based substantive interpretation of the model's structure and parameters. The availability of such an interpretation, in my view, greatly enhances the range of what Goldilocks will deem acceptable; if only because, without a process model, all one has is a statistical structure and a statistical structure, by itself, hardly ever convinces as a substantive model. I think we have covered the question of which kinds of interpretations are available reasonably well from a meta-theoretic perspective.

However, you are certainly correct when you say that putting a causal interpretation on top of a factor model and being done with it would be a step backwards. So an important question, that we have hardly tackled at all, is how to go about and test the causal interpretation of a measurement model. I think that three sources of data are particularly important for a causal interpretation. First, a measurement model should be invariant over background variables: effects of, say, genetic factors or childhood experience on, say, neuroticism at age 18 should run via the latent variable—otherwise a measurement interpretation is hard to uphold. So I see a significant role for MIMIC modeling and measurement invariance testing. Second, I think that at some point one needs to address the individual person; if one wants to submit a measurement interpretation, one cannot forever limit one's attention to individual differences at time t. This issue will, I think, become pressing rather quickly because we are now witnessing a trend towards gathering "datastreams," to which new data are added continually, rather than datasets that are closed. The development of mobile data gathering methods, for instance, is likely to lead to data that are sampled in time and to which new data can be added all the time. Such data would allow for testing theories at the intra-individual level, and this is exactly what one needs to test process models and to connect them to the measurement structure. Hence, I think that *time series data* are going to play an important role. Third, psychometrics is not necessarily limited to the analysis of correlational data, and I think that an entire field can be opened up when psychometricians start intervening in their subject matter and testing the effects of these interventions. Here, it is important to note that psychometric interventions can often concern interventions that change items, rather than people. Thus, I would see the development of *experimental psychometrics* as an important stride forward.

KM: I agree about the importance of moving from look-and-see psychometrics to try-and-see psychometrics. I think that another theme from chapter

1 developed in chapter 10 and to some extent in chapter 12 sheds some useful light on this issue. We described the background of Kane's (2006) validation chapter as a shift from realism to pragmatism. An important aspect of validity arguments that Kane has developed involves audience specificity. Another involves a dynamic quality that distinguishes them from mathematical proofs. It seems to me that these ideas more or less seal the coffin for checklist approaches to validation. It is not possible to follow a checklist because the evidence required to support the validity of a test, however construed, will differ depending upon the audience and the current state of knowledge. Checklists, like mathematical proofs, do not share these properties of validity arguments. This shift in thinking about validity has the consequence of making it more difficult to provide specific methodological advice. One can provide different advice for different types of tests and different audiences. It seems neither possible nor desirable, however, to attempt to anticipate every contingency. Instead, it seems to me that one of the big take-home messages is that test validators should not attempt to work in isolation to produce a universal knock-down argument. Instead, they should reach out as early as possible to their various audiences—various stakeholder groups—and begin a dialog that will help them refine their choice of validation methods, enrich their understanding of the issues, and tailor their validation efforts to specific stakeholder concerns. Science is fallible. Checklists cannot provide immunity from unanticipated criticism. Moreover, the values that animate validation come from the community of stakeholders. (This is illustrated by the constructive tension between psychometricians who want tests longer and clinicians who want them shorter.) For all these reasons, it is better to seek out criticism early in the process and work collaboratively. Working in isolation and dictating standards unilaterally is not only bad public relations, it is bad science.

That said, there are certainly prevailing norms of scientific inference that bear in a general way on test validation. Even these vary to some degree by substantive topic. However, I think that another take-home message involves triangulation. A variety of sources of evidence that test an assumption in different ways will generally offer stronger validity evidence than a single line of evidence that tests the assumption in just one way. A third recommendation that falls out of current test validity theory involves a focus on what the literature calls critical experiments, although they need not use experimental methods. The key point involves the following two-step process. First, seek plausible alternative explanations of test scores that differ in ways important to testing policy or other practical decisions. Then, design studies that pit these contrasting theories against one another. Framing validation research this way should really put those conducting validation studies on familiar ground, adopting methods that prevail in the substantive literature related to the test in question.

DB: Naturally, one should always keep in mind one's audience when communicating. However, I am wary of incorporating audience specificity into the definition of validity. Even though it is certainly true that arguments for validity will take a different form depending on one's audience, one should avoid defining the quality of that argument in terms of whether it succeeds in persuading one's audience. Especially if validity theory is to keep a normative component (which I think it should), stating what *ought* to be involved in a validity argument implies that at least some kind of checklist should be an essential element of validity theory.

I also think that we can say quite a lot about what should be in such a checklist. For instance, if one wants to argue for the predictive value of a test score, then one should always present a measure of association or regression coefficient that justifies such use. I do not think that such requirements should be taken to be all too audience specific. I have had quite a few experiences where the predictive value of neuroscientific measures (fMRI and such) was simply assumed by an audience for reasons utterly unclear to me (naturally, white coats and big machines do not ensure high correlations). Methodology is largely a normative business, and so is validity theory. Any normative business involves correcting people's beliefs when they are mistaken. For instance, standing up to remind the audience that predictive use of test scores is senseless if they do not have predictive ability. I think this is an essential task for psychometricians and validity theorists.

So I construct the pragmatic element in the interpretative-argument theory somewhat differently. Namely: different test score interpretations require different arguments. Some of these arguments may involve measurement, others may not; some may involve constructs, others may not. However, the standards for any given argument are not, in my view, up for grabs.

I do agree that checklist methodology is naturally limited, because as you note correctly there is always some degree of context sensitivity. However, this does not preclude the formulation of relatively uniform standards; it merely licenses motivated deviations from these standards. I also agree that the triangulation of evidence is very important to establish good arguments to support or refute test score interpretations. This is also something I think psychometricians should be more concerned with. It fits the general scheme of moving beyond fitting models to a given dataset and towards testing theories against various strands of evidence, towards manipulating item and person attributes to assess causal models, and towards modeling processes involved in responding to items.

13.2. Test Validity Theory and Meaning

DB: Meaning is a delicate issue in any field in which it arises. Validity theory is no exception. From the discussion in this book, it appears that test score meaning is the least developed of the topics we addressed. For both measurement and causation there exist formalized theories that can be used to test one's hypotheses to the data. In addition such models allow one to reason precisely and evaluate the relative importance of different assumptions in one's theory. For meaning, there appears to be no analogous framework. Of course, both measurement models and formal models for causation are relatively recent additions to the psychometric arsenal. So it might be the case that we will see the development of "meaning models" in the future. On the other hand, there may be fundamental problems that preclude this. So: could such a framework exist at all? Or is the entirely informal treatment of meaning just something that we have to live with?

KM: This is an issue that has interested me for some time, from test validity to collective cognition to jurisprudence. The fundamental problem remains the same in each of these guises. A formal model begins with an agreed-upon set of terms, formation rules for well-formed formulae, and inference rules for deriving conclusions from premises. Each of these, in its own way, begs the question of meaning. In the Greek tradition, logic is closely tied to logos, which can be understood as a sort of collectively shared comprehension of the world. In the European tradition, what was logically possible was for a long time understood as that which was conceivable to the mind of the Christian God (Mason, 2000). These conceptual linkages help illustrate the problem with formal models of meaning. The formulation of the model itself constitutes a perspective, a point of view, from which facts are understood, formulated, and expressed. One can relatively unproblematically use formal systems to describe and model games of chance because the formal systems have no direct involvement in the games of chance. The same holds for many other processes. However, meaning is central to the application of formal systems. Without meaning, they offer only pointless symbol manipulation. As such, formal systems cannot offer a means to get outside of meaning and map it onto an external representation.

This situation need not preclude the application of formal semantic models. In some sense, it offers a useful reminder that our formal models do not yield universal truths when applied to other content either. They only yield conclusions relative to their assumptions, and the assumptions are always open to criticism. So, perhaps it is nothing special that formal systems cannot provide a representation of meaning that is not also subject to dispute. What does seem clear is that one cannot begin in the traditional way by stipulating a fixed and pervasive set of agreed-upon meanings. To do so would simply assume away the very phenomena one wants to capture in the formal system. Here lies the challenge.

Bach (1989) discussed an interesting approach developed in a dissertation by Irene Heim. In this approach, a discourse is formalized like a drawer of file cards. Different participants put various cards into the drawer and each participant has access to the drawer to review all the cards. One could extend this approach to represent different systems of meaning as different file boxes. One way to do this might be to make use of paraconsistent logics (Priest, 2006). As Priest notes, classical logics allow the inference of any conclusion from a contradiction. Paraconsistent logics make it possible to reason from contradictory premises by limiting the inferences that one can draw from contradictory premises. Even if each file drawer remains consistent, the combination of any two file drawers need not. This might offer a way of formalizing heteroglot test item interpretations.

DB: I think that you have identified a number of interesting points here. First, you note that discussions of meaning, in contrast to those about causality or probability, have no external vantage point (since they themselves require terms to be invested with meaning). To me this resonates with the way meaning can be set up to chase its own tail through self-reference. This is for instance the case in the Liar paradoxes (e.g., L: The sentence denoted "L" is false), Russell's set theoretical problem ("does the set of all sets that contain themselves contain itself?"), and the famous Gödel theorems. In these cases, the problems arise when the system produces statements about its own statements, and any system that is capable of producing such statements is capable of getting into such troubles. In the context of validity, it is indeed questionable whether a system that contains statements about the meaning of test scores could avoid speaking about the meaning of these statements about the meaning of test scores. Could such a system be made to chase its own tail like other self-referential systems?

How respondents make sense of items might be a different issue altogether, and one that may in fact be more accessible. Clearly, when answering an item like "do you like parties?" the respondent will assign meaning to the terms in the item. It must be possible to use cognitive science theories about meaning assignment and interpretation to model this process. In addition one should be able to spot differences between different groups; the term "party," even if abstractly similar (a number of people gathered together to celebrate), might concretely mean something very different to different people (e.g., in different ethnic communities, or in different social classes). To the extent that it does, heteroglossia may be the norm rather than the exception. I find it surprising that no formal models exist to model the process of item interpretation. It would seem that a wealth of cognitive science theory is available.

KM: Perhaps it would be useful to illustrate what I see as making heteroglossia so tricky with a standard example from the legal indeterminacy literature. Imagine a local ordinance forbidding vehicles in the park. The ordinance applies to some clear cases such as private automobiles that almost everyone would agree that it does not allow. There are also many clear cases, such as baby buggies, that most would agree that the ordinance does allow. However, there are also many cases upon which the interpretation does not seem as clear. Are bicycles allowed? Mopeds? Trucks used by landscapers? Various interpretations of the ordinance differ with respect to these kinds of cases. Now suppose we convert this example to a survey question asking whether respondents agree with the ordinance that prohibits vehicles in the park. Each of these various interpretations corresponds to a different interpretation of the survey item.

At a theoretical level, one can think of this as different ways of mapping words such as 'vehicle' onto reality. One interpretation includes bicycles and another does not. However, to model this phenomenon, one needs to represent reality in some optimally neutral way in order to then represent in the model the ways that different interpretations map onto reality. The problem comes with formulating a sufficiently neutral representation. If one begins by specifying what types of things counts as vehicles, one immediately favors some interpretations over others. The obvious thought is to leave the extension of 'vehicle' open in the formal representation. However, the problem is that heteroglossia about the term 'vehicle' interweaves with heteroglossia about other related terms. So, one cannot begin by simply assuming fixed meanings for terms like 'car', 'bicycle', or 'truck'. These terms remain open to different interpretations in relation to what counts as a vehicle. Ultimately, this phenomenon spreads outward, denying the formal representation any neutral means of representing the world onto which these various interpretations map. So, even if one can safely treat the model language as outside of the system and fully fixed in its interpretation, one still runs into a serious problem in using such a language to represent and model heteroglossia between different interpretations of the ordinance.

I lay this out in an attempt to articulate the depth of the problem, not as an argument against the possibility of a solution. If one makes some severe simplifying assumptions limiting the range of interpretations to a small fixed set of alternatives, one can think of this in terms of classical test theory. Each participant has a true score corresponding to each interpretation. The overall model expands to $X = {}_1T_1 + {}_2T_2 + \ldots + {}_kT_k + E$, where the ${}_1$terms represent the proportion of individuals adopting the corresponding interpretation. Of course, it does not hold much interest to know the proportion of item variance attributable to all the various true scores taken together. The test user is presumably interested in just one of the true scores. Moreover, the simplifying assumptions are both false and restrictive.

13.3. The Yardstick by Which Validation is Judged (If There is One)

KM: One might encapsulate the view of validity developed throughout the book as follows. First, decide what the test should do: assess (perhaps even measure) a construct, predict something, facilitate a fair contest, or something else. Then, seek validation evidence appropriate to what the test should do. If one intends a test to assess something, then one needs to articulate an appropriate theory of assessment. Examples include the causal account(s) from chapters 6 to 8 or the behavior domain sampling account from chapter 5. Causal or not, the idea is that one needs some sort of explicit account of what it means to assess a construct in order to know what evidence would support that conclusion. Looked at from another angle, a theory of the construct does not suffice. One also needs a theory of how the test does what it does in relation to the construct.

A number of interesting and difficult questions emerge about matters of research design for validating what a test does. For instance, how do traditional techniques like content validation, correlations with external variables, analyses of internal structure, and so on bear differently on different things that a test can do? In the case of assessment, a prior set of questions involves how one selects an appropriate account of assessment for a given test or construct. For instance, must tests that assess the same construct rest on the same account of assessment? At a more fundamental level, throughout the book we juggle empiricist, realist, and pragmatic perspectives on various validity issues—often finding a mix of these within a specific issue. With all of these alternatives in flux, perhaps the most fundamental question is this: How does one justify choices between different validation procedures themselves? Interpretive and validity arguments help organize these choices, but what makes a good argument remains a prior question. We tackle this piecemeal throughout the book, but do not offer a general answer.

From an empiricist perspective, one posits an axiomatic deductive system to help organize inferences about sense data. Justifications for inquiry methods typically come from axiomatic definitions and first principles. From a realist perspective, methodological prescriptions are broadly continuous with substantive research and methodological advice should have empirical support. From a pragmatic perspective, all forms of inquiry rest in collective efforts to address practical problems and are ultimately justified by the success that they bring in such endeavors—even if that means adopting an empiricist or realist stance for pragmatic reasons. Moreover, ongoing collective efforts to address problems can transform the bases on which success is judged. In addition to their central theoretical importance, these questions are quite practical. Faced with diverse alternatives, how does a test developer or user chart a course to successful validation of a testing procedure with respect to its doing what it should? Absent a simple fixed foundation, what provides the basis for such choices? Is a general account possible, or must such questions be answered piecemeal as a matter of principle?

DB: In my view, different uses of tests imply different standards for evaluating how well they perform. When one intends to measure something, these standards are wholly different from when one intends to predict something. Thus, it makes no sense to me that one should use the same yardstick to assess the quality of prediction instruments versus that of measurement instruments. In this respect, I consider it unfortunate that validity theory has, in the past, insisted that the justification for test use should be tied to the measurement of theoretical constructs. I think there are legitimate test uses that have no issue with measurement or constructs, and in these cases one should not be forced to build validity arguments in these terms. In that sense, I think that the old tripartite model of validity (content, criterion, and construct validity) did something right that was lost in later treatments; these later treatments insisted (dogmatically, in my view) that construct validity was the whole of validity. The old tripartite model may have had its flaws, but it may be used to profitably coordinate different goals to different types of evidence in a systematic way: the goal of covering a domain corresponds to content validity, the goal of prediction to criterion validity, and the goal of measurement to construct validity. Thus, at this level, standards should vary with the goals of the test user, which means that they are partly pragmatic (in the sense of being context-sensitive). Working out the many ways in which this can happen, rather than insisting on a single one, is a main strength of the way we have approached validity.

Having said that, however, I do not think that this pragmatic dimension carries us all the way through. For instance, once you have chosen to design your instrument as a prediction instrument, you cannot adhere to adequate measurement properties or to content coverage, in order to defend predictive utility. Instead, you will have to show, minimally, that the test score is associated with the property to be predicted. I do not see much space for negotiation in this respect. If one's prediction instrument does not predict anything, then it is useless for its purpose however good its measurement properties may be. The same, in my view, holds for measurement. If one wants to interpret an instrument as a measurement instrument, then one is obliged to explicate what measurement is and when it is achieved. There is some room for negotiation on this issue, as we have discussed in chapters 2–4, but even here it is the case that once one fixes the semantics of measurement, one has thereby explicated what sort of evidence one needs. The point is that, if one settles on a particular goal for test use, the possibilities for choosing between different standards tend to disappear. Naturally, there is always a deeper level at which one can ask ever more involved philosophical questions, and these questions do not have easy answers. However, I do not think that one has to solve every such question to meet the challenge of developing a validity argument or to establish the measurement qualities of an instrument.

KM: A common yardstick for evaluating validation efforts differs from a common procedure for validating test uses. The absence of the latter might make the former more attractive. When one reviews research reports one has a general yardstick and applies it, as appropriate, to a particular study. Likewise, when one reviews validation efforts, it seems worth asking whether one can have a common yardstick that one then applies appropriately depending upon the specific types of evidence appropriate to the test use being validated. Renaming validation for certain test uses would not alter the basic question, only the terminology.

Content validation strategies offer an instructive example. Messick's criticism was that while failure to represent a domain provides evidence that a test does not assess the ability common to tasks in the domain, success does not provide evidence that the test does assess the ability. It can fail for other reasons. The smuggled premise is that the test is intended to assess. If one limited content validation to non-assessment applications in which the test merely samples, then Messick's and related criticism would not apply. However, the fact is that today content validation strategies are widely applied in assessment contexts. So, the applications of various validation strategies sometimes overlap.

Predictive tests are also instructive. Imagine a new job knowledge test designed to predict job performance. The validity generalization argument asserts that the meta-analytic evidence for an association swamps whatever the local validation study might add. So, hypothetically, validation efforts might be better directed toward evaluating reliability and potential sources of construct-irrelevant variance that could lead to selection biases. It also seems to me that predictive evidence absent an underlying construct explanation offers much less of a basis for generalizing into the future. So, the best evidence may depend upon background information. Moreover, predictive and assessment issues may overlap.

Here is a sketch of how I might try to answer the question. At the level of specific validation strategies, both empiricist and realist approaches offer advantages with respect to particular aspects of validation. However, at the level of evaluating validation efforts, they share a common weakness: They both begin by attempting to box validation into a limited range of options. Empiricism does this with axioms, realism does it with naturalized definitions of various empirical categories. Both bracket off alternatives to constrain the problem space. This is where pragmatism comes into its own: Its fundamental advantage rests precisely with its open-ended approach that does not close off unanticipated possibilities.

If there can be a common yardstick, I would envision it as an evaluation of the extent to which the validation effort has addressed the concerns of various parties and moved them as far as possible toward consensus. Whether this should reflect rational deliberation idealized away from political influences or whether the politics of testing constitute an essential part of validation remains an open question for further work in test validity theory. If all test uses require justification, however, that fact may provide the common yardstick.

DB: You are hitting on a central problem here, and I think it concerns the very relation between science and society. If we are to consider standards that should apply to successful measurement, prediction, assessment, or content sampling, I think we may justifiably take these to be part of psychometrics. That is, the rationales for these standards are to such an extent infected with psychometric theory that they can be constructed as lying within the domain of psychometrics: psychometrics covers them. This has the important implications that (a) the standards in question can, to a considerable extent, be grounded in science, and (b) psychometricians may justifiably claim special expertise in this matter, just like, say, geologists can claim special expertise in developing standards for soil treatment in construction work. Naturally, validation strategies for assessment, measurement, and prediction may overlap, but we can figure out how and why; importantly, we could consider a research project that analyzes the overlap to also be part of psychometrics. Although issues of conceptualization matter even at this level, I think they do not matter enough to turn to pragmatism (which, perhaps as a part of my continental heritage, I regard as a last conceptual resort).

However, there is also a different issue, namely whether there could be common yardsticks to decide when a validation effort (of whatever nature) is good enough. I personally do not believe that any uniform yardsticks to decide this are feasible (unless one relativises them to such an extent that they are no longer uniform, as I think your proposal does). However, more importantly, I think that my opinion here simply does not matter much; no more, at least, than that of others. I can claim expertise in constructing all kinds of psychometric standards. But I do not want to claim expertise in deciding when a validation effort is good enough, precisely because (as you correctly note) that depends crucially on who is to be convinced. In addition, this is an issue that I believe should be in the public space, so to speak, and not a topic that psychometrics should treat as its subject matter. It is especially important to avoid the use of jargon in this respect, because a lay audience generally does not know where the psychometric expertise begins and where it ends. If one starts talking about general yardsticks for validation research, and dresses such talk with jargon, the audience can easily interpret these general yardsticks as being part of one's expertise. I think my expertise ends quite a long way before general yardsticks for validation are in sight.

13.4. Validity and Response Processes

DB: For the past twenty years or so, there has been a promise in the air that (cognitive) process modeling will help address the issue of validity.

The case seems obvious: whatever assessment we get is produced in the moments between item administration and item response. So whatever it is we are measuring must have some bearing on that process. Investigating the item response process, and if possible actively modeling it, should therefore give useful information on validity, if only because it forces the researcher to spell out how the attribute of interest affects (is or is affected by) the item responses. There is a significant array of cognitive theory that could be used to inform psychometric models. For instance, many psychometric items require people to make a decision (which box to tick) in response to a question (e.g., "are you a nervous person?") which in turn require the integration of evidence (How do I typically behave? What do other people say about me? How do I feel now?) for and against the expressed hypothesis (i.e., that the respondent is in fact a nervous person). There are many cognitive models for this type of task. However, with the exception of cognitive diagnostic modeling in educational testing, there is very little activity on substantively informed psychometric modeling that utilizes this kind of information. Almost all testing applications use the same one-size-fits-all model, typically a factor or Item Response Theory (IRT) model, without paying attention to the item response process or even showing that the item response process indeed supports such a model. Why is this? Can we expect this to change or are there factors that prohibit successful process models in many cases?

KM: This topic has several aspects. One is technical. For my master's thesis, I combined a confirmatory factor analysis with a protocol analysis to evaluate the validity of a job satisfaction measure. Integrating the results of the two halves of the study posed one of the greatest challenges at the time. Today, a researcher willing to invest the time required to learn some new software can make use of sophisticated integrative models (de Boeck & Wilson, 2004). However, options that can handle polytomous items that differ in discrimination remain limited. Moreover, there remains some distance to go before the casual user who wants to conduct just one such study can complete the required analyses without a significant learning curve.

Another aspect is sociocultural. The private sector does not seem to incentivize such research for commercial test developers nor does the public sector incentivize it for government test developers. It seems plausible that published examples that researchers can follow will help (Mislevy, 2006). It also seems plausible to conjecture that a few well-positioned testing specialists offering courses in this area could graduate a steady flow of new academics in various fields who have the required expertise to apply such methods to substantive research programs.

I would like to focus on a third aspect, the nature of explanation in the behavioral sciences. These sciences follow Humean practices that can sometimes work against other practices within the same sciences.

From the Humean inheritance comes the tradition of seeking explanations for some happenings only in terms of other happenings. However, this explanatory minimalism conflicts with the idea that an explanation points to something that brings about what it explains. For example, consider the observed regularity that people feel more confident about making an inference from a general category (all birds have an ulnar artery) to a typical subtype (all robins have an ulnar artery) than to an atypical subtype (all penguins have an ulnar artery; Sloman, 1993). From a Humean perspective, there really is nothing more to explaining this than pointing to the regularity that people express more confidence about the former type of inference that the latter. (Thus Chomsky associates behaviorism with a prohibition against theory; Chomsky & Foucault, 2006.) Sloman's explanation was that instead of storing categories hierarchically, human memory stores similarity between categories in terms of shared features and infers hierarchical relationships from similarity. It is important to note that either type of explanation can use explanatory item response models. However, only the non-Humean process explanation gives us a story about what brings about the observed regularity. The Humean impulse toward minimalism in behavioral science has a tendency to co-opt methods like explanatory item response modeling and thus preempt process explanations. Practices for collecting, analyzing, and reporting data remain very Humean. One finds little incentive for process explanation when a well-fitting model suffices for publication. Adding theory risks rejection or reviewer objections. These entrenched Humean practices may pose the greatest challenge to widespread item response process research.

DB: The methodology of psychologists is a big hammer with which they violently flatten any topic until it is sufficiently flat to be treated as a dime. Almost every research question is tortured until it fits the general scheme of "is there an effect of X on Y under conditions Z?" (very seldom deepened to "how large is the effect in question?"). In that sense, large areas of psychology are still captive of dustbowl empiricism and are extremely Humean in spirit. I agree that this does not work to the advantage of process theory and modeling. (An interesting aside is how methodologists could counteract the simplistic methodological tendencies of psychology; yet another interesting question is why many other fields, whether natural sciences or humaniora, have not fallen prey to comparable methodology-induced theoretical flatness.) So I tend to agree that there is little fertile ground for process models.

However, I do think that at least some inspired individuals have pulled the cart to work out modeling endeavors that could be used to some profit; you mention De Boeck and Wilson (2004) but there are several other people working along similar lines. Right now several modeling strategies are available in accessible software packages and there has also been some professed enthusiasm about the models (e.g., Leighton & Gierl, 2006). Still, I have not seen any major substantive breakthroughs. Maybe a problem is that whenever sets of processes or skills determine an order in the respondents' performance, such that we can order that performance from better to worse, the total score will capture that information as well as any more fine-grained statistic. In addition, there may be only a few cases in which a breakdown of ability level into its constituent skills maps on to clear actions (e.g., taking different educational measures or therapeutic approaches depending on the respondent's profile). The only indisputable gain of process-based models, in my view, resides in areas where performance cannot be ordered and in which different processes map on to different categories (as with the well-known balance scale task; Jansen & van der Maas, 1997) so that the total score really is not usable. Thus, maybe the problem is that the total score is so powerful across a wide range of conditions, and is good enough for most practical purposes psychologists might contemplate.

KM: That is a very important point. I think that we agree that, in broader terms than you framed the above comments, there has been some excellent progress in certain areas cited as examples at various points throughout the book. Perhaps one of the greatest incentives for process models comes from their application to item generation. With many testing programs adopting a model that requires many new items each testing cycle, response process modeling offers a means of facilitating more effective and efficient item generation.

Another incentive might come from better understanding how different responses processes can produce the same total score. Imagine three test takers earning the same profile of scores on a vocational interest test. Ae-Cha responds by imagining people she knows who perform the task in the item stem, and rating the task in proportion to her esteem for those people. Bon-hwa responds by imagining himself performing the task and rating how much he imagines enjoying it. Bong-Cha responds by drawing from her experience performing various tasks and remembering how much she enjoyed them. Despite the identical scores, one might have more confidence in the scores as accurate indicators of Bong-Cha's interests than Bon-hwa's, and more still than Ae-Cha's. Similarly, a better understanding of response processes can help refine construct definitions and fine-tune choices about what a test should assess. Attention to response process can thereby lead to better total scores.

One of the challenges faced by response process modeling involves conceptualizing what to model. Most work in this area adopts cognitive individualism in which an individual respondent accepts input, represents that input, manipulates the input, and produces output. This approach takes as given the meaning of internal representations, perhaps simply projecting the meanings assigned by the researcher. An alternative to this approach involves modeling the individual cognitive agent as a participant in a larger process with other cognitive agents. This approach leads to the idea of meanings shared by a linguistic community. However, this approach still gives primacy to linguistic meaning as consciously understood by the cognitive agent. Discursive approaches go a step further by emphasizing meanings formed in the shared discourse and transmitted through individual language users with or without their conscious awareness. Modeling test item responses using each of these approaches involves different strengths, limitations, and challenges. It is not immediately obvious which offers the best approach in a given situation.

Possibly, test developers intend some constructs to abstract over response processes. Imagine an engineering certification test in which all that matters is that the engineer can solve certain kinds of problems. It makes no difference to the test user how the engineer solves the problem. This would constitute an example of multiple-realizability. Engineers can realize the same basic competency with more than one response process. Despite their heterogeneity, it is possible that all such response processes share a common feature that corresponds to a quantitative dimension reflecting a specific engineering skill (Humphreys, 2009). Nonetheless, a validity argument should make this assumption explicit.

13.5. Attributes

KM: We chose measurement, causation and meaning as the three central questions to structure our treatment of test validity theory and its open questions. In so doing, we opted to omit a prior set of issues that could easily have filled an additional three chapters between chapters 1 and 2. What is an attribute or property? Test theory habitually takes the notion of an attribute as a primitive foundational concept that does not require explanation. Certainly it is true that in everyday talk people manage to communicate with one another about assumed attributes and properties. Users of educational tests do not need a theory of properties to communicate about student success, readiness, or mastery of a particular curriculum. Users of clinical assessments do not need a theory of properties to communicate about diagnoses, treatment plans or prognoses. Nonetheless, a clear theoretical account of attributes remains lacking. Do attributes exist independently of individuals that have them? Do they exist at all? Is it possible to specify the set of individuals with a given attribute in a way that does not presuppose understanding of the attribute? Can one give a non-circular and non-vacuous account of what it means for an individual to have an attribute? It seems plausible that many problems in test theory trace back to an underlying lack of theoretical clarity on these and related issues.

Let me use a common example from the literature on attributes to clarify the sort of issue that I have in mind. As context, let us suppose, just hypothetically, that someone proposed a theory of test validity that required that an attribute exist in order for a test to validly assess that attribute. Alternatively, more generally, assume that any causal theory of measurement entails that the assessed attribute exists as a corollary of attribute variation causing test score variation. One can read the existence requirement in at least two ways. One can read it in Chiara's (1990) sense that one can mathematically construct the attribute out of suitable materials. One can also read it in a stronger sense that the attribute exists outside the test user's or researcher's representation, as an actual element of the world that one seeks to represent. This stronger sense of existence seems to be at play in a causal theory of measurement that understands causation as something in the world and not just part of a mental or linguistic representation.

Even those who champion the existence of attributes, however, defer to Occam's Razor by avoiding multiplying entities without necessity. Suppose one asked a yes or no survey question "Are you a bachelor?". Furthermore, suppose that test takers who are bachelors are exactly those who are male and eligible for marriage. This holds exactly, like the standard deviation being the square root of the variance, not as an imperfect empirical association. Finally, assume that gender and eligibility are basic attributes that exist in the strong sense without controversy. The usual interpretation of this situation, even among realists about attributes, is to deny that bachelorhood exists as an independent entity. Instead, gender and eligibility exist and bachelorhood is a derived property that does not exist independently of these two attributes. However, this makes mischief for a causal theory of measurement that requires that what the test assesses exists in the strong sense. A causal model that explained item responses in terms of gender and eligibility and their interaction would provide a completely satisfactory (and true) explanation. Inserting bachelorhood as a mediator with no residual variance would add nothing to the explanation. Yet, it seems both natural and appropriate to interpret the item as assessing bachelorhood despite the fact that most would deny any independent existence to this property as a distinct attribute.

DB: This is an interesting—and challenging—question. I would like to pursue the example you present in some detail. Suppose that someone in fact devised a test to assess bachelorhood, and it consisted of questions like "Are you a bachelor?", "How old are you?", "Are you male?", and "Are you married?". I assume a person's responses would be combined into a rule that would assign that person a score 1:Bachelor, 0:Married. I am all right with supposing that the *actual* values of the antecedent variables (sex, eligibility, age, etc.) combine in a logical way to determine whether someone is *in actual fact* a bachelor or not (without residue).

If we actually made the test in question, it is likely we would encounter the unfortunate fact of psychometric life that even the answers to these simple items will not align deterministically (e.g., some people will consent to being a bachelor and to being married). Neither will the outcomes of the test align perfectly with the theoretical definition of bachelorhood (e.g., some people may believe that they are married but will in fact be bachelors due to their marriage being unlawful). So, there is likely to be a probabilistic mapping from the variable bachelor/no bachelor to the item responses; if one bothered, one could probably work out the latent class model appropriate for the situation. However, the latent classes may not align perfectly with the structure of the attribute. A classic set of validity problems.

Now, does the attribute of "bachelorhood" exist? My answer would be positive. Even though it is a complexly constituted attribute (i.e., is a function of a number of more basic attributes) I do not see that as a reason to doubt its existence. Can the attribute be assessed with a test? Yes, certainly—we just discussed a test for this purpose. Is there a causal link between the attribute of "bachelorhood" and the person's response to the items, so that we can claim validity? I see no reason to doubt it for the items that actually aim to assess this (e.g., "Are you a bachelor?"; of course the item "How old are you?" cannot count as assessing bachelorhood). Even though the item response process involves a complex constitution of symbol recognition, semantic processing, category formation, and decision-making, it would seem to me that, in essence, the item response story is this: the person is (or is not) a bachelor, and whether the person is a bachelor is a decisive causal factor in the process that leads to the decision to the answer box "yes" directly under the question "Are you a bachelor?" because (a) the person knows whether he is a bachelor, and (b) the person is willing to supply the relevant information to the tester. So, I think that in this particular case the theory fits like a glove.

Finally, from a *psychometric* perspective, I do not think that we need to worry about whether or not bachelorhood will be mentioned in the ultimate description of the universe by the ultimate scientific theory (although for what it's worth I personally think it would). What rather counts is that the attribute has sufficient structure to define actual values for a variable we may want to assess. Bachelorhood has such structure, and hence can be assumed a real attribute.

KM: I want to stick to the case where a putative property is entirely reducible to other more basic properties. The technical problem of working that out bears less importance. The theoretically interesting issues involve how best to understand attributes in a causal theory of measurement. If bachelorhood reduces to more basic properties like eligibility for marriage and gender, then bachelorhood will not appear in a final theory because removing it would produce an equally strong theory with more simplicity. One cannot appeal to minor discrepancies between bachelorhood and the Boolean product of eligibility and maleness to support the independent existence of bachelorhood because any discrepancies only occur in observed indicators purely as a result of measurement error. One way of thinking about this is that in such a case bachelorhood simply is the Boolean product and thus if eligibility and maleness exist, then so does their product. The hard part comes with fleshing that out. I agree that test development can get quite far on the basis of a cavalier common-sense construct theory. However, winging it this way eventually catches up to us.

As one vantage point, consider that both classical test theory and modern test theory in the forms of factor models or IRT models divide test score variation between variation in what the test measures (true scores or latent variables) and random error. Thus, these models presume that tests cannot assess constants because assessment involves variation and random error does not assess anything. However, even a weak regularity theory will allow a constant as a regularity. For instance, the fact that all applicants to a particular college have SAT scores above 1300 constitutes a regularity, albeit not a law. Stronger theories of causation also allow for constant causes producing constant effects. So, on a causal theory of measurement, the college checking that all applicants have SAT scores above 1300 constitutes a valid assessment despite the absence of variation. One way of interpreting this example is that classical and modern measurement theories would preclude constants as assessable attributes but a causal theory of measurement allows for these.

Further, contrast bachelorhood with H-bachelorhood. The term H-bachelor applies to bachelors just in case a certain coin is facing heads up (Fodor, 1987). If the coin faces heads, then our original bachelorhood item may offer a valid assessment of H-bachelorhood. If the coin faces tails, then the same item has no validity for this purpose on any view. It seems to me that broadly Humean approaches to causation, either regularity- or counterfactual-based, can allow H-bachelorhood as a cause of bachelor-item responses. However, a less Humean view, like a process or mechanism view, might not because the coin position is not suitably connected to the bachelor-item responses and thus one cannot take H-bachelorhood as a cause of the responses. In this case, different theories of causation might differ in terms of what they allow as causal attributes assessed by test items. Clearly, these suggestive examples only scratch the surface of the issue.

DB: In my view, we need to separate two issues: (a) whether some attribute exists, and (b) whether some attribute exists independently of some set of more basic components. Issue (a) is an important criterion for measurability, but (b) is not. For instance, H-bachelorhood clearly exists *as* a function of more basic components (namely bachelorhood and the coin facing heads). It is a strange unprojectible property that does not license much natural-kind-type generalization, perhaps, but it is clearly a property that could in principle be assessed. Importantly, I do not think that the item "Are you a bachelor?" assesses H-bachelorhood as you suggest;

rather it assesses bachelorhood but only works conditional on the coin facing heads. H-bachelorhood is a conjunction (Boolean product) and hence items that assess this property (in the causal view) must depend causally on the conjunction itself. An obvious candidate would be "Are you an H-bachelor?" (assuming the person knows how to judge this). I think that this holds both under the counterfactual view and under the process view. In the counterfactual view, it is required that differences in H-bachelorhood are necessary for differences in the (expected value of) the item response, which is plausibly the case for "Are you an H-bachelor?" but not for "Are you a bachelor?". In the process view, it requires that there is a process that connects H-bachelorhood to the item response, which is also plausible: the person understands the question, judges his or her condition, and responds truthfully.

Certainly different conceptions of causation and causality will give different validity verdicts in a causal theory of measurement (the same holds for different conceptions of measurement). This is conceptually interesting and likely a rich topic to investigate; even scratching the surface is quite a formidable task. However I do think it is independent of the precise nature of the existence of attributes. Conjunct attributes are eligible for assessment in a causal view, even though they cannot be manipulated apart from their constituents (not that I believe that there are many attributes to which such a clean reductionist picture will apply).

Whether a regularity, counterfactual, or process view is applicable to the case of psychological assessment is quite hard to generally say. I think it may in fact depend on context. Clearly if one wants to uphold a causal theory about the assessment of an individual attribute of an individual person at an individual time point, one has to minimally subscribe to a counterfactual view (which can be quite problematic in psychology). But there are also many attributes that simply do not exist without individual differences and for which such a counterfactual link at the individual level is just nonsensical. For instance, heritability estimates of intelligence are just not applicable to the individual because they are undefined in the absence of individual differences. The same holds for the classical test theory reliability of my test score: it is zero by definition, and it makes no sense to require that I somehow counterfactually generate the value of .80 as found in the general population.

13.6. Tests and Interpretations

DB: There are two questions, both important, that surface invariably in discussions on validity. First: does the test measure what it should measure? Second, is my interpretation of the test scores justifiable? The literature on construct validity theory has usually focused on the second question, holding the idea that validity is a property of a test score interpretation. However, textbooks almost always discuss validity in terms of the first notion, which presents it as a property of tests. Naturally, the justifiability of a test score interpretation does not necessarily cover the validity of a test. For instance, one's intended test score interpretation may have nothing to do with measurement or may even deny that the test scores are measures (for instance by challenging the definition of measurement), and still be justifiable. On the other hand, one may have a perfectly valid measurement instrument but interpret the score incorrectly so that one arrives at mistaken conclusions about test takers; for instance because one has failed to read the test manual properly.

To me, it appears unproductive to cover both of these meanings of validity with the same theory. The justification of propositions is properly taken as a very general topic covered in the philosophy of science, whereas the validity of tests is a specific topic in psychometrics that covers the substantive component of a measurement model. In this book, we discuss broad and narrow ranges of validity theory, but we do not make a choice on this issue partly because we do not entirely see things in the same way. To me, it seems that if one takes seriously the idea that validity is about test score interpretations in general, chapters on validity ought not to be written by psychometricians. Why should psychometricians have anything special to say about justification? One would rather expect a general philosopher to work on these issues. But one never sees philosophers involved in test development. Aren't psychometricians treading beyond their specialization in the test score interpretation conception of validity? Isn't it better to just adhere to the textbook definition and spell out exactly what is involved in ascribing measurement qualities to an instrument?

KM: Conversely, if one takes 'Test *t* validly assesses attribute *x*' to mean the same as 'Test *t* assesses attribute *x*' then validity becomes a redundant concept. In that case, test theory is better off without the concept of validity (Michell, 2009). However, spelling out the ascription of assessment to tests comes down to justifying such ascriptions, which comes down to justifying interpretations of test scores as assessments. The only choice is whether one does this explicitly or implicitly. Making it explicit encourages critical reflection on assessment ascription, and that is the primary contribution of the argument approach to validity framed in terms of test score interpretations.

I do not see anything inherently wrong with interpreting a coin flip as a random number generator, or validating such an interpretation. Lottery auditors provide a valuable service. However, this has nothing to do with test validity because one has not interpreted the coin flip or lottery draw as a test. If a test is a standardized observation procedure designed to assess, then that constrains the range of test score interpretations that fall within the domain of test validity.

Likewise, the distinction with which you began dissolves the apparent paradox with respect to examples like a phlogiston test (Borsboom et al., 2009). The interpretation was once justified based on the best available science (validity$_2$) but it never assessed anything (validity$_1$). The important point is that even if today's science were in error and the test did assess phlogiston, one could not justify such an interpretation based on today's science. So, assessment does not suffice. Test use requires validity evidence to support assessment ascriptions.

Moreover, everyone seems to agree that assessment ascription holds relative to an attribute. A pan scale may assess weight but not temperature. As I read it, the notion of test score interpretation comes down to nothing more than this relativity. If we consider logical form, assessment ascription involves a relational property, $a(t, x)$, asserting that the assessment relation holds between test t and attribute x. The attribute is not eliminable. A simple predicate of the form $a^*(t)$ would require either that each attribute has its own assessment property or that one quantifies over attributes by merely asserting that this test assesses something. The former approach would preclude a general systematic test validity theory. The latter approach does not suffice to warrant test use. Evidence that the scale assesses something does not provide evidence that it assesses temperature.

Validity$_2$ also has the advantage of emphasizing rival hypotheses in the form of alternative interpretations. It further emphasizes the social context of validation in which test takers, test users, and other stakeholders may not share all the assumptions that test developers make in a validity argument. For these reasons, I do not view 'validity' as a redundant term in test theory. Validity$_2$ involves the quality of the inference to validity$_1$ and contributes to test theory in important ways. Moreover, I understand validity$_2$ as consistent with a causal theory of measurement, not as an alternative.

DB: Naturally, the textbook variant of test validity (validity$_1$: does t measure a?) is a question that for any *individual* test reduces to the question of whether the test measures the indicated attribute; in this sense, to ascribe validity to that test is to say nothing more than that it measures the relevant attribute. I do not think we disagree on this. Under a causal theory of measurement, this does not establish the redundancy of validity as a *general* psychometric concept, because that theory homogenizes a wide variety of instruments that assess a wide variety of attributes in a wide variety of ways (namely, all instruments that measure a are such that variation in their test scores depends causally on variation in a). Thus, to say that the instrument is valid for a means it is a member of this class. This is not an empty categorization, at least in my view. Naturally, if you have already spelled out exactly why a particular test score depends on the attribute, then to say "and the test is valid" is in a sense redundant. I find this type of redundancy not harmful because being able to theoretically define what the category of valid tests for *a* have in common is a notable achievement.

Of course validity$_2$ is consistent with a causal theory of measurement or assessment, as you note correctly; this is because validity$_2$ is consistent with *any* theory of measurement. And this is because it has very little to do with measurement or even with psychometrics in general. I have no interest in arguing against your conclusion, because it is precisely this conclusion that makes me uncomfortable. If we take validity$_2$ to be, say, about the question of whether we are justified in believing an empirical proposition involving observations, then it does not separate itself from general philosophy of science. There is no reason why psychometricians could claim particular expertise in this regard, or is there? Why should chapters on test validity be written by test theorists? Why should *we* be the authors of this book, rather than any two randomly drawn philosophers of science? I think there is a good answer to this question, and it is that test validity theory should *not* be about just any test score interpretation (except maybe for purposes of exposition). It should be about test score interpretations whose truth conditions can be formulated in terms of psychometric models that we have expertise on, so we can spell out what these truth conditions are and provide suggestions on how to check them. I am not comfortable with claiming much more expertise than this.

KM: The importance of validity$_2$ involves fallibilism. Validity$_1$ treats the content as the figure and the evidence as the ground whereas validity$_2$ does the reverse. If test theory dropped validity$_2$ and retained only validity$_1$, then it would have a harder time encouraging critical reflection on evidence.

I welcome contributions by philosophers to test theory. However, I do not see much danger of the recognition of validity$_2$ undermining the centrality of test theory to test validity. I see the fact that validity$_2$ limits itself to the interpretation of test scores as adequate to keeping test validity within the domain of test theory.

I agree that validity$_2$ opens the door to interpretations of test scores as something other than assessments. However, I see more disadvantage than advantage to trying to define such interpretations out of test validity. Leaving the nature of the interpretation open allows for a broad range of test uses within the domain of test theory. Consider the example of a biodata blank that depends only on a regression model predicting a criterion. I do not want to advocate the use of empirically keyed biodata forms. However, it seems to me that the validity of such instruments ought to remain an empirical question. Restricting the definition of validity to models that exclude empirically keyed forms would make biodata invalid by definition. I can imagine circumstances in which biodata might offer the best available alternative. I would not want to preclude such forms with a restrictive definition of test validity. Likewise, a restrictive definition holds the danger of excluding new approaches to testing before they even have a chance to develop. A further disadvantage of a restrictive definition is that it excludes disconfirming evidence from validity theory. Disconfirming evidence involves interpreting test scores as poor or problematic assessments.

It seems preferable to maintain a clear distinction between the validity of an interpretation and the value of the interpretation. Interpreting scores assigned by fair coin flips as random numbers can have high validity$_2$ even if it offers a useless interpretation for the purposes of assessment. Likewise, a very useful test score interpretation might lack validity$_2$ in light of the available evidence. So, the two properties of an interpretation vary independently of one another. If a test score interpretation has no bearing on assessing a construct of some sort, then it is likely to be of little value to test developers as a test score interpretation. So, it seems best to me to allow test validity theory handle such interpretations but also recognize that they do not offer especially useful interpretations of test scores from a testing perspective.

The critical point that your comments emphasize is that nobody should mistake validity$_2$ per se as evidence in favor of a test being an effective test. Validity$_2$ of an inference to good validity$_1$ speaks in favor of the test. Validity$_2$ of an inference to poor validity$_1$ speaks against it. Support for effective testing requires the right kinds of evidence for the right kind of conclusion.

13.7. Chapter Conclusion

Through the course of the book we discovered that we agreed on much more than we anticipated. Many disagreements evaporated into semantic issues. However, even at the end of a book-length treatment, there remain many unresolved issues and much room for further research. Contrasting perspectives are an important driving force in the development of validity theory. Many perspectives in the field still await careful development. Clear development of various perspectives offer immediate opportunities for substantial contributions to test theory. Having explored causal theories of measurement in some detail, we would both welcome further development of non-causal approaches by those who find them more promising.

Many questions may have arisen in the reader's mind while reading through the book, as they have in ours. One point on which we both certainly agree is that we both reject the idea that test validity theory is nearly complete. Even in this book-length treatment we have barely scratched the surface. We hope that our book will stimulate and advance further research in test validity theory.

Notes

2 Philosophical Theories of Measurement

1   It is of some importance to note that Stevens' own work was on the line (see also Michell, 1999): The Ferguson committee had chosen his Sone scale of loudness (Stevens & Davis, 1938) as a paradigm example of psychological measurement in its deliberations. One can imagine that he was highly motivated to rescue his measurement procedures from a negative verdict by the scientific community; and, perhaps unsurprisingly, his Sone scale came out as a ratio scale (Stevens, 1946, p. 680).

2   To be precise, the empirical and numerical systems are *homomorphic*, because several objects may be assigned the same number. Therefore, the mapping is many-to-one rather than one-to-one (an isomorphism requires a one-to-one mapping). In the text, we will use the term isomorphic because it is more familiar to most psychologists.

3   When the axiomatic theory of measurement was first articulated (Scott & Suppes, 1958; Suppes & Zinnes, 1963), the construction of the quantitative out of the qualitative was quite a philosophical feat that solved some important problems facing positivist reconstructions of science, especially with regard to the problem of theoretical terms (Stegmüller, 1979).

4   Borsboom, Mellenbergh, and Van Heerden (2003) take a stronger position by arguing that realism is inherent to the models; see also Haig (2005, 2006), who discusses the relation between realism and latent variable models in terms of abductive inference and concludes that latent variable models are naturally situated in a realist philosophy of science, and Markus, Hawes and Thasites (2007) who draw a different conclusion.

5 Test Scores as Samples: Behavior Domain Theory

1   An earlier version of this chapter appeared online in *New Ideas in Psychology* (doi:10.1016/j.newideapsych.2011.02.008). We thank Taylor & Francis and Elsevier for making this possible.

2   There is some disagreement regarding the total number of Haydn symphonies. The 105th is not properly classified as a symphony and the 106th does not survive in its full form. For simplicity, the present discussion nonetheless adopts 108 sequentially numbered symphonies for the example.

3   The phrasing is evocative of an argument familiar from introductory psychology courses suggesting a circularity in explaining behavior in terms of dispositions to behave a certain way. A similar argument arose with respect to the circularity of explaining behavior in terms of reinforcers, when they are

understood as anything that reinforces behavior. However, one can interpret the present passage as presenting a more subtle argument.

11 Open Questions About Test Score Meaning

1   Our thanks to Gabrielle Salfati for this example.
2   In an otherwise highly accessible essay, Quine unfortunately assumes that the reader has prior familiarity with the Greek term pou sto (που στω) at the end of section I. The term refers to an external vantage point from which to evaluate one's own worldview or conceptual scheme.

References

Aggen, S. H., Neale, M. C., & Kendler, K. S. (2005). DSM criteria for major depression: evaluating symptom patterns using latent-trait item response models. *Psychological Medicine, 35*, 475–487.

American Educational Research Association, American Psychological Association & National Council on Measurement in Education (1985). *Standards for educational and psychological testing.* Washington, DC: American Psychological Association.

American Educational Research Association, American Psychological Association & National Council on Measurement in Education (1999). *Standards for educational and psychological testing.* Washington, DC: American Educational Research Association.

American Psychological Association (2003). Guidelines on multicultural education, training, research, practice, and organizational change for psychologists. *American Psychologist, 58*, 377–402.

Angoff, W. H. (1988). Validity: An evolving concept. In H. Wainer & H. I. Braun (Eds.), *Test validity* (pp. 19–32). Mahwah, NJ: Erlbaum.

Apgar V. A. (1953). A proposal for a new method of evaluation of the newborn infant. *Current Researches in Anesthesia and Analgesia, 32*, 260–267.

Aristotle. Metaphysics. In Adler, M. J. (Ed.) (1990). *Great Books of the Western World* (vol. 1). Chicago: Encyclopaedia Britannica Inc.

Ayer, A. J. (1952). *Language, truth, and logic.* New York: Dover.

Ayer, A. J. (1959). *Logical positivism.* New York: The Free Press.

Bach, E. (1989). *Informal lectures on formal semantics.* Albany, NY: State University of New York Press.

Bagozzi, R. P. (2007). On the meaning of formative measurement and how it differs from reflective measurement: Comment on Howell, Breivik, and Wilcox (2007). *Psychological Methods, 12*, 229–237.

Baker, F. Fundamentals of Item Response Theory. Retrieved from: http://echo.edres.org:8080/irt/

Bakhtin, M. M. (1981). The dialogic imagination: Four essays (C. Emerson & M. Holquist, Trans.). Austin, TX: University of Texas Press. (Russian text published 1975; especially essay four: Discourse in the novel.)

Bakhtin, M. M. (1983). *The dialogical imagination* (M. Holquist & V. Liapunov, Eds., K. Brostrom, Trans.). Austin, TX: University of Texas Press.

Bakhtin, M. M. (1986). *Speech genres and other late essays* (V. W. McGee, Trans.). Austin, TX: University of Texas Press.

Bartholomew, D. J. (1987). *Latent variable models and factor analysis*. London: Griffin.

Bartholomew, D. J., Deary, I. J. & Lawn, M. (2009). A new lease of life for Thomson's bonds model for intelligence. *Psychological Review, 116*, 567–579.

Barofsky, I. & Legro, M. W. (1991). Definition and measurement of fatigue. *Reviews of Infectious Diseases, 13*, 94–97.

Bechger, T. M., Maris, G., Verstralen, H. H. F. M., & Béguin, A. A. (2003). Using classical test theory in combination with item response theory. *Applied Psychological Measurement, 27*, 319–334.

Bechtel, W. & Richardson, R. C. (1993). *Discovering complexity: Decomposition and localization as strategies in scientific research*. Princeton, NJ: Princeton University Press.

Bechtoldt, H. P. (1959). Construct validity: A critique. *American Psychologist, 14*, 619–629.

Beck, A. T., Ward, C. H., Mendelson, M., Mock, J., & Erbaugh, J. (1961). "An inventory for measuring depression". *Archives of General Psychiatry, 4*, 561–571.

Beebee, H., Hitchcock, C. & Menzies, P. (2009). *The Oxford handbook of causation*. Oxford, UK: Oxford University Press.

Bejar, I. I. (2010). Recent development and prospects in item generation. In S. E. Embretson (Ed.), *Measuring psychological constructs: Advances in model-based approaches* (pp. 201–226). Washington, DC: American Psychological Association.

Bell, J. S. (1964). On the Einstein Polodolsky Rosen paradox. *Physics, 1*, 195–200.

Belov, D. I. (2005). Applications of Uniform Test Assembly for the LSAT (Research Report 05-01). Newtown, PA: LSAC.

Belov, D. I. (2006). A Stochastic Search for Test Assembly, Item Pool Analysis, and Design (Research Report 04-01). Newtown, PA: LSAC.

Berkel, H. J. M. van (1984). De diagnose van toetsvragen. [The diagnosis of test items.] Amsterdam: Centrum voor Onderzoek van het Wetenschappelijk Onderwijs.

Bernstein, R. J. (1983). *Beyond objectivism and relativism: Science, hermeneutics, and praxis*. Philadelphia, PA: University of Pennsylvania Press.

Billingsley, P. (1995). *Probability and measure* (3rd ed.). New York: Wiley.

Binet, A. (1916). New methods for the diagnosis of the intellectual level of subnormals. In E. S. Kite (Trans.), *The development of intelligence in children*. Vineland, NJ: Publications of the Training School at Vineland. (Originally published 1905 in *L'Année Psychologique, 12*, 191–244.)

Birnbaum, A. (1968). Some latent trait models and their use in inferring an examinee's ability. In F. M. Lord & M. R. Novick (Eds.), *Statistical theories of mental test scores* (pp. 397–479). Reading, MA: Addison-Wesley.

Bix, B. (1993). *Law, language, and legal determinacy*. Oxford, UK: Clarendon.

Blalock, H. M. (1964). *Causal inferences in nonexperimental research*. Chapel Hill, NC: University of North Carolina Press.

Bollen, K. A. (1989). *Structural equations with latent variables*. New York: Wiley.

Bollen, K. A. (2007). Interpretational confounding is due to misspecification, not type of indicator: Comment on Howell, Breivik, & Wilcox (2007). *Psychological Methods, 12*, 219–228.

Bollen, K. A., & Lennox, R. (1991). Conventional wisdom on measurement: A structural equation perspective. *Psychological Bulletin, 110,* 305–314.

Bollen, K. A., & Ting, K. (1993). Confirmatory tetrad analysis. *Sociological Methodology, 23,* 147–175.

Bond, T. G., & Fox, C. M. (2001). *Applying the Rasch model: Fundamental measurement in the social sciences.* Mahwah, NJ: Lawrence Erlbaum Associates.

Borgatta, E. F., & Bohrnstedt, G. W. (1981). Level of measurement: once over again. In E. F. Borgatta & G. W. Bohrnstedt (Eds.), *Social measurement: current issues.* (pp. 23–37). Beverly Hills: Sage.

Borsboom, D. (2005). *Measuring the mind: Conceptual issues in contemporary psychometrics.* Cambridge: Cambridge University Press.

Borsboom, D. (2006a). The attack of the psychometricians. *Psychometrika, 71,* 425–440.

Borsboom, D. (2006b). When does measurement invariance matter? *Medical Care, 44,* S176-S181.

Borsboom, D. (2008a). Latent variable theory. *Measurement, 6,* 25–53.

Borsboom, D. (2008b). Psychometric perspectives on diagnostic systems. *Journal of Clinical Psychology, 64,* 1089–1108.

Borsboom, D. & Dolan, C. V. (2006). Why g is not an adaptation: A comment on Kanazawa (2004). *Psychological Review,* 113, 433–437.

Borsboom, D., Cramer, A. O. J., Kievit, R. A., Zand Scholten, A., & Franic, S. (2009). The end of construct validity. In R. W. Lissitz (Ed.), *The concept of validity* (pp. 135–170). Charlotte, NC: Information Age.

Borsboom, D., & Mellenbergh, G. J. (2004). Why psychometrics is not pathological: A comment on Michell. *Theory & Psychology, 14,* 105–120.

Borsboom, D. & Mellenbergh, G. J. (2007). Test validity in cognitive assessment. In Leighton, J. P. & Gierl, M. J. (Eds.), *Cognitive diagnostic assessment for education: Theory and applications* (pp. 85–115). New York: Cambridge University Press.

Borsboom, D., Mellenbergh, G. J., & Van Heerden, J. (2002). Different kinds of DIF: A distinction between absolute and relative forms of measurement invariance and bias. *Applied Psychological Measurement, 26,* 433–450.

Borsboom, D., Mellenbergh, G. J., & Van Heerden, J. (2003). The theoretical status of latent variables. *Psychological Review, 110,* 203–219.

Borsboom, D., Mellenbergh, G. J., & Van Heerden, J. (2004). The concept of validity. *Psychological Review, 111,* 1061–1071.

Borsboom, D., Wicherts, J. M., & Romeijn, J. W. (2008). Measurement invariance versus selection invariance: Is fair selection possible? *Psychological Methods, 13,* 75–98.

Borsboom, D. & Zand Scholten, A. (2008). The Rasch model and additive conjoint measurement theory from the perspective of psychometrics. *Theory & Psychology, 18,* 111–117.

Bourdieu, P. (1984). *Distinction* (R. Nice, Trans.). Cambridge, MA: Harvard University Press.

Bourdieu, P. (1994). *Language and symbolic power* (J. B. Thompson, Ed., G. Raymond & M. Adamson, Trans.) Cambridge, MA: Harvard University Press.

Brennan R. L. (2001). *Generalizability theory.* New York: Springer.

Brennan, R. L. (1992). Elements of generalizability theory (rev. ed.). Iowa City, IA: American College Testing.

Bridgman, P. W. (1927). *The logic of modern physics.* New York: Macmillan.

Brodbeck, M. (1957). The philosophy of science and educational research. *Review of Educational Research, 27,* 427–440.

Brodbeck, M. (1963). Logic and scientific method in research on teaching. In N. L. Gage (Ed.), *Handbook of research in teaching* (pp. 44–93). Chicago: Rand McNally.

Brown, G. & Yule, G. (1983). *Discourse analysis.* New York: Cambridge.

Buckingham, B. R. (1921). Intelligence and its measurement: A symposium— XIV. *Journal of Educational Psychology, 12,* 271–275.

Burge, T. (1979). Individualism and the mental. *Midwest Studies in Philosophy, IV,* 73–122.

Buss, D. M., & Craik, K. H. (1983). The act frequency approach to personality. *Psychological Review, 90,* 105–126.

Camilli, G. (2006). Test Fairness. In R. L. Brennan (Ed.), *Educational measurement* (4th ed., pp. 221–256). Westport, CT: American Council on Education/Praeger.

Campbell, D. T. (1982). Experiments as arguments. In E. R. House, S. Mathison, J. A. Pearsol, & H. Preskill (Eds.), *Evaluation studies review annual* (vol. 7, pp. 117–128). Beverly Hills, CA: Sage Publications.

Campbell, D. T. (1986). Relabeling internal and external validity for applied social scientists. *New Directions for Evaluation, 31,* 67–77.

Campbell, N. R. (1920). *Physics, the elements.* Cambridge: Cambridge University Press.

Campbell, D. T. & Fiske, D. W. (1959). Convergent and sicriminant validation by the multitrait–multimethod matrix. *Psychological Bulletin, 56,* 81–105.

Cann, R. (1993). *Formal semantics: An introduction.* New York: Cambridge University Press.

Cannon, T. D., & Keller, M. C. (2006). Endophenotypes in genetic analyses of mental disorders. *Annual Review of Clinical Psychology, 2,* 267–290.

Carnap, R. (1967). *The logical structure of the world and pseudoproblems in philosophy* (R. A. George, Trans.). Chicago: Open Court. (German text published 1928)

Cartwright, N. (1989). *Nature's capacities and their measurement.* Oxford, UK: Oxford University Press.

Cartwright, N. (1999). *The dappled world: a study of the boundaries of science.* Cambridge, UK: Cambridge University Press.

Cartwright, N (2007). *Hunting causes and using them: approaches in philosophy of economics.* Cambridge, UK: Cambridge University Press.

Carver, C. R. (2007). *Explaining the brain: Mechanisms and the mosaic unity of neuroscience.* New York: Oxford University Press.

Cervone, D. (2004). Personality Assessment: Tapping the Social-Cognitive Architecture of Personality. *Behavior Therapy, 35,* 113–129.

Cervone, D. (2005). Personality architecture: Within-person structures and processes. *Annual Review of Psychology, 56,* 423–452.

Cervone, D. & Caldwell, T. L. (2008). From measurement theory to psychological theory, in reverse. *Measurement: Interdisciplinary Research and Perspectives, 6,* 84–88.

Chan, D., Schmitt, N., Jennings, D., Clause, C. S., & Delbridge, K. (1998). Applicant perceptions of test fairness: Integrating justice and self-serving bias perspectives. *International journal of selection and assessment, 6,* 232–240.

Chernyshenko, O. S., Stark, S., Drasgow, F., & Roberts, B. W. (2007). Constructing personality scales under the assumptions of an ideal point response process: Toward increasing the flexibility of personality measures. *Psychological Assessment, 19,* 88–106.

Chihara, C. S. (1990). *Constructibility and mathematical existence.* Oxford, UK: Clarendon.

Chomsky, N. & Foucault, M. (2006). *The Chomsky–Foucault debate on human nature.* New York: The New Press.

Cliff, N. (1992). Abstract measurement theory and the revolution that never happened. *Psychological Science, 3,* 186–190.

Cole, N. S. (1973). Bias in selection. *Journal of Educational Measurement, 10,* 237–255.

Collins, J., Hall, N. & Paul, L. A. (2004). *Causation and counterfactuals.* Cambridge, MA: MIT Press.

Cook, T. D., & Campbell, D. T. (1979). Quasi-experimentation: Design & analysis issues for field settings. Boston: Houghton Mifflin.

Colwell, J., Schröder, S., & Sladen, D. (2000). The ability to detect unseen staring: A literature review and empirical tests. British Journal of Psychology, 91, 71–85.

Cowan, J. L. (1964). The uses of argument—An apology for logic. *Mind, 73,* 27–45.

Cramer, A. O. J., Waldorp, L. J., van der Maas, H., & Borsboom, D. (2010). Comorbidity: A network perspective. *Behavioral and Brain Sciences, 33,* 137–193.

Cronbach, L. J. & Meehl, P. E. (1955). Construct validity in psychological tests. *Psychological Bulletin, 52,* 281–302.

Cronbach, L. J. (1971). Test validation. In R. L. Thorndike (Ed.), *Educational measurement* (2nd ed., pp. 443–507). Washington, DC: American Council on Education.

Cronbach, L. J. (1988). Five perspectives on validity argument. In H. Wainer & H. Braun (Eds.), *Test validity* (pp. 3–17). Hillsdale, NJ: Erlbaum.

Cronbach, L. J., & Meehl, P. E. (1955). Construct validity in psychological tests. *Psychological Bulletin, 52,* 281–302.

Cronbach, L. J., Gleser, G. C., Nanda, H., & Rajaratnam, N. (1972). *The dependability of behavioral measurements: Theory of generalizability for scores and profiles.* New York: Wiley.

Cureton, E. E. (1950). Validity. In E. F. Lindquist (Ed.), *Educational measurement* (pp. 621–694). Washington, DC: American Council on Education.

Davey, G., Lian, C. D., & Higgins, L. (2007). The university entrance examination system in China. *Journal of Further and Higher Education, 31,* 385–396.

Davidson, D. (1984). *Inquiries into truth and interpretation.* Oxford, UK: Clarendon Press.

Davidson, D. (2005). *Truth, language, and history.* Oxford, UK: Oxford University Press.

de Boeck, P. & Wilson, M. (2004). *Explanatory item response models: A general linear and nonlinear approach.* New York: Springer.

De Champlain, A. R. (1995). Assessing the Effect of Multidimensionality on LSAT Equating for Subgroups of Test Takers (Statistical Report 95-01). Newtown, PA: LSAC.

De Finetti, B. (1974). *Theory of probability* (vol. 1). New York: Wiley.

Dennett, D. C. (1991). *Consciousness explained*. Boston: Little Brown.

Derrida, J. (1978). *Writing and difference* (A. Bass, Trans.). Chicago: University of Chicago Press.

Derrida, J. (1988). *Limited Inc*. Evanston, IL: Northwestern University Press.

Derrida, J. (1989). *Memories for Paul de Mann* (C. Lindsay, J. Culler, E. Cadava, & P. Kamuf, Trans.). New York: Columbia University Press.

Dewey, J. (1926). *Experience and nature*. LaSalle, IN: Open Court.

Dewey, J. (1938). *Logic: the theory of inquiry*. New York: Henry Holt.

Diaconis, P. & Freedman, D. (1980). Finite exchangeable sequences. *Annals of Probability, 8*, 745–764.

Digman, J. M. (1990). Personality structure: Emergence of the five-factor model. *Annual Review of Psychology, 41*, 417–440.

Dinnel, D., Glover, J. A., & Ronning, R. R. (1984). A provisional model of mathematical problem solving. *Bulletin of the Psychonomic Society, 22*, 459–462.

Doignon, J. P., & Falmagne, J. C. (1999). *Knowledge Spaces*. New York: Springer.

Dowe, P. (2000). *Physical causation*. Cambridge, UK: Cambridge University Press.

Dusky v. United States, 362 U.S. 402 (1960)

Ebel, R. L. (1961). Must all tests be valid? *American Psychologist, 16*, 640–647.

Edwards, J. R., & Bagozzi, R. P. (2000). On the nature and direction of relationships between constructs and measures. *Psychological Methods, 5*, 155–174.

Ellis, J. L., & Junker, B. W. (1997). Tail-measurability in monotone latent variable models. *Psychometrika, 62*: 495–523.

Ellis, J. L., & Wollenberg, A. L. v. d. (1993). Local homogeneity in latent trait models: A characterization of the homogeneous monotone IRT model. *Psychometrika, 58*, 417–429.

Embretson, S. E. & Gorin, J. (2001). Improving Construct Validity with Cognitive Psychology Principles . *Journal of Educational Measurement, 38*, 343–368

Embretson, S. E. (1983). Construct validity: Construct representation versus nomothetic span. *Psychological Bulletin, 93*, 179–197.

Embretson, S. E. (1998). A Cognitive Design System Approach to Generating Valid Tests: Application to Abstract Reasoning. *Psychological Methods, 3*, 380–396

Embretson, S. E. (2010). Cognitive design systems: A structural modeling approach applied to developing a spatial ability test. In S. E. Embretson (Ed.), *Measuring psychological constructs: Advances in model-based approaches* (pp. 247–273). Washington, DC: American Psychological Association.

Embretson, S. E. (2010). *Measuring psychological constructs: Advances in model-based approaches*. Washington, DC: American Psychological Association.

Erdmann, J. B. (1992). Law School Admissions Test. *Mental Measurements Yearbook, 11*, 592–594.

Fechner, G. T. (1860). *Elemente der psychophysik*. Leipzig: Breitkopf & Hartel.

Feigl, H. (1950). Existential hypotheses: realistic versus phenomenalistic interpretations. *Philosophy of Science, 17*, 35–62.

Feigl, H. (1975). Russell and Schlick: A remarkable agreement on a monistic solution of the mind-body problem. *Erkenntnis, 9*, 11–34.

Fischer, G. (1995). Derivations of the Rasch model. In G. Fischer & I. W. Molenaar (Eds.), *Rasch models: Foundations, recent developments, and applications* (pp. 15–38). New York: Springer.

Fodor, J. A. (1987). *Psychosemantics: The problem of meaning in the philosophy of mind.* Cambridge, MA: MIT Press.

Fodor, J. A. (1992). *A theory of content and other essays.* Cambridge, MA: MIT Press.

Fombonne, E. (1991). The use of questionnaires in child psychiatry research: Measuring their performance and choosing an optimal cut-off. *Journal of Child Psychology and Psychiatry, 32*, 677–693.

Foster, S. L. & Cone, J. D. (1995). Validity issues in clinical assessment. *Psychological Assessment, 7*, 248–260.

Foucault, M. (1972). *The archaeology of knowledge & the discourse on language* (A. M. S. Smith, Trans.). New York: Pantheon.

Frederiksen, N., Mislevy, R. J., & Bejar, I. I. (1992). *Test validity for a new generation of tests.* London: Routledge.

Garson, B. (1994). *All the livelong day: The meaning and demeaning of routine work* (rev. & upd. ed.). New York: Penguin.

Glennan, S. S. (2002). Rethinking mechanistic explanation. *Philosophy of Science, 69*, S342–S353.

Geisinger, K. F. (1992). The metamorphosis of test validation. *Educational Psychologist, 27*, 197–222.

Genova, A. C. (1970). Institutional facts and brute values. *Ethics, 81*, 36–54.

Global Times (7 June 2010). 9.57 mln students take national college entrance exams. (Downloaded 28 July 2010 from http://life.globaltimes.cn/life/2010–06/539354.html)

Glymour, C. (2001). *The mind's arrows.* Cambridge, MA: MIT Press.

Goodenough, F. L. (1949). *Mental testing.* New York: Rinehart.

Goodman, N. (1983). *Fact, fiction and forecast.* Cambridge, MA: Harvard University Press.

Granger, C. (1969). Investigating causal relationships by econometric models and cross-spectral methods. *Econometrica, 37*, 329–352.

Grayson, D. (1988). Two-group classification in latent trait theory: Scores with monotone likelihood ratio. *Psychometrika, 53*, 383–392.

Green , C. D. (2001). Operationism again: What did Bridgman say? What did Bridgman need? *Theory & Psychology, 11*, 45–51.

Green, D. R. (1998). Consequential aspects of the validity of achievement tests: A publisher's point of view. *Educational Measurement: Issues and Practice, 17(2)*, 16–19.

Guilford, J.P. (1946). New Standard for Test Evaluation. *Educational and Psychological Measurement, 6*, 427–439.

Guion, R. M. (1980). On trinitarian doctrines of validity. *Professional Psychology, 11*, 385–398.

Habermas, J. (1990). *Moral consciousness and communicative action* (C. Lenhardt & S. Weber Nicholsen, Trans.). Cambridge, MA: MIT Press.

Habermas, J. (2003). *Truth and justification* (B. Fultner, Trans.). Cambridge, MA: MIT Press.

Hacking, I. (1999). *The social construction of what?* Cambridge, MA: Harvard University Press.

Haig, B. D. (2005). Exploratory factor analysis, theory generation, and scientific method. *Multivariate Behavioral Research, 40,* 303–329.

Haig. B. D. (2006). An abductive theory of scientific method. *Psychological Methods, 10,* 371–388.

Hale, B. & Wright, C. (1997). Putnam's model-theoretic argument against metaphysical realism. In B. Hale & C. Wright (Eds.), *A companion to the philosophy of language* (pp. 427–457). Oxford, UK: Blackwell

Hall, N. (2004). Causation and the price of transitivity. In J. Collins, N. Hall, & L.A. Paul (Eds.), *Causation and counterfactuals* (181–203). Cambridge, MA: MIT Press.

Hamaker, E. L., Nesselroade, J. R. & Molenaar, C. M. (2007). The integrated trait–state model. *Journal of Research in Personality, 41,* 295–315.

Hambleton, R. K., & Swaminathan, H. (1985). *Item Response Theory: Principles and applications.* Boston: Kluwer-Nijhoff.

Hambleton, R. K., Merenda, P. F. & Spielberger, C. D. (2005). *Adapting educational and psychological tests for cross-cultural assessment.* Mahwah, NJ: Erlbaum.

Harrison, P. (2001). *The Bible, Protestantism, and the Rise of Natural Science.* Cambridge, UK: Cambridge University Press.

Hayduk, L. A. (1987). *Structural equation modeling with LISREL: Essentials and advances.* Baltimore, MD: Johns Hopkins University Press.

Hayduk, L. A., Pazderka-Robinson, H., Cummings, G. G., Boadu, K., Verbeek, E., & Perks, T. (2007). The weird world and equally weird measurement models: Reactive indicators and the validity revolution. *Structural Equation Modeling, 14,* 280–310.

Hemker, B. T., Sijtsma, K., Molenaar, I. W., & Junker, B. W. (1997). Stochastic ordering using the latent trait and the sum score in polytomous IRT models. *Psychometrika, 62,* 331–347

Hemker, B. T., Sijtsma, K.. Molenaar. I. W., & Junker, B. W. (1996). Polytomous IRT models and monotone likelihood ratio of the total score. *Psychometrika, 61,* 679–693.

Hempel, C. (1965). *Aspects of scientific explanation and other essays in the philosophy of science.* New York: Free Press.

Hofstadter, D. R. & Dennett, D. C. (1981). *The mind's I: Fantasies and reflections on self and soul.* Toronto: Bantam.

Hölder, O. (1901). Die Axiome der Quantität und die Lehre vom Mass. *Berichte über die Verhandlungen der Königlich Sachsischen Gesellschaft der Wissenschaften zu Leipzig.* Mathematische-Physicke Klasse, 53, 1–64.

Holland, P. W. (1986). Statistics and causal inference. *Journal of the American Statistical Association, 81,* 945–960.

Holland, P. W. (1990). On the sampling theory foundations of item response theory models. *Psychometrika, 55,* 577–601.

Holland, P. W., & Rosenbaum, P. R. (1986) Conditional association and unidimensionality in monotone latent variable models, *Annals of Statistics, 14,* 1523–1543.

Hood, S.B. (2009). Validity in psychological testing and scientific realism. *Theory & Psychology, 19,* 451–473.

House, E. R. & Howe, K. R. (1999). *Values in evaluation and social research.* Thousand Oaks, CA: Sage Publications.

Howell, R. D., Breivik, E., & Wilcox, J. B. (2007). Is formative measurement really measurement? *Psychological Methods, 12,* 238–245.

Howell, R. D., Breivik, E., & Wilcox, J. B. (2007). Reconsidering formative measurement. *Psychological Methods, 12,* 201–218.

Hubley, A. M. & Zumbo, B. D. (1996). Dialectic on validity: Where we have been and where we are going. *The Journal of General Psychology, 123,* 207–215.

Hume, D. (1896). *A Treatise of Human Nature* (L. A. Selby-Bigge, Ed.). Oxford, UK: Clarendon Press.

Hume, D. (1962). *On human nature and the understanding.* New York: Macmillan. (Originally published 1739–1751)

Humphreys, P. (1989). *The chances of explanation: Causal explanation in the social, medical, and physical sciences.* Princeton, NJ: Princeton University Press.

Humphreys, P. (2009). Causation and reduction. In H. Beebee, C. Hitchcock & P. Menzies (Eds), *Oxford handbook of causation* (pp. 632–646). Oxford, UK: Oxford University Press.

Hunkins, R. V. & Breed, F. S. (1923). The validity of arithmetical-reasoning tests. *The Elementary School Journal, 23,* 453–466.

Jackson, D. N. & Messick, S. (1978). Problems in human assessment. Huntington, NY: Krieger.

James, W. (1950). *The Principles of Psychology* (vol. 1). New York: Dover. (Originally published 1890; Chapter VII: The methods and snares of psychology.)

Jansen, B. R. J., & Van der Maas, H. L. J. (2002). The development of children's rule use on the balance scale task. *Journal of Experimental Child Psychology, 81,* 383–416.

Jensen, A. R. (1999). *The g factor: The science of mental ability.* Westport, CT: Praeger.

Jöreskog, K.G. & Sörbom, D. (1974). LISREL III. Chicago, IL: Scientific Software International, Inc.

Kane, M. T. (1992). An argument-based approach to validity. *Psychological Bulletin, 112,* 527–535.

Kane, M. T. (2001). Current concerns in validity theory. *Journal of Educational Measurement, 38,* 319–342

Kane, M. T. (2006). Validation. In R. L. Brennan (Ed.), *Educational measurement* (4th ed., pp. 17–64). Westport, CT: Praeger.

Kane, M. T. (2009). Validating the interpretations and uses of test scores. In R. W. Lissitz (Ed.), *The concept of validity: Revisions, new directions, and applications* (pp. 39–64). Charlotte, NC: Information Age.

Kane, H. D. & Krenzer, D. (2006). A confirmatory analysis of the WAIS-III using data from standardization and independent samples. *Counseling and Clinical Psychology Journal, 3*(3), 113–136.

Kant, I. (1929). *Critique of pure reason* (N. Kemp Smith, Trans.). New York: Saint Martin's Press. (German text published in 1787)

Kaplan, D. (2005). Reading "On denoting" on its centenary. *Mind, 114,* 934–1003.

Kaplan, D. (2008). *Structural equation modeling: Foundations and extensions* (2nd ed.). Thousand Oaks, CA: Sage Publications.

Kim, N. S., & Ahn, W. (2002). Clinical psychologists' theory-based representations of mental disorders predict their diagnostic reasoning and memory. *Journal of Experimental Psychology*, 131, 451–476.

Krantz, D. H., Luce, R. D., Suppes, P., & Tversky, A. (1971). *Foundations of measurement* (vol. I). New York: Academic Press.

Kripke, S. A. (1979). A puzzle about belief. In A. Margalit (Ed.), *Meaning and use* (pp. 239–283). Dordrecht, Netherlands: Kluwer.

Kripke, S. A. (1980). *Naming and necessity*. Cambridge, MA: Harvard University Press.

Kyngdon, A. (2008). The Rasch model from the perspective of the representational theory of measurement. *Theory & Psychology*, 18, 89–109.

Landy, F. J. (1986). Stamp collecting versus science: validation as hypothesis testing. *American Psychologist*, 41, 1183–1192.

Law School Admissions Counsil (nd). *LSAT Preparation*. (retrieved 28 November 2009 from http://www.lsac.org/pdfs/LSATPreparationweb.pdf)

Lawshe, C. H. (1952). What can industrial psychology do for small business (a symposium) 2. Employee selection. *Personnel Psychology*, 5, 31–34.

Lazarsfeld, P. F. (1959). Latent structure analysis. In S. Koch (Ed.). *Psychology: A study of a science.* (pp. 476–543). New York: McGraw-Hill.

Lefkowitz, J. (2003). *Ethics and values in industrial-organizational psychology.* Mahwah, NJ: Erlbaum.

Levelt, W. J. M., Riemersma, J. B., & Bunt, A. A. (1972). Binaural additivity of loudness. *British Journal of Mathematical and Statistical Psychology*, 25, 518.

Lewis, D. (1973). *Counterfactuals.* Cambridge, MA: Harvard University Press.

Lissitz, R. W. (2009). *The concept of validity: Revisions, new directions, and applications.* Charlotte, NC: Information age.

Lissitz, R. W. & Samuelsen, K. (2007). A Suggested Change in Terminology and Emphasis Regarding Validity and Education. *Educational Researcher, 36*, 437–448

Locke, E. A. (1969). What is job satisfaction? *Organizational Behavior and Human Performance, 4*, 309–336.

Loevinger, J. (1957). Objective tests as instruments of psychological theory. *Psychological Reports, Monograph No. 9, 3*, 635–694.

Lord, F. M. & Novick, M. R. (1968). Statistical theories of mental test scores. Reading, MA: Addison-Wesley.

Lowman, R. L. (1998). *The ethical practice of psychology in organizations.* Washington, DC: American Psychological Association.

Luce, R. D. & Tukey, J. W. (1964). Simultaneous conjoint measurement: A new type of fundamental measurement. *Journal of Mathematical Psychology, 1*, 1–27.

MacCorquodale, K., & Meehl, P. E. (1948). On a distinction between hypothetical constructs and intervening variables. *Psychological Review, 55*, 95–107.

Mackie, J. L. (1980). *The cement of the universe: A study in causation.* Oxford, UK: Clarendon.

Maraun, M. D. (1997). Metaphor taken as math: Indeterminacy in the factor analysis model. *Multivariate Behavioral Research, 31*, 517–538.

Maraun, M. D. (1998). Measurement as a normative practice: Implications of Wittgenstein's philosophy for measurement in psychology. *Theory and Psychology, 8*, 435–461.

Maraun, M. D. & Peters, J. (2005). What does it mean that an issue is conceptual in nature? *Journal of Personality Assessment, 85,* 128–133.

Markus, K. A. (1998a). Science, measurement, and validity: Is completion of Samuel Messick's synthesis possible? *Social Indicators Research, 45,* 7–34.

Markus, K. A. (1998b). Validity, facts, and values sans closure: Reply to Messick, Reckase, Moss, and Zimmerman. *Social Indicators Research, 45,* 73–82.

Markus, K. A. (2002). Statistical equivalence, semantic equivalence, eliminative induction, and the Raykov-Marcoulides proof of infinite equivalence. *Structural Equation Modeling, 9,* 503–522.

Markus, K. A. (2004). Varieties of causal modeling: How optimal research design varies by explanatory strategy. In K. Van Monfort, J. Oud & A. Satora (Eds.), *Recent developments on structural equation models: Theory and applications* (pp. 175–196). Dordrecht: Klewer Academic Publishers.

Markus, K. A. (2008a). Constructs, concepts and the worlds of possibility: Connecting the measurement, manipulation, and meaning of variables. *Measurement, 6,* 54–77.

Markus, K. A. (2008b). Hypothesis formulation, model interpretation, and model equivalence: Implications of a mereological causal interpretation of structural equation models. *Multivariate Behavioral Research, 43,* 177–209.

Markus, K. A. (2010). Structural equations and causal explanations: Some challenges for causal SEM. *Structural Equation Modeling, 17,* 654–676.

Markus, K. A., Hawes, S. W., & Thasites, R. J. (2007). Abductive Inferences to Psychological Variables: Steiger's Question and Best Explanations of Psychopathy. (Accepted for publication.)

Mason, R. (2000). *Before logic.* Albany, NY: State University of New York Press.

McCrae, R. R., & Costa, P. T., Jr. (1987). Validation of the five-factor model of personality across instruments and observers. *Journal of Personality and Social Psychology, 52,* 81–90.

McCrae, R. R., & Costa, P. T., Jr. (2008). Empirical and theoretical status of the Five-Factor Model of personality traits. In G. Boyle, G. Matthews & D. Saklofske (Eds.), *Sage Handbook of personality theory and assessment* (vol. 1, pp. 273–294). Los Angeles: Sage.

McCrae, R. R., Costa, P. T., Jr., Ostendorf, F., Angleitner, A., Hrebickova, M., & Avia, M. D. (2000). Nature over nurture: Temperament, personality, and lifespan development. *Journal of Personality and Social Psychology, 78,* 173–186.

McCrae, R. R., Zonderman, A. B., Costa, P. T., Jr., Bond, M. H., & Paunonen, S. V. (1996). Evaluating replicability of factors in the Revised NEO Personality Inventory: Confirmatory factor analysis versus Procrustes rotation. *Journal of Personality and Social Psychology, 70,* 552–566.

McDonald, R. P. & Mulaik, S. A. (1979). Determinacy of common factors: A nontechnical review. *Psychological Bulletin, 86,* 297–306.

McDonald, R. P. (1999). *Test theory: a unified treatment.* Mahwah, NJ: Erlbaum.

McDonald, R. P. (2003). Behavior Domains in Theory and in Practice. *Alberta Journal of Educational Research, 49,* 212–230.

McGrew, K. S. (1997). Analysis of the major intelligence batteries according to a proposed comprehensive gf-gc framework. In D. P. Flanagan, J. L. Genshaft, & L. P. Harrison (Eds.), *Contemporary intellectual assessment: Theories, tests, and issues* (pp. 151–179). New York: Guilford Press.

McLachlan, G., & Peel, D. (2000). *Finite mixture models.* New York: Wiley.

Mehrens, W. A. (1997). The consequences of consequential validity. *Educational Measurement: Issues and Practice, 16(2),* 16–18.

Mellenbergh, G. J. (1989). Item bias and item response theory. *International Journal of Educational Research, 13,* 127–143.

Mellenbergh, G. J. (1994). A unidimensional latent trait model for continuous item responses. *Multivariate Behavioral Research, 29,* 223–236.

Mellenbergh, G. J. (1994). Generalized Linear Item Response Theory. *Psychological Bulletin, 115,* 300–307.

Mellenbergh, G. J. (1996). Measurement precision in test score and item response models. *Psychological Methods, 1,* 293–299.

Mellenbergh, G. J. (2001). Outline of a faceted theory of item response data. In A. Boomsma, M. A. J. Van Duijn, & T. A. B. Snijders (Eds.), *Essays in Item Response Theory.* New York: Springer.

Menzies, P. (2004). Difference making in context. In J. Collins, N. Hall, & L.A. Paul (Eds.), *Causation and counterfactuals* (139–180). Cambridge, MA: MIT Press.

Meredith, W. (1993). Measurement invariance, factor analysis, and factorial invariance. *Psychometrika, 58,* 525–543.

Messick, S. (1989). Validity. In R. L. Linn (Ed.), *Educational measurement* (pp. 13–103). Washington, DC: American Council on Education and National Council on Measurement in Education.

Michell, J. (1986). Measurement scales and statistics: A clash of paradigms. *Psychological Bulletin, 100,* 398–407.

Michell, J. (1997). Quantitative science and the definition of measurement in psychology. *British Journal of Psychology, 88,* 355–383.

Michell, J. (1990). *An introduction to the logic of psychological measurement.* Hillsdale, NJ: Erlbaum.

Michell, J. (1999). *Measurement in psychology: A critical history of a methodological concept.* Cambridge: Cambridge University Press.

Michell, J. (2008). Is psychometrics pathological science? *Measurement, 6,* 7–24.

Michell, J. (2009). Invalidity in validity. In R. W. Lissitz (Ed.), *The concept of validity* (pp. 111–133). Charlotte, NC: Information Age.

Michell, J., & Ernst, C. (1996). The axioms of quantity and the theory of measurement: Part I, an English translation of Hölder (1901). *Journal of Mathematical Psychology, 40,* 235–252.

Michell, J., & Ernst, C. (1997). The axioms of quantity and the theory of measurement: Part II, an English translation of Hölder (1901). *Journal of Mathematical Psychology, 41,* 345–356.

Mill, J. S. (1874). *A system of logic, ratiocinative and inductive: being a connected view of the principles of evidence and the methods of scientific investigation* (8th ed.). New York: Harper & Brothers.

Millsap, R. E. (2007). Invariance in measurement and prediction revisited. *Psychometrika, 72,* 461–473.

Millsap, R. E. (1997). Invariance in measurement and prediction: Their relationship in the single-factor case. *Psychological Methods, 2,* 248–260.

Mislevy, R. J. (2006). Cognitive psychology and educational assessment. In R. L. Brennan (Ed.), *Educational measurement* (4th ed., pp. 257–305). Westport, CT: Praeger.

Mislevy, R. J. (2008). How cognitive psychology challenges the educational measurement tradition. *Measurement: Interdisciplinary Research and Perspectives.* [Downloaded 21 March 2010 from http://bear.soe.berkeley.edu/measurement/docs/CommentaryHaig_Mislevy.pdf]

Mokken, R. J. (1971). *A theory and procedure of scale analysis.* The Hague: Mouton.

Molenaar, P. C. M. (2004). A manifesto on psychology as idiographic science: Bringing the person back into scientific psychology, this time forever. *Measurement: Interdisciplinary Research and Perspectives, 2,* 201–218.

Molenaar, P. C. M., & von Eye, A. (1994). On the arbitrary nature of latent variables. In A. von Eye & C. C. Clogg (Eds.), *Latent variables analysis.* Thousand Oaks: Sage.

Moore, G. E. (1903). *Principia ethica.* Cambridge, UK: Cambridge University Press.

Morgan, S. L. & Winship, C. (2007). *Counterfactuals and causal inference: Methods and principles for social research.* Cambridge, UK: Cambridge University Press.

Mosier, C. I. (1947). A critical examination of the concepts of face validity. *Educational and Psychological Measurement, 7,* 191–205.

Mulaik, S. A. & James, L. R. (1995). Objectivity and reasoning in science and structural equation modeling. In R. H. Hoyle (Ed.), *Structural equation modeling: Concepts, issues, and applications* (pp. 118–137). Thousand Oaks, CA: Sage.

Mulaik, S. A. & McDonald, R. P. (1978). The effect of additional variables on factor indeterminacy in models with a single common factor. *Psychometrika, 43,* 177–192.

Mulaik, S. A. (2009). Linear causal modeling with structural equations. Boca Raton, FL: Chapman & Hall.

Newton, P. E. (2012). Clarifying the consensus definition of validity. *Measurement: Interdisciplinary Research and Perspectives, 10,* 1–29.

Neyman, J., & Pearson, E. S. (1967). *Joint statistical papers.* London: Cambridge University Press.

Nichols, P. D. & Williams, N. (2009). Consequences of test score use as validity evidence: Roles and responsibilities. *Educational Measurement: Issues and Practice, 28,* 3–9.

Norris, S. P. (1983). The inconsistencies at the foundations of construct validation theory. *New Directions in Evaluation, 19,* 53–74.

Novick, M. R. (1966) The axioms and principal results of classical test theory. *Journal of Mathematical Psychology, 3,* 1–18.

Nunnally, J. C. & Bernstein, I. H. (1994). *Psychometric Theory* (3rd ed.). New York: McGraw Hill.

Ober, W. U. (1981). *The story of the three bears: The evolution of an international classic.* Delmar, New York: Scholar's Facsimiles & Reprints.

Orom, H. & Cervone, D. (2009). Personality dynamics, meaning, and idiosyncrasy: Identifying cross-situational coherence by assessing personality architecture. *Journal of Research in Personality, 43,* 228–240.

Paul, L. A. (2009). Counterfactual theories. In H. Beebee, C. Hitchcock & P. Menzies (Eds.), *The Oxford handbook of causation* (pp. 158–184). Oxford, UK: Oxford University Press.

Pearl, J. (2000). *Causality: Models, reasoning, and inference.* Cambridge, England: Cambridge University Press.

Pearl, J. (2009). *Causality: Models, reasoning, and inference* (2nd ed.). Cambridge, UK: Cambridge University Press.

Pearson, K. (1896). Mathematical contributions to the theory of evolution: III. Regression, heredity and panmixia. *Philosophical Transactions of the Royal Society A, 187,* 253–318.

Penke, L., Denissen, J. J. A. & Miller, G. F. (2007). The evolutionary genetics of personality. *European Journal of Personality, 21,* 549–587

Pepper, S. C. (1942). *World hypotheses: A study of evidence.* Berkeley, CA: University of California Press.

Perline, R., Wright, B. D., & Wainer, H. (1979). The Rasch model as additive conjoint measurement. *Applied Psychological Measurement, 3,* 237–255.

Petersen, N. S. (1976). An expected utility model for "optimal" selection. *Journal of Educational Statistics, 1,* 333–358.

Petersen, N. S. & Novick, M. R. (1976). An evaluation of some models for culture-fair selection. *Journal of Educational Measurement, 13,* 3–29.

Plumer, G. E. (2000). A review of the LSAT using literature on legal reasoning (Computerized Testing Report 97-08). Newtown, PA: LSAC.

Pollock, J. L. (1990). *Nomic probability and the foundations of induction.* New York: Oxford University Press.

Popham, W. J. (1997). Consequential validity: Right concern—wrong concept. *Educational Measurement: Issues and Practice, 16(2),* 9–13.

Priest, G. (2006). *In contradiction: A study of the transconsistent* (2nd ed.). Oxford, UK: Clarendon.

Psillos, S. (2002). *Causation and Explanation.* Montreal, CA: McGill-Queens University Press.

Putnam, H. (1975a). *Mathematics, matter and method: Philosophical papers* (vol. 1, 2nd ed.). Cambridge, UK: Cambridge University Press.

Putnam, H. (1975b). The meaning of "meaning". In K. Gunderson (Ed.), *Minnesota Studies in the Philosophy of Science, VII* (pp. 131–193). Minneapolis, MN: University of Minnesota Press.

Putnam, H. (1981). *Reason, truth and history.* Cambridge, UK: Cambridge University Press.

Putnam, H. (1983). *Realism and reason: Philosophical papers* (vol. 3). Cambridge, UK: Cambridge University Press.

Putnam, H. (2002). *The collapse of the fact/value dichotomy and other essays.* Cambridge, MA: Harvard University Press. (Especially chapters 6 and 8).

Quine, W. V. O. (1960). *Word and object.* Cambridge, MA: MIT Press.

Quine, W. V. O. (1969). *Ontological relativity and other essays.* New York: Columbia University Press.

Quine, W. V. O. (1980). *From a logical point of view: Nine logico-philosophical essays* (2nd ed., rev.). Cambridge, MA: Harvard University Press.

Quine, W. V. O. (1981). *Mathematical logic* (rev. ed.). Cambridge, MA: Harvard University Press.

Radford, A. (1988). *Transformational grammar: A first course.* New York: Cambridge University Press.

Ramsey, F. P. (1990). *F. P. Ramsey: Philosophical papers* (D. H. Mellor, Ed.). Cambridge, UK: Cambridge University Press.

Rasch, G. (1960). *Probabilistic models for some intelligence and attainment tests.* Copenhagen: Paedagogiske Institut.

Reckase, M. (1998). Consequential validity from the test developer's persepctive. *Educational Measurement: Issues and Practice, 17(2)*, 13–16.

Reese, L. M. (1999). A Classical Test Theory Perspective on LSAT Local Item Dependence (Statistical Report 96-01). Newtown, PA: LSAC.

Reese, L. M. & Cotter, R. A. (1994). A Compendium of LSAT and LSAC-Sponsored Item Types 1948–1994 (Research Report 94-01). Newtown, PA: LSAC.

Reichenbach, H. (1956). *The direction of time.* Berkeley: University of California Press.

Rogers, R., Jackson, R. L., Sewell, K. W., Tillbrook, C. E., & Martin. M. A. (2003). Assessing dimensions of competency to stand trial: Construct validation of the ECST-R. Assessment, 10, 344–351.

Rogers, R., Tillbrook, C. E., & Sewell, K. W. (2004). *Evaluation of Competency to Stand Trial—Revised (ECST-R).* Odessa, FL: Psychological Assessment Resources.

Roskam, E. E., & Jansen, P. G. W. (1984). A new derivation of the Rasch model. In E. Degreef & J. v. Bruggenhaut (Eds.), *Trends in mathematical psychology.* Amsterdam: North-Holland.

Rozeboom, W. W. (1966). Scaling theory and the nature of measurement. *Synthese, 16*, 170–233.

Rubin, D. B. (1974). Estimating causal effects of treatments in randomized and nonrandomized studies. *Journal of Educational Psychology, 66*, 688–701.

Russell, B. (1903). *Principles of mathematics.* Cambridge: Cambridge University Press.

Russell, B. (1913). On the Notion of Cause. *Proceedings of the Aristotelian Society, 13*, 1–26.

Salmon, W. C. (1998). *Causality and explanation.* Oxford, UK: Oxford University Press.

Scheiblechner, H. (1999). Additive conjoint isotonic probabilistic models. *Psychometrika, 64*, 295–316.

Schmidt, F. L., & Hunter J. E. (1977). Development of a general solution to the problem of validity generalization. *Journal of Applied Psychology, 62*, 529–540.

Schmidt, F. L., & Hunter, J. E. (1999). Theory testing and measurement error. *Intelligence, 27*, 183–198.

Scott, D., & Suppes, P. (1958). Foundational aspects of the theory of measurement. *Journal of Symbolic Logic, 23*, 113–128.

Scriven, M. (1962). Explanations, predictions, and laws. In H. Feigl & G. Moxwell (Eds.), *Minnesota studies in the philosophy of science* (vol. 3, pp. 170–230). Minneapolis, MN: University of Minnesota Press.

Scriven, M. (1991). *Evaluation thesaurus* (4th ed.). Thousand Oaks: Sage Publications.

Scriven, M. (2001). Evaluation: Future tense. *American Journal of Evaluation, 22*, 301–307.

Scriven, M. (2002). Assessing six assumptions in assessment. In H. I. Braun, D. N. Jackson & D. E. Wiley (Eds.), *The role of constructs in psychological and educational measurement.* Mahwah, NJ: Erlbaum.

Searle, J. R. (1969). *Speech acts: An essay in the philosophy of language.* Cambridge, UK: Cambridge University Press. (Chapters 6 and 8)

Sechrest, L. (1963). Incremental validity: A recommendation. *Educational and Psychological Measurement, 23,* 153–158.

Sechrest, L. (2005). Validity of measures is no simple matter. *Health Services Research, 40,* 1584–1604.

Shadish, W. R., Cook, T. D., & Campbell, D. T. (2002). *Experimental and quasi-experimental designs for generalized causal inference.* Boston: Houghton Mifflin.

Sheppard, L. A. (1997). The centrality of test use and consequences for test validity. *Educational Measurement: Issues and Practice, 16(2),* 5–8.

Shope, R. K. (1983). *The analysis of knowing: a decade of research.* Princeton, NJ: Princeton University Press.

Sireci, S. C. (1998). The construct of content validity. *Social Indicators Research, 45,* 83–117.

Sloman, S. A. (1993). Feature-based induction. *Cognitive Psychology, 25,* 231–280.

Spearman, C. (1904). General intelligence, objectively determined and measured. *American Journal of Psychology, 15,* 201–293.

Spirtes, P., Glymour, C. N., & Scheines, R. (2000). *Causation, prediction, and search.* Cambridge, MA: MIT Press.

Stegmüller, W. (1979), *The structuralist view of theories. A possible analogue of the Bourbaki programme in physical science* , Berlin: Springer-Verlag.

Stenner, A. J., Burdick, H., Sanford, E. E. & Burdick, D. S. (2006). How accurate are Lexile text measures? *Journal of Applied Measurement, 7,* 307–322.

Stevens, S. S. (1946). On the theory of scales of measurement. *Science, 103,* 667–680.

Stevens, S.S., & Davids, H. (1938). *Hearing: Its psychology and physiology.* New York: Wiley.

Steyer, R. (2005). Analyzing Individual and Average Causal Effects via Structural Equation Models. In *Methodology European Journal of Research Methods for the Behavioral and Social Sciences, 1,* 39–54.

Stilwell, L. A., Dalessandro, S. P., & Reese, L. M. (2005) Predictive Validity of the LSAT: A National Summary of the 2005–2006 Correlation Studies (LSAT Technical Report 07-02). Newtown, PA: LSAC.

Stitch, S. (1985). *From folk psychology to cognitive science.* Cambridge, MA: MIT press.

Suppe, F. (1977). *The structure of scientific theories.* Urbana: University of Illinois Press.

Suppes, P. & Zinnes, J. L. (1963). Basic measurement theory. In R. D Luce, R. Bush, & E. Galanter (Eds.), *Handbook of mathematical psychology* (pp. 3–76). New York: Wiley.

Terman, L. M. (1916). *The measurement of intelligence.* Boston: Houghton Mifflin.

Thomas, H. (1989). *Distributions of Correlation Coefficients.* New York: Springer.

Thomson, G. H. (1916). A hierarchy without a general factor. *British Journal of Psychology, 8,* 271–281.

Thurstone, L. L. (1927). *A law of comparative judgement. Psychological Review, 34,* 278–286.

Toulmin, S. E. (2003). *The uses of argument* (upd. ed.). Cambridge, UK: Cambridge University Press.

Van der Linden, W. J. (2006). *Optimal assembly of tests with item sets (Computerized Testing Report 99-04)*. Newtown, PA: LSAC.

Van der Linden, W. J., & Glas, C. A. W. (2000). (Eds.), *Computerized adaptive testing: Theory and practice*. Dordrecht: Kluwer.

Van der Maas, H. L. J., Dolan, C. V., Grasman, R. P. P. P., Wicherts, J. M., Huizenga, H. M., & Raijmakers, M. E. J. (2006). A dynamical model of general intelligence: The positive manifold of intelligence by mutualism. *Psychological Review, 113*, 842–861.

Van Fraassen, B. C. (1980). *The scientific image*. Oxford, UK: Clarendon.

Varela, R. J., Thompson, E., & Rosch, E. (1991). *The embodied mind: Cognitive science and human experience*. Cambridge, MA: MIT Press.

Vygotsky, L.S. (1978). *Mind and society: The development of higher psychological processes*. Cambridge, MA: Harvard University Press.

Wakker, P. P. (1989). *Additive representations of preferences: A new foundation of decision analysis*. Dordrecht: Kluwer.

Waller, N. G. (1999). Searching for structure in the MMPI. In S. Embretson & S. Hershberger (Eds.). *The new rules of measurement: What every psychologist and educator should know*. (pp. 185–217). Mahwah, NJ: Erlbaum.

Weick, K. (1979). *The social psychology of organizing*. New York: McGraw-Hill.

Weick, K. (1995). *Sensemaking in organisations*. Thousand Oaks, CA: Sage.

Weiss, H. M., Nicholas, J. P., & Daus, C. S. (1999). An examination of the joint effects of affective experiences and job beliefs on job satisfaction and variations in affective experiences over time. *Organizational Behavior and Human Decision Processes, 78*, 1–24.

Westen, D., & Rosenthal, R. (2003). Quantifying construct validity. *Journal of Personality and Social Psychology, 84*, 608–618.

Wicherts, J. M., & Millsap, R. E. (2009). The absence of underprediction does not imply the absence of measurement bias. *American Psychologist, 64*, 281–283.

Wicherts, J. M., Dolan, C. V., & Hessen, D. J. (2005). Stereotype threat and group differences in test performance: A question of measurement invariance. *Journal of Personality and Social Psychology, 89*, 696–716.

Wiley, D. E. (2002). Validity of constructs versus construct validity of sores. In H. I. Braun, D. N. Jackson, & D. E. Wiley (Eds.), *The role of constructs in psychological and educational measurement* (pp. 207–227). Mahwah, NJ: Erlbaum.

Wittgenstein, L. (1958). *The blue and brown books*. New York: Harper Torchbooks.

Woodward, J. (2003). *Making things happen: A theory of causal explanation*. Oxford, UK: Oxford University Press.

Zumbo, B. D. (2009). Validity as contextualized and pragmatic explanation, and its implications for validation practice. In R. W. Lissitz (Ed.), *The concept of validity: Revisions, new directions, and applications* (pp. 65–82). Charlotte, NC: Information Age.

Zumbo, B. D. (2007). Validity: Foundational Issues and Statistical Methodology. In C. R. Rao and S. Sinharay (Eds.), *Handbook of Statistics (vol. 26: Psychometrics)*. (pp. 45–79). Amsterdam: Elsevier.

Author Index

Subject Index

Example Index